Public Speaking
as a Liberal Art

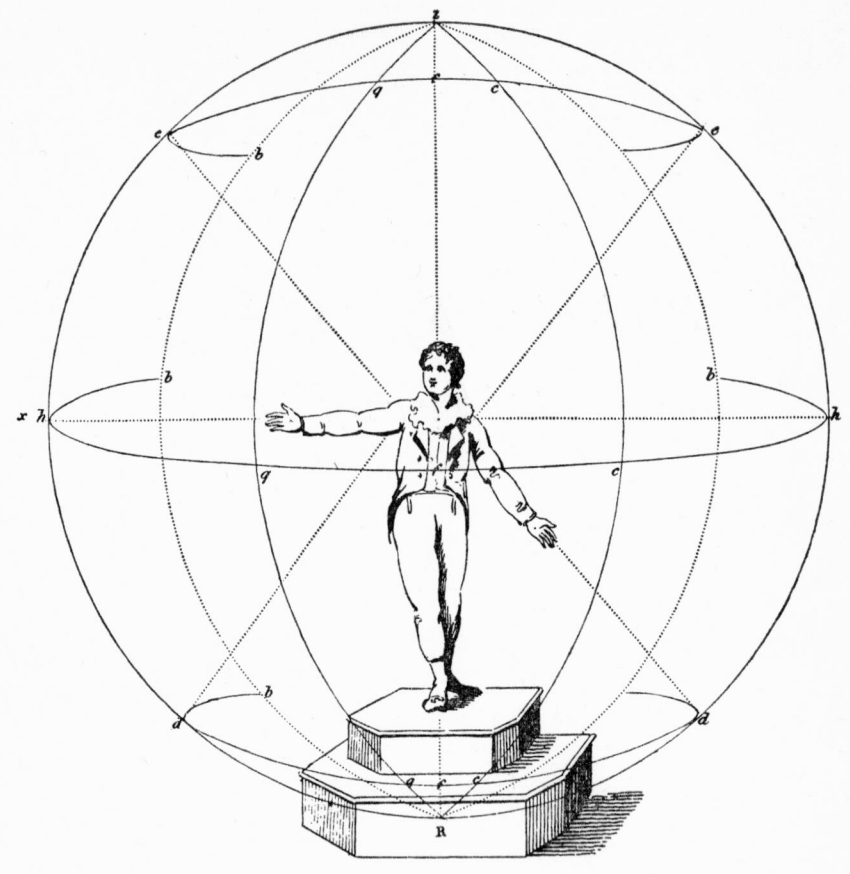

Key to Illustrations

Illustrations on chapter opening pages are from Chironomia; or a
Treatise on Rhetorical Delivery *by Gilbert Austin, London, 1806.*

Frontispiece (*above*)   *Positions, motions, and elevations of the arms*

Public Speaking as a Liberal Art

John F. Wilson
Cornell University

Carroll C. Arnold
Pennsylvania State University

Allyn and Bacon, Inc.   Boston

First printing .... April, 1964
Second printing .... September, 1964
Third printing .... January, 1965

Preface

Liberal education is that education which focuses on aspects of experience and environment having the most universal significance. Its special aim, we believe, is to spread before students whatever records and processes of discovery are most likely to intensify command of self and environment in the interests of humanity, present and future. In other times and in our own the place of the arts in this kind of education has been ambivalent.

The criticism of art has for centuries been firmly established within the framework of liberal education; the making of art worthy of criticism has not. This seems especially strange in the twentieth century when we are sharply aware that a comparable emphasis on contemplation, to the exclusion of learning through direct experience, ill served the development of scientific knowledge in mediaeval and later times.

We have chosen to place ourselves beside those who have left affirmations that speech making *is* an art. We hold with them that its general principles are identifiable and their application feasible, once taught. By virtue of this position ours is a "traditional" book. It is so not because we feel an obligation to emulate tradition. It is so because we believe the art of public speaking is truly "liberal" only if *the choices men have* become the focal points of study. These choices considered, speech making inevitably becomes the study of inherited theory and creative processes intensifying the student's capacity to understand himself and society. So approached, we believe it is unquestionably a liberal study. In our view the "ancient tradition" furnishes the only starting point for such inquiry.

This book approaches the study of public speaking from the position that the ultimate significance of oral communication is demonstrated by man's unflagging interest in it as a source of knowledge about himself and his relations with others. The pages that follow were written in the belief that modern college students *will* make and pass judgment on speeches. With what understanding they speak and with what competence they judge are important. We have, therefore, prepared a book which is insistent that neither the contemplation of speeches nor the making of them, alone, establishes full understanding of how men command themselves and their environments through speech.

The plan of our book provides an organized body of theory to be contemplated, judged, and practically applied. We have centered upon the demands present in every public speaking situation because the dynamic interactions among speaker, audience, material, and occasion define the choices open to a speaker and furnish questions by which to judge man speaking in public.

We hope that students will perceive speeches as speeches before trying to classify them on the basis of their dominant purposes. We have, therefore, tried to avoid a treatment which implies that there are ways of invention, disposition, style, and delivery which are the exclusive properties of speeches to inform, inquire, reinforce, persuade, and entertain. At the same time we have designed our inquiry so that those who prefer to emphasize the forms speech purposes engender may do so.

We have tried to provide a brief book without sacrificing thoroughness. Some topics such as group discussion and broadcasting are omitted. We believe that given the limited time available to students in public speaking courses it is desirable to concentrate on a cohesive body of basic principles. However, we have attempted to treat theories and problems fundamental to all oral communication as they apply to public address.

At points we have explored alternative ways of defining and viewing aspects of speech. We hope students will make personal decisions in reaching definitions and interpretations of their own. Such speculation is a first step in exercising the freedoms characteristic of truly liberal inquiry.

Our teachers and colleagues have influenced what we present here, and we are grateful for the stimulation and insight they have given us. Our students have taught us much. We repay them by passing to their successors a book reflecting their contributions.

No book is published without assistance. We are particularly indebted to Professor Edelwina C. Legaspi of the University of the Philippines at Los Baños and Nancy Wolfers, Assistant Editor, Allyn and Bacon, Inc., for valuable editorial assistance, to Bie Arnold for preparing the final manuscript, to Barbara L. Rowan for reading proof, and to Wayne A. Barcomb, Senior Editor, Allyn and Bacon, Inc., for his encouragement and suggestions.

J.F.W.
C.C.A.

Contents

Public Speaking as a Liberal Art

I

The Art of
Public Speaking

We ought, therefore, to think of the art of discourse just as we think of the other arts, and not to form opposite judgements about similar things, nor show ourselves intolerant toward that power, which, of all the faculties which belong to the nature of man, is the source of most of our blessings. For in the other powers which we possess . . . we are in no respect superior to other living creatures; nay, we are inferior to many in swiftness and in strength and in other resources; but, because there has been implanted in us the power to persuade each other and to make clear to each other whatever we desire, not only have we escaped the life of the wild beasts, but we have come together and founded cities and made laws and invented arts; and generally speaking, there is no institution devised by man which the power of speech has not helped us to establish.

Isocrates, "Antidosis"[1]

It is difficult to picture a world of silence—a world in which there is no human speech. Yet, most of us take our ability to communicate with others for granted. We have been talking for years, but few pause to consider what it is we do when we talk or why we talk. We are scarcely aware that approximately 75 percent of a normal communication day is spent listening and speaking. The fact seems to be that roughly one-third of our time is spent associating with others through the medium of speech.[2]

---

[1] Reprinted by permission of the publishers and the Loeb Classical Library from Isocrates, "Antidosis," trans. by George Norlin in *Isocrates* (Cambridge, Mass.: Harvard University Press, 1956), II, p. 327.

[2] The most reliable estimate we have on this matter is somewhat dated. This estimate claimed that 45% of our time is spent listening, 30% in speaking, 16% in reading, and 9% in writing. Paul T. Rankin, "The Importance of Listening Ability," *English Journal* (College Edition), XXVII (Oct. 1928), 623–630.

Speech is learned quite by chance from those around us; from our friends, our parents, our teachers, and our religious leaders. Some of us learn to speak well because our models are good ones; and some of us develop speech of less than satisfactory quality, marked by poor habits, because our models are bad ones. Even those of us who have accidentally learned to speak well can improve our ability to express thoughts and feelings.

Most of us take speech so much for granted that only when it is defective or breaks down do we accord it attention. We pity the deaf and the mute, or the boy who stutters, or the girl who lisps. Indeed, "communication breakdown" has become one of the great tragic themes of our time. The physiological breakdown of communication is vividly portrayed in the writings of Helen Keller. Breakdown due to psychological difficulties is exemplified for us in Herman Melville's *Billy Budd* and in Robert Anderson's *Tea and Sympathy*. Far too often we must experience a crisis in spoken communication before we accord speech any attention, but we do not wait for a breakdown in our writing abilities before paying attention to that form of communication. It is sensible to consider human speech at least as seriously as any other communicative behavior.

There are many misconceptions concerning speech and public speaking. First, there is the idea that good speech cannot be learned, that good speech is inherited or just "rubs off on you." While it is true that a good environment is conducive to good speech, the number of improved speakers, the last-day speeches delivered in a public speaking course compared to the first, the letters from graduates of such courses, all testify to the fact that one can learn to speak better.

Second, the idea exists that if you have *something to say* you don't have to worry about *how to say it*. The *content* of the message will insure its understandable delivery. Professorial lectures poorly organized, delivered with blurred articulation and inadequate volume, and directed to the trees outside the classroom window eloquently refute the content-is-enough allegation of people who regard studying speech as something unworthy of their time.

Just as unfounded as the misconception that content is enough is a third misconception that no content is needed. The purveyors of hot air who believe, "It isn't what you say, it's the way you say it," tread on even more dangerous ground. These Willy Lomans of the world will eventually find, as he did, that verbal tricks won't do. They will find that empty, vacuous phrases reflecting empty, vacuous minds can never be strengthened by dulcet tone or sweeping gesture. The discerning listener will see the emptiness. The exhibitionist who speaks primarily to be admired has forgotten the true functions of speech.

A fourth misconception goes hand-in-hand with the third. It is that all courses in speech, including those in public speaking, are primarily concerned with manipulation of the body and the voice, with how to pound the lectern and sound the "O." While it is true that there are courses in voice and in a few of our universities there are courses in bodily action, it must be noted that these courses deal with fundamental components of speech but represent only single facets of the experiences that are speech. Courses in public speaking, essentially courses in speech composition, do consider the voice as a transmitting medium for the ideas; but considerations of diction, of articulation and enunciation, of quality and rate of utterance, are incidental to the broader task of preparing ideas for public reception. Attention is also incidentally paid to gesture in public speaking courses and elsewhere, but only as gesture gives meaning to ideas by punctuating and reinforcing them. Those who are under the impression that to study speech is to study the physiological transmission of ideas are simply misinformed.

Speech as a Liberal Study

With major misconceptions swept away, we are ready to approach speech, of which public speaking is an aspect, as a liberal study. We say *as a liberal study* for while it is true that public speaking, as so many textbooks proclaim, is a tool leading to success in legislatures, law courts, classrooms, pulpits, engineering laboratories, and market places, it is even more true that to understand the nature of public speaking is to understand man in all these settings. To study speech in general or public speaking in particular is to explore highly intricate processes by which man apprehends truths about himself and his environment. To say that speech is a tool that yields power and success is of less consequence than to say study of it yields insight into the nature of man through examining an ever-present facet of his behavior. A study of speaking man and his works entails discrimination in observing and producing action and reaction. It requires one to learn much about how ideas become meaningful through the selective, sifting, and structuring processes that govern thought's emergence in the human mind. The study of man speaking explores systems of symbolization—verbal, vocal, gestural—that regulate the significance of thought when uttered. To study man's speech in virtually any aspect frees the mind from parochial concentration upon self, for this study not only proclaims with Socrates, "Know thyself," but admonishes, likewise, "Know others!" So, while it is not deplorable to learn to give public speeches for the sake of future careers, it is more important to learn, through speaking and studying speech making, how it is that mind links to mind through speech, regardless of who you are or what your profession.

In this book we are not concerned with examining human speech in all its aspects; our attention will focus on that aspect of speech usually referred to as public speaking. In every modern era of Western civilization there have been those who have insisted that this aspect of human speech is one depending upon practiced skill far more than upon understanding. We think this view ignores a most important fact about the creation of anything that has impact upon the minds of men. That fact is that whether the created thing is a painting, a musical score, a poem, an essay, a speech, or any other artistic work capable of influence, someone purposefully *selected* what he would work with, gave it distinctive form or shape, and released it in a particular manner calculated to influence the rest of mankind. Significant works of fine art do not happen by setting monkeys to practicing on typewriters, canvases, or clavichords; significant works of art come into being when an artist, both skilled and sensitive, successfully matches idea, medium, and purpose in such a fashion as to bring to bear upon his idea all resources of his medium. Using all possible means, he endows ideas with just the qualities his purpose requires. This is precisely the achievement of the ideal public speaker. In this sense he, too, is an artist. He is a good artist if he understands enough about the world in which he lives to distinguish a significant from an insignificant idea, if he understands the full range of resources and limitations embodied in his medium—human speech—and if he can bring to bear upon his ideas those resources of human speech that will endow worthy ideas with the qualities his social purposes require. Practice without understanding will never bring him to this achievement except by sheer, unrepeatable accident. This is the sense in which we choose to call public speaking an art. We do not suggest that every intelligent and understanding person can by thought and diligence become a Daniel Webster, a Clarence Darrow, or a Franklin D. Roosevelt. We do insist, however, that there is an important place for disciplined study and practical experience in applying such principles as these men successfully used in shaping the society we live in. Such experience will, at the least, produce knowledge of self and of others and, at best, produce the sensitivity and skill essential to artistic use of speech in formal communication.

There are those who, in writing about public speaking, focus almost entirely on personality and the persuasive elements emanating from character, thus making the study of public speaking exclusively speaker-centered. Others focus on ideas and their symbolization, on the mental processes, avowing that the study of public speaking ought to be speech-centered or message-centered. Still others emphasize motivation and adaptation, claiming that the study should be audience-centered. Though such emphases can be justified, each is partial. The study of public speaking as a liberal art ought to be *all* of these. It can, and should, be man-centered. A liberal view of the public speaker acknowledges him as a complete man—versatile and potentially artistic—projecting himself as a thinking, feeling being. It is a view that reveals him as man relating personal experience to the diverse experience of others, projecting and reinforcing his meaning through voice and gesture, adapting his message and being adapted to. Fully understood, the public speaker becomes Emerson's "man thinking" under the influence of nature, drawing not only upon minds of the past but upon the lessons of action as well. Such is the speaker of whom we shall think in the chapters that follow.

Wisely conducted, the study of public speaking can and should correlate with other liberal studies. In deciding what to say in practice speeches you will need to draw upon other subjects such as history, government, literature, and more specialized courses of study. In deciding how to say what you have to say in reasonable and systematic fashion, you will need to call upon your experience with logic and that practice in thinking acquired through the study of philosophy, the physical sciences, and mathematics. You may assimilate what you learned in literature, English composition, linguistics, and foreign languages as you select word symbols to convey your messages. The process of voicing your thoughts may make you see connections with physics, music, or acoustical engineering. The management of your body to reinforce your ideas may prompt you to bring to bear knowledge acquired in biology, physiology, physical education, and dance. If you approach the study of public speaking with a view to learning about yourself and your kind, you will have occasion to draw upon many phases of your general education; for public speaking is an eclectic art, the resources of which are as varied as man's shared knowledge.

We have been treating public speaking as a liberal *art*. There is a sense in which it may be viewed as a liberal *science*. Throughout education, society insists that in science at least it is not enough to speculate—to comtemplate—one's subject matter. Scientific processes, we say, must be directly explored. Theories must be tested in the laboratory and the methods of scientific exploration must be mastered. Without such direct learning through personal experience scientific education is nowadays thought to be incomplete. As has already been hinted, any thoroughgoing study of public speaking involves similar practical, personal experience with the art. You will, therefore, be wise to consider each speech you give as an experiment in human relations. You will gain from asking yourself: "Given a particular body of material, a particular speaker, and a particular audience, all existing in a particular moment of time, what effects or reactions will occur when a given set of ideas is presented in a particular order and reinforced with a particular set of vocal and gestural behaviors?" You will find, of course, that you are dealing with an experimental setting in which there are many variables. A change of word, the fact that the audience has lived a day longer, the temporary effect of a cold—these and dozens of other varying factors—mean that no speaking situation can be so rigidly constructed as to be capable of perfect duplication elsewhere. Even so, a scientific, objective attitude toward the experimentation that goes on in the speech laboratory, the classroom, is invaluable in drawing genuine knowledge about yourself and others from the study of public speaking. You will establish no universal laws through observing speech making with a scientific detachment, but you will be able to see more clearly the choices men make in order to be understood as they intend.

Public speaking as an academic study is a crossroads of the arts and sciences. It is a hybrid art, run through with the strands of other studies. It is a social art using speech as its medium, thought and feeling as its

content, and influence upon the experience of others as its end. To understand its processes requires reflection and experimentation: study of the
constituents of the art and practice to discover their potentialities.

What Is Speech?

Public speaking falls within the broader phenomenon, speech. In order
to understand the distinctive nature of public speaking we must first understand what is meant by that very common but seldom examined term:
speech.

Speech has been viewed and defined from diverse vantage points and
by diverse methods. Gray and Wise have examined speech in their book,
The Bases of Speech, from nine different points of view: the social, physical, physiological, neurological, phonetic, linguistic, psychological, genetic,
and semantic.[3] Speech has also been defined by synonym, analytic dissection,
function, and description. Speech has been broken down into its parts; it
has been diagrammed and charted. There has been little agreement on
any single definition, but by placing several kinds of definition side by side
we may gain insight into the nature of speech. Realizing that no one
definition achieves perfection, let us examine some useful definitions with
an eye to constructing one of our own.

If we were to define speech by synonym, we would use such terms as
"oral communication and expression," "orally verbalized thought," "spoken
rhetoric and poetic," or "oral discourse." We might simply call speech
"talk." Yet, not everyone would agree that these labels were entirely
accurate since it might be argued that all speech is not "talk" and that not
all speech is oral. If gesture and pantomime and silent but visible signals
are to be included in the broad study of the human organism as it expresses
meanings and elicits responses, some of our synonyms would have to be
rejected as too confining.

Some have defined speech by breaking it down into its elements.
Borchers and Wise did so from an almost exclusively physical point of view
when they wrote, "Speech is a code of audible signs made with the muscles
and other tissues producing voice, and of visible signs made with other

[3] See Giles W. Gray and Claude M. Wise, *The Bases of Speech,* 3rd ed. (New York:
Harper & Brothers, 1959).

muscles and tissues of the body, both codes being used for the purpose of communication."[4] Charles Henry Woolbert, who wrote a good deal about speech in the 1920's, also identified elements of speech; but he included mental as well as physical components. He said:

A man speaking is four things, all of them needed in revealing his mind to others. First he is a will, an intention, a meaning which he wishes others to have, a thought; second, he is a user of language, molding thought and feeling into words; third, he is a thing to be heard, carrying his purpose and words to others through voice; and last, he is a thing to be seen, shown to the sight, a being of action to be noted and read through the eye.[5]

Woolbert suggests that these "Four Phases of Speech" (thought, language, voice, and bodily action) be studied in reverse order. Many speech textbooks and many speech courses are organized in this pattern with the result that thought is relegated to the last position and is consequently too often de-emphasized in study. In the two definitions we have just cited the authors seem to be attempting to answer the question, "What is speech made of?"

Elwood Murray defines speech by highlighting its function. He says speech is the chief means by which we carry on personal adjustments and social relations. He sees in every speech act "phonetic skills," "semantic skills," and "social skills."

The emphasis to be presented here is that the essence of speech is in its social aspect . . . the most important means of carrying on human relations. To improve speech, therefore, is to improve effectiveness in human relations. . . . *Speech is defined as a tool of social adjustment, which reflects the efficient personality, and as a psychological and sociological technique of modifying human behavior by means of body, voice, thought and language.*[6]

We see in this definition a tentative answer to the question, "What is speech good for?"

Speech has also been defined by describing or charting the cycle of sequential actions and reactions that takes place when we speak. Alan H. Monroe characterized this chain of events by calling it the "circular response."

---

[4] Gladys L. Borchers and Claude M. Wise, *Modern Speech* (New York: Harcourt, Brace, 1947), p. 2.

[5] C. H. Woolbert, *The Fundamentals of Speech* (New York: Harper & Brothers, 1920), p. 3.

[6] *The Speech Personality*, rev. ed. (Chicago: Lippincott, 1944), pp. 3, 10.

An idea forms in the speaker's mind where it is translated into language symbols; reacting to impulses from the nervous system, the muscles used in speech convert these language symbols into audible speech; the sounds are carried as wave patterns in the air until they strike the eardrums of the listener; as nerve impulses, they travel to the brain, where they again become language symbols which convey meaning to the listener's mind; the listener reacts to what he has heard; the speaker observes this reaction and responds to it.[7]

Monroe, through description, provides an answer to the question, "What happens when we speak?"

Weaver and Ness suggest another answer to this question by identifying and diagramming the sender, receiver, and message as the basic elements of a speaking event. They tell us that when we speak a phenomenon called "feedback" occurs. "Feedback" here means that audience reactions or cues stimulate the speaker's subsequent actions and reactions. Weaver and Ness go on to compare speakers to self-regulating machines like thermostatically controlled heating systems, radar-directed missiles, and automatic chemical plants.[8]

While it is certainly helpful to trace the path of action and reaction in the speech act, we must note that while speech is not just a one-way process, neither is it just a two-way process. In most of the descriptive constructs available to us, no account is taken of the fact that during the speech act the speaker not only stimulates and is stimulated by others but he also stimulates himself. Wendell Johnson has explored this aspect of reaction in his book entitled *Your Most Enchanted Listener*. There he explains that *that* listener is *you!*[9]

A group of educators, whose specialties vary from public address to drama and radio, agreed at a workshop meeting of the Speech Association of the Eastern States in 1952 upon a definition of speech for purposes of discussion.[10] This definition read: "Speech is the process by which ideas and feelings are transmitted through the integration of words, voice, and

---

[7] *Principles and Types of Speech*, 3rd ed. (Chicago: Scott, Foresman, 1949), pp. 28–29.

[8] See Andrew T. Weaver and Ordean G. Ness, *An Introduction to Public Speaking* (New York: Odyssey Press, 1961), pp. 4, 10.

[9] See Wendell Johnson, *Your Most Enchanted Listener* (New York: Harper & Brothers, 1956), especially pp. 23–29.

[10] Members of this group were: Carroll C. Arnold, J. Calvin Callaghan, Giraud Chester, Donald L. Clark, Martin T. Cobin, John Crawford, Magdalene Kramer, Orvin P. Larson, James M. Mullendore, Loretta Wagner Smith, Walter H. Stainton, and Buell B. Whitehill, Jr.

action."[11] We are in substantial agreement with this rather general definition, though we realize the values of definitions formulated from other vantage points and emphasizing special aspects of speech be they physiological or physical, sociological or psychological. If we choose to look at speech as a phenomenon consisting of substance, process, and function, we arrive at this definition: *Speech is thought conceived, transmitted, and expressed by brain, voice, and body, producing stimuli for auditors and for the speaker himself; and influencing subsequent thoughts, feelings, and actions.*

Public Speaking and Related Forms of Speech

Public speaking falls within what is generally conceived of as *speech:* oral communication and expression. A logical next question is: What distinguishes public speaking from other forms also falling under the labels and definitions applied to speech? To be specific, how does public speaking differ from conversation, reading aloud, or acting, all of which are also forms of speech?

PUBLIC SPEAKING AND CONVERSATION

Public speaking differs from conversation in that public speaking is usually directed at more listeners than are most conversational utterances. While an audience for a speech may be relatively small or for a conversation relatively large, it can still be said that in most instances you will be facing more people when you give a public speech than you will in your daily exchange with friends.

A second readily observable difference is that *you* will do *most* of the talking during a public speech. *Public speaking is relatively uninterrupted discourse.* This does not mean there are no one-sided conversations. Many conversations with your dogmatic elders are in reality *almost* speeches directed at you. A professor or an advising father, such as Polonius was,

[11] From the unpublished proceedings of a Speech Association of the Eastern States workshop, 1952, "Excerpts from Findings," mimeographed.

may brook little interruption. On the other hand, he is still not delivering a public speech. What he says is meant for one set of ears and one set only. Private discourse is not public speaking. The point we are making here is that private talk is more often interrupted and lends itself to observable give and take. Applause, laughter, and the lustily shouted "Amen, Brother!" of the revival meeting are interruptions, but in most instances such interjections and audible responses account for but a small percentage of the total time during which a public speech takes place. Thus, the primary burden for directing the flow of stimulation falls more exclusively on the public speaker than on the conversationalist.

In addition to the usual presence of more auditors and the relative continuity of discourse, there are prevailing conditions which demand greater volume of voice and greater amounts of bodily action. The larger the audience the greater the physical demands upon you. You must make yourself easily seen and easily heard. Before a small, intimate audience gestures can be more subtle and voice less forceful than when you appear before thousands assembled in a large auditorium or field house. In these larger situations a greater amount of energy must be exerted to achieve adequate volume and that degree of bodily motion than can be plainly seen and interpreted by hundreds or thousands. Wider brush strokes are demanded in most public speaking situations than are demanded in conversation.

Finally, public speaking is prepared utterance while most conversation is not. It is true that rare individuals, like Oscar Wilde, have prepared conversations for the salon, but such preparation is the exception rather than the rule. It is also true that some speeches—those of the impromptu variety —are not prepared beforehand but are delivered "off the cuff" or "off the top of the head." Yet, in most instances, public speaking engagements occur only after a period of prior notice, be it several hours or several months. Prior planning, ranging from a careful prethinking of content to writing out the utterance, word-for-word, marks most successful public speaking performances.

These readily observable differences which *usually* prevail do not mean that good public speaking is totally unlike good conversation. Good public speaking has many of the features of good conversation. Directness, spontaneity, animation, and emphasis are characteristics of both these activities. To be successful in either, you must look the audience in the eye and adapt to the listeners and to the occasion as you go. Such adaptation often means incorporating phrasings and examples not previously anticipated. Furthermore, you will succeed best in both public speaking and conversation if your body and voice have a readiness to respond to your material, your audience, and the occasion. Visual and vocal activity ought to take place in such a way that the listener attends to what you say and realizes the relative importance of your ideas. In each of these ways public speaking and conversation are similar, but while it is easy to say, "Be conversational" when presenting a public speech, being conversational is not the whole answer. It is more to the point to say, "Adopt with appropriate modifications those characteristics of conversation suitable to the moment." Conversationality in public speaking results from control *and modification* of elements to be found in conversation. To speak on a public platform in exactly the way you would speak in situations calling for private, reciprocal communication or to reproduce conversation on the platform for other than illustrative purposes is likely to prove ineffectual.

PUBLIC SPEAKING AND ORAL READING

Public speaking differs from oral reading in the nature of the material presented, the purposes of the presentation, and the process of preparation. The oral reader, unless he is reading what he himself has composed, acts as an interpreter of someone else's ideas. It is necessary for him to discover the intellectual and emotional meanings of the ideas he presents. He must discover the author's intentions. He stands between the composer and the audience and becomes the instrument of transmission. This position calls for greater imaginative capacity than is required of a public speaker, especially the speaker who composes his words as he utters them. Moreover, the two modes of speaking involve different processes of selectivity. The oral reader has had the ideas and words selected for him; he must exercise selectivity in arriving at decisions concerning emphasis and his modes of transmission. The public speaker selects his own ideas and the symbols for those ideas; then, he chooses the ways in which he will emphasize and transmit them. Sometimes the task of the reader demands that he become someone other than himself, that he indulge in impersonation in varying degrees. At other times the oral reader remains himself but *suggests* the character of some other person. Most often, he merely reveals himself and the meanings he has discovered in what he reads. In the last of these circumstances it is only sometimes that his *purpose* is the same as a public speaker's.

The reader's purpose may or may not be a rhetorical one. He may read to provide information, to instruct, to persuade, or to entertain his audience. His purposes, like those of the public speaker, may be distinctly utilitarian. On the other hand, his purpose may be largely aesthetic, which means that he seeks a response to the beauty of his material. Such a response is often sought when works of literature—short stories, drama, portions of novels, or pieces of poetry—are read aloud before an audience. A good public speaker rarely invites primarily aesthetic responses. While he may evoke feelings and engender emotional responses, his aim is seldom that of focusing attention upon the universality or the poetic quality of his message.

Unless the reader reads a speech he has composed himself, his preparation of materials and his oral rehearsal will differ markedly from the procedures followed in readying a speech for public presentation. The preparation of a selection for oral reading involves research to discover the author's true meaning and the selection's emotional content. The reader searches through his selection many times, sometimes word-for-word, to make sure that he discovers the meanings intended by the author. He may also read other selections by the same author or what has been written about the author to gain further insight into the material he is preparing. A public speaker reading his own speech knows the meanings he intends to convey since he invented them. He obviously knows the author more intimately than anyone else. But if he reads a speech by some other person, he follows the same procedures in preparation as the oral interpreter.

The distinctive differences between reading aloud and extemporaneous public speaking, as opposed to public speaking read from a manuscript, lie in the rigidity with which the ideas are set. Speakers who memorize their speeches from manuscripts are really practicing a form of speech reading. The reading of a speech from manuscript or from memory is common practice today. The speaker who reads from manuscript usually does so because he has not had time to gain command over his ideas and has little confidence in his control of them. Before the advent of electronic recording devices, it was common practice to memorize speeches or to read them from manuscript in order to insure accurate reproduction of the speech in print. Such a requirement no longer exists; yet, on some significant occasions such as dedications, anniversaries, and commencements, tradition prompts the speaker to write out and read his message or to deliver it from memory.

PUBLIC SPEAKING AND ACTING

Public speaking differs from acting in that the speaker rarely, if ever, reveals any character or personality traits other than his own. A central problem of the actor is to create a character for his audience. There are other differences. The public speaker usually works alone. The actor, unless he is performing a monodrama, usually works with a group. A public speaker does not ordinarily use scenery, costume, or make-up to help him express and communicate as the actor does. He may on some occasions employ special lighting effects and platform decorations to reinforce his message. Further, the public speaker deals only with his own composition while the actor, like the oral reader, has all the problems of interpreting the words of another. He serves as a sort of middleman for the playwright and reveals the intentions of a director. Thus, the purposes of the actor are at once like and unlike those of the public speaker. The actor may seek to elicit primarily utilitarian responses or to gain aesthetic responses depending upon the nature of the material with which he works.

The Demands of Public Speaking

In distinguishing public speaking from other forms of speech we may say: *Public speaking is that form of speech which is relatively uninterrupted, which involves more than two persons, and in which the communicator invents and symbolizes his own ideas in order to elicit primarily utilitarian rather than aesthetic responses.*

Public speaking is an audience-centered, problem-solving, nonexhibitionistic art wherein time-tested principles are applied to specific situations.

Public speaking is adaptive in nature. The study of man speaking in public is a study of adaptation. Such study calls upon us to perceive a series of interacting relationships and to probe some or all of them to effect the most harmonious relationships possible. Diagrammed, the relationships indicate the various connections between the components of public speaking situations.

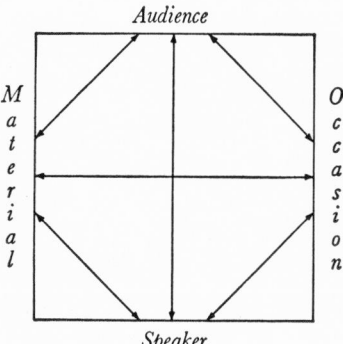

Given these relationships, the questions a speaker must seek to answer in preparing for a public engagement are these:

1. What is my relationship to the audience?
2. What is the audience's relationship to me?
3. What is the relationship between the audience and occasion?
4. What effect does the occasion, the particular circumstance in which the speech is to be delivered, have upon the audience?
5. What influence does the audience exert upon my material, upon what I have to say?
6. What is the relationship of my speech content, my material, to the audience?
7. What is my relationship to my material? That is, What do I as a person bring to my material to determine its final substance and form?
8. What effect does my material (my subject choice, the facts, opinions, and illustrations) have upon me as a person?
9. What is my connection with the occasion?
10. What is the effect of the occasion upon me as a speaker?
11. What influence does the occasion have upon my materials, upon what I intend to say?
12. What does the content of my speech do to modify the nature of the occasion?

Exploration of these twelve questions constitutes the work of a would-be public speaker. Given a particular situation, he must seek to answer each of these questions. Answers to some of them will be hard to come by. Indeed, in some cases, the potential speaker may be unable to provide even probable answers. In some situations some questions will be more important than others. Sometimes the best the speaker will be able to do is to formulate some educated guesses. Given the information available to him, it is his duty to calculate the probable answers to as many questions as he can. Should the speaker ignore a crucial question or arrive at answers which prove to be in error, he may fail to achieve his purpose, to elicit the response he seeks, or to achieve the degree of adaptation necessary to insure success.

We believe that the study of speech is a man-centered activity of which public speaking is but one branch which has as its main concern the eliciting of utilitarian responses. In order to study man speaking we must know not only the responses he seeks, we must know what aspects of the speech situation he must satisfy in order to elicit the responses he wants. Demands are made upon the public speaker by each major element of the speaking situation. First and foremost, the speaker must meet the demands of the audience at almost every turn if he is to gain the reactions he desires. Second, he must so fashion his communication that it meets demands inherent in the speech material itself. Next, he must meet certain demands which his own organism makes upon the message. And lastly, he must meet demands made by the physical space-time setting which constitutes the occasion. Thus it is that a speaker, as indicated in the preceding paragraphs, must consider data concerning the audience, himself, the content, and the occasion. Refusing to consider all four of these components and their interrelationships can easily cause failure in communication.

It is our purpose in this book to look at public speaking largely as a process of acceding to and satisfying the demands of audience, content, self, and occasion. Our approach will be to explore speech preparation and delivery by inquiring into the probable demands imposed upon the speaker during each phase of the communicative experience.

After some initial background which will serve as a context for study and for your first performances, we shall devote the remainder of this book to discussion of five general aspects of speech making. These aspects are those often called the "classical canons of rhetoric." We shall first examine the problems of *invention*, considering the nature of audiences and the means by which ideas for speeches may be discovered and sifted. Next we shall consider the *disposition* of materials selected for inclusion in a speech—the principles according to which they may be assembled and structured. Our third and fourth considerations will be those having to do with the symbolization of ideas—*style,* and *delivery* of the finished speech. What ancient writers called *memoria* or command of the entire speech as planned and composed will be discussed at various points in the chapters that follow. Many of the decisions speakers make during discovery, disposition, and symbolization of ideas have direct bearing on ability to retain command over the speech until delivery is completed. In considering each of these five major aspects of public speaking we shall seek to determine what demands the speaker must meet and the reasons they must be met if the speaker is to be understood as he intends.

The "demand" approach may seem too practical to some; yet we feel that this view of public speaking is essential if one is to acquire a comprehensive understanding of man communicating formally and orally. Intellectual and social adaptation for the purpose of gaining and giving responses is the central feature of speaking-listening man. What to do to achieve a desired response is and has been the chief concern of every public speaker in every age; modulation of his own responses in the face of purposive adaptation is the chief concern of every listener. Adaptation, then, is inevitably a very practical matter. This is why we shall focus in succeeding chapters upon the demands under which each speaker inevitably works and to which he must adjust if he is to effect those responses he seeks in listeners.

In this chapter we have taken notice of the pervasiveness of speech as human experience. Despite misconceptions concerning it, public speaking is not fundamentally different from man's other arts. Like most arts and all sciences, it cannot be fully commanded without direct experience in using principles and processes. Artistic achievement requires that the resources peculiar to speech making be brought into the service of the maker's purposes. Our approach to the study of public speaking as a liberal art will lead us to explore the demands made upon the speaker by audience, self, material, and occasion. We first turn briefly to certain broad principles that have been observed through the centuries by eminent theorists, among them historic figures of western civilization.

Exercises

Written

1. Write your own definition of speech.
2. Write your own definition of public speaking.
3. Write a paragraph in answer to each of the following questions:
   A. What is speech made of?
   B. What do we do when we speak?
   C. What is speech good for?
4. Keep a diary of a single day of your activities in which you note all the occasions upon which you found speech to be necessary. In noting these occasions try to describe briefly the distinctive nature of each.
5. After viewing a movie, television, or live theater performance, list those things you observed in the performances of the actors which were similar to or different from those things you have observed in the performances of public speakers.

Oral

1. Make a short speech in which you describe a specific speaking situation and in which you point out aspects of the situation of which you would have been unaware had you not attended this class and read this chapter.
2. Make a brief public speech on a subject of your own choosing during which you read from the printed page or impersonate some real or fictional character.

2   *Heritage: The*

Evolution of

Rhetorical

Theory

A clear understanding of any subject is strengthened by a knowledge of its history. The origins of the study, the concepts and ideas handed down for contemporary judgment, the accepted and suspect traditions of theory and practice establish the essential character of the subject and are parts of its fabric. You may not be able to survey all that has been written about public speaking or any other subject, but you will be better equipped to think and to apply your thinking if you are acquainted with the high points of its development and are aware of how present knowledge evolved. With these considerations in mind we shall trace in broad strokes the evolution of that part of rhetorical theory especially relevant to public speaking.

We shall not be concerned in this chapter with the orators whose practices shaped theories and who used them once they were formulated. Neither shall we consider all those whose writings on rhetoric would have to be included in a complete and comprehensive history of rhetorical hypotheses. We shall concentrate instead on the evolution of leading ideas about the art of speech making—on the points of change, the additions and omissions that have appeared in our culture's suppositions about the rhetoric of speaking from the time of the ancients to the present. We invite you to examine this briefly sketched and sometimes oversimplified record for the purpose of acquiring background against which to judge the theories and suggestions of this book and your own experience with the complicated art of public speaking.

The Greek Period

The story of the study of public speaking as a liberal art begins at Syracuse in Sicily in the fifth century B.C. Descriptions of speech making and scattered bits of advice concerning oral communication are to be found in such places as the Prisse papyrus from ancient Egypt and Homer's works, but it is from the Golden Age of Greece that we have the first record of an organized theory of the art of oratory.[1] Corax and Tisias are usually credited with authorship of a now lost manual of public speaking. We are not sure of its contents but what scholars have been able to discover leads them to believe that Corax and Tisias developed a theory of how arguments ought to be developed from probabilities and that they laid the first foundations for a theory of rhetorical organization. These ancient rhetoricians seem to have taught that a speech ought to have *at least* three parts including a proem or introduction to win the favor of the listening judges, a narration or demonstration, and an epilogue. Their primitive work contained only the germ of a rhetorical system but one to which the citizens turned in their argumentative efforts to reclaim lands and other rights.

It was no accident that rhetoric made its first appearance in Sicily where a succession of tyrants held sway. In the wake of the revolts which deposed those tyrants came the inevitable disputes over land and citizenship claims. These pressing matters for arbitration coupled with the warm nature of the Sicilian nourished the first systematization of the art of speaking, or more specifically, the art of courtroom speaking.

"Sophist" was the name given to some Greek teachers about the middle of the fifth century B.C. Most were itinerants who founded no schools. They have left us little by which to judge them. Isocrates, himself a Sophist, refers to them in his speeches "Against the Sophists" and "Anti-

---

[1] For further information on the Egyptians see Giles W. Gray, "The 'Precepts of Kagemni and Ptah-Hotep,'" *The Quarterly Journal of Speech*, XXXII (Dec. 1946), 446–454. A discussion of oratory in Homeric works may be found in George Kennedy, *The Art of Persuasion in Greece* (Princeton: Princeton University Press, 1963), pp. 35–39.

dosis." His allusions and some others in Plato's works are about all we know of other prominent Sophists. Many of these teachers were allegedly insincere, apathetic toward former students, and motivated by money. They were accused of corrupting youth and of regarding success as more important than learning. In truth, they had no uniform standards. They operated quite independently and their methods and ideas differed greatly. Most, it appears, gave much attention to speech making. Some of them were well educated and encouraged pupils to think speculatively, an activity contemporary society unfortunately eyed with suspicion.

Protagoras of Abdera (c. 480–c. 410 B.C.) was one of the earliest and most important Sophists. He maintained that the existence of the Gods was uncertain, that truth was relative, and that "man is the measure of all things." In teaching speech he held that there were two sides to every proposition and that speakers ought to be able to argue either. He practiced his pupils in what were called "commonplaces," speeches constructed in praise or dispraise of such human qualities as friendship, patriotism, and cupidity. These exercises had no reference to any particular occasion but provided students with a stock of set passages they could use when called upon to speak in public. Protagoras founded our system of grammar by classifying and distinguishing parts of speech, tenses, and moods.

Another Sophist, known as the founder of the art of prose, was Gorgias of Leontini (c. 485–c. 380 B.C.). His chief interest was in occasional oratory. His teaching and practice seem to have emphasized beauty in diction and style. He held that prose rhythm and word choice were more important than grammar. His own style was florid and exaggerated. Aristotle condemned him for his emphasis upon memorization and delivery of speeches written by others. The portrait in the Platonic dialogue that bears Gorgias' name depicts him as one prone to disregard ethics in his attempts to excite emotions. If we may rely on Plato and Aristotle, Gorgias did not care what means he used as long as he realized his rhetorical ends. His lost book, *On the Nature of the Non-Existent*, postulated: nothing exists, if anything exists it cannot be known, even if it could be known it could not be communicated. It appears that from Gorgias the rhetorical theories of Corax and Tisias received their most complete exposition and most artful practice.

Prodicus of Ceos (c. 465 B.C.), whose teaching was recommended by Socrates, taught that to face death courageously was a virtue. He propounded the ideals of labor, hardihood, and simplicity in a famous lecture,

"The Choice of Hercules." As a kind of early semanticist, he loved to study language and collected and compared words of similar meaning the better to insist upon accurate usage.

A Sophist we have already mentioned, Isocrates (436–338 B.C.), established a school to train speakers and wrote speeches for others to deliver. His rhetorical teachings are occasionally ranked above those of Aristotle because he equated the study of speaking with preparation for citizenship. A weak voice and innate shyness kept him from speaking in public, but the excellence of his written speeches earns him a place in the list of foremost Attic orators. The views he expressed in "Against the Sophists" and "Antidosis" reveal that he took the fullest development of the highest human faculties as the goal of speech training and that his ultimate aim was to prepare his students for public life. He condemned those who taught rhetoric solely for money and those who claimed that all is possible to him who learns the art of discourse. Isocrates' real love was teaching, and his most lasting contributions rest upon the breadth of learning he associated with the art of speaking. He is distinguished from other Sophists by this broader view of the functions of training in public speaking, by his ethical bent, and by his efforts to improve the prose of his day. His work influenced such Roman writers as Cicero and Quintilian.

Few of the Sophists were perfectionists. More were practical in their teaching of rhetoric and other subjects. Some used rhetoric for exhibition while others aimed for pragmatic results in speech making. A few ennobled the communicative arts. We can see that despite their reputation for being unscrupulous exhibitionists, the group of teachers called the Sophists was responsible for new thought, for discerning the practical applications of speech, for our grammatical system, and for other miscellaneous contributions to the field of diction. They did contribute to the knowledge of their own society and indirectly to ours.

The main contributions which Plato (427?–347? B.C.) made to the theory of the art of rhetoric appear in two of his dialogues: *Gorgias* (c. 387 B.C.) and *Phaedrus* (c. 380 B.C.). These works view speech making from opposed positions. The *Gorgias* criticized rhetoric and inspired others to come to its defense. The *Phaedrus* advanced theories which contribute to rhetorical excellence.

The theoretical considerations in the first of these two dialogues revolve about the nature of rhetoric. An attempt is made to answer two questions: "What is rhetoric?" and "Is it an art?" Rhetoric, Plato concedes, depends upon speech, but to define it as speech alone he thinks invalid. At one point in the dialogue, rhetoric is conceived as producing persuasion for belief rather than for instruction about right and wrong. It is declared to be neither a true art nor a true source of power. Following this line of thought Plato classes rhetoric with cookery and cosmetic as one of the arts of flattery. The only good use of rhetoric, he here contends, is in self-accusation though it may be nobly used to prevent the punishment of one's enemies. Good rhetoric, the *Gorgias* contends, is based upon knowledge and revelation of truth; bad rhetoric, upon exhibitionism which is not beneficial to the audience and induces belief without knowledge. Those reading the *Gorgias* today will not find the criticism it directs at training in public speaking new.

The *Phaedrus* considers the composition of three speeches on the subject, love. Here Plato reversed his position and took the affirmative side in the debate over rhetoric. In this dialogue he made several valuable points all speakers should bear in mind. In essence Plato said:

1. Writing speeches is not in itself deplorable; it is writing them poorly that is a disgrace.
2. A speaker must know the truth about the matters of which he speaks.
3. Those wishing to develop an art of rhetoric must be able to define and systematically partition the subjects they deal with.
4. Correctness in diction is necessary to good oratory.
5. Knowledge and practice must be added to natural endowments if one is to become a notable orator.
6. Anyone who teaches rhetoric must have a full knowledge of the souls of men.
7. Writing produces forgetfulness, and words once set down cannot defend themselves or know when or to whom to speak.

The impression left by this dialogue is that all speech making is not good speech making but that well conceived, well intended, and permeated by truth, public speaking is a powerful instrument which may be employed for social and spiritual good.

Aristotle (384–322 B.C.) was Plato's pupil and rival. He was probably the greatest Greek philosopher and certainly the greatest theorist ever to write on public speaking. His *Rhetoric* is the most influential work ever to be written on the subject. Theories set forth in this book, written about 330 B.C., emerge in all respectable speech textbooks today, and you will find much dependence on Aristotle's thought in the pages that follow.

The heritage Aristotle left to us is a rich one. In the three books of his *Rhetoric,* the books of the speaker, the audience, and the speech—as translators and commentators have labelled them—he treats speech making in such a way that his theories are still usable. Aristotle saw popular speaking as a problem in audience adaptation, a position we have adopted in this book. He believed that a speaker must know himself and his intellectual capacities, that he must understand his audience and its emotions, dispositions, wants and fears, and that he must know his material and the ways of presenting it logically, systematically, and strikingly.

In Book I of his *Rhetoric* Aristotle discusses popular speaking as it contrasts to dialectic (analytical discourse among experts). He condemns the speech handbooks of his day for dwelling on irrelevant matters and neglecting the treatment of proofs while concentrating exclusively on pleading in the law courts. He defines rhetoric as ". . . the faculty of discovering in a particular case what are the available means of persuasion."[2] This function, he says, belongs to no other art. He sees the character of the speaker (*ethos*), emotion (*pathos*), and reasonableness (*logos*) as the forces that bring about persuasion. He discusses at length the nature of rhetorical reasoning and the use of topics or "lines of argument" as guides to invention. Three kinds of speaking, deliberative (of the legislature), forensic (of the law court), and epideictic (of the ceremonial situation), are discussed with reference to their subject matter, their elements, and their ends. This tripartite analysis of speech making which Aristotle popularized continues influential and useful after twenty-four centuries.

Book II of Aristotle's *Rhetoric* concentrates mainly on the audience. It contains discussions of how emotions affect the judgments of listeners and how such feelings as anger, love, fear, shame, benevolence, pity, and the like are evoked by what is said. Age, too, is considered as a factor influencing the probable responses of listeners. (See pp. 81–83.) The influence of fortune, wealth, and power upon human character is explored.

---

[2] From *The Rhetoric of Aristotle* translated and edited by Lane Cooper. Copyright, 1932, Lane Cooper, p. 7, Bk I, Ch. 2. Reprinted by permission of the publisher Appleton-Century-Crofts.

Then Aristotle returns to a further consideration of reasoning and the topics of argument. (See pp. 96–106.)

The "book of the speech," Book III, says of delivery that it is something we must pay attention to because of the "sorry nature" of the audience. On the problems of effective delivery, however, Aristotle wrote little. When he turns to style, Aristotle discards most of his predecessors' strictures on the requisites of good style, preferring to emphasize clarity above all else. The additional characteristics needed for effective style, Aristotle thinks, are propriety and liveliness, the latter to be gained chiefly through using metaphors, similes, antithesis, realism, and rhythm. The final section of Aristotle's work deals with disposition (speech organization). It offers suggestions for developing the proem (introduction), the narration and ordered arguments (the body), and the epilogue (the conclusion).

Subsequent to Aristotle little of note was done to advance rhetorical theory until Roman times. As far as we know, it was about 250 years before the next work of major influence on present practice appeared.

The Roman Period

The rhetorical contributions of the Romans were largely those of systematizing and refining the theories of the Greeks. Theorists of the Roman era formulated the speaker's problems into five "canons of rhetoric": invention, disposition, elocution (style), pronunciation (delivery), and *memoria* (command of the speech). Classifications of style, methods of amplification, the functions of each division of a speech, and the several kinds of speaking held special interest for these theorists.

The first extant Latin treatise on public speaking, *Rhetorica ad Herennium*, was written about 82 B.C. It is sometimes attributed to Cicero.[3] This concise, plain, technical manual, which resembles a student's notebook, contains the oldest surviving discussion of the canon of *memoria* and the second oldest treatment of the canon of style. Style, which includes figures of speech, is given most space. Delivery, treated prescriptively, also receives much emphasis. Little attention is accorded disposition. The book is filled

---

[3] Professor Harry Caplan, who has made the most authoritative English translation of this work, is of the opinion that Cicero was not the author. See *Rhetorica ad Herennium* (Cambridge, Mass.: Harvard University Press, 1954), pp. vii ff.

with classifications, some of which are rather complicated. Where definitions appear, they seem oversimplified today.

Rhetorica ad Herennium gives extensive but unoriginal treatment to the three kinds of oratory (legislative, ceremonial, and legal) and the five canons of rhetoric. It contends that art in speech making must be attained through study of theory, study of models, and by practice. There are, says this author, six parts in a discourse: introduction, statement of facts or narration, division, proof, refutation, and conclusion. His handbook is especially noteworthy for providing advice on keeping the details of a speech in the memory, for adding to theories of style, and for its general review of Greek rhetorical teachings.

Cicero (106–43 B.C.) wrote several works dealing chiefly with rhetoric and left many other scattered references on the subject. The books that exerted the most significant subsequent influence were his *De Inventione* (86 B.C.), *De Oratore* (55 B.C.), and *Orator* (46 B.C.). Less important were his *Partitiones Oratoriae* (54 B.C.), *Brutus* (46 B.C.), *De Optimo Genere Oratorum* (c. 46 B.C.), and *Topica* (44 B.C.).

Cicero added little to Greek rhetorical theories, but he clarified and refined them. He was Rome's foremost orator, more famed for his speeches than for his writings. Well over fifty of his speeches survive. He wrote as an orator for other orators, brilliantly and well. His works reflected the practical cast of mind characteristic of the Roman of his day. His treatment of rhetoric was not novel, but it was thorough. He stressed the relation between wide general knowledge and excellence in speaking. He also discussed at length the constituents and the uses of the plain, middle, and grand levels of style. (See p. 253.) Since the language of public speaking interested Cicero greatly it is worth noting that correctness, clearness, appropriateness, and ornateness were the qualities he most admired.

Cicero was a great artist turned great theorist. That his own speaking met the standards of his theories is a distinctive aspect of his contribution. His mature judgment and long experience as a public speaker, his ability to synthesize and illuminate older theories, and his polished writing made his works classics. Not even Aristotle had a greater influence upon the rhetoric of subsequent generations. Some of Cicero's versions of theory became the bases for rhetorical treatises of the Middle Ages and Renaissance.

Quintilian (c. 35–95 A.D.) was the first teacher to be paid by the

Roman Empire. He contributed the *Institutio Oratoria* to the literature of speech making. This sole surviving work by Quintilian comprises twelve short volumes. It prescribes the education of the orator from the cradle to the grave. Its often quoted definition of the orator as "the good man speaking well," reveals the emphasis upon *ethos* with which Quintilian's name has become linked. He looks first to the character of the orator, his competence, his integrity, and his good motives. Given these qualities, Quintilian insists that the student acquire the skills necessary to reveal them and to perfect subject matter for communication.

Books I, II, and XII of *Institutio Oratoria* reveal Quintilian's philosophy of education and give special consideration to such topics as the curriculum for the early training of the orator, the individuals who should be allowed to influence him, the importance of adapting training to the individual, and the role of punishment. Because of their subject matter these three books are still discussed in courses in the philosophy of education. The remaining nine books of Quintilian's work contain the curriculum for the orator's liberal education. To be sure, he covers the five canons in detail, but he also prescribes what the student should read and suggests the value of such studies as geometry, music, and gymnastics for the development of the fully educated man.

Quintilian's central thesis that the orator has to be a good person and conduct himself honorably and responsibly if he is to be more than adequate in speech making appears as valid today as it was in Quintilian's time. Many speech teachers, as a matter of fact, have adopted it as doctrine. But Quintilian does not make his major contribution to our present patterns of speech education as a theorist or practitioner of speaking. Rather, our debt to him is that he wrote primarily as a teacher of public speaking. Because he was a teacher his primary concern is, appropriately, the student. That the education of a speaker must be individualized, broad, painstaking, and an integral part of general education is Quintilian's constant reminder to those coming after him.

On the Sublime, attributed to an unknown usually called "Longinus" and written sometime between the first and third centuries A.D., discusses elevation and inspiration, nobility of soul, and diction. The author sees as the requisites for eloquence: boldness with regard to sentiments, vehement and enthusiastic feeling, facility with the figures of speech, and majesty of expression derived from judicious word selection and dignified and elevated

27

views. Conciseness, amplification, and imagery are recommended as especially valuable resources in management of language. The attention "Longinus" gives to the roles of inspiration and largeness of conception in producing superior rhetoric gives his work its most distinctive cast. *On the Sublime* stands also as the first great work on rhetorical and literary criticism.

The Mediaeval Period

Little is known of the evolution of rhetorical theory during the Middle Ages. Chief among those who contributed to the theory of speech making during this period was St. Augustine (354–430 A.D), a teacher of rhetoric before his conversion to Christianity. His *Confessions* reveals his turning away from the artificial and exhibitionistic rhetoric taught him in his youth. But many still regard Book IV of his *De Doctrina Christiana* (c. 426) as the best treatise on preaching ever written. To St. Augustine, the purpose of speaking was to teach, to remind the listener of the truth that was within. He discouraged the irresponsibility and insincerity prevalent in the rhetorical training of his time. He urged preachers to study the speeches of others as models and to attain realization of full meaning as a foundation for good oral reading. In a time when the popular rhetoric resembled that of the ancient Sophists, St. Augustine focused attention upon speaking as a functional art rather than as exhibitionism.

Such names as Venerable Bede (673–735), Alcuin (735?–804), and John of Salisbury (c. 1115–1180) are linked with rhetoric in the dark period which followed St. Augustine. We know little of what happened to rhetorical theory during the fourteenth and fifteenth centuries. It is only in the early years of the sixteenth century that notable contributions to the theory of the art again emerge.

The Renaissance Period

During the Renaissance, rhetoric absorbed poetic and became completely confused with it. The prevalent theory of public speaking became a theory of ornamentation, as shown in Lydgate's *Court of Sapyence* (c.

1510). The chief purpose of rhetoric was to give pleasure to the ear. In fifteenth- and sixteenth-century England the word *rhetoric* came to mean skill in diction. The view of the period was exemplified by Stephen Hawes (c. 1475–1530) who wrote *The Pastime of Pleasure* (1506). This allegorical treatment of the liberal arts characterized rhetoric as honied speech best found in the works of poets. In this era, invention, discovering what to say in speaking, was lifted from rhetoric and was thought of as a poetic experience—the exercise of wit, fantasy, discernment, memory, and judgment. Disposition was also treated as a problem peculiar to poetic, as was delivery. Delivery was conceived of only as the oral reading of poetry. Only *memoria*, command of what is to be said, retained anything like its classical meaning. Rhetorics of the period gave greatest stress and most space to style, and for most of the theorists of the time "rhetoric" and "style" became synonymous.

At the start of the sixteenth century, what classical writers had treated as rhetorical invention was thought of as matter to be studied in logic. Even Thomas Wilson in his book, *The Rule of Reason, conteinyng the Arte of Logike* (1551), saw the relationship between logic and rhetoric less perceptively than in his later work on rhetoric. In his earlier work he gave these definitions:

> Bothe these Artes are moche alike, sauying that Logike is occupied about all matters, and doeth plainlie and nakedly set forth with apt wordes, the sum of things by way of argumentacion. Again of the other side, Rhetorike useth gaie painted sentences and setteth forthe those matters with freshe colours, and goodly ornamentes, and that at large.[4]

Petrus Ramus (1515–1572) saw logic as consisting of *judicium* and invention, the apt framing of things and knitting of words together and the finding out matter and searching out "stuffe" agreeable to the cause. As Donald Lemen Clark says:

> . . . while the survival of the mediaeval notion that rhetoric was concerned mainly with style thus gave over in the English Renaissance *inventio* and *dispositio* to logic, there naturally remained nothing of classical rhetoric but *elocutio* [style] and *pronuntiatio* [delivery].[5]

[4] *The Rule of Reason, conteinyng the Arte of Logike*, 1563, fol. 3a, pp. 7–13.
[5] *Rhetoric and Poetic in the Renaissance* (New York: Columbia University Press, 1922), p. 58.

Books supporting this view were Richard Sherry's *A Treatise of Schemes and Tropes gathered out of the best grammarians and orators* (c. 1550), Henry Peacham's *Garden of Eloquence* (1577), and the *Artes of Logike and Rhetorike* (1584) attributed to Dudley Fenner. Many other books of this era, including John Smith's *The mysterie of Rhetorique unvailed* (1657), continued the faulty tradition of viewing rhetoric as a study concerned only with style and delivery.

Only two important rhetorics were remarkable for preserving classical precepts. They were Leonard Cox's *The Arte or Crafte of Rhetoryke* (1530) and Thomas Wilson's *Arte of Rhetorique* (1553). Cox's primer of ninety-one small pages did not pretend to be complete in coverage but had the distinction of being the first known book on rhetoric in the English language. It told the schoolboy how to put a speech together and emphasized invention, the canon of ancient rhetoric which had received least attention from contemporary writers. Wilson's volume, which came after the *Arte of Logike* already mentioned, passed through eight editions and is important because it contributed to the evolution of rhetorical theory by preserving classical tradition at a time when the vision of rhetoric had been badly distorted.

D. L. Clark attributes the perversion of rhetorical theory in the Middle Ages and early Renaissance to the bad judgment of rhetoricians and to their ignorance of the classical tradition. In England particularly the most important classical treatises on rhetoric and poetry, those by Aristotle and "Longinus," were unknown and only fragments from Cicero and Quintilian were used. The most popular and best-known work was the *Rhetorica ad Herennium. De Oratore* and *De Inventione* ranked second. The mediaeval tradition based upon the *Rhetorica ad Herennium* and *De Inventione* persisted in England for over a hundred years after it had been displaced in Italy. Quintilian's *Institutio Oratoria* was published in Europe early in the seventeenth century but proved too long to be used extensively; and even when Aristotle's works became available, his *Rhetoric* had almost no immediate influence upon English rhetorical theory. On account of the persistence of mediaeval tradition, rhetoric in England did not again come to mean what it had in classical antiquity until the seventeenth century.

At a time when rhetorical theorists had divided into two camps, one very small and with a marked classical influence, the other large and with a conspicuous emphasis on style, it is impressive that a comprehensive rhetorical theory emerged in the works of the period's most noted philosopher, Sir Francis Bacon (1561–1626). His theory is not presented as a compact set of rules, but Professor Karl R. Wallace has done a masterful job of organizing and assembling the scattered pieces on the subject found chiefly in *The Advancement of Learning* (1605) and *De augmentis scientarium* (1623).[6] On the whole, Bacon's theory condemns excessive stress upon style while emphasizing invention and highlighting the adaptation of speeches to specific audiences, an almost totally neglected aspect of rhetoric's classical foundation.

Bacon assigns rhetoric the function of applying reason to imagination for the better moving of the will. Rhetoric fulfills the office of influencing human conduct. It is persuasion based upon psychological precepts. Bacon declares that we know very little of the actual substance of the mind but are conversant with its faculties which are the concerns of the logical and ethical sciences—understanding, reason, imagination, memory, appetite, and will. A knowledge of these faculties will aid us in securing action, the goal of all rhetoric, as opposed to the securing of belief. Bacon's theory also has an ethical base, for it insists upon a portrayal of the good as an additional function of true rhetoric. Imagination is to be controlled and subordinated to reason, which must govern all of man's activities.

Bacon does not limit rhetoric to oral discourse. True, he refers to the orator and the speech, but he applies what he has to say to both speaking and writing of the utilitarian sorts.

Bacon's most unique contributions were his observations concerning invention. His treatment of commonplaces and topics as aids to invention influenced subsequent writers on the subject more than any other part of his work. Also influential was his discussion of the errors of the human mind deriving from mistakes of inference. In this connection he considered sophistical fallacies; fallacies of interpretation; and his famous Idols of the Tribe, Cave, Marketplace, and Theatre. He viewed rhetoric in broader perspective than others of his time. He saw utilitarian communication as a social art in which reason is applied to imagination for persuasive ends, subjugating passion and establishing good and just causes.

[6] See Karl R. Wallace, *Francis Bacon on Communication and Rhetoric* (Chapel Hill: The University of North Carolina Press, 1943).

The Modern Period

At this point we must look briefly to France to see a rhetorician of the pulpit who was doing for preaching what classically oriented rhetoricians were doing elsewhere for speaking in general. François de Salignac de la Mothe Fénelon (1651–1715) wrote three dialogues on rhetoric which were first published in 1717, after Fénelon's death.[7] In them he considered preaching in relation to other arts of expression but by no means limited his discussions to sermonizing. Rhetoric, he thought of as a social instrument wherein matter is more important than manner. He preserved the principles of the ancients but did not treat them systematically nor did he apply them with the rigidity other rhetoricians of the day observed. In Fénelon we find a liberal, modern application of a rhetorical theory based upon an insistence that man imitate nature in his speaking, that naturalness is a prime requisite for effective communication.

Fénelon disagreed with those who believed that the arts of logic and rhetoric must be kept separate. Nor did he confine his dialogues to style and delivery as was the custom in most rhetorics. Fénelon stressed the close connection between rhetoric and logic, the necessity for proof, vivid portraiture and movement, and the logical and aesthetic dimensions of all acts of literary evaluation.

Unlike others of his day, Fénelon did not find things beautiful unless he first found them true and useful to listeners. In this his teaching resembled St. Augustine's. He believed that real eloquence is an inspired and inspiring thing resting upon an ethical base. Once he has given his listeners the "bread" of meaning, the preacher may properly add the "spice" needed to arouse the feelings of the audience, to stir up emotion and to strike the heart. The philosopher, said Fénelon, acts only to convince, but the orator must go beyond, adding everything capable of arousing sentiments and demonstrating the truth.

Fénelon did not approve the rigid, artificial rules of disposition in vogue in his time; he felt that organic unity in the content of discourse is destroyed by complicated, unnatural divisions of subject matter. Style, too,

[7] Wilbur Samuel Howell, *Fénelon's Dialogues on Eloquence* (Princeton: Princeton University Press, 1951), pp. 36–37.

was a matter of aptness, simplicity, and clarity for Fénelon; and delivery was to be unaffected and artless rather than artificial or mechanical.

Fénelon's creed was that man must follow nature in her changes. He saw both oratory and poetic art rooted in the imitation of nature. Their methods are, thus, imitative. Their aims are also similar—to instruct pleasingly. Fénelon's, says Wilbur Samuel Howell, was "the earliest statement we have of what may be said to have become the dominant modern attitude toward rhetoric."[8]

In contrast to Fénelon's viewpoint and separated from it by less than a hundred years was a body of theory called "elocution," the results of which were the antithesis of naturalness. Of this mutation in rhetoric Frederick W. Haberman writes:

Elocution was an offshoot of rhetorical study. It was an exhaustive and systematic analysis of delivery. The elocutionary movement, which began about 1750, was a response to the demands of the age. This widespread and intense study of delivery was an answer to the eighteenth-century denunciations of oratorical frigidity, to the pressure for professional and educational training in speech, to the new consciousness of the need for standardization of spoken language, to the desire of the people to obtain facility in speaking a language of which they were becoming proud and to demands of those who dealt with democratic movements. The elocutionary movement, however, was more than a simple renaissance of a particular canon of rhetoric. It was rather, a new ordering of an old subject.

This new ordering resulted from the application of the tenets of science and of rationalism to the physiological phenomena of spoken discourse. The new study of delivery was affected by the impact of science or of rationalism in precisely the same way that the study of history, of economics, of poetry, and of prose style was affected. . . .[9]

Three kinds of textbooks for speakers came out of the elocutionary movement: works treating voice, rhythm, and gesture in extremely thorough fashion; elementary rule books; and books of elegant extracts containing prefatory essays useful for practice. In an attempt to approach speech theory scientifically, methodologies were developed by the elocutionists for observing voice, gesture, and language and for recording their

---

[8] *Ibid.*, p. 46.
[9] Frederick W. Haberman, "John Thelwall: His Life, His School, and His Theory of Elocution," *The Quarterly Journal of Speech,* XXXIII (Oct. 1947), 294.

observations. Elaborate systems of notation and representation resulted from exhaustive analyses based upon careful observation. At its roots, the movement rested upon a philosophy which posited that man is controlled by natural laws. Nature is a compelling force. It has immutable laws in the physical universe and immutable codes in the social universe. These laws and codes are systematic and can be disregarded only at one's peril. Speech, along with the other things of this world, these theorists thought, is capable of scientific systematization and they embarked upon their mission to reduce speaking to system.

Professor Haberman in his authoritative work on the movement identified its four founders.[10] Thomas Sheridan (1719–1788), who published *Lectures on Elocution* (1756), examined the individual sounds of speech as he sought a scientific phonetic basis for pronunciation. Joshua Steele (1700–1791) in his *Prosodia Rationalis* (1775) devised a system of musical notations for the management of the voice, an enterprise which stemmed from his interest in melody, rhythm, and pitch in speech and music. John Walker (1732–1807), an actor turned elocutionist, investigated the interplay between inflection and grammatical form. He invented a complete system by analyzing the four inflections (rising, falling, and two circumflex kinds) found in nature and generalizing concerning their applications in the utterance of various grammatical forms. His chief work was *Elements of Elocution* (1781). James Burgh (1714–1775) contended that "nature had given every emotion of mind its proper expression" in his book, *The Art of Speaking* (1761). This belief was not original with him, but the system in which he explained ninety-eight emotions surpassed others in thoroughness and influenced the conception of bodily action during the entire elocutionary movement.

Others, such as Gilbert Austin, John Thelwall (1764–1834), and David Charles Bell (1817–1902) and Alexander Melville Bell (1819–1905), played leading roles in the elocutionary movement. Austin's *Chironomia* (1806) exerted the greatest influence on the theory of gesture by analyzing bodily action in four systems of notation and producing descriptions or chartings for over fifty foot movements, over one hundred arm positions and thousands of hand positions. Thelwall's distinctive contribu-

---

10 Frederick W. Haberman, "The Elocutionary Movement in England, 1750–1850" (Unpublished Ph.D. thesis, Cornell University, 1947).

tion was formulation of a principle of "rhythmus" derived from his explorations in physiology, music, and speech. He applied this principle and elocutionary vocal exercises in his work with the speech handicapped. The Bells devised a physiological or visible alphabet in which there were symbols to represent every speech sound. Through the use of physiological pictographs they formulated the first modern system of phonetic symbols to gain prominence and serve really useful purposes.

The elocutionists, in their desire to apply the laws of nature to man's behavior, produced systems which were often characterized by artificiality. The inflexibility of their notations and rules made their theories inapplicable to any but those public speeches which had been written out in their entirety. Their systems, in fact, were designed for and mostly applied to the oral reading of literary works and to acting. Their methods would not work for the extemporaneous mode of delivery and so were of little influence after 1915. Yet, the elocutionists performed valuable service by their thorough investigations, descriptions, and analyses of delivery. Some of these are useful to us still in arriving at an understanding of the operation and management of the voice and body during speaking.

During the period of the elocutionary movement there also developed a counter effort on the part of British writers on rhetoric to revivify, clarify, and strengthen ancient classical theories. Chief among these writers were George Campbell (1719–1796), Hugh Blair (1718–1800), and Richard Whately (1787–1863). All three were Christian ministers.

Campbell's *Philosophy of Rhetoric* (1776) is a markedly theoretical but useful work which explores the foundations of rhetoric as they evolve from philosophical, literary, psychological, and epistemological considerations. Campbell's topics are: the sources of knowledge; evidence; the influences upon man's passions; the speaker; the analysis of audiences; wit, humor, and ridicule; and the purity, clarity, and vividness of language. He conceives rhetoric's ends to be enlightening the understanding, pleasing the imagination, moving the passions, and influencing the will. Though his psychology is outdated, he was the first rhetorician since Bacon to perceive the inseparability of rhetorical and psychological theories. He treats evidence differently from his predecessors in that he sees analysis of evidence as a solution to the persistent problem of the finding of truth. He does not treat the ancient canons of rhetoric systematically; but tries to explain audience

35

adaptation which, in turn, leads him to discuss invention, arrangement, style, and delivery in deliberate if unorthodox fashion.

Blair's *Lectures on Rhetoric and Belles Lettres* (1783), as the last half of its name implies, approaches rhetoric with a focus that emphasizes taste, style, and critical appraisal. Ten lectures in this work are devoted to public speaking. Two trace the history of eloquence from the ancient Greeks to the time of writing. The next three examine oratory in its settings —the popular assembly, the law court, and the pulpit. Another is a critical examination of a sermon. These six lectures are followed by two on the "Conduct of a Discourse in All Its Parts," meaning the parts of the speech. Two more lectures are on delivery and on the "Means of Improving in Eloquence." The popularity of Blair's work has been attributed to its form rather than to its content. It was widely read in both Great Britain and America. The reader examines public address from a vantage point unlike that provided by other classical theorists. Style, occasion, structure, and delivery are all elements of Blair's unique view of rhetoric. He had nothing constructive to say of inventive processes but revitalized other classical precepts and presented them freshly, stimulating new insights.

Richard Whately in his *Elements of Rhetoric* (1828) defined rhetoric uniquely as "argumentative composition, generally and exclusively." He saw rhetoric as an offshoot of logic. His book on rhetoric was written after his *Elements of Logic* (1826) and was divided into four parts: "An Address to the Understanding," an extensive analysis of invention and arrangement; "An Address to the Will or Persuasion," primarily an examination of emotional appeals; Style; and Delivery.

Whately has been regarded as the first to treat argumentation as a separate branch of speech making. He assigned a high place to argument from probability, and reason occupied the central position in his rhetorical theory.

Refinements which earn further praise for Whately's work include his distinction between argument from example and argument from analogy and his introduction of the idea that he who argues for a change in the *status quo* must assume the burden of proof. His treatment of *ethos* was original in that he discussed the speaker's character in terms of the diverging taste and intelligence of his hearers. Whately's remarks on the disadvantages of being thought eloquent were also original with him. His views on delivery (see pp. 290–292) represented his revolt against the mechanical delivery cultivated by the elocutionists; he insisted that a speaker must focus upon what he is saying to speak naturally. His theory of delivery to some extent resembled Blair's.

Whately's treatise was based more directly upon Aristotle's *Rhetoric* than upon any other source though he also relied on Campbell, Cicero, and Bacon.

The two streams of rhetoric we have been discussing, the elocutionary movement and the classical revival, have both influenced the understandings of our day. The transmission of rhetorical theory from England to America was, of course, inevitable. The theories we have described as flourishing in Great Britain appeared and reappeared in many versions in the textbooks imported from England and in those written here. They thus became familiar to American students in both the secondary schools and colleges.

Classical and elocutionary ideas have survived, but since the 1920's the elocutionary methods have almost passed from the scene. In reorganizing and reshaping rhetorical theory for formal study in the classroom American speech teachers have refined the inherited theories of disposition, strengthened the psychological interpretations upon which theories of audience adaptation must rest, enlarged the theory and perfected the practice of extemporaneous delivery, and otherwise added detail and example to the tradition stemming chiefly from the time of Aristotle.

An American speech teacher who added significantly to the heritage of rhetorical theory was James A. Winans (1872–1956). Professor Winans made perhaps the most notable contribution to rhetorical theory in this century when he introduced the psychology of attention as the basis for a system of public address. This psychology, which he borrowed chiefly from William James and Edward Titchener, is threaded through his book, *Public Speaking* (1915). Walter Dill Scott (1869–1955) had published *The Psychology of Public Speaking* in 1907, but he had not made attention the basis for a comprehensive theory of public speaking. Winans defined persuasion as gaining and maintaining fair, favorable, and undivided attention; and also insisted that logical argument as well as appeals to emotion are usually necessary to attain belief. His contribution came in the fullness of time, for without the psychologists' investigations of attention his rationale would not have been possible.

Winans' passages on delivery are also notable for his distinctions between conversational *style* and conversational *quality*. Many today believe his discussion of the theory of delivery remains the soundest available.

The evolution of rhetorical theory, the heritage as traced in the preceding pages, appears to be marked chiefly by changes in emphasis. Of the five ancient canons of rhetoric, invention, disposition, style, delivery, and *memoria* or command of the speech, only disposition and *memoria* have missed their hour in the limelight. Neither of these canons has ever dominated rhetoric in a given period.

The ancient Greeks laid a foundation for the art of speech making which in many respects still serves us today. The Romans refined and amplified the Greek teachings. Following a mediaeval period of little growth a distorted rhetoric was revived in the Renaissance, confused with poetic, and absorbed into logic. But in this period when rhetoric became style, there were those who clung to classical tradition and regarded invention as the key process in speech composition and delivery. With the modern period came an emphasis upon naturalness. The elocutionists' attempt to convert delivery into a science resulted in mechanical methods which were at least partially responsible for the simultaneous attempt on the part of British writers to revivify the more comprehensive classical theory with new approaches and accents. Most recently the injection of modern psychological theory into the stream of rhetorical theory has provided a new insight into the speech maker's art. Interest in psychology and application of scientific method to the study of the humanities may bring about as yet unthought-of emphases in the study of the liberal art of public speaking. In the United States public address is today studied with increasing intensity by more diverse methods of research and experimentation than ever before. The yield of such study may well direct us to new understandings of rhetorical theory in the years to come.

Exercises

Written

1. Write a book review of 1500–2000 words treating one of the works on rhetorical theory discussed in this chapter.
2. Write an essay comparing the treatment of a canon of rhetoric (inven-

tion, disposition, style, delivery, or *memoria*) in two of the books cited in this chapter. For example, compare Aristotle's theories of style with those of Blair or Quintilian's theories on delivery with those found in Whately.

Oral

1. Prepare and deliver a two- to three-minute speech introducing a person whose name is mentioned in this chapter. Assume he is living and is about to deliver a speech on rhetorical theory to your class.
2. After reading in one of the works mentioned in this chapter deliver a short report in which you point out an element of theory which you feel is applicable to speech making today.

3

First
Considerations

A public speech has been assigned. A time for speaking has been allotted you. You are expected to appear and perform. A dozen questions crowd your brain. "What must I do to carry off this assignment successfully?" "How can I make sure that what I have to say won't sound as though it had been said dozens of times before?" "What must I do to prepare a speech?" "How can I organize what I have to say?" "How can I be sure I won't faint?" "What speech principles must I expose myself to before I make my first try?"

It would be ideal for you to know all the theoretical and practical knowledge in the remaining pages of this book before making a speech, but a crucial portion of the art of public speaking can only be acquired from experience. It is therefore essential that your personal experiments in formal, spoken communication begin early. Each opportunity for performance will be an opportunity to explore your own nature as a communicator and to study the behavior of other persons when they undertake the distinctive human functions of listening and reacting to what they hear from the speakers' platform. It is, then, only through steady accumulations of re-lated knowledge drawn from experience and reflection that you can arrive at a full understanding of your own potentialities in oral composition.

Your development as a speaker, aware of the true nature of his art, will be gradual. As your understanding and powers of control grow, you will become equal to meeting higher standards of performance and more difficult problems in communication. But one must begin with practical experiments immediately if there is to be time for personal growth. In order that your beginning may be a constructive experience, we ask you to study the elemental but important observations in this chapter before you make your first major attempt at learning about yourself and others through public speaking. These "first considerations" are relevant to all your speaking, but it is important for you to know about them now—before you take the platform.

In the following pages we shall deal with five topics concerning which you must have at least a rudimentary awareness if you are to address an audience with a realistic understanding of yourself and the thing you are about to do. These topics are: originality in speech making, the elemental processes involved in preparing a communication for oral presentation, stage fright, the modes of delivery, and the nature and limitations of listening. Each of these topics will be further dealt with in other ways in later chapters.

Originality[1]

Good speech making by beginner or veteran requires originality. So the question of what constitutes originality is a basic one which must be explored and clarified.

A speaker may draw his information and ideas from printed or oral sources. He may acquire his materials from personal knowledge, magazine articles, essays, editorials, or books. He may glean ideas from lectures, plays, movies, television and radio programs, or conversations with fellow students and professors. But once his information is gathered, he must reflect upon it and stamp it with his own personality. Then it must be presented in his own words. *The original speaker is one who is able to discover and convey fresh meaning in matters the world is already acquainted with.* It is a rarity for even the greatest speaker to speak about what was before the speech totally unknown. To realize a truth clearly because one has experienced it in his own mind produces a degree of originality gained in no other way, even though the base for such originality is to be found in readily accepted axioms.

[1] This section is based upon a portion of the mimeographed Assignments and Materials Booklet for the beginning public speaking course at Cornell University. The original version was written by Herbert A. Wichelns and subsequently modified by the authors of this book and by others.

Any speaker concerned with self respect and the respect of his audience must be prepared to convey newly discovered meanings or new interpretations. Any listener demands as the price of attention that the speaker shall have actively thought for himself, shall have reached his own point of view, and shall have reacted as an individual to the information he has digested through reading and personal experience. To be heard with attention and confidence each speaker must exercise judgment in sifting the materials to which he has been exposed, and he must test his own reasoning. He must say what he has to say in his own way, choosing his own words. Since individualized choices in both matter and structure are involved, the speaker should be extremely wary of constructing speeches based on a single source. The speaker who relies too heavily on ready-made outlines to be found in debate manuals or study files or upon ideas expressed in a *single* book or magazine account cannot hope for originality even though he actually speaks the words conveying the final message. Ready-made facts, style, and tone promote parrot-like discourse.

Thorough, systematic preparation is the key to originality in public speaking. First, the speaker must become intimately acquainted with the facts on his subject. Next, he must apply his own judgment to the material under surveillance. Sifting the important from the unimportant takes time and reflection. For this reason the likelihood of discovering fresh significance in a subject will increase if the speaker begins work early. Ideally, a period of at least several days should elapse between the period of research and final organization and rehearsal of the speech. During this "gestation" or "cooling-off" period the speaker may mull over the meanings and possibilities of what he knows. Ideas should be allowed to grow, to flower into final form, before the finished utterance is evolved.

It takes imagination to bring freshness to a subject. The speaker must realize the distinct shapes and the distinct functions of the materials he uses to support and amplify his points. He must try to see what is unique in these materials, in his relationship to them, in their meaning and interest for his audience. The function of imagination in this case is not to create the unreal or imaginary but to bring about a true understanding of reality. Imagination ought to reinforce and animate fact and probability.

Clear speech plans reflecting the speaker's views, views framed in his own best language and related to his listeners' life experiences, result from acquiring knowledge, reflecting on that knowledge, and application of the imagination to it.

What are some tests of originality in speaking? The speaker will be able to defend his speech in subsequent discussion. He will be able to add to the information he has presented should he be called upon to do so. He will know more about it than he has time to tell. He will be able, willing, and eager to trace his ideas to their sources and to credit these sources by citing them in his speech or in discussing their reliability afterward. If he uses illustrations or exact expressions borrowed from others, he will acknowledge them. He will be sincere in stating his own ideas and beliefs, and he will publicly evaluate the ideas and beliefs of those he has consulted.

At no time will a truly original speaker wish to rely upon others to the extent of repressing his own individuality. He will be sensitive to the dangers of plagiarism and will steer clear of passing off the work of others as his own. He will avoid the hackneyed and be free from clichés. He will rely upon his own initiative to produce the fresh synthesis of ideas and wordings which constitute original public address. Like any other work of artistic merit, his work—the speech—will be the product of his personal experience and insights.

Basic Procedures in Speech Preparation

The processes of preparing any speech are processes of directing your own intellectual behavior in such ways as the nature and frailties of human thought, the conventions of communication, and the nature of listening require. We shall consider these processes in detail in later chapters but certain necessities must be understood before you undertake your first experiment in public speaking.

Before you can give a speech you must consider what is to be said. If you do not know what to say, you must decide on some subject worth talking about or someone must assign you a subject. Given a subject, you must decide what sort of response you may legitimately seek from the particular audience you will address. For example, you must determine whether to inform, conduct an inquiry, reinforce, persuade, or entertain. This decision made, your next decision must be to determine what central idea is to dominate your information, inquiry, reinforcement, persuasion, or entertainment. Let us briefly examine how and why each of these decisions must be made.

Your first classroom assignment in public speaking is not unlike the assignment you might receive elsewhere, and it is far better to think of a classroom speech as a real speaking event than as an unrealistic academic exercise. Suppose you were asked to speak to a dramatic club "about drama." After agreeing to give the speech, you would have to decide what sort of response you wished to elicit. Should you inform the group of something they do not know about drama and seek the response, "Yes, I understand"? Or should you review and amplify familiar knowledge, thus adding to their information about some phase of drama, seeking the response, "Yes, I understand better (or more fully)"? Or should you persuade the group to change some aspect of its philosophy or some phase of its activity, thus engendering the response: "Yes, we ought to think or do that" or "I agree"? Should you inquire with this group, raising some question with them to excite the response: "We ought to look into that further" or "That bears further thinking"? Or should you reinforce what your audience already believes and inspire them to strengthen their prior affirmations so they respond with, "We ought to reflect more strongly what we stand for" or "Yes, drama *is* a cultural force"? Should you simply amuse the audience with satire or irony or other diverting discussion, seeking smiles, laughter, and "That's amusing" as your responses? These are your normal options in preparing any speech. A subject may be treated in many ways; how *you* should treat it depends first of all on how you want your listeners to react to it.

The five purposes or response aims we have just reviewed need not be mutually exclusive in your speech. You may inform in order to persuade or reinforce. You may persuade in order to get a group to conduct an inquiry. But despite such intermixing and overlapping of purposes, *one* purpose must dominate your utterance and the others must be subordinate, providing a substructure upon which the dominant purpose rests. The reason is as simple as it is inexorable: neither you nor your listeners can think clearly about any subject unless you plainly understand the chief reason for thinking about it at all.

CHOOSING YOUR SUBJECT

As we said earlier, the group or the instructor that asks you to speak may specify neither subject nor purpose for your speech. A program chairman may simply say, "Come and talk to us about anything you want to." Here you are faced with deciding both your subject and the response you seek.

When you must decide upon a subject there are several guidelines you should follow.

1. The first of these is your own *experience.* Usually it is unwise to choose a subject about which you know absolutely nothing. Experience, however, is not the whole answer to this problem of subject choice. We think of the student who had had much experience with turtles. In fact, he was an expert. He spoke first to the class on diamond-back turtles. The audience was fascinated with his special qualifications, breadth of knowledge, enthusiasm, and thoroughness. Experience and the sources of information with which he was very familiar served him well. But the second time he spoke he chose to talk about snapping turtles. He was still interested in turtles and he was still experienced, but the audience had heard enough of turtles and turned its attention elsewhere. In this case experience and personal interest did not serve.

We also think of the students who, told to consider their personal experiences in arriving at subject choices, gave speeches on "my summer job as a milkman" and "my days as a lifeguard." Their subjects were not well received, not because the speakers were unqualified. They had experience and were enthusiastic. They felt that they had learned a good deal on their jobs. But what they had to say was trite and familiar, incapable of stimulating their audiences to think.

2. *Prior knowledge* is a second factor to be considered. If you do not possess knowledge about your subject, you must gain it before you have earned the right to take the time of listeners. Remember, the five minutes you spend on the platform before an audience of twenty people consumes one hundred minutes of the world's time. Therefore, you will need to decide upon a subject about which you already know a great deal or about which you *can* know a great deal before your speaking engagement.

3. The *availability of material* becomes a third determinant of the

subject choice. Don't choose speech subjects without making a preliminary survey of the resources for obtaining the information you will need. We have mentioned possible sources of speech materials on page 41 and will discuss them further in Chapter 5. Our point here is that unless you make a preliminary inventory you may find that there is just not enough material to warrant a speech.

4. The *audience* will also have a bearing upon your subject choice. Age, sex, expectations, knowledge, and socioeconomic level may rule out some subjects which otherwise may seem to be excellent possibilities. We treat these matters more fully in Chapter 4.

5. A fifth determinant of your subject may well be the *occasion* with its inherent limitations: the reason for your listeners' coming together, the situation, and the time of day. Some subjects will be inappropriate because of the occasion or assignment.

6. The *time allotted* to you for your speech will place further limitations on the subject. In your preliminary survey of materials you may come to realize that your subject is too complex to be handled in the time you have, or too narrow. You may find some subjects too simple to profitably occupy the minutes.

7. Lastly, subjects for speaking ought to *challenge* the audience and the speaker. Something ought to be gained by both. There ought to be "news." Brain stretching and creative cogitation ought to be products of good subject choices. Puerile and parochial subjects do not encourage the kinds of thinking which ought to characterize public speaking as a liberal art.

Sometimes it is not the subject area which is responsible for poor subject choice but your selection of the aspect to be treated. The decisions that determine the merit of a speech often have to do with how to approach and treat a subject rather than with what that subject is.

If you or a program chairman or your instructor should propose the general topic, drama, for your first speech, your real business in deciding upon a subject begins with deciding what kind of response you want from your audience and with determining how you can narrow this topic to suit your purpose and your time limit. If your assignment or your preference particularizes your subject to something like, "Off-Broadway theatre during the 1950's," you may turn at once to deciding whether to inform, conduct an inquiry, persuade, or amuse your listeners in treating this subject. On the other hand, an inclination or a request to "tell about your experience with drama" leaves you with some decisions to make concerning *which* experiences to talk about. But these decisions, once more, will be chiefly determined by what kind of response you choose to seek from listeners. This topic seems to suggest a speech aiming at giving information, but your experiences could be so culled and selected as to persuade or amuse. Here as elsewhere, *which* materials ought to go into a speech and how broad or narrow your subject ought to be depend first and foremost upon one crucial decision: What response are you trying to get from your listeners?

LOCATING YOUR CENTRAL IDEA

In a classroom or in a public meeting you may be assigned a "report." This indicates that you are expected to inform. If the assignment goes one step farther and says you must report on a specific subject such as the outcome of a project or an interpretation of a concept, your purpose and your subject are already decided. Having been brought to this stage, by whatever means, your next task is to locate a central idea, a proposition or thesis or subject sentence around which to structure what you will say. In framing this central or core idea it is helpful to think of it as the hub of a wheel from which supporting spokes extend, as the roof of a pavilion which is supported by pillars, or as the apex of a pyramid supported by blocks of specific information which substantiate the epitomizing statement.

Any praiseworthy speech has *a* central idea or proposition to which the audience's attention is directed and for which a specific response is sought. Ideas, reasons, or assertions that are more detailed may form primary points in the general framework of your speech; but these ought to lead to, be subsumed by, funnel into, the central subject sentence. So, once your subject and purpose are known, your task invariably becomes to decide upon some statement that will express with pith and point the encompassing thought to which all that you will say ultimately refers. Once this is determined, you are ready to search for lesser ideas and special material with which to substantiate, amplify, and vivify the central thought in such a way as to evoke from listeners the response you earlier identified as your goal.

To sum up: sometimes you must choose your own subject; sometimes it is assigned; sometimes you must locate a narrower, more specific subject within a suggested topic or subject area; *always* you must define the responses you seek from listeners; *always* you must formulate a central idea that epitomizes the content you envision putting into the speech; *always* you must proceed to locate the subordinate ideas with which to render your central thought humanly meaningful. The reasons for our emphasis on conscious identification of sought-for responses, and conscious and precise formulation of central ideas lie in the nature of man. All listeners look for "the point of it all" in what they hear, so their demand must be met.

PHRASING YOUR SUBJECT SENTENCE

We add that some ingenuity in the framing of your central idea and statement of purpose will be welcomed. "I shall inform you this morning. . . ." or "Let me instruct you. . . ." or "It is my purpose this evening to persuade you that. . . ." are often unsatisfactory phrases with which to begin this sentence. Such wordings suggest lack of regard for the mentality of your audience. They tell the listeners so bluntly just what you are up to that the audience may back away from you and your message because they feel you are too strongly controlling or manipulating them. To say, "This morning I will inform you of the four ways in which pulp is processed," may fulfill the formal requirements for a good subject sentence, but it is rather bald. The purpose stands out obtrusively and is tritely phrased. Though when embedded in content this subject sentence may be acceptable to some, it may offend others by its kindergarten tone. A better subject sentence might be: "I hope you will be willing to work to eliminate Inner Cities like East Harlem, which can be found in every urban area." It invites attention and intrigues the listener.

Given the subject, a listener ought to be able to detect a speaker's rhetorical purpose and the kind of theme he is working with from the way in which his subject sentence is worded. Assertions are usually used for speeches of information and entertainment. Questions usually indicate that the purpose is inquiry. Propositions are reserved for persuasive speeches of various kinds. Suppose a speaker's subject is community theatre in the United States. For each of the usual rhetorical purposes his subject sentence might be worded in the following ways:

For informing: The history of the community theatre movement in the United States clearly reveals its purpose and nature.

For persuasion: The federal government ought to subsidize the community theatre movement.

For inquiry: Ought the federal government subsidize the community theatre movement?

For reinforcement: The community theatre movement in the United States is a worthwhile institution which enriches the lives of many people.

For entertaining: The community theatre movement is too bizarre for words.

Note that each of these sentences does three things: (1) reveals the subject of the speech, (2) states the central idea clearly, and (3) plainly implies the kind of response sought.

SUPPORTING THE CENTRAL IDEA

Let us suppose you have completed the initial steps of finding a subject, determining your purpose, narrowing your subject, and framing your subject sentence. You must now discover varied and interesting materials to clarify, to add detail to, or to prove and reinforce your theme. You must, in short, discover (1) facts; (2) testimony; (3) examples, whether long or short, real or hypothetical; (4) stories; (5) statistics; (6) comparisons, contrasts, and analogies; and (7) definitions for the purpose of proving or amplifying your subject sentence. At a later point in this book we shall explain these forms of support and amplification fully. (See pp. 150–161.) For now, it is enough to point out that you must find such pertinent materials and that you must structure them as simply as possible into a coordinated, organically unified whole that becomes a speech. In your first attempts to discover and arrange materials, it will be well to concentrate upon a clear, simple main theme rather than upon an elaborate and complicated structure of points and supporting material. It will also be wise to locate a number of pieces of support and from these to select a half dozen of the best for arrangement in clear, connected order. Once you have delivered one or two simple speeches consisting of one or two main points adequately supported or clarified, you will see that a longer speech is but a series of simple units, each developed individually and originally, and juxtaposed so as to form a larger, more elaborate, more complicated structure.

THE SEQUENCE OF PREPARATION

Thus far we have been dealing with the stages of speech preparation prior to arrangement and wording. The full pattern of basic steps in preparing a speech can be completed by adding to the steps already discussed the remaining tasks to be performed in sequence. While some of the following steps may be rearranged in order, you must ordinarily perform all of them to assure proper preparation and final success:

1. You must analyze your audience.
2. You must analyze the occasion.
3. You must discover a subject area.
4. You must discover the response you seek, often referred to as the rhetorical purpose.
5. You must narrow or expand the subject area to locate your specific subject.
6. You must wed the rhetorical purpose and your central idea in a clear-cut statement which stands as the theme of your speech and which may be expressed in a single, unambiguous sentence revealing both the content coverage and the rhetorical purpose of your speech.
7. You must gather materials for your speech through such activities as viewing, interviewing, reading, and discussing.
8. You must organize your materials into a comprehensive pattern which may be written in outline form.
9. You must try out wordings and experiment with language in your mind, or orally, in order to find the sharpest, clearest, and most vivid expression for your thoughts.
10. You must rehearse your speech orally in order to gain control of the pattern of ideas, of tentative wordings, of your body and your voice so that you gain a sense of emphasis, of timing, and time consumption.

Though this list may seem prescriptive and rigid, a careful consideration of the basic steps we have marked out will soon reveal that they are more flexible than they may seem to be when listed. For example, a speaker called upon by a women's club program chairman to give a speech on his recent experiences as a member of a rehabilitation project in Peru may skip step 3 but must at some time or other complete all other processes of preparation. Even though he may feel that he can dodge step 7 (after all, he knows all about the subject in question), he will find that to look outside himself and seek subject matter from others will provide reinforcement for his own supply of content. If he pursues step 7 as he ought to, he will find fresh illustrative materials so that all of his generalizations need not be based on personal experience alone. He may also find the observations of others suggest usable patterns of organization which he might not have thought of otherwise. A speaker who is simply asked to "come and speak for our group" will find that he had better complete all the steps we have outlined. A speaker who is asked to "come and give us the history of the National Association for the Advancement of Colored People" may omit steps 3 and 4, and he may find that his invitation has virtually completed step 6 for him.

Here, we have set down the elemental procedures essential in preparing any speech, long or short, composed of one or many points, for purposes of informing, inquiring, reinforcing, persuading, or entertaining. We do not say these procedures must be carried out in the exact order in which we have presented them; but we do reiterate that all decisions about a speech, for which subject, audience, and occasion are known, are contingent upon a clear and unequivocal identification of the response to be elicited from the audience. Step 4 in the list of procedures offered above must, therefore, be taken as early as possible in the preparatory process. Beyond this we have no wish to prescribe. On the other hand, it should never be forgotten that a listener's confusion about any speech is usually the consequence of some moment of illogical, unsystematic preparation on the part of the speaker.

Preparing a First Assignment

Now that you have an overview of the procedures involved in preparing a speech, you may ask what should be done to construct a first speech consisting of a single point, one which might well be a segment of a longer speech. Your specific procedure may be as follows:

1. First, select from a subject area of interest to you and your audience a relatively simple, single idea which you wish to clarify for your audience or which you wish them to accept. Sometimes you can arrive at such an idea by making a rough plan for a longer speech and then selecting from it one main point for development.

2. Once this idea has been selected, phrase it accurately in a single subject sentence.

3. Concentrate on a single, simple method of development—a structural pattern. Explain or persuade, for example, by arranging your materials in chronological, spatial, effect-to-cause, or problem-solution order.

4. Draw upon several sources other than personal experience for material to amplify or support your idea.

5. Carefully plan even this short speech; prepare a full-sentence outline though it may consist of only six or eight items.

6. Make each of these items bear upon your subject sentence. Show the audience that each item does clarify or support your subject sentence.

7. In delivering this single point and its amplifying or supporting material, make each item stand out clearly.

8. A final test of the speech will be an affirmative answer to one of two questions: "Does my audience understand the subject better now that I have spoken?" or "Does the audience more nearly accept the idea I have been proposing?"

A simple outline will serve in planning this first speech. To illustrate how you might locate and outline a single point appropriate for a brief talk, let us imagine that you think a major speech might be given on the subject sentence: "We need to support mental health organizations better than we do." If you ask yourself what might be the main headings of such a speech the following could occur to you:

    I. Anxiety is a disturbing phenomenon.
    II. Anxiety is widespread in our society.
    III. Mental health organizations help people to reduce their anxieties.
    IV. Mental health organizations deserve more help than we give them.

Any of these four points could be used as a central idea for a shorter speech although the fourth is least promising because it depends for support on the other three. If you chose the first of these points for a one-point speech, you would need to prepare a simple outline or plan of its development. It might look like this:

Subject Sentence: Anxiety is a disturbing phenomenon.[2]

Supporting Material:

| (Example, brief) | 1. A recent article in the *Saturday Evening Post* tells the story of a woman's unwarranted anxiety over the fate of her handicapped son. |

[2] This sample outline was prepared by John K. Thorne. Used by permission.

(Fact)   2. The anxiety response is often characterized as objectless.

(Definition,   3. A group of prominent psychologists, including Harold
Testimony)   Basowitz and Roy Grenker, define anxiety as ". . . the
                    conscious and reportable experience of intense dread and
                    foreboding, conceptualized as internally derived and un-
                    related to any external threat."

(Comparison)   4. Anxiety produces a result like that experienced when
                   marching in place; we only raise the dust around us.

(Quotation)   5. An old saying is that "Anxiety and worry, not work, tire
                   one out."

(Quotation)   6. In Book I of Plato's *Republic* you may find the statement:
                   "Nothing in the affairs of men is worthy of great anxiety."

A comparable plan for a one-point speech on a proverb might well
look like this:

Subject Sentence: "A bird in hand is worth two in the bush" is widely applicable
in our day.[3]

Supporting Material:

(Restatement of   1. Aesop related this concept in stronger language in *The
Central Idea)   Fisher and the Little Fish:* "A little thing in hand is
                       worth more than a great thing in prospect."

(Fact)   2. The future is unpredictable; so great expectations may
                   easily become only false hopes.

(Fact)   3. Psychologically, when one continually gambles on the
                   prospect of a "great thing" and loses, he may develop
                   complexes and may become mentally unbalanced.

(Example,   4. A young girl may physically decay as a result of wait-
brief)   ing for "a great thing in prospect."

(Example,   5. The value of a "bird in hand" is exemplified by Cor-
brief)   nell's policy in football: going for the sure extra point
                   rather than gambling on the two-point conversion.

(Example,   6. It is better to have a date with a Cornell coed for a
extended)   big week end than to have no date at all. (Tell story.)

You will notice that these sample outlines omit title, opening, and
closing. Although it will be necessary for you to have some sort of intro-

[3] This sample outline was prepared by James Hamasaki. Used by permission.

duction and conclusion for your speech, we have exemplified only the amplification or proof for the main point. The pieces of support are labelled to show the types the speakers used and to suggest to you that variety in supporting materials enlivens communication.

Modes of Delivery

There are four general methods of delivering a speech. One may present a speech impromptu. He may deliver it extemporaneously. He may read it aloud, or he may deliver it word-for-word from memory.

The best and most widely used method of delivery among beginners is the extemporaneous method, for more than the others it promotes development of conversational quality in speaking.

Many people confuse the word *extemporaneous* with the word *impromptu*. The two are not synonymous terms. The extemporaneous mode of delivery is one in which your speech is thought out in advance; planned with care; usually carefully outlined on paper; rehearsed orally, and delivered sometimes with, sometimes without, notes. This mode allows freedom and spontaneity in the final wording of thoughts. It also permits the speaker the flexibility he needs if he is to adapt easily to unforeseen circumstances.

The impromptu mode is one in which there is no formal preparation of any kind until a few minutes before speaking begins. The most an impromptu speaker usually does before speaking is to gather his thoughts together by jotting down a few words on a paper napkin or note card. Impromptu speaking is, for the most part, spur-of-the-moment activity which is rarely profitable except as an exercise in self-command and in emergencies.

It is easy to mistake extemporaneous speaking for impromptu speaking when you are unsure of the preparation, planning, and rehearsal involved. Many lecturers and some legislators and lawyers appear to their audiences to speak impromptu when in reality they have made extensive preparation during years of authoritative investigation, experience, and practice. Those who seem to speak impromptu when they are really speaking extemporaneously are commonly people who engage in public speaking almost daily, so that formal practice sessions though desirable are not an absolute necessity for them. Most of you, lacking such experience and practice, must conduct a specific investigation to enrich each utterance and must gain command over each particular set of ideas by rehearsing them in special, oral practice sessions.

You may or may not be allowed to use notes for classroom extemporaneous speeches. If they are used, they should be unobtrusive and kept to a minimum. They are not to be used in such a way as to call attention to themselves. On the other hand, it is best not to try to hide them in the palm of your hand or under your sleeve. Few in the audience will expect you to memorize a particularly troublesome set of statistics or a long literary quotation, the flavor of which is best preserved by verbatim presentation. Fewer, however, will feel that you are direct and in control of your ideas if your eyes are constantly on your notes or if you are reading from them most of the time. In some cases you will be allowed to take your outline to the platform and in other cases not. When you are using an outline or notes your aim should be to refer to them as little as possible.

In your classroom performances your aim ought to be to free yourself from preset wordings and from mechanical delivery. Should you freeze fast all your ideas, you will deliver them with exactness and rigidity in wording and gesture; they will have little prospect of coming alive. There will be small chance for what Professor J. A. Winans called a "vivid realization of the idea at the moment of utterance." Should you persist in draining your performance of spontaneity by verbatim memorization, by lackluster reading of what you have written prior to speaking, or by clinging to specific wordings at the expense of the re-creation of ideas, your audience will probably receive your efforts coldly and with little enthusiasm. They may react as they would to left-overs of any kind. Cold mashed potatoes served without reheating are hardly as appetizing to most people as those freshly prepared. While you cannot serve up a "just-prepared" speech, you ought to come as close as possible to creating that illusion. Prepare, rehearse, let the speech lie. Let it go through a gestation period as seeds do. Then re-create your speech with enthusiasm, poise, and verve.

The extemporaneous method of delivery is best for the beginner. By using this mode you avoid the pitfalls inherent in other methods. You will avoid the disorganized, unsupported train of ideas usually apparent in the beginner's impromptu efforts. You will avoid the rigid, mechanical transmission of ideas evident in the efforts of the unpracticed oral reader and inexperienced memorizer. We are not at this point disparaging the reading or memorizing of speeches per se. Some people read aloud very well, and some can memorize material and recite it so their listeners never know that it is memorized. In Chapter 11 we shall discuss reading in some detail. (See pp. 312–320.) We are saying that the beginner is more likely to achieve the most conversationality in his speaking if he uses the extemporaneous mode. This mode allows not only for careful, thorough preparation, but also for audience adaptation and for spontaneous regeneration of ideas at the time the speech is given. We discuss oral rehearsal for extemporaneous speaking in a later section of this chapter. (See pp. 60–61.)

Stage Fright

Stage fright or "speech fright," as it has been more progressively called, is a universal experience. You no doubt know its physical symptoms. When some situation demanded that you speak with another individual in interview or required you to stand up alone before an audience, you may suddenly have experienced feelings that told you you had stage fright. You may have discovered to your dismay that your knees were shaking, that your mouth felt as if it were stuffed with wads of cotton, that your voice quavered, or that your heart beat all too swiftly. You may have felt faint, perspired in the palms of your hands. You may have experienced a churning in your stomach or felt as if twenty-two butterflies were using it as a football field. Some of these physical manifestations of stage fright were real. Others were imaginary. You actually did perspire, but your saliva flow did not really dry up. All these signs, whether actual and overt or imaginary and covert, were manifestations of a state of anxiety which stemmed from fear. You know that what you experienced was stage *fright*, but you may have overlooked the fact which the name implies, that *fear* was at the heart of the matter. Fear provoked the anxieties manifested in your emotional disorganization. These anxieties may have become so severe that you were actually physically ill. Instead of realizing that you were afraid, you may have become preoccupied with the imaginary or real manifestations of your condition and sought to remedy the situation by concentrating on getting rid of the "shakes" or by wetting your lips over and over again. You may have tried to get rid of the physical symptoms without trying to do anything about the real cause of your condition: fear itself.

The fear which caused your anxiety did result in physiological changes. Many who undergo these changes think they are actually organically ill, that they have a tumor somewhere or some sort of secretion imbalance. What actually happened was that the flow of adrenalin set off other changes. Blood pressure, the rate of respiration, and nerve conductivity increased. More blood sugar furnishing energy entered the system. More thyroxin, speeding the burning of the blood sugar, may have been secreted. More oxygen was taken into the blood. More poisons were removed from your system. As a result of these changes fatigue probably lessened, and you may have experienced the kind of increase in strength that frequently accompanies the release of tensions during a period of anger. These bodily changes may be of interest to you, but they are not the causes of your fear.

The real causes of your fear were psychological. A lack of self-confidence resulted in fear when insecurity threatened. The insecurity stemmed from the uncertainties of the situation in which you found yourself. You may have been apprehensive about how your audience would react. Literally, you were afraid that you would lose control of the audience. Or, you may have been apprehensive about your mastery and control of what you were going to say. You were afraid you wouldn't be perfect or that you would fail. You may have been anxious about how well your voice and body would function, or whether you would choose the right words to express your thoughts and feelings accurately. In public speaking situations the mere fact that you were physically separated from a group of peers may have been responsible for feelings of insecurity and aloneness. You may have been afraid of listeners' disapproval or of the criticisms you thought they might make. Or you may have felt you *had* to speak, that you were compelled to do so against your better judgment, and conflict within resulted. You may have fought with yourself. Your wishes to avoid the situation, to flee from it, may have caused you to make such serious excuses that you finally did not have to speak at all. (After all, you *were* ill.) You may have invented alibis or have inwardly prayed, "If ever I am going to break my leg, let it be now."

If, however, you were unable to avoid speaking or if you faced up to reality and decided that now was the time to speak, you may have been unable, still, to channel your excess energy so that it worked for rather than against you. You squirmed, fidgeted, grimaced, croaked out the words, and visibly shook in the face of fear. Each of these actions called the attention of the audience away from what you were saying. Because of your manifestations of discomfort, those to whom you spoke couldn't hear what you were saying.

The problem, then, would seem to be: How can you reduce fear and, subsequently, the tensions which afflict you? The solutions to the problem can be discovered only by going back to the causes to see what can be done to remove them.

A good first step is to realize that everyone else at some time or other experiences the same apprehensions you do. Nothing except this is certain in the public speaking situation. The most any speaker can do is to guess how an audience will react, then calmly calculate how best to promote the responses he seeks and to meet the demands the audience makes. Insights into the nature of human behavior come with experience, but they are always less than perfect. Realize this fact, but do not dodge the business of making educated guesses on how you can best adapt to your particular audience in order to get them to react in the ways you wish them to. They are human beings like you. They may vary in age, interest, and creed; but they are similar to you in more ways than you probably realize. We know it is easy to say, "Feel at one with the audience," "Know that they will be more uncomfortable than you are if you don't succeed," "Remember that they are faced with the same problems, the same fears, and the same reactions to fear as you are." All of this is to say, "Get yourself in the right frame of mind." But, it is quite another matter to *feel*, once you have adopted attitudes conducive to the feeling. Yet you must make first tries, you must gain composure by repeatedly going through the experience of making a speech in the face of all the varying conditions attending it. So it is that a striving for realistic attitudes, coupled with practice, will be of help in assuaging your fear.

Thorough preparation, once the calculated guesses are made, is a further step in combating fear. If the apprehensions you have result from distrust of your material and your memory of it, then close, careful attention to your pattern of organization, to your supporting and amplifying materials, to your wordings and to particularly troublesome spots in your train of thought is needed. The best antidote to fear is thoroughgoing preparation—but this does *not* mean memorization.

Proper attitudes, practice, and preparation, then, may all play a part in dispelling fear and decreasing anxiety. Above and beyond these, however, is your desire to speak. If you want to speak, you have won half the battle in many instances. If you have more than enough to say and are filled with a determination to make the audience understand or accept your point of view, you will have come a long way toward releasing your tensions into meaningful, constructive actions which will contribute to the accomplishment of your goals. If your desire to communicate is strong enough, you will forget to worry about your hands or feet or what they are doing. This is not to say that you will forget you have a voice and body which you must control. It is to say that with all efforts bent in the direction of gaining specific audience responses, you will have your best opportunity to accomplish what you set out to do. You will be like a swimmer in a race who, once he has hit the water, lets nothing divert his attention until he reaches the finish line. All distractions will be swept aside or ignored. With proper practice, wasted motion can be eliminated. Controlled gestures will be made—gestures that are necessary but which never occur as superficial flourishes or decorations. Wordings will become economical, because with your mind filled with the business of communicating that which you know securely, you will say just enough and no more to elicit the reactions you seek. Losing yourself in your speech without losing your self-control will cause you to forget your fears.

Of course, you cannot desire to speak unless you are sure that the subject you have chosen is a worthy one. It must be worthy of you and of the time spent in preparation, and it must be worthy of your audience. If you have misgivings about the ideas and materials you are presenting, you are a prime target for fear. Only by choosing wisely and carefully what you will say can you hope to approach a speech situation with confidence. If you feel that what you are going to say isn't worth much to you or your audience; if you feel that your ideas are shabby, that you have settled for words that are dull or imprecise, or that your speech is just something to get over, of course you will be afraid, and you deserve to be!

Rehearsal   and   Attitudes
Toward   Speaking

Oral rehearsal for extemporaneous delivery assures mastery of your speech plan, control of the succession of points embodied in it, and confidence in your ability to present the speech as you intend. The problem in extemporaneous speaking is to transfer your plan to your mind and become thoroughly familiar with its sequence of ideas. As you gain control of ideas and their order specific word choices will vary with each rehearsal, thus building for you a large stock of verbal resources by which to express yourself during the final presentation of your speech. Sound practice in rehearsing extemporaneous speeches is the first and foremost avenue to confidence in public speech; sensible, realistic attitudes toward the act of speaking constitute the second. The suggestions outlined below will repay you in clarity of mind and serenity of spirit if you follow them closely whenever you prepare to speak extemporaneously.[4]

1. Read through your written plan fixing your mind on the succession of main points. Read through it again, this time concentrating not only on the main points but on the details supporting each.

2. Still referring to your outline, speak through the speech in whatever words happen to come. Talk out loud, not under your breath. You will find it helps to stand up and face an imaginary audience. Try out gestures as you verbalize. Get through the whole speech. If you bungle a part, go right on to the end without stopping to straighten out the troublesome section. Come back to that when you have finished your run-through of the entire speech.

3. Without using your outline or any memoranda except those notes you will use on the platform, stand up and speak through the speech as before. If you can find a patient listener or group of listeners, so much the better.

4. When you can get through your total speech fairly well, time yourself and adjust the speech to the time allotted for your actual presentation. Such an adjustment may call for omissions or condensations, or it may call for additions or expansions of points. It is important to acquire a sense of time on the platform and the habit of keeping within time limits.

5. If, in anticipating the moments of speaking, you have a tendency to

---

[4] The material that follows is adapted from *Manual for Public Speaking, I,* p. 22, by H. A. Wichelns and others (1932) and *Manual for an Elementary Course* by H. A. Wichelns, G. B. Muchmore, and others, p. 19. Used by permission.

panic, fix your mind on the realities of the situation. Focus on facts; do not imagine difficulties you don't yet face.

6. In the moments before taking the platform keep the plan of your speech uppermost in your mind; review it. This is the most constructive outlet for tensions.

7. During preparation and just before speaking renew your desire to share a worthwhile message with others. Remind yourself that the experience before you is not a "performance" but an opportunity. You have earned that opportunity through the knowledge you have acquired and your position as a respected human being in a communicating society.

8. Recall that your auditors are persons not very different from yourself, that they want you to succeed.

9. Don't expect to avoid all tension. Some tension is good for you. Properly channeled, tension can serve you positively by increasing your alertness and your available supply of energy.

10. When you are nervous, exercise autosuggestion. Act alert, at ease, and in control of your subject, and you will actually tend to be alive, relaxed, and in command. You will also find deep breathing and an erect rather than a slumped posture will contribute to your comfort. You *do* need extra oxygen.

11. As a general rule, avoid last-minute changes in your speech, especially during your maiden efforts. Don't add to uneasiness by entertaining misgivings about choices already made. Adapt to the moment and to other speakers but do not make changes that undermine the over-all plan you established in your mind by systematic rehearsal.

Oral rehearsal is insurance. Fluent discourse demands it. Beginning speakers are often tempted to omit this important stage of speech composition because of self-consciousness or because they have not allocated sufficient time for it in scheduling their preparation. This is a mistake of the gravest order. It is control over content that contributes most to control over self; both kinds of control are established and enhanced in oral rehearsal.

Listening

We have thus far examined basic considerations important to you as a speaker. But where there are public speakers there are listeners. Listening is an integral part of the public speaking experience. There are some elemental facts about listening in general and about listening as a student of speech making which also are "first considerations."

All of us listen all the time, and we listen more than we speak. We find ourselves listening more often than speaking. Because our role is so frequently that of listener, we ought to ask how we can carry out this role with profit. What ought we to do as listeners? *How* should we listen?

Before we can profitably listen to any speech or consider how to do so, we must discover our purposes in listening. Are we listening to the speech to gain information? To absorb information we will later be tested on? Are we listening out of mere courtesy, to appear to be ladies and gentlemen? Are we listening in order to experience pleasurable sensations, to be entertained? Are we listening to assess critically the speaker's arguments or interpretations? Are we listening to hear the other side of a case? Are we listening to gain information on only one aspect of the subject a speaker is considering? Are we listening in order to appraise the speech as an artistic endeavor?

To answer "yes" to any of these questions or to others like them would be to give a legitimate reason for listening. But to give a "yes" to more than one question (a definite possibility) would make it necessary to qualify some one answer with the adverb, *primarily*. Only so could one determine what posture he ought to adopt as a listener. Only by knowing his *primary* reason for listening can any of us discover *how* to listen. Secondary reasons for listening, though appropriate, do not focus attention any more than secondary ideas focus upon the total meaning of a speech. Efficient listening for any primary purpose requires that attention be focused *in a particular way* upon what is heard.

When one's primary purpose in listening is discovered, the items in a speech which demand closest attention become apparent. What a listener will note depends on what he is listening for. How critically he will examine ideas and their detail, how carefully he will observe the manner in which ideas are phrased or spoken, is determined by his purpose in listening. Conversely, any listener relaxes his attention when he decides what he is hearing is irrelevant to his needs and interests. In sum, we all have learned to select what we want to hear, note, and absorb. As a speaker you must seek to get your listeners to select for attention what *you* think is of primary importance in your speech. As a listener you invariably weigh whether the speaker's view of importance coincides with your own.

Self-discipline is necessary in all comprehensive listening. Careless listening is simply randomly or erroneously directed. Efficient, comprehensive listening is hard work. It entails clarity about purpose and it requires bringing the sense organs sharply to bear on what one hears or sees. Comprehensive listening can be a fatiguing enterprise. Louis Nizer says of the work it involves: "So complete is this concentration that at the end of a court day in which I have only listened, I find myself wringing wet despite a calm and casual manner."[5] To listen critically, taking in the sum of information conveyed through speech requires that one curb his tendency to let attention wander, despite many temptations. A barking dog, a flickering light, a noisy radiator are stimuli competing with what is being said. These are distractions external to speech, but other distractions emanate from the speaker. He may fidget, speak monotonously, or become confused and disorganized in his train of thought. Still other distractions arise within the listener himself. He is strongly drawn to his own immediate problems; he thinks of a coming examination, of a letter just received, or a remark recently overheard. Biases and prejudices, too, may provoke strong reactions if a speaker touches a sensitive topic. There is, indeed, clear evidence that one of the most common interferences with effective listening is the tendency to construct counter arguments in imagination whenever an old belief is in any way challenged by those to whom we listen. To pay attention to what is said in the face of such distractions demands considerable self-control. Purposive, efficient listening does not just happen. It requires a measure of discipline appropriate to the demands of one's primary purpose in attending.

Questions concerning speakers' and listeners' *obligations* often arise in speech classes. It is proper that they should, for both speaking and listening must be examined and understood if communication itself is to be understood. It is useful to ask, Must the whole burden for holding attention rest on the speaker? Does the listener have a duty to perform? Are you, as listener, obligated to attend to what every classroom speaker says whether you want to or not? How far do listening to learn content and listening to observe examples of speech making demand that you pay close attention to all that is said? As a student of public speaking your best answer to such questions is probably the Golden Rule. When your role is that of speaker, you will want others to listen to you so they may make constructive sug-

[5] *My Life in Court* (New York: Doubleday, 1961), pp. 297–98.

gestions for your improvement. You will hope they will listen carefully to what you have to say and to how you say it. And if this is the sort of listening that you hope for from others, you must be able and willing to listen to them in the same way—for the primary purpose of evaluating speaking as artistic endeavor. Outside the classroom you are the only listener to whom you can prescribe "duties." But the liberally educated citizen ought at least to recognize that if he does not listen cooperatively and objectively to both the content and method of what he hears, he will seldom be qualified to judge "what is going on here" in the speaking offered him. The exacting task of listening to evaluate speeches as artistic creations demands that attention be focused upon the suitability of method to content; there are, then, few more constructive laboratories for the practice of the educated citizen's skills in listening than the laboratory-classroom where public speaking is practiced.

Often what you hear as a listener may puzzle you. You cannot see the sense of it, the rationale behind it, or the relationships between one idea and another. Depending on your purpose, your job as listener may dictate that you reorganize the material which the speaker has neglected to organize or has organized badly. In order for you to understand, you may have to go over the notes you have taken during listening and put them in a new order that makes sense to you. Some college lectures demand this kind of attention. Conversely, in speaking you will want to avoid placing this kind of burden on your audience, so you will make it easier for them by clearly organizing what you have to say.

The public speaking classroom is a listening laboratory in another sense. As a speaker you will have opportunity to detect whether others are listening to you and opportunity to adjust to what you discover. If a member of your audience stares listlessly into space, fidgets uncomfortably, frowns or shakes his head, lolls sleepily in his chair, or chats with his neighbor, you will know you are not holding his full, favorable attention. Given such cues, and you will learn others as well, you will know you must do something to recapture wavering attention, to start listeners nodding in recognition of what you say, to get them to lean forward in spirit if not in fact. How you can accomplish this is a major consideration in the chapters that follow. But from the beginning of your study of public speaking you will need to recognize that efficient, purposeful listening is not an invariable condition of communicative settings. You will misunderstand your own responses to the speeches of others if you fail to perceive (1) that any but haphazard listening is the product of deliberate and organized effort, (2) that what you will gain from hearing other speakers will depend on what purpose governs your listening responses, (3) that what responses any speaker wins from listeners depends upon how well he accommodates his speaking to the natural difficulties of listening, and (4) that the public speaking classroom is a laboratory in which you may study the nature of man in the act of listening as well as man in the act of speaking.

The listening role of the student of public speaking is tripartite, but the primary goal of this kind of listening is to discover in what ways design or method in oral communication affects the intelligibility and impact of content. You will find yourself listening to absorb the ideas that other speakers present, to improve your own communication by observing what methods enhance or debilitate other speakers' meanings, and to discover that which you can offer your colleagues as constructive criticism calculated to enlarge their potentialities as speakers. To so listen, you must discipline your perceptions by searching for answers to this primary question: *Why* did what was said affect me, and other listeners, as it did? Every answer you can defensibly make to that question will add to your understanding of speaking and listening—and in the process of answering you will also acquire much new information of a general sort.

In this chapter we have dealt with matters you need to consider before engaging in formal speech making. Originality, we have said, is the first requisite of all effective public speaking. Careful and systematic preparation gives discourse the focus and clarifying structure so necessary to both speaker and listener. Since the beginning speaker's need is to acquire conversational directness and flexibility in speaking, the extemporaneous mode of presentation will benefit him most, at least in the early stages of his experience as a speaker. Stage fright, we have seen, is not to be exorcized by any tactics except those that eradicate fear. Again, extemporaneous speaking, properly prepared for, is the mode of delivery that will best permit you to develop constructive attitudes easing tension. It is not enough, however, to view the study of public speaking as a study in how speeches are composed and given utterance; speeches are made *for* listeners who, themselves, have difficulties accommodating to the practices of speakers. The public speaking classroom must therefore become a laboratory of both speaking and listening, if its full resources are to be used. To this end you will probably need to develop in yourself a new kind of listening—that which concentrates on the ways by which methods of oral communication affect the impact of content.

E x e r c i s e s

Written

1. Read a speech of your own choosing. Note as you read those aspects of the speech which seem to you to be original and those which do not. Hand in a paper containing two lists of items: Original, Unoriginal. Add two paragraphs in which you justify your choices in each of the two lists.
2. Write down five simple, single ideas which you think would be good ones for development in a speech of 2–3 minutes.
3. Select a subject area. Frame a subject sentence for each of the rhetorical purposes: informing, persuading, inquiring, reinforcing, and entertaining.
4. Listen carefully to a speech by one of your classmates. Take notes in outline form on what he is saying. Following the speech, compare your outline with the one the speaker used. Check to see (a) how accurately you noted what was said, and (b) how much you missed noting.

Oral

1. Deliver a three-minute speech in which you develop a single point which could be one of several main points in a longer speech. In developing your point use at least three different kinds of supporting material. In preparation, prepare a simple outline like that found on pages 52–53.
2. Prepare and deliver a brief speech on a proverb of your own choosing. Select at least six items to support its truth or falsity. In preparation devise a simple outline like that on page 54.

4   *Understanding*

Audiences

Until a man knows the truth of the several particulars of which he is writing or speaking, and is able to define them as they are, and having defined them again to divide them until they can be no longer divided, and until in like manner he is able to discern the nature of the soul and discover the different modes of discourse which are adapted to different natures, and to arrange and dispose them in such a way that the simple form of speech may be addressed to the simpler nature, and the complex and composite to the complex nature—until he has accomplished all this, he will be unable to handle arguments according to rules of art, as far as their nature allows them to be subjected to art, either for the purpose of teaching or persuading. . . .

PLATO, *Phaedrus*[1]

Whenever you talk to another person you expect him to respond in some way. You speak to be heard, and you want a reaction. The poet, the novelist, and even some essayists may concentrate upon the long-range excellence and beauty of what they write, but you are usually interested in the reception accorded your message now—at the moments of speaking. Even if you are ambitious for your message to reach beyond the immediate audience, you are still aiming for a particular set of effects in specifiable other places or other times. In either case you loose speech to do specific kinds of practical work under conditions you can describe rather precisely. This is why successful speakers do not dwell on the beauty of their speeches; they concentrate, rather, on the practical effects of what they plan to say. For the same reasons a speaker's success is not measured so much by the

[1] Plato, *Phaedrus*, trans. B. Jowett in *The Works of Plato* (New York: Tudor Publishing Company, n.d.), III, p. 446.

timelessness of his remarks as by the responses they evoke at the time of the speech. Speakers seldom address all men in all ages as other literary artists often seek to do; speeches are, before all else, composed and delivered to and for a particular audience in a particular time and place. If they become part of the cultural heritage it is because their subject matters *happen* to have importance for many audiences.

Since practical effect is the chief measure of success in speaking, the degree of your achievement will depend heavily on your knowledge and understanding of how men listen and respond to what they hear. It is not always easy to regulate one's speech making according to the dictates of what we know about listeners. Like the serpent tempting Eve, self-love often whispers that the world ought to be as we wish it. Listeners ought to wait attentively to hear what we have to say. "I know what they ought to hear," we tell ourselves; and, if we discover that "they" didn't listen, we frequently complete the self-delusion saying, "Well, they should have listened for I am right and I spoke for their own good. They could have caught my meaning had they tried." But all the while the mistake was our own, for we prepared the speech to please ourselves, not with our listeners' necessities in mind. This very self-deceit, which we all practice at some time, should be to each speaker a proof that everyone prefers his own discourse to the talk of another. Just as you prefer your own ways of thinking about any question, every other person—every listener—prefers his way. The situation of the speaker is clear, if a bit difficult. If he is to reach the minds of listeners, he must fit his thought to their preferences, understandings, and interests.

You have certainly felt, when talking to a friend, that although he seemed to hear you, he was not thinking about what you were saying. Each of us has played this role of polite but evasive listener, actually engrossed in his own private thoughts. And most of us have also witnessed the same phenomenon in public situations. In the novel, *Phineas Finn,* for example, Anthony Trollope invented such a circumstance when he imagined Mr. Daubeny announcing to the House of Commons the resignation of a Ministry. That part of Daubeny's speech which dealt with what his party might have done had it been left in power, Trollope says, "was generally felt by gentlemen on both sides of the House to be 'leather and prunella,' . . . very little attention was paid to it. The great point was that Lord de Terrier had resigned, and that Mr. Mildmay had been summoned to Windsor." The listening politicians had no time for Mr. Daubeny's speculations on what might have been but was not going to be. They were too busily occupied with calculating how *they* would be affected by the change of Ministers. Like all listeners everywhere, their own thoughts and concerns were, for them, the most important things in the world. Mr. Daubeny's speculations were equally important to *him*, but he might as well have kept them to himself that day for no one was really listening. What the *new* government was going to do was the only discussable subject just then.

The speaker's necessity, then, is unavoidable even if it is troublesome. He must secure the attention of his hearers; if he cannot do this there is little use in speaking. He cannot assume audiences will give him attention just because they and he are in the same physical place. It is the *psychological* meeting place that counts. So, speakers must learn under what circumstances listeners can and cannot be brought to prefer what is being said to what they carry in their own minds. It is this knowledge, acquired from instruction or from experience, that distinguishes the effective from the ineffective speaker.

What Is an Audience?

We all use the word, *audience,* in everyday speech and writing, yet we do not always think clearly about the characteristics of audiences. There are those who conceive of an audience as a mass of faceless—even will-less —beings who have left their individualities at the door and present a kind of gelatinous common front on which the speaker may make whatever imprint he chooses. There are also those who imagine that any group of listeners will respond, like automatons, to this or that appeal or to some technique alleged surely to influence behavior.

But an audience is not a faceless, will-less mass of beings. Neither are its responses mindlessly automatic. Whether it consists of one person or many, an audience is made up of individuals, each intent upon his own and his group's life and happiness, preferring the pursuit of these private interests to any other form of activity. True, each member of the audience tends to conform in some degree to the standards and expectations of those about him, but he seldom surrenders his individuality to the audience group. Whether any member will *choose* to attend to what you say depends much more upon his own inclinations and upon your astuteness in designing the communication than on the behavior of the other people also in the audience. (One can imagine extreme circumstances where this statement would be inaccurate, but it is true for typical speaking situations.) Thus the two most important things a public speaker must remember about listeners are: *they are individuals* and *they do not have to listen unless they want to*. If you consider your own behavior you will see the truth of these propositions.

At some time you undoubtedly sat in a class in American history. Sometimes you gave active attention to almost everything your instructor and classmates said. At other times you found nothing especially interesting in what was being discussed, so you allowed your thoughts to wander to more inviting matters. If you liked the subject or the teacher, you probably attended more carefully than if you disliked either or both. It was also true, no doubt, that every now and then some historical fact or an especially clear, interesting, or impressive statement seemed literally to seize your attention and your thoughts. But in all of these experiences of listening *you* retained control over what you would admit into your consciousness and over the ways you would respond to what you admitted. Doubtless there were many times when you restrained your enthusiasms or fought your boredom out of regard for others and for the social situation, but in the main you always remained yourself. Though you were among many, you were neither the spineless creature of the group nor the speaker's will-less puppet. You were part of an audience; you were to some extent affected by the behavior and opinions of those about you; but you and each of your classmates remained individuals, granting or withholding attention according to your own different interests, ideas, attitudes, and desires.

But, you may say, "The role of a listener in a classroom need not be that of listeners everywhere. How is it that large numbers of people are deeply moved as in religious revivals or great political rallies?" There are probably several answers, but the one of most importance to public speakers is that in circumstances like revival meetings and political rallies people take encouragement from discovering that others feel as they do. They *seem* to be swept along by the power of a speaker when in reality they are only allowing themselves the luxury of acting in an unusually uninhibited fashion on the basis of prior attitudes, enthusiasms, or dislikes. We cannot say such demonstrations illustrate mass conversion through speech and pageantry; rather, they illustrate the greater freedom with which listeners will express or demonstrate strong beliefs and feelings once these have been intensified by the words of a powerful speaker and encouraged by the support of like-minded fellow listeners. The facts, so far as they are now understood, seem to be that although audiences are made up of individuals who retain their own preferences and concerns, these individuals do not like to appear very far ahead or very far behind the opinions held by their fellows; and they are anxious to have their predispositions confirmed by others. Few follow the herd blindly, but most want to be within the bounds of what the group accepts and approves. Just as, in your American history class, you curbed some of your enthusiasm or hid some evidences of your boredom, so all of us, when we become members of audiences, trim the sails of our behavior to the winds of group opinion and practice. Each sails his own vessel, but each prefers to have the fleet at least in sight.

How then shall we define an audience? It is an aggregation of individuals with some tendencies to behave alike. But it is an aggregation in which each member maintains his own personality, acts on the basis of his private needs and knowledge, and retains his own power to shut out or admit the influences about him, whether these come from a speaker or from other members of the audience. An audience presents no collective mind to which you can direct mass appeals. On the other hand, one cannot, practically, motivate each audience member independently of the others. To move an audience, then, you must know some of the ways in which people and groups of people tend to behave alike just because they are people. Since you cannot learn all about each person to whom you will speak, you must learn generalizations about what individuals responding to speaking have in common. These generalizations will never furnish bases for solving all the problems of adapting to audiences, but they will help you to deal with audiences as aggregations of human beings who share at least their humanity.

The remainder of this chapter is devoted to an exploration of the generalizations a speaker may safely make about human beings as listeners. With such broad but practical understandings you will be better able to reach the minds of those who hear you and to do so with efficiency and effectiveness.

Sources of Attention

Imagine yourself entering a room and sitting down beside a friend. What happens inside your friend? First, he becomes conscious that you have come into the room. Probably he looks at you. He may smile or speak a greeting which says he is aware of you—even that he is glad to see you. In the same moment he may casually notice what you are wearing or whether you look tired or refreshed. So far, he has been carrying on a kind of swift conversation within himself; his greeting was probably only an automatic reaction of which he was hardly conscious. What really occupied him was his feeling toward you and toward your sudden appearance. In these earliest seconds of your meeting his thoughts were focused on you as a person and not at all on communication with you. But if you speak, he will begin to listen, for he was already focusing his attention on you. All that is newly required of him is that he shift attention from your person and his feelings about your presence to what you are saying. This he will usually be willing to do—but only for as long as your remarks strike him as interesting or worthwhile. If your talk begins to bore him, he may turn his thoughts back to your person, or to the way you sound when you talk, or to someone or something else in the room, or to other thoughts of his own. Should he do this, your meanings no longer affect him.

Of course, what has just been said is neither a complete nor an entirely scientific description of how one individual grants and takes away his attention. It is, however, an approximate description that you should always carry in your mind as the portrait of your every listener, whether he be a single friend or the unknown member of a crowd before you. Each listener first grants attention to your presence; then, he responds to whatever feelings your presence arouses in him; next, he transfers his attention, tentatively, to whatever communication is initiated. Thus far he will go *voluntarily;* what happens after depends on whether the communication keeps him interested and favorably disposed toward its source.

Plainly, to *secure* attention is relatively easy. Perhaps that is why unsophisticated public speakers lavish so much loving care on introductory "gimmicks"—they always seem to work because they weren't really needed in the first place. To secure attention is easy. To *hold* a listener's attention is what requires inventive effort and design.

The attention of a listener is a fickle thing to be enticed, guided, managed, commanded by the speaker. Samuel Taylor Coleridge's "The Rime of the Ancient Mariner" touches on the control over attention of which speakers dream:

> He holds him with his glittering eye—
> The Wedding-Guest stood still,
> And listens as a three years' child:
> The Mariner hath his will.
>
> The Wedding-Guest sat on a stone:
> He cannot choose but hear;
> And thus spake on that ancient man,
> The bright-eyed Mariner.

But a wordy observation, dullness of expression, or an ill-adapted theme may tell your listener there is nothing for him here and set his mind to wandering in search of more pleasant exercise. So irrelevant a thing as a flashy tie, graceless speech, or awkwardness of manner may overpower your words and throw attention back to your person or demeanor. It is, in short, unobtrusiveness of manner and vitality and appropriateness of theme and expression that hold attention in your command.

PURPOSES AND INTERESTS

Our problems as speakers would be simplified if we possessed the Ancient Mariner's wonderful power to hold attention by a glance; but lacking that mysterious faculty, we must seek other keys to the minds of men. One thing experience tells us is that *every listener is anxious to hear about things that affect his own purposes and interests.* Conversely, he will usually deny attention to things having no apparent bearing on his affairs as he understands them. Here is a safe and reasonably sure generalization you can make about listeners. They behave this way simply by virtue of being human beings. "Man is aware," says an eminent social psychologist, "of only those aspects of his environment that have some bearing on his purposes in the 'now' that he must judge and act on."[2]

You read this book because you suppose your personal affairs may be affected by something said here. If you decide what we are saying can be

[2] Hadley Cantril, *The "Why" of Man's Experience* (New York: Macmillan, 1950), p. 175.

of no use to you, you will soon lay the book aside or begin turning the pages in search of something that does promise to be useful. In this you are like every listener who has heard or will hear you. "Of what use is it to me?" your listeners are always asking. If you can find the things most men prize or with which they are concerned, you will have found the stones on which to build successful speeches; ignore these matters, and you will soon be ignored.

BIOLOGICAL NEEDS

There are things that affect our interests and purposes simply because we are mammals of the species called *man*. We have certain bodily and organic needs, and we are interested in satisfying them. We want gratifications for hunger, thirst, our need for oxygen, for the many and complex ways in which sexual drives manifest themselves, and for other natural demands made by our peculiar biological nature. We want to preserve ourselves from injury, punishment, or other forms of physical discomfort. All these are creature wants which each of us spends much time satisfying or trying to satisfy. Thus, we get another useful generalization: *every human being is anxious to learn how his biological wants and needs can be satisfied with the least sacrifice of his other goals and purposes in life.*

In this group of things which all men and women want lies a whole series of possible answers to the listener's question, "Of what use is it to me?" Show him that what you have to tell him will help him find such satisfactions as we have just discussed, and he will listen to you—at least until he begins to doubt your promise or to suspect the goals toward which you lead him are in conflict with some of his other, stronger wants and needs. Whenever we can link talk with the physical needs of listeners, we increase the probability that we will hold attention.

SOCIAL NEEDS

Human beings are also something more than creatures driven by physiological needs. When people live together they develop social as well as biological desires. These, too, offer avenues for approaching their minds, holding their attention, and influencing their behavior.

Almost all people, wherever they live, want to be rich (or to be thought rich) in whatever values their societies hold in high regard. A Spartan or an American Indian warrior was specially interested in what would increase his strength or prove his bravery. Athenian listeners of ancient times were greatly concerned that their decisions should prove their good judgment in practical affairs. North Americans readily attend to those who seem able to tell how to win out in the various competitions for success that make up so much of our life. Each society and each self-acknowledged group within a society has its special ways of thinking about life, the rest of the world, and the sources of happiness. In turn, each member of the society or group always carries within him some of these special goals, judgments, and points of view derived from the milieu in which he lives.

STEREOTYPES

It is possible for a speaker to change the preconceptions listeners draw from their societies and groups, but the task is difficult and can be accomplished only through using other previously acquired beliefs and knowledge. Listeners—like all people in all situations—tend to perceive what they expect to perceive, and they can find in speeches only what their knowledge and expectations allow them to find. If they cannot see and hear something familiar, something like what they expected or have come to know about, they lose interest or begin to resist the strange concepts put before them. Thus, what a listener is willing and ready to understand limits what can register in his consciousness. On the other hand, the listener is usually quite ready to inspect ideas—even new ones—that are evidently linked to the values and ways of thinking he has learned from the groups with which he is associated.

This point was especially well stated by Walter Lippmann in his famous chapter, "Stereotypes":

For the most part, we do not first see, and then define, we define first and then see. In the great blooming, buzzing confusion of the outer world we pick out what our culture has already defined for us, and we tend to perceive that which we have picked out in the form stereotyped for us by our culture.[3]

[3] Walter Lippmann, *Public Opinion* (New York: Harcourt, Brace, 1922), p. 81.

75

It may be unfortunate that listeners tend to respond so much in terms of their prior experiences, but one who would speak well and effectively cannot safely ignore the facts of the matter. When we speak to anyone, we must talk to him of values, facts, and needs he already understands, else we shall be speaking of a part of the world he has never imagined, much less seen. To show him a new facet of the world of thought, we must begin with the parts of that world already known to him, then lead him by easy stages into the new provinces we wish him to see. Hence, we can formulate another generalization about how we may reach and influence the minds of listeners: *if we speak of what listeners already know and want to reinforce, we shall more probably win and hold attention; if we show disregard or disrespect for their beliefs and expectations, our listeners are likely to resist or ignore what we say.*

To tear a listener away from the comforting assurances his stereotypes give him is probably to lose him, perhaps to irritate and frighten him. It will certainly impair his ability to understand. Carried out of his world of familiar things, ideas, customs, goals, each of us becomes uncomfortable, uncertain, and insecure. The effects are much the same whether a jet airliner sets us down suddenly in an unfamiliar land or a speaker rushes us precipitately into a realm of unfamiliar ideas and language. In either case we miss the friendly landmarks and the old direction signs. Each listener wants some assurance that his old direction signs are still accurate; perhaps this is why he regards so highly the reassurances of respected authority.

AUTHORITY

One pair of psychologists has put the matter this way:

Size and magnitude yield only to the prestige of authority as inhibitors of reflective thought. . . . *Prestige of authority* is a general term which refers to many forms of influence. The source of authority may be expert opinion, official pronouncements, religious symbols, the pomp and ceremony of institutional practice, the sayings or doings of the socially elect, or even the printed word or the tone of voice.[4]

[4] Daniel Katz and Richard L. Schanck, *Social Psychology* (New York: Wiley, 1938), p. 313.

The practical applications of this universal tendency to accept without much question the assurances and advice of favored authority (of whatever sort) are easily illustrated. Are you speaking to engineers, physicists, or other scientists? Show them the system you are explaining rests on physical laws they know and trust, and you will probably hold their attention and secure their belief. Would you address a group of businessmen? Make it clear your proposals have support in the business world. And if your listeners are especially devout? Identify your thought with the voices of leaders from whom these listeners received their creed. All men do not have the same values or the same hierarchies of authorities, but they all have some values and some sources of authority, so we may generalize that: *to reach listeners' minds and influence their behavior, you must discover their favorite sanctions and authorities and use these to illumine or justify the new thought you offer.*

FAMILIARITY AND NOVELTY

For reasons that probably lie very deep in the psyche, though we all tend to reject, even fear, what is alien to our experience, certain levels of novelty still attract and fascinate us. In greater or lesser degrees we are all both timidly bound to the familiar and adventurously drawn toward the strange and the unknown. Thus it is that while it is true to say speakers must discover and use their listeners' favorite sanctions and authorities, it is equally true to say speakers must offer their hearers "news."

For all of us, whatever is familiar (especially if it appears in a strange setting) or whatever seems strange (especially if it appears in a familiar setting) can crowd almost everything else out of our perceptions. You do not notice the flawless playing of sixty musicians when the sixty-first player blows a discordant note. On the other hand, you do not pay much attention to twenty cars in a parking lot or to twenty different hats worn at a meeting; but your eye unerringly picks out the one car that is yours or the single hat that closely resembles your own. These dual tendencies of the mind to embrace the familiar and inspect the new afford the speaker many opportunities to catch and hold attention by mingling elements of the new and old.

Parables are, of course, the classic examples of how one can secure and hold attention for a new thought by imbedding it in stories about well-known activities or familiar kinds of persons. Likewise, one can see in the King James Version of "The Sermon on the Mount" the attention-compelling power of the new when linked to the familiar—especially when what is familiar has the prestige of authority. In this sermon Jesus introduced six successive sections of new instruction with the words: "Ye have heard that it was said by them of old time. . . ." In these two clauses Jesus was able to reassure His audience that the new thoughts to be offered only extended and amplified what was already accepted on the authority of the law-givers. So, also, when Abraham Lincoln wanted to convey his fears about the spread of slavery, he used a familiar figure to express the disturbing view that unrestricted slavery must surely be a constant threat to the nation. "A house divided against itself cannot stand," he said. Parables, references to old and familiar law, and Lincoln's metaphor illustrate some of the means by which speakers may supply the needed reassurance of the familiar while placing before their listeners ideas that are essentially new or strange.

Though too much that is unusual or unexpected disturbs us, we still expect worthwhile experiences to contain some elements of the novel. As Aristotle expressed it in his *Rhetoric:*

> Words are like men; as we feel a difference between people from afar and our fellow townsmen, so it is with our feeling for language. And hence it is well to give the ordinary idiom an air of remoteness; the hearers are struck by what is out of the way, and like what strikes them.[5]

He was speaking of style, but the unexpected idea, like the unexpected or out-of-the-way word, has power to catch and hold attention, at least briefly.

Speaking at Cambridge, Massachusetts before the Phi Beta Kappa Society, Ralph Waldo Emerson caught up attention and held it by striking a note not usually heard at such bookish gatherings. He was speaking about the importance of independent thought and was contrasting independent thinking with learning for its own sake, when he gave a novel turn to his argument:

> Books are the best of things, well used; abused, among the worst. What is the right use? What is the one end, which all means go to effect? They are for

[5] From *The Rhetoric of Aristotle* trans. and ed. by Lane Cooper. Copyright, 1932, Lane Cooper, p. 185, Bk III, Ch. 2. Reprinted by permission of the publisher Appleton-Century-Crofts.

nothing but to inspire. I had better never see a book than to be warped by its attraction clean out of my own orbit and made a satellite instead of a system. The one thing in the world of value is the active soul. . . . In its essence it is progressive. The book, the college, the school of art, the institution of any kind, stop with some past utterance of genius. That is good, say they—let us hold by this. They pin me down.[6]

And, having in this manner seized his listeners' attention by unexpectedly questioning the value of books, Emerson restored the balance of forces in his speech by driving home his central but by no means startling theme: "*Man thinking* must not be subdued by his instruments."

Such is the power of the familiar to focus attention on the new, and of the new and unexpected to make memorable the familiar. But the speaker who uses—as he must—man's curiosity about the new and his affection for the old should also remember that attention is a fleeting thing. Men do not usually look deeply into what is new nor contemplate the familiar for very long. They tire easily, especially when listening. The key to holding their attention through the means we have just been discussing is that *it is the shift from the familiar to the unfamiliar and back again that pleases and holds the mind.* It is *change* that controls attention. The speaker who remembers this important generalization will see to it that his listener has, at every possible point, something familiar to which he can cling for assurance and something new which will give him a sense of learning and, possibly, adventure. Too much of the old bores; too much of the new baffles.

We have been considering what forces seize and hold attention. We have seen that people tend to grant their attention first to your presence; second, to the feelings your presence arouses; and finally, to what you communicate. We have observed that the special concern of a speaker must be to work wisely and carefully in order that he may hold and control this attention which was casually granted and may as casually be withdrawn. To accomplish this object, speakers must be guided in every utterance by the general truth that listeners are usually eager to hear about things that seem likely to affect their immediate purposes and interests, but will deny attention to things that have no apparent bearing on their affairs as they understand them. In amplification of this important generalization about audi-

[6] "The American Scholar," delivered August 31, 1837.

ences, we have located these subsidiary propositions that should be always in every speaker's mind:

1. Whatever can be closely linked with the immediate physical needs of those who are listening will probably receive their sustained attention.
2. Whatever can be shown consistent with and favorable to the social standards and purposes of those who are listening will probably receive attention, provided it does not conflict with some stronger physical desire or drive.
3. Whatever can be shown to have the sanction of known and respected sources of authority has a better chance of being received attentively than that which must be presented without evidence of such approval.
4. To sustain attention, any subject matter must be presented to listeners in such a way that the new and the familiar will engage their minds alternately or in combination.

These are the basic generalizations that must govern selection of materials and planning for any public speech.

Against these standards you, as a public speaker, must test your choice of a speech subject, your mode of developing each point, your choice of each piece of supporting material, and the language in which you couch your thoughts. Your first business is to enter the minds of those who hear you and to deposit there the propositions which you have brought to the rostrum. You can gain admittance to the mind of another by any number of means, but you cannot remain there long enough to transact your business unless you demonstrate that your errand meets one or more (preferably all) of these charges which every listener levies as the price of his continued attention.

Attributes of Listeners
Affecting Attention

That there are characteristic ways in which nearly all human beings respond to events, we have just seen; however, there are also special conditions of life that affect the ways in which auditors attend to what is said. These, too, the speaker must recognize. Where they work against his cause or obstruct the traffic of ideas between his mind and the minds of his listeners, he must neutralize them by offering other compensatory justifications for full and favorable attention. Naturally, where these forces could make interest in his cause more intense or where they can be brought directly into the service of clarity and understanding, the speaker must take full advantage of them.

What are the special circumstances that most significantly affect what human beings attend to in the act of listening? They are many, but five are invariably at work within every listener. These are *age, sex, expectation, amplitude of knowledge and information*, and what social scientists have come to call *socioeconomic level*.

AGE

Consider first how the age of your listener affects the ways in which you can appropriately deal with a given topic. The young, the middle aged, and the old give their closest attention to different aspects of ideas, examples, arguments, behavior, and language. Shakespeare's famous description of the ages of man, in *As You Like It*, and Aristotle's more detailed analysis of how age influences the interests of auditors form, together, an unsurpassed survey of this condition of life as a force affecting the receptivity of human kind. Shakespeare's Jacques thus characterized the ages of man:

> At first the infant,
> Mewling and puking in the nurse's arms.
> And then the whining school-boy, with his satchel
> And shining morning face, creeping like snail
> Unwillingly to school. And then the lover,
> Sighing like furnace, with a woeful ballad
> Made to his mistress' eyebrow. Then a soldier,
> Full of strange oaths, and bearded like the pard,
> Jealous in honour, sudden and quick in quarrel,
> Seeking the bubble reputation
> Even in the cannon's mouth. And then the justice,
> In fair round belly with good capon lin'd,
> With eyes severe, and beard of formal cut,
> Full of wise saws and modern instances;
> And so he plays his part. The sixth age shifts

Into the lean and slipper'd pantaloon,
With spectacles on nose and pouch on side,
His youthful hose, well saved, a world too wide
For his shrunk shank; and his big manly voice,
Turning again toward childish treble, pipes
And whistles in his sound. Last scene of all,
That ends this strange eventful history,
Is second childishness and mere oblivion,
Sans teeth, sans eyes, sans taste, sans everything.[7]

Aristotle addressed himself more specifically to "the proper means of adapting both speech and speaker to a given audience." His characterizations of the young, "men in their prime," and the elderly can only be summarized here, but they are well worth a full reading in the original source. Most of what Aristotle had to say of the men of his day applies as well to modern men and women.

In youth "men have strong desires, and whatever they desire they are prone to do. Of the bodily desires the one they let govern them most is the sexual; here they lack self-control. They are shifting and unsteady in their desires. . . ." They are "quick to anger, and apt to give way to it," and they are "fond of honor" but even "fonder of victory." Money means relatively little to them "for they have not yet learned what the want of it means." They are not cynical; rather, they are trustful "for as yet they have not been often deceived." Being quick to hope, and living much in anticipation, "they are easily deceived." Though brave and spirited, they are also shy. Being idealistic, "in their actions they prefer honor to expediency" and are dogmatic. "All their mistakes are on the side of intensity and excess. . . ."

In middle life, Aristotle thought, people "will be neither excessively confident . . . nor yet too timid; they will be both confident and cautious. They will neither trust everyone nor distrust everyone; rather they will judge the case by the facts. Their rule of life will be neither honor alone, nor expediency alone. . . ." They will temper valor with self-control, and they will be neither parsimonious nor prodigal with their possessions. Generally, "all the valuable qualities which youth and age divide between them are joined in the prime of life."

The aged, according to Aristotle, have characteristics opposed to those

---

[7] *As You Like It*, Act II, Scene 7.

of the young. Thus, "they err by an extreme moderation" and are "positive about nothing" for they have lived long and been deceived and disappointed much. They tend to be cynical and "put the worst construction on everything"; they are suspicious, and sometimes small-minded. They "aspire to nothing great or exalted, but crave the mere necessities and comforts of existence." They are constantly apprehensive and "live their lives with too much regard for the expedient and too little for honor." What other people think counts for little with them, for they do not expect much more from life and "live in memory rather than in anticipation."

Aristotle closes his review of the effects of age upon mankind with these words: "Now the hearer is always receptive when a speech is adapted to his own character and reflects it. Thus we can readily see the proper means of adapting both speech and speaker to a given audience."[8] It is true. In Shakespeare's and Aristotle's descriptions you may find almost the sum of things on which men and women in each age of life bestow eager attention. Here are truly useful generalizations about the changing interests of man—generalizations that tell the wise speaker how he must approach his themes to come within the interests of each age group represented among his listeners. He cannot, of course, always gratify the idealism of youth and the caution of age with the same argument. But more often than most speakers realize, ideas have both idealistic and practical aspects, promise "the bubble reputation" for some without threatening the security of others, are at once expedient and honorable, and so on. At least the speaker who is aware that age influences the interests and judgments of listeners will investigate the possibilities of gratifying more than a single age group when his own purpose requires that he win acceptance from an audience of mixed ages.

SEX

Whether the listeners are mostly male or female or evenly divided must also be considered in selecting and using materials for speeches. In an era when women receive essentially the same education and share many of the same responsibilities as men, it is certainly possible to overemphasize alleged differences in the interests and motivations of the sexes. Neverthe-

[8] From *The Rhetoric of Aristotle* trans. and ed. by Lane Cooper. Bk II, Ch. 12–14, pp. 132–37. Reprinted by permission of the publisher Appleton-Century-Crofts.

less, anyone who wishes to influence the behavior of both sexes or of audiences in which one sex predominates must remember that men and women do not share all kinds of experience. They will accordingly attend to some topics with differing degrees of willingness.

It may surely be said that matters of business policy, mechanical construction, team sports, and the like touch the experience of most men while being foreign to the experience of many women. Though it seems relatively easy to focus the attention of women on problems of government, few have a comparable interest in problems of corporate or international finance. Similar examples are plentiful. The chief reasons for these differences probably lie in the special values inculcated by experiences peculiar to one group or the other and which, in turn, influence the kinds of knowledge and interest each group prizes. But whatever the reasons, the practical fact for speakers is that common sense and experimental evidence plainly tell us that men and women are not equally persuasible on all subjects. Though we do not know much about the precise nature and degrees of these sex differences, we do know enough to say that, given any specific topic, it is important for a public speaker to ask himself whether the normal differences between masculine and feminine experience are such that he needs to accommodate his treatment of the subject to these differences.

Chivalric and romantic attitudes are not entirely dead in our society. They, too, affect the tone of discourse. Among many of us there persists a feeling that while argumentative pressures, cumulation of overwhelming amounts of evidence, and bluntness of statement are possible and even appropriate in dealing with masculine listeners, these harsher modes of communication are inappropriate in discourse addressed to women. Female listeners ought to be treated with some degree of indirection and be persuaded by gentle suggestion, or so the convention seems to say. At any rate when speakers argue aggressively or attempt "the hard sell" in dealing with female listeners, some men and some women are moved to withhold serious attention, deeming the manner of the communication inappropriate for feminine ears. Whether in public speaking as in love women listeners must always be treated as beings

> nobly planned,
> To warm, to comfort, and command;
> And yet a Spirit still, and bright
> With something of angelic light

84

is a moot point; but speakers certainly have little to lose and often much to gain by respecting some of the conventions of chivalry when dealing with women as listeners.*

EXPECTATION

The expectations of your listeners will also affect their willingness and ability to attend to what you say. What we expect to perceive has much to do with what actually invades our consciousness, as has already been pointed out. The intention, inclination or expectation of a listener makes him peculiarly alert to whatever suits his will or is consistent with his prevision of the speaker, the speech, and the occasion. A psychologist has put it this way: "The organism goes out and determines what it is going to respond to, and organizes that world. One organism picks out one thing and another picks out a different one, since it is going to act in a different way."[9] In short, your listener is already prepared to attend to some things (the expected ones) but by the same token he shuts out certain other things (unexpected thoughts and ideas). Practical examples are easy to find.

If you go to church to worship and hear a preacher deliver a political harangue, you are likely to become uneasy and consequently inattentive. If you expect radio and television broadcasters to report the news without editorializing, you will be irritated by a reporter who injects opinion into his newscast. You may even agree with the preacher-turned-politician or the newscaster-turned-editorialist, but you still become disturbed over whether his comments are appropriate for the time, his position, and the occasion. When this happens you cannot keep your mind on the *whole* of what he says. You focus on the fact that he is violating your expectations and, afterward, you may not be able to remember what he actually said. Conversely, when your expectations are realized, you are able to attend fully and can afterward usually recall the gist of the communication. Your prevision "is in a way a rehearsal of an expected experience. When the experience comes it is like meeting an old friend."[10]

A listener may base his prevision of your remarks on what he knows

[9] George H. Mead, *Mind, Self and Society* (Chicago: University of Chicago Press, 1934), p. 25.

[10] Edwin G. Boring, Herbert S. Langfeld, and Harry P. Weld, *Foundations of Psychology* (New York: Wiley, 1948), p. 220.

* Excerpt from "She Was a Phantom of Delight" by William Wordsworth.

about you, on what he thinks would be appropriate for the moment or the occasion, on his understanding of your announced subject or on some other ground. If the occasion is formal and dignified (a commencement exercise, a formal business conference, the inauguration of a high officer) he prepares himself to hear a formal address touching themes that grow out of the situation. If the occasion is small and informal, he prepares himself to hear pithy, relevant remarks delivered without much fanfare or formality. A juryman expects the attorney to give him reasons for making this or that decision, and the alumnus at a homecoming banquet expects to hear reminiscences of college days and news of his alma mater. The point is that people prepare themselves for most experiences in listening. They usually do this without consciously thinking about it, but that does not change the fact that they do set up standards which they expect speakers will live up to, and they are disturbed if those standards are not observed. Speakers are left with these alternatives: they can conform to their listeners' expectations or they must justify their deviations from expected practice. The speaker whose purpose permits and whose foresight has prepared him to fit the whole of his speech to the expectations of his hearers is fortunate; the speaker whose purpose requires him to violate these preconceptions may safely do so only by drawing the listeners' thoughts from the "old friend" they expected to meet to the new and better "friend" whom the speaker feels bound to introduce. The heart of the matter is: listeners do not respond predictably if taken unaware.

KNOWLEDGE

The amount of education and general information your listeners possess will affect responses to your speech. We have already seen that what human beings know will govern what they are ready to hear and what they can understand. Unfortunately, it is almost impossible to generalize about the specific effects education has on attention and understanding, but it is broadly true that the more catholic their knowledge and experience the wider will be the variety of things that can grip listeners' attention and interest. Another way to put the matter is: the more things listeners are already familiar with, the fewer new things there will be to baffle or frighten them. This is scarcely a profound observation, and it certainly provides no very specific guidelines for the speaker to follow as he sorts speech materials in the hope of selecting those that will hold the attention and interest of an audience. Still, the speaker who makes a point of trying to evaluate what his listeners know and don't know will come closer to meeting his hearers on their own grounds than one who forgets that every listener's power to respond and comprehend is regulated by the knowledge he brings to the speech.

A veteran of World War II who was stationed in China reports that American airmen transporting Chinese troops from one battle area to another found it extraordinarily difficult to make soldiers from remote parts of China understand the hazards of flying. There were even instances of soldiers, not realizing they would be killed by the fall, trying to step out of planes in flight. Since they had no experience to which they could relate this danger, they could not understand it despite explanations. Such extreme difficulties in communication should remind us that all listeners have their blind spots. The more one can find out about a specific audience the better able he will be to anticipate and compensate for their limitations. Beyond this reminder that he needs always to make inquiries, anticipations, and compensations for each audience he addresses, our knowledge about patterns of human behavior can furnish little additional advice of a general sort. But this does not change the speaker's need to adapt his message to his listeners' knowledge and experience.

SOCIOECONOMIC LEVEL

Among the conditioning factors that deeply affect the knowledge and expectations of listeners are their cultural, social, and economic experiences. So important are these forces that they deserve some special treatment here. How these background factors condition the lives and perceptions of everyone is one of the most fascinating topics of inquiry in anthropology, sociology, and social psychology. It is a subject we can touch but lightly in a work on public speaking, but it is one of enormous importance to an understanding of audiences.

One of the limitations of studying public speaking in college is that you will have all too few opportunities to explore directly the influences of cultural, social, and economic forces upon audiences. You may not come into contact with their full play until you enter the nonacademic world. Just now most of your listeners are essentially like yourself in age, educational attainment, expectations; even sex differences are probably about as limited in influence over opinions and judgments as at any time in life. Even more important, college or university life makes more alike those whom it touches. This is true even where cultural, social, and economic differences are concerned. The authors of one recently published study of attitudes held by college students have said:

. . . you can infer a college student's economic philosophy if you know only what political party has his sympathies and what college he is attending, and further information about the economic level of his family will not substantially improve the prediction. The same clues will lead to a rather accurate inference regarding his stand on an economic issue with humanitarian overtones. If, however, you wish to infer a college student's attitude towards a current economic issue which reflects conflicting class interests, then additional information about his family's economic level will increase the accuracy of your guess.[11]

Later, the same authors conclude:

Our study suggests . . . that the overall impact of the college years, at least during this period of widespread conservatism in the country at large, nurtured a conservative economic philosophy, and was unsympathetic to a contrary viewpoint.[12]

The fact that you are a college student speaking to college students means you will probably find more common ground and more identity of interests with your listeners than you would find if you addressed a nonacademic audience. You must, then, be on guard against assigning to nonacademic audiences the uniformity of opinion and the relative indifference to cultural, social, and economic conditioning that you find among fellow students. Outside the college or university these conditioning forces produce marked differences in viewpoints such as you only occasionally see in student life.

To illustrate how disparate are the attitudes and opinions held by people from different walks of life we have no need to contrast the extremely varied outgrowths of primitive and sophisticated cultures. There are numer-

[11] Rose K. Goldsen, Morris Rosenberg, Robin M. Williams, Jr., and Edward A. Suchman, *What College Students Think* (Princeton: Van Nostrand, 1960), p. 116.
[12] *Ibid.*, p. 123.

ous sharp differences of outlook within our own society. For example, according to one often-quoted study, white American males of "lower occupational strata" are more likely than males of "higher occupational strata" to insist that woman's place is in the home. Higher occupational groups of males have more faith in the value of machines than do manual workers. The higher groups tend to think success and wealth are achieved through ability, but significant numbers of males from lower occupations attribute success to "luck, pull, and superior opportunities." The same study indicated that men from the lower strata of occupations tended to think those from the higher strata were overpaid.[13] These distinctive views only suggest the vast array of differences that distinguish listeners whose cultural, social, and economic experiences are dissimilar. Plainly, any speaker will err if, when preparing to address a general audience, he fails to investigate the viewpoints and expectations that varied experiences of these kinds have implanted in the minds of his prospective hearers.

It deserves repetition that your college experience as a speaker is unlike the experience you will have outside the college in respect to the impact of cultural, social, and economic forces upon your listeners. The moment you turn from your college-oriented audience to a general, unsifted audience, sociological differences among auditors become critical factors to which you must adjust. It is not too much to say that when any speaker asks, "Who will be there?" he ought to insist upon as precise a *sociological* answer as can possibly be secured.

In this chapter we have been trying to discover some useful generalizations about audiences. In essence we have said that audiences are composed of listeners who must be thought of as individuals, though each will behave as it is the nature of human beings to behave. Listeners, like human beings everywhere, can be depended upon to give attention to what seems likely to affect their immediate physical needs or social purposes; to what presents an interplay of the familiar with the new; and to ideas that seem associated with whatever sources, institutions, and patterns of experience already hold their confidence and trust. These are things that have inevitable claims on the attention of all men and women in all circumstances—in-

[13] Richard Centers, "Attitude and Belief in Relation to Occupational Stratification," *Journal of Social Psychology*, XXVII (1938), 158–185.

cluding the circumstance of listening to public speakers. The speaker who always designs his message and his speaking to touch these concerns will have a very much better chance of being heard and believed than one who neglects them or touches them sporadically and without design.

Listening is also a special kind of activity as we have pointed out in Chapter 3. We have therefore tried to discover what distinct but ever-present conditions of life peculiarly affect men's ability or willingness to listen comprehendingly. We have suggested that five such conditions have special importance for public speakers: age, sex, expectation, amplitude of knowledge and experience, and cultural-social-economic background. Every listener is of some age, is either male or female, has some preconceptions about what he is going to hear or ought to hear, has some limitations and strengths in knowledge and experience, and is the product of a particular cultural-social-economic environment. Whether listeners will it or not, these conditions of life invariably regulate their ability and readiness to respond to what is said to them.

If we knew precisely what things command the attention of, let us say, a man of thirty who holds a law degree and is attending a chamber of commerce luncheon, speech making would be more nearly a science than an art. But we do not know all the ways age, sex, expectations, knowledge, and cultural-social-economic factors can, as individual or combined influences, affect a given man's responses to a particular message. We have, instead, a few crude generalizations. With these admittedly rough tools it is still possible for the diligent speaker to refine his command over the minds of those who hear him; for, if he remembers to use the tools he does have and to make the inquiries he ought to make, he will recognize at least some of the opportunities and limitations laid before him by the inevitable conditions of auditors. As Plato implied in the passage quoted at the head of this chapter, it is by knowing what needs to be found out about hearers, by experience in bringing different kinds of messages before differing audiences, and by imaginatively adapting content to the natures of listening men that speakers can ultimately achieve artistic, insightful social control. It is possible to do this even though the tools for analyzing audiences remain crude. Here as elsewhere, art in public speaking consists in working subtly and perceptively with rough resources. Our purpose in this chapter has been to clarify the demands audiences impose upon those who would speak with art.

A superficial reading of what we have said might suggest that to speak effectively one has only to display a useful and desirable proposal to win the assent of listeners. Of course this is not the case. As we pointed out in Chapter 3, in every moment every member of an audience is being challenged to respond to an almost inconceivable number of stimuli. Most are irrelevant—sometimes contradictory—to the speaker's message. The public speaker is only *one* of the competitors for command of the hearer's mind. He competes against the rustling of paper, the stuffiness of an ill-ventilated room, discomforts caused by an indigestible meal or a hard chair, the roving eyes of the girl in the fourth row, political beliefs, preconceived attitudes growing out of the socioeconomic level of society represented, and so on almost without end. The public speaker's task is to make *his* bid for attention strong enough to win out in this incessant competition. It is crucial that he be the winner at those points in his speech when his most important ideas are being presented. Here, if ever, what he says must be more compelling than the other stimuli clamoring for control over the listener's consciousness.

Careless or cynical interpretation of these facts about audiences might also yield the view that listeners can never be confronted with messages to which they are not already prepared to give assent. To so read this chapter would be a grave mistake indeed. We have emphasized that all listeners are the products of their humanity and their conditioning. But audiences are no more changeless than faceless or will-less. True, the speaker who would change the viewpoint of a listener must begin by accepting him as he is and proceed by adapting a message to the listener's condition. But the very object of adapting is to enable that listener to see what he did not see before. It encourages him to reorganize his awareness so he may discover that the speaker's message is relevant to his life. Rhetorical adaptation of ideas to the natures of audiences is a means of achieving *change* in listeners—the only means open to man, short of force.

It is ideas, and feelings about them, that must be adapted if audiences are to respond as speakers wish. But ideas and listeners are alike in that they are pliable only to a degree. Force is not weakness; nor love, hate. Speakers therefore must understand the role of content in speaking, as well as the role of the audience. In the next three chapters we shall concentrate on the problems of discovering and sifting that which needs to be said, given what we now know about audiences.

Exercises

Written

1. Write a careful description of some specific audience with which you are familiar (fraternal group, political or other club, religious congregation, or other) giving special consideration to the following:
    a. Chief biological wants and needs, if any, that affect this audience;
    b. Chief social wants and needs, if any, that affect this audience;
    c. Favorite sanctions and authorities of this audience;
    d. Any special characteristics of age, sex, expectation, knowledge, and socioeconomic level that all speakers addressing this audience should take into account.

2. You are to prepare a short speech using the central idea: "Reading is superior to listening to radio or watching television as a means of acquiring education." Outline the major points you might make in such a speech if it were to be given to audience *a* below; then outline the major points you might try to make if the speech were for audience *b* below. Justify any differences there may be in the two outlines.
    a. An audience of 20 college students aged 17–22, made up of 10 men and 10 women, assembled for an informal class on study habits organized for students whose academic records do not "meet the potentialities indicated by standardized aptitude-test results."
    b. An audience of 20 college students aged 19–22, all cadet teachers in an elementary school attending one of a series of weekly seminars. The seminar topic for this meeting is "Motivation." There are 18 women and 2 men in the group.

3. Using the text or a recording of any speech, identify the points at which the speaker seems to have adapted content for the specific purpose of suiting it to one or another of the audience characteristics discussed in this chapter.

Oral

1. Give an expository speech on one of the following subjects: stereotypes, the psychological process called suggestion, the psychological process called conditioned response, social (or ethical or other) values of the American college student, the expectations of audiences assembled on ceremonial occasions, unique expectations of audiences assembled to legislate or determine policy, theories of crowd behavior, authority as a source of persuasion.

2. Prepare and deliver an oral report on the methods of audience analysis and adaptation used by an outstanding trial lawyer, preacher, or political speaker.
3. Prepare and deliver a talk on some aspect of audience research and advertising or market research and industrial design.

5

Invention:

Basic Processes

I would not be hurried by any love of system, by any exaggeration of instincts, to underrate the Book. We all know, that as the human body can be nourished on any food, though it were boiled grass and the broth of shoes, so the human mind can be fed by any knowledge. And great and heroic men have existed who had almost no other information than by the printed page. I only say that it needs a strong head to bear that diet. One must be an inventor to read well. . . . When the mind is braced by labor and invention, the page of whatever book we read becomes luminous with manifold allusion. Every sentence is doubly significant, and the sense of our author is as broad as the world. We then see, what is always true, that as the seer's hour of vision is short and rare among heavy days and months, so is its record, perchance, the least part of his volume.

RALPH WALDO EMERSON, "The American Scholar"

Let us suppose. You are a psychology major standing in the foyer of the library. A friend hails you: "I just saw Professor Perception. He says there's a meeting of underclassmen on Friday afternoon at the Student Union. Some of the academic departments have been asked to pick upperclass majors to talk at the meeting about their departments. The Psych Department wants you to speak for them. So get in that library and hit the books; you've got to write a speech."

This is the way most of us become involved in speech making. Some-one sends word, or calls. The request is a little indefinite. A speech subject may be suggested or not, and even if the subject is suggested the plea is vague. "We'd like you to talk about _____," the caller will say. Whether the subject is given or we find it ourselves, we soon learn that the work of creating a speech has scarcely begun when the speech subject has been located.

So, returning to our supposition, you are standing in the foyer, suddenly aware that you are going to make a speech on undergraduate study in psychology. Shall you rush into the library and begin reading? Does a speech suitable for an audience of underclassmen spring full-blown into your mind? If you are candid, you will admit that in this moment you would not know what to read if you did go into the library; nor could you say you possessed any coherent, cogent speech. You probably could not even tell a friend, clearly and precisely, what it is like to be a psychology major. Some random thoughts about psychology and the social sciences may flit through your head; a good phrase or two may come to mind. In the first moments of realizing that a speech must be made you, like all other speakers, find no speech in your thoughts nor very many of the makings of a speech. The situation is entirely normal. It simply demonstrates what introspective speakers have known for centuries: *the first step in speech making is to decide where and how to look for ideas* appropriate to the new speaking assignment.

The Discovery of Ideas

The authors of this book believe it is not very profitable to enjoin speakers to THINK, READ, DIGEST, and then to leave them with these noble injunctions. Neither do we think speakers are helped much by textbook writers and teachers who exhaust vocabulary in deploring the undeniable superficiality of much student and other contemporary speaking. Something more practical is wanted. *Method* in inventing what is to be said is more important than hours spent in intellectual and emotional agitation.

As you stand in the library foyer, your problem is not really whether to enter the library, to rush to the Department of Psychology, or to seek refuge in your room. Your immediate problem is to direct your thoughts toward identifying the "places" in the world of concepts and feelings where you can find the most useful ideas relative to an academic major.

Not every idea connected with psychology will be appropriate in talking to underclassmen about psychology as a field of study. Some available ideas will be too technical, some too remote from the experience of underclassmen, some you will be unable to formulate clearly and exactly. What you need are ideas that are *negotiable* between you and your hearers—ideas that can be exchanged between the parties like coins, with each negotiator understanding the nature and value of the items traded. But how does one begin the search for negotiable ideas?

FINDING LINES OF THOUGHT

One of the earliest and most useful systems for guiding speakers' intellectual explorations was detailed by Aristotle in his *Topics* and his *Rhetoric*. Simplified and slightly modified, this system can draw your thoughts toward the best hunting grounds where ideas suitable to your particular speaking assignment may be found.

The Aristotelian theory of how a speaker should search for negotiable ideas rests on this assumption: the situations for speeches and the expectations of audiences fall into a few, identifiable categories.

First, the theory runs, there are times when the main business of the speaker and the main interests of the audience have to do with *courses of action*. When this is so, the question at issue is: What shall be done or left undone? Aristotle called this the *deliberative* setting. In the language we have adopted in this book it would be called a *persuasive* setting, in which a proposition of policy is to be discussed—one in which the speaker's central idea contains the words "should" or "ought to" or their equivalents. Put another way and in contemporary terms, Aristotle's idea was that there are times when the speaker knows he must persuade and that his central idea is going to be something like "The United States government ought to recognize the Communist government of China" or "The federal government ought to own and operate the railroads" or "You ought to vote for John P. Findley." It was Aristotle's contention that when the speaker knows this much, he should realize that he is going to function as a kind of *adviser*. For purposes of advising, ideas that have to do with the *expediency* of alternative courses of action are the ones that are most negotiable. These are ideas that have to do with rewards and punishments lying in the future and with the prospects for happiness or unhappiness should one course of action or another be chosen. According to this reasoning, whenever the demands of an audience, occasion, and your central idea concern the *future* behavior of your listeners, you will need to hunt for ideas touching the expediency or inexpediency of the various kinds of actions your hearers might adopt. Of course you may need other kinds of ideas for incidental use; but if your audience wants or needs advice, most of your initial preparation time ought to be spent finding ideas that concern the consequences of whatever actions your listeners are free to choose.

A second class of situations in which men speak are those in which the audiences function as judges rather than as deciders on future action. In discussing these circumstances Aristotle talked almost exclusively of judgments at law, but we need not take so narrow a view. There are many other situations in which audiences render *judgments* about facts and events. Every speech to inform is such a case. Most of what one says in a speech of inquiry deals with what the facts are, though when possible solutions are being considered the situation shifts to one concerned with policies and future actions. All persuasion about propositions of fact succeeds or fails according to the *judgments* finally rendered by the listeners. A further way to distinguish this kind of speaking situation is to ask what the central idea of the speech is likely to express. If the central idea focuses on whether a thing exists or what it is, it becomes plain that whether you intend to persuade, inform, or inquire you will be asking your listeners to function as judges of accuracy, truth, propriety, legality, or something else. And just here is the most significant point about any situation in which listeners are going to judge: to make judgments they must interpret the facts or events presented to them *in the light of some "code."* The code may be the law of the land, the theory of probabilities, the standards of historical research, the canons of artistic excellence, or their own standards for distinguishing truth from error. Whoever judges in these ways, then, needs two distinct kinds of knowledge: (1) knowledge about the facts or events he is to judge and (2) knowledge about the standards against which he is to measure the facts or events.

This extension of Aristotle's thinking produces an exceedingly valuable guideline for speakers who are trying to decide what kinds of content to put in their speeches. The guideline is this: if in informing, inquiring, or persuading you are going to ask for *judgments*, the ideas you will need most are those that define and clarify the details of whatever is to be judged and the standards to be used in judging. Other information you may need too, but these two kinds of content are crucial for any listener who is to render a judgment.

Rhetoricians who came after Aristotle suggested that three kinds of information about facts and events were especially useful in speeches of the sort we are now considering. Speeches of this kind, they said, tend to focus on: (1) information about whether there really are any facts or events to talk about; (2) information about what the facts are, if they do exist; and (3) information about how any acknowledged facts or events are to be interpreted in the light of whatever codes properly apply to them. These suggestions are simply extensions of what we have already said, but they are as useful today as they were to the great Roman orator, Cicero, and to the pupils of Quintilian in the first century A.D. The heart of the matter is that all speakers, especially those who inform or persuade about propositions of fact or conduct inquiries, face situations where facts and events are to be judged or interpreted. It makes no sense for them to rush about collecting information on what the future holds because, above everything else, their audiences are going to want to know how to measure accurately yesterday's and today's events.

The third class of speaking situations that Aristotle and other writers of classical times thought they perceived was one in which audiences behaved more as spectators or admirers of speech making than as deciders or judges. For a variety of reasons this conception needs to be modified a bit in order to be useful in our own day.

We can begin by saying that there are many situations in which audiences expect to have old ideas strengthened, familiar beliefs rendered more firm, convictions deepened, new or old knowledge rendered amusing or diverting. Using the language we have adopted for describing the purposes of speaking, these are situations in which speakers try to persuade by reinforcing belief or feeling, or in which they try to entertain their listeners. In these settings *new* judgments and *new* courses of action are neither sought nor wanted in any high degree. Commencement exercises are such occasions. So are many worship services, service club meetings, fellowship meetings, dinners and banquets, political rallies, etc. Those who attend commencements already accept the worth of education; worshippers accept the greatness of their deity; convivial club or fellowship groups accept the worth of being together and wish their association to be strengthened by being made more enjoyable or still more worthy. Whoever prepares to speak to such audiences must, then, locate the kinds of ideas that deepen, enrich, magnify, or even exaggerate what the listeners already know about. The chief end of the worship service may be to strengthen faith that already exists; the chief end of the club dinner may be, not calorie intake, but some magnification of the joys of friendship.

To sum up the implications of this third line of thought concerning the situations in which we speak, it is possible to say that when one's purpose is to reinforce beliefs and feelings, or to entertain, his need is for ideas peculiarly familiar to the audience he is going to face. Aristotle's advice on preparing for the more serious of the occasions we are now discussing was: look for ideas that connect your subject with such well-known virtues as justice, courage, temperance, grandeur, magnanimity, liberality, gentleness, prudence, wisdom, or with the opposites of these. The advice is sensible. Whatever has these virtues becomes impressive and admirable, and whatever lacks them or is incompatible with them becomes the object of ridicule and disdain if not disgust. And we can add one thing more: if lightheartedly done, assigning these virtues and their opposites where they do *not* belong is a standard way of rendering things and people amusing.

Thus, your task, when preparing for this kind of speaking situation, is to hunt for the virtues possessed by whatever you and your audience are committed to and for the non-virtues possessed by what you and your audience disapprove. Except for incidental uses you do not need ideas that deal with what is an expedient action or with the existence and legitimacy of facts and events.

Such, in outline, are some of the ancient suggestions for speakers in search of useful, negotiable ideas. If we imagine, again, that you are wondering how to begin "thinking up" a speech on psychology as a study in college, we can quickly see the applications of the advice we have so far summarized.

Though they didn't say so, the Psychology Department probably hopes you will tell the underclassmen what kinds of psychology courses are open to them and what requirements govern those who major in that department. On the other hand, since other departments are to be represented at the same meeting, it appears the meeting at which you will speak is not organized as a recruiting session for any particular department. Still, no one would object if you tried to make studying psychology seem inviting. Once you accept these presumptions about your assignment, you know something about how to proceed toward preparing your speech: (1) you do *not* need much material on whether psychology majors have better professional opportunities than other majors; (2) you *do* need to find the facts about specific courses and the regulations governing the psychology major, because enabling your audience to pass some kind of *judgment* on the study of psychology as it is regulated in your college is a major part of your assignment; (3) you *do* need to know by what standards underclassmen and other people measure the worth of a course of study, because these are the codes by which the facts you present are going to be judged. Having discovered your prospective listeners are going to function primarily as judges, you are in a position to begin gathering information with some efficiency. Having decided not to try to make these listeners commit themselves to any course of action just now, you can bypass much, but not all, information having chiefly to do with the rewards of studying psychology. And since your audience is not already devoted to the study of psychology, there would be little point in hunting for ways of associating that study with the generally accepted virtues.

On the basis of these decisions you need stand indecisively in the library foyer no longer. Two things must be done immediately: (1) obtain information about psychology as it is taught in your college and (2) find out how underclassmen distinguish "good" from "not-so-good" in academic subjects. If you enter the library, it is the college announcement or catalogue you will want to read; if you don't go in, you will be wise either to set off for the Psychology Department's offices or to begin conducting some interviews among underclassmen to see how they make judgments about courses and subjects. Any other actions on your part will probably be irrelevant to your speech preparation.

These are general ways by which you can point your thinking and research in potentially useful directions. But the system we have reviewed suggests only very broad topics: expediency, happiness, justice, accuracy, truthfulness, virtuousness, their opposites, and the like. Ancient writers on speech making went much farther than this in trying to identify the specific ideas speakers need in one or another of the usual circumstances for speaking. Aristotle enumerated literally hundreds of specific "lines of argument" in his *Topics* and his *Rhetoric*. It seems hardly possible that even the most astute speaker could remind himself of so detailed a catalogue of what he might say in a given case. Some more concise scheme of reminders of what it is possible to say can help a speaker once he knows the general kinds of material he will need.

Actually, speakers use a relatively limited number of "topics" or themes in discussion. This is because in matters of human affairs the *customary* ways of looking at things or thinking about them are limited. Notice, for example, the specific ideas Professor William G. Carleton identifies as those necessary to establishing a sound and comprehensive case for what he believes would be an *expedient* American foreign policy.

In a speech entitled "Effective Speech in a Democracy," Professor Carleton at one point spoke thus:

Will you permit me to illustrate my point by demonstrating for a moment how I would construct a speech on current American foreign policy? It so happens that I favor the following foreign policy: In the countries of Asia and Europe where the non-Communists are in control, I would, where conditions indicated, put the United States squarely behind a policy of social democracy or even democratic socialism as a way of combating Communism; and in the countries where the Communists are in control, I would play upon the nationalistic tendencies everywhere evident in Communist governments and Communist parties, to attempt to divide Communist countries from each other on national grounds and thereby contribute to the restoration of a multiple balancing-of-power system, a system which would prevent the Communists from acting together in a Communist front and threatening to upset the balance of power. For if we can remove the Communist threat to the balance of power we can remove the real cause of another great war.

In order to present effectively my point of view on the importance of playing wise social politics, it seems to me that I would have to show how and why conditions in Europe and Asia are converging to produce collectivist movements there and why laissez-faire capitalism there is not feasible [1]; also I would have to show the difference between totalitarian socialism and democratic socialism [2] and examine the reasons why I believe America's backing of social-democracy and even democratic socialism in Europe and Asia would check Communism and serve America's national interests [3]. In order for me to present effectively my belief that nationalism within Communist countries and parties could be used to divide Communism and restore a multiple balance-of-power system, I would have to examine in some detail the degree to which Communist revolutions and movements are in fact nationalistic in aim, method, and development [4], and actually point out the specific grounds of possible national conflict between specific Communist countries [5].

However, even when I had done all this my intellectual task would not be completed. I would have to point out why other courses in foreign policy would not serve America's national interests as well as the policy I favored [6]. This would involve my examining the reasons why political isolation would not work today; why a policy of mere military containment of Communism through the United Nations would not be enough and would not work permanently [7]; and why if it worked it would be the hard way to do something that could be done with less possibility of war and fewer long-time sacrifices [8]; why a policy of mere military containment of Communism by the United States alone—a policy of American imperialism—would be even less workable and less desirable than a policy of military containment through the United Nations [9]. In short, in order to carry intellectual conviction on so large and controversial a question, it seems to me I would have to construct a speech that analyzed critically all courses —those I oppose as well as those I favor [10].¹

In this passage we have a realistic representation of how a serious speaker explores what it is necessary to say in a given situation. The kinds of ideas Professor Carleton says need to be covered in the speech he is imagining are "lines of thought" that almost any speaker talking about any matter of policy would have to consider as topics for *possible* development.

What are these "lines of thought" or "themes"? *Feasibility* is one— how and why a thing can or cannot work: note the remarks just preceding [1] in the quotation. *Similarities and dissimiliarities* is another: see the statement that differences would have to be defined, in the clause before [2]. *Causality* would have to be established before anyone would think Carleton's preferred policy would in fact "serve America's national interests" [3]. *Degree* must be discussed if Carleton is to show there is enough nationalism in Communist systems to allow his plan to work [4]. And the *existence* of circumstances that make national conflicts likely must also be treated, says Carleton in the passage preceding [5]. In the sentence ending at [6] Carleton sees another set of *similarities and differences* that ought to be treated; and to explain these, a new set of *causalities* would have to be discussed [7]. Incidentally, a comparison of the *potency* or power of alternative policies to bring *desirable* results would have to be treated [8].

---

¹ William G. Carleton, "Effective Speech in a Democracy," *Vital Speeches of the Day*, XVII (June 15, 1951), 540-544. Reprinted by permission of the publisher and author.

Then, Carleton finds he would need to consider a further set of *similarities and differences* among the *desirable* and *feasible* features of several policies [9]. All these specific lines of thought would need to be discussed, says Carleton, in order that his speech might have the kind of *substance* or quality ("carry intellectual conviction") he would want it to have [10].

The themes or lines of thought or topics which Professor Carleton enumerates include most of the themes we normally develop in speeches about popular affairs. A tolerably complete list of such themes might be set forth thus:

A. Attributes commonly discussed:
1. *Existence* or nonexistence of things.
2. *Degree* or quantity of things, forces, etc.
3. *Spatial* attributes, including adjacency, distribution, place.
4. Attributes of *time*.
5. *Motion* or activity.
6. *Form*, either physical or abstract.
7. *Substance:* physical, abstract, or psychophysical.
8. *Capacity to change*, including predictability.
9. *Potency:* power or energy, including capacity to further or hinder anything.
10. *Desirability* in terms of rewards or punishments.
11. *Feasibility:* workability or practicability.
B. Basic relationships commonly asserted or argued:
1. *Causality:* the relation of causes to effects, effects to causes, effects to effects, adequacy of causes, etc.
2. *Correlation:* coexistence or coordination of things, forces, etc.
3. *Genus-species* relationships.
4. *Similarity or dissimilarity.*
5. *Possibility or impossibility.*

Not every speaker talks about all of these themes, but there are few things one can say to popular audiences that are not suggested as soon as one pauses to ask whether he needs to talk about one or another of these eleven attributes and five relationships which things may have.

Let us suppose you are preparing a speech on how space exploration has affected industries. If you discipline your thinking as we propose, your first step will be to note that your audience will look chiefly for understanding rather than for a course of action to follow. Hence, the materials most important to you will be those that concern *facts* about the impact of the space age and the *standards* your listeners ought to apply in judging the truth or significance of those facts. But can you be more precise about the specific kinds of facts you will need? The checklists of attributes and relationships can help you. Will you need any facts showing the *existence* of, say, the space age? Not unless yours is a primitive audience. How about the *existence* of a "space industry"? Possibly. Simply by asking yourself this question, you will probably be reminded that it could be worth while to show your audience that something properly called a space industry actually does exist within the general thing we call industry. Here is a kind of fact truly appropriate to your speech and probably useful to your audience. Notice, too, that you could as easily have come to this thought by asking whether any genus-species relationships ought to be discussed. You could begin research for the speech at this point—looking for information that will satisfy the demands of your audience and your own purpose of establishing that something properly called "space industry" has actually come into being. Your best practice, however, will be to make a note that the *existence* of a space industry must be discussed and then continue your review of the other "topics."

Continuing your canvass of what *may* be worth talking about in this speech, you might ask, Will I need to talk about the *degree* or quantity of anything? Unquestionably. How much change has taken place is one of the primary things you want your listeners to understand. How much of industry is now space industry? The theme of *degree* is a central theme in your speech. What about *time*—the order in which the features of space industries emerged? This theme may prove important in developing some details, but it will probably not be a major topic in your speech. The changes you are talking about have happened swiftly. Your audience will know they have occurred. Possibly, but not necessarily, your hearers should know more about their timing. The theme of *motion* or activity does not suggest much in the way of material to be included in your speech. Were you explaining how a space-shot is accomplished, information about preparatory, launching, and orbital movements would be exceedingly important, but the probability is that you will have little need to discuss activities by which space industry or the materials for space exploration are produced.

Form, as a theme, ought to suggest that you can say something about such matters of abstract form as whether space industries grow up inside more familiar types of industrial organizations or independent of them. *Substance* seems unlikely to suggest many kinds of information you will need, unless you choose to discuss such things as the importance of research in space science, opportunities for industrial growth, the youthfulness of those who work in space industries. On the other hand, *capacity to change* ought to remind you that whether the present space industries are stable or subject to radical changes as scientific technology advances is something you will certainly need to comment on. And the topic, *potency*, ought to suggest that you must be ready to consider what things further or hinder an industry's capacity to compete in production of space goods.

The *desirability* and *feasibility* of various industrial practices will also need to be touched upon in your speech—not because your audience must approve any courses of action but in order that your hearers may understand *why* certain practices or production systems had to change as space industries developed.

When you turn to the commonly discussed relationships to see if they suggest specific kinds of information you should acquire, your judgment will probably tell you that information about genus-species relationships will be relatively unimportant to you—except when you distinguish space and non-space industries from one another. Otherwise, you will do little classifying in this speech. But the *causes* and *effects* of various special attributes of space industries will certainly have to be discussed if these attributes are to be understood. For example, what are the *effects* of our space industries' having grown so large (*degree*)? And whether it is *possible* or *impossible* for a space industry to function like any other industry may be important as you discuss unique features (*substance*) of the new kind of industry. In treating this particular point, and others, the *similarities* and *dissimilarities* between space and traditional industries will have to be treated, so you must know a good deal about them. To take another likely kind of idea: whether there is any reliable *correlation* between the way an industry is organized (*form*) and its *capacity* to produce space goods may also be worth inquiring into.

These are samples of the directions in which thought and research may be stimulated and guided by reviewing sixteen familiar themes for discussion. The values of reviewing these themes before and during research for a speech are several. Your examination of your own knowledge is likely to be more thorough, fruitful, and relevant to the business at hand. Your initial researches can be made more efficient because you readily discover what kinds of ideas you need to search for. But most important, a checklist of possible themes for treatment in a speech gives some assurance that you will not overlook important kinds of information, as you might easily do were you to prepare without any systematic analysis of what is actually thinkable and sayable about your subject.

Our system of identifying the kinds of material useful in speeches can, of course, also assist you in planning the development of individual points within a speech. For example, if you see that at some point in a speech you must distinguish between the effects of sales taxes and income taxes, the checklist we have provided might help. It might remind you that one way of making this distinction is to emphasize that the income and sales taxes are different *species* of taxation and, therefore, exert their influence (*causal effects*) in different ways. This observation would in turn send you in search of such detailed materials as examples, comparisons and contrasts, formal definitions, and other data that are useful in defining or describing the nature of things.

RESEARCH

Systems of classifying speech situations and systems for suggesting discussable themes cannot, in themselves, provide information. All they can do is show you what to look for. When you have decided what kinds of information you need, the routine work of research for speaking begins, and a few general suggestions about this stage of speech making may be useful. None of the advice we are about to give is unfamiliar to you, but all of us need to be reminded from time to time that some ways of digging for information are more practical than others. We shall not attempt to provide a list of bibliographic aids. We take for granted that you know how to use a library and that you are acquainted with its reference department. If you do not know how to use these facilities, we assume you will soon take the time to learn. We shall by way of example mention some sources we expect you to know about, but we feel it would be presumptuous to provide specific lists of encyclopedias, indexes, and dictionaries.

Though books are among the very best places to go for information, they are not the only wells of knowledge from which you may draw. We have already pointed out that *you* are a valuable source of information. Perhaps instead of talking about research for speeches, we ought to speak of "recall, recovery, and research for speeches," for we all possess knowledge we too seldom recover from ourselves. What have I already read about this subject, or this point? What have I heard in conversation, in lectures, on radio or television? What have I seen at firsthand or in photographs? Just asking such questions often stirs the memory and enables one to recall and recover forgotten information. Hence, it is fitting to record again the obvious but nonetheless worthwhile advice that each speaker ought, as an early step in research, to explore the recesses of his memory and check his notebooks.

Other people are excellent resources too. What photographer is not happy to answer questions about photography? What traveller is not all too pleased to reminisce about what he has seen and felt while visiting new places? What professional man is unwilling to talk about the problems and accomplishments of his profession? We are all in constant contact with people who would be happy to supply information; yet, just as we often forget to probe our own minds, we neglect convenient, willing resource persons.

Authorities, public officials, teachers, popular personalities, and their kind are often overlooked as sources of valuable information. One must be cautious about seeking assistance from such persons because of the heavy demands on their time, but even the busiest people are usually willing to grant a limited amount of time and aid to those who know what they want and are able to draw out needed information efficiently. The carefully pre-arranged interview is the usual vehicle for securing help from such people, and the speaker who has already carefully identified the kinds of ideas he needs should be able to conduct himself as a business-like interviewer. In any case, interviewing available authorities ought to be a normal part of an effective speaker's preparation for communication with an audience.

Personal investigation is another neglected avenue of research. We would think ill of a speaker who, after urging us to read the works of Joseph Conrad, turned out to have read only one of Conrad's books. What, then, of speakers who deplore the low level of television programming without having checked the full program listings and explored the viewing options open to their particular audiences? To take other examples, you are fortunate if you have never been subjected to speeches on juvenile delinquency or some other youth problem by speakers who had never visited a youth court, a settlement house, or even discussed their subjects with young people of the kinds they speak of. One need not be an ex-convict to speak of prisons or a parent to discuss children, but to neglect obvious and convenient opportunities for firsthand inquiry is to miss some of the most vital and immediately relevant information available.

We do not mean to disparage reading as a source of materials for speeches. We wish only to stress the fact Emerson speaks of in the quotation at the head of this chapter: the printed word is never the sole resource available. Printed materials are, of course, your most varied sources and, best of all, they are available when you want them and need them. But the printed page, like people and personal experience, needs to be approached thoughtfully, systematically, and imaginatively if it is to render its best service.

The kind of content one wants should determine the kind of reading material he explores. Comprehensive books, encyclopedic articles, surveys, and reviews in periodicals are the most promising sources of background material, and usually these are the sources to which one goes first when preparing a speech. Before looking for detailed information on the classical Greek theatre, you will be well advised to read some brief, general, but authoritative work on ancient Greek society. G. Lowes Dickinson's *The Greek Way of Life* or Edith Hamilton's *The Greek Way* or the general article on ancient Greece in a good encyclopedia are sources of this kind. The way you read such works makes a difference too. The object of reading general works is to accumulate enough broad understanding so that when you find more detailed materials you can see them in their proper context. To this end one reads general works attentively but swiftly.

But general source materials usually do not contain the detailed information a speaker needs if he has to establish, say, the precise *degree* or *desirability* of what he speaks about. If your speech subject concerns the role of advertising in our society, you may need to know something about how much advertising is handled through advertising agencies and how much is purchased directly by the advertiser. You are unlikely to find these details in general books or articles on advertising. To putter among the encyclopedias at this stage is to waste time and effort. Examine your library's card catalogue and such indexes as *The Readers' Guide to Periodical Literature* or the *International Index to Periodicals* to locate up-to-date reports and studies on the organization and economics of the advertising industry. The procedure is the same no matter what your subject: after obtaining general knowledge, you must locate specialized information, usually in specialists' reports and studies.

Your mode of reading will change also. The point is easily illustrated. Assume you are working on a speech dealing with John C. Calhoun as a public figure. You would certainly find Professor Richard Hofstadter's "John C. Calhoun: the Marx of the Master Class" (in his *The American Political Tradition*) a fascinating, general essay relevant to your subject. However, you could hardly talk competently about Calhoun's political influence without acquiring a clear understanding of what Hofstadter calls "the king pin of his political system"—his proposal to amend the Constitution to provide for settling contested national issues by "concurrent majority." Hofstadter's essay, like most general works, gives but a few lines to this theory of Calhoun's. An obvious place to go for more detail would be Calhoun's own *Disquisition on Government*. There the idea and reasons for it are spelled out in full. Some sections of the *Disquisition* would demand your most intensive study, but others, such as those dealing with the Polish, Iroquois, Roman, British, and other constitutions, would probably be irrelevant to your needs. From full but relatively light reading of Hofstadter's essay, it would be necessary to shift to highly selective but intensive reading when attacking the more technical and specialized *Disquisition*.

There also comes a time when exact bits of evidence—statistics, authoritative estimates, dates, facts about topography or design or authorship—are needed to fill small gaps in what is to be said at a given point in your speech. What were the exact dates of Calhoun's life? What was the population of the North and South at the time he popularized his "concurrent majority" concept? If your speech were on some other subject you might find yourself needing to know the area of a battlefield, the height of a building, the probable authorship of the "Letters of 'Junius,'" or the sequence of formal communications between the United States government and the USSR prior to the American blockade of Cuba in 1962. When this is the class of information required, it is time to explore some of the many volumes of classified data: biographical dictionaries, *The World Almanac, The Statistical Abstract, Facts on File,* concise histories of this or that literature, *Bartlett's Quotations,* Jane's *Ships of the World* or *Aircraft of the World,* etc. These are the kinds of resources you need when in search of isolated items of fact, and study of such materials is still more selective than one's general reading or intensive reading on special topics.

In all the exploratory activities that most speeches impose upon you, you ought never to forget that the purpose of it all is to extract what is necessary in order to *create a communication that will be your own,* a message designed for a particular group of auditors gathered on a specific occasion at a given time. One does not gather a speech together; he gathers raw materials out of which to mold a speech—a new and unique thing. Research for speech making ends, and is well finished, whenever the raw materials for an original, informed communication on a significant subject have been assembled in the interests of the audience that will hear it. When this is accomplished, it is time to get on with the task of composing the speech.

Before we pass to considerations that should control your efforts while you are composing speeches, something needs to be said about recording research findings in ways that will aid rather than hinder composition. Speaker after speaker compounds his difficulties by jotting research information in random fashion on page after page of notebook paper. If he paused to ask how he was going to use these notes later, he would adopt different methods of note taking.

Given the information he needs, a speaker must discover which of the facts and ideas he has found deserve inclusion in the speech he will actually give. But how can he decide whether he ought to spend much or little time talking about, say, the types of cancer, if what he has found out about the forms of cancer is scattered through six or a dozen pages of miscellaneous notes on the control of diseases in general? He must literally dig out the bits of information that deal with the types of this particular disease. This would be a far simpler task if all his notes were on individual cards or slips of paper, each labelled according to the special subject covered. Were this so, he could in a few moments shuffle the cards marked "Cancer —Kinds" out of his complete pack of notes, examine them, and determine whether this sort of information seemed important enough to deserve presentation to his audience.

There are many satisfactory ways of recording information for convenient use during speech composition. This is one:

Biographies—Attitudes in

John Clive, "More or Less Eminent Victorians: Some Trends in Recent Victorian Biography," *Victorian Studies*, II (Sept., 1958), 22.

"First, it is probably fair to say that the approach to the period taken by most Victorian biographers writing today is sympathetic. . . . No longer do we dare mock the victorians or condescend to them."

(John Clive: Asst. Prof., History and General Educ., Harvard. Specialist in 18th and 19th century English thought.)

The requisites of a good record of information are simply that it be complete enough so a second trip to the original source will not be necessary, that it provide an accurate representation of what was found, and that it allow individual items of information to be separated, sorted, and compared in any conceivably useful way.

Thus far in this chapter we have been dealing with procedures that precede the actual composition of the speech. We have suggested that a relatively simple series of topical questions can direct thought toward the types of information you need for a given speech. We have also seen that these same topical questions can guide and render more efficient explorations of your own mind, the minds of others, and the world of print. We have pointed out that different kinds of source materials are needed at different stages in research and that they must be studied in ways appropriate to their natures and to what you need to draw from them. Finally, we have observed that it is at best laborious and at worst confusing to record the results of research in any way that does not allow you to sort and study easily pieces of information that are related to one another. But a speaker is more than a bibliographer or research clerk. He investigates *in order that he may compose* an informed speech that will do what it needs to do with the particular audience he is going to meet.

Shaping Ideas

Let us go back to the supposition with which this chapter began. You are to speak to underclassmen on the character of the psychology program at your college. Suppose, now, that you have picked the brains of professors and underclassmen and have read generally and specifically on your subject. Your pockets may fairly bulge with notes carefully inscribed on suitably labelled three-by-five-inch cards, but you have not yet begun to create a speech out of this information. Your first attempt to sketch an outline of possible remarks will bring you face to face with a kind of problem that confronts you more insistently in preparing oral communications than anywhere else.

The gist of your intended talk may be perfectly clear in your mind: "The psychology program here makes sense; it offers a course of study that helps a person to understand himself and other people. It will never be irrelevant to anything you afterward do in life." To crystallize what thought and research have taught you is the first and indispensable step toward composing a meaningful communication; but because your communication is to be a speech rather than an essay, you are peculiarly restricted as to ways in which you may develop your thoughts. The position you have taken about the study of psychology is yours, and you have a right to it. You have no cause to give it up, no matter what audience you address or under what circumstances you meet them. But whether it is sensible to present your ideas in just the form in which they appeal to you and with just the supports that impress you is quite a different matter. *You* are not the one who is going to receive this communication. Nor are the people who will receive it going to hear you in circumstances just like those under which you worked out your position about the subject.

Those who are going to hear you speak are people who have lived different lives, whose knowledge differs from yours and from each other's, who have all the general and special susceptibilities discussed in Chapter 4. Yet *they, not you,* are going to be the final judges of whether the study of psychology is justifiable, compelling, inviting. And they are going to make these judgments or spurn them at a time when other people are "talking up" other kinds of study offered in your college. The whole tenor of the meeting will be one that says to your listeners: "Look over all your opportunities for study. Don't decide quickly or thoughtlessly on any concentration of courses." Your job, then, is to prepare a communication that will clarify the study of psychology and its benefits *despite all the human variables represented by the kind of audience you have and the tone of the occasion on which you speak.*

Here is the speaker's peculiar problem: no matter what seems compelling to *him*, he dares not apply only his personal judgments as criteria of adequacy, clarity, or persuasiveness in the communication he composes. In these respects no communicator is a completely free agent; but because they always face particular audiences on specific occasions, speakers are less free than essayists, poets, or writers of imaginative literature. An essay, a poem, or a novel can be composed as an expression of private feelings and can be published to the world on a take-it-or-leave-it basis. Your listener cannot pick up your speech when the moment is right and his spirit coincides with yours. A listener *gets* the speech at whatever time and in whatever place he and the speaker happen to come together. If the listener is ready for the speaker and his message, that is good fortune; if the listener is unready, the speaker must create readiness through his speech. He cannot retire to the bookshelf to wait until the listener falls into a mood to seek out what he has to say. *The composition of a speech thus becomes an exercise in transforming your knowledge and feelings about a subject into the kinds of stimuli that will evoke a like understanding in people who are different from you and who are going to respond to you and your message at a place and time that may or may not be ideal for either of you.*

It is not enough for you to know a truth. Through the design of your speech, you must give that truth vitality within another person's life—whether or not he is entirely ready for the experience. Through the design of your speech, data must be made humanly significant—significant for the human beings who are to assimilate them. Through the design of your speech, you must establish mutual acceptance between yourself and other people whose lives are momentarily linked with yours by the fact that you happen to have the platform and they the seats. All of this means that you, as speaker, must accommodate yourself and your ideas to whatever demands of audience, time, and place you can foresee. This means accommodating, in particular, to the age, sex, expectations, knowledge, and socioeconomic characteristics of your listeners. Only so can you be understood as you intend.

There are people who feel that personal integrity and accommodation to the demands of an audience are scarcely compatible. The issue they raise can be put thus: How can you sort, pare, rearrange, and perhaps even suppress things you know or think you know, and still be faithful to yourself and to your audience? Quite rightly, those who ask this kind of question are impatient with answers that say only, "You have to do these things in order to win your audience." The authors of this book think both the question and the answer misconstrue what adaptation or accommodation in speech making really requires of the speaker.

In the first place, the question implies that integrity and candor require publication of everything known about a subject—that simplification is necessarily misrepresentation. This can be the case, but it is not inevitably so. Second, the question presupposes that there is but one faithful version of a discussable subject. This is almost never so in the realm of human affairs, and even physicists and mathematicians would be prepared to say it is not always so in the matters with which they work.

There are, in fact, few things men discuss that can be understood in one way and one way only. Most discussable matters are susceptible to various presentations, all equally valid though not equally comprehensive. Assume it is true that by studying psychology one comes to understand himself and his fellows better. The following propositions are, then, also true, though they are not as inclusive as the first: By studying psychology one comes to understand himself. By studying psychology one comes to understand his fellows. In trying to accommodate himself to the demands of his audience a speaker's thinking might run as follows: "I have only five minutes to talk. That means I can either treat both benefits of studying psychology superficially or one of them fully. To show I really know what I'm talking about, it's better to be thorough than comprehensive but superficial. I'll develop one benefit only. Which? Most people are more interested in themselves than in others. Also, I can be more specific about how we can observe and understand our own behaviors. I shall put my emphasis on the thesis that the study of psychology helps one to understand himself. Maybe some other time I'll have an opportunity to talk to someone about the social insights a knowledge of psychology can give."

This little imaginary monologue fairly represents one aspect of the accommodation speakers must make to audiences and occasions. Unquestionably some of what this speaker thinks is going to be suppressed in his speech, not for purposes of misrepresenting anything but for the purpose of giving a full and proper representation to a *portion* of what he thinks. This speaker's responsibilities to his audience would be even less well served if he attempted more and so gave his subject a shoddy treatment.

Adaptation of subject matter is not always a problem in simplification or partition, however. The subtle decisions speakers are sometimes called upon to make are illustrated by this justly famous example of audience adaptation: St. Paul's sermon on Mars Hill in Athens. The Revised Standard Version of the account in The Acts of the Apostles, Chapter 17, runs as follows:

And they took hold of him and brought him to the Areopagus, saying, "May we know what this new teaching is which you present? For you bring some strange things to our ears; we wish to know therefore what these things mean." Now all the Athenians and the foreigners who lived there spent their time in nothing except telling or hearing something new.

So Paul, standing in the middle of the Areopagus, said: "Men of Athens, I perceive that in every way you are very religious. For as I passed along, and observed the objects of your worship, I found also an altar with this inscription, 'To an unknown god.' What therefore you worship as unknown, this I proclaim to you. The God who made the world and everything in it, being Lord of heaven and earth, does not live in shrines made by man, nor is he served by human hands, as though he needed anything, since he himself gives to all men life and breath and everything. And he made from one every nation of men to live on all the face of the earth, having determined allotted periods and the boundaries of their habitation, that they should seek God, in the hope that they might feel after him and find him. Yet he is not far from each one of us, for
'In him we live and move and have our being';
as even some of your poets have said, 'For we are indeed his offspring.'

"Being then God's offspring, we ought not to think that the Deity is like gold, or silver, or stone, a representation by the art and imagination of man. The times of ignorance God overlooked, but now he commands all men everywhere to repent, because he has fixed a day on which he will judge the world in righteousness by a man whom he has appointed, and of this he has given assurance to all men by raising him from the dead."[2]

---

[2] (New York: Thomas Nelson, 1959), Acts, XVII, 19–31. Copyright by the Division of Christian Education of the National Council of the Churches of Christ in the United States of America. Reprinted by permission.

The story of this speech closes with these words:

> Now when they heard of the resurrection of the dead, some mocked; but others said, "We will hear you again about this." So Paul went out from among them.
>
> But some men joined him and believed. . . .[3]

Looking at this account of a speech carefully designed to win a hearing within Greek culture raises some questions about rhetorical adaptation on which reasonable men may differ. Would Paul's personal religious convictions have been better honored had he not suppressed, for this speech, his strong distaste for paganism? This was his first meeting with Athenian philosophers, all of whom were pagans in Paul's eyes; yet he chose not to deplore their views outright but to use one facet of their paganism as a means of getting into his own subject. Certainly what he chose to say did not represent his complete view of Greek religious doctrines, nor did he merely simplify his own views. Still, the tolerant spirit he expressed was not essentially at variance with his private opinions. One can also ask a very different question about this speech: Would Paul's mission of converting the Greeks to his faith have been as well served if he had chosen to be completely outspoken? We do not choose to pronounce upon St. Paul's ethics in adapting speech materials to his audience. "Truth" and "right" are elusive here as elsewhere. On the other hand, we see no good reason for charging St. Paul with disseminating anything that was, for him, falsehood. He took his hearers as he found them, adapted to their natures, and proceeded as far as he thought it practical to proceed toward changing them.

In the opinion of the authors of this book one must distinguish between those accommodations to audience and occasion that leave the communication *essentially* faithful to what the speaker knows or thinks he knows and those accommodations that convey to the audience a meaning *other than* what the speaker knows or thinks he knows. Certainly the latter practice is either very clumsy or it is unethical. A remark attributed to Confucius constructively suggests another direction in which adaptation ought to tend: "The nobler sort of man emphasizes the good qualities in others and does not accentuate the bad. The inferior sort does the reverse."[4]

In addition to accommodating his materials to the requirements of audiences and occasions a speaker must recognize that not all kinds of

---

[3] *Ibid.*, 32–34.
[4] *The Sayings of Confucius*, trans. by Lionel Giles in *An Anthology of World Prose,* Carl Van Doren, ed. (New York: Literary Guild, 1935), p. 4.

content pass through the medium of speech with equal efficiency. Thus another kind of adaptation is required. An attorney normally prepares a brief to accompany his oral plea; the judge studies the brief at his leisure. This custom of our courts recognizes that some content is better communicated in print than in speech, and vice versa. If an engineer or any other speaker *must* deal with highly technical details, he is likely to reinforce what he speaks with visual or other more efficient means of communication. The architect prepares floor plans, sketches, sectional drawings, models, and the like, all in recognition that some kinds of information are better communicated in one mode than another and that building plans are never adequately communicated verbally—whether by speech or writing. Likewise, each speaker must discriminate between what can be communicated through speech and what is better conveyed in some other way.

Despite the examples we have just cited, the balance of effectiveness is not always against speech as a communicative medium. A man's attitude toward a proposition or toward another person is exceedingly difficult to picture and more difficult to convey through writing than through speech. A degree of feeling or emphasis is better conveyed in person than in print. What speech best communicates are the relationships between ideas and human experience. Aspects of an idea or event that have strong human significance are "naturals" for oral communication, and ideas that lack human significance must either be deliberately associated with other matters of human concern or be recognized as considerations better consigned to another medium.

As a public speaker you have *both* auditory and visual resources at your disposal. (Never forget that *you* are your most versatile visual resource.) One of your assignments as a composer-adapter of ideas and feelings is to choose and emphasize that content which lends itself to communication through your media. Another assignment is to subordinate or exclude from your speech whatever materials cannot be effectively communicated through speech and action.

Adaptation of content for a speech has still another dimension. What an audience can "take" and what the medium of speech can efficiently communicate sometimes vary with the time and place in which the communication occurs. We would miss much of St. Paul's artistry in adapting his material if we did not know that he had previously been speaking in the market place at the foot of Mars Hill and that it was a group of philosophers who "brought him to the Areopagus" at the top of the hill. We would miss more of Paul's achievement if we did not know that this hilltop had for centuries been the site of Athenian deliberations on matters of law, ethics, and morality. Some scholars have even thought that the philosophers who brought Paul there were members of a formal council that met regularly on Mars Hill. Whether this is true or not, we see more clearly the fitness of Paul's choice of ideas when we realize that few places and few audiences in all Greece more naturally invited discourse about comparative religion and ethics. The very details of the setting gave St. Paul cause to reason about whether a true god needed man-made offerings, for the speaker's stone on the hilltop was flanked by altars for sacred offerings. This, then, was a place and an occasion for reasoning and discussion, but not for pronouncing and evangelizing. What better topics than the proper *substance* of worship and the *potency* of the "Unknown God"?

Every speaker sooner or later faces similar situational problems in adaptation. The after-dinner situation establishes a tone of conviviality and relaxation. This tone must be respected, at least at the beginning of a speech. A Great Books discussion group will tend to establish reflective and informal communication as its norm, so unusually vigorous expression will be looked upon as inappropriate. Most radio and television situations demand more personalized and informal communication than is customary on public platforms. The reason is that sitting at home before their receivers, listeners tend to identify more easily with direct and conversational speakers than with orators addressing thousands in rally halls. Such are the special, delicate demands that settings for speeches impose upon speakers, and the composer of a speech needs to be sensitive to them from the beginning.

To return to the thought with which we ended Chapter 4, it is unfortunate that academic study of speech making can seldom give students opportunities to move from one unique speech situation to another except in imagination. Just because there are limited opportunities to test your skill in adapting to a wide variety of settings, it is important for you to recognize that upon entering the nonacademic world, you will almost never find speaking occasions as free from special demands as the academic settings within which you practiced. It is true that Winston Churchill was able to turn a Westminster College convocation platform in Fulton, Missouri, into an international forum that would accommodate his famous address, "Sinews of Peace," in 1946. But most of us will never have Churchill's prestigeful power to rule occasions instead of being ruled by them. We shall have to be content with adapting ourselves and our materials to the requirements of the occasions, places, and special times in which we are granted the privilege of speaking.

In the last several pages we have focused on external forces that hem you in as you plan and compose speeches. It is time to recognize that though subjects, audiences, and occasions do circumscribe your choices, there are resources upon which you can draw to compensate for these restrictive pressures. In succeeding chapters we shall discuss these resources in detail. Here we shall present only preliminary observations about these compensatory opportunities.

There is seldom only *one* way of handling an idea, however complex or difficult it may be. For example, if you find it virtually impossible to demonstrate the *existence* of life on another planet, you have other options. You can discuss whether conditions on the planet are *potentially* capable of supporting life as we know it. Again, many distinctive qualities of a great piece of music are scarcely communicable through words, but this need not prevent you from speaking about the musical work. Though you cannot say all, you can with words draw attention to some aspects of its structure or *form*. This, by the way, is precisely the method Leonard Bernstein, conductor of the New York Philharmonic Orchestra, used to make meaningful the verbal portions of his justly famous televised lectures on musical comedy, jazz, rhythm, conducting, etc. If one attribute or relationship of a subject does not lend itself to oral communication in a given setting, there is always the possibility that some other theme or line of thought, almost equal in importance, *is* orally communicable.

Speech makers confronted with ideas that are difficult to communicate or with purposes difficult to accomplish are subject to the same dangers as scientists confronted by the fact that absolute certainty and rigorously demonstrable answers are not always possible:

There is in the first place the temptation to sloppy thinking—if one knows that rigor can never be attained one is tempted to do less than one's best and let a piece of analysis go that one sees could be improved if one took more time and pains with it. There are situations where a defeatist attitude is too easily adopted instead of pressing the attack to one's utmost.[5]

[5] P. W. Bridgman, *The Way Things Are* (Cambridge. Mass.: Harvard University Press, 1959), p. 9.

It is almost never true that there is no usable analogy, no example, no familiar principle, no easily imagined experience that will create at least an approximate impression of what you want to speak about. We have seen how St. Paul turned to the methods of philosophical deduction when he wanted to show the superiority of his "Unknown God" to the philosophers so used to this kind of discourse. Thomas Huxley once explained the principles of scientific investigation to an audience of English working men by showing how this kind of investigation resembled investigations of crimes. Huxley's speech is still a classic model of exposition, but it would certainly not be had he decided to disregard the limitations of his auditors and proceed by rigorously defining induction, evidence, generalization, and the like.

Edmund Burke had a similar problem: how to explain the proper relation between political representatives and their constituents. Speaking to his constituents, he said:

Parliament is not a *congress* of ambassadors from different and hostile interests, which interests each must maintain, as an agent and advocate, against other agents and advocates; but Parliament is a *deliberative* assembly of *one* nation, with *one* interest, that of the whole—where not local purposes, not local prejudices ought to guide, but the general good, resulting from the general reason of the whole. You choose a member, indeed; but when you have chosen him he is not a member of Bristol, but he is a member of *Parliament*. If the local constituent should have an interest or should form a hasty opinion evidently opposite to the real good of the rest of the community, the member for that place ought to be as far as any other from any endeavor to give it effect. . . . Your faithful friend, your devoted servant, I shall be to the end of my life: a flatterer you do not wish for.[6]

Some six years later the same subject came up in Parliamentary debate. Addressing fellow members of Parliament, Burke spent little time *defining;* rather, he clarified his point by focusing on how a proper representative acts and feels toward himself and his constituents:

Faithful watchmen we ought to be over the rights and privileges of the people. But our duty, if we are qualified for it as we ought, is to give them information, and not to receive it from them: we are not to go to school to them, to learn the principles of laws and government. In doing so, we should not dutifully serve, but we should basely and scandalously betray the people, who are

[6] "Speech to the Electors of Bristol," November 3, 1774. *Works* (London: John C. Nimmo, 1887), II, pp. 89–98.

not capable of this service by nature, nor in any instance called to it by the constitution. I reverentially look up to the opinion of the people, and with an awe that is almost superstitious. I should be ashamed to show my face before them, if I changed my ground as they cried up or cried down men or things or opinions,—if I wavered and shifted about with every change, and joined in it or opposed as best answered any low interest or passion,—if I held them up hopes which I knew I never intended, or promised what I well knew I could not perform. Of all these things they are perfect sovereign judges without appeal; but as to the detail of particular measures, or to any general schemes of policy, they have neither enough of speculation in the closet nor of experience in business to decide upon it. They can well see whether we are tools of the court or their honest servants.[7]

A fainthearted or easily defeated speaker might have said the constituent-representative relationship was too abstract a subject to be explained to ordinary voters. But Burke found, in contrasts between agents and representatives, between hostile interests and the interests of people of the same nation, between "member of Bristol" and "member of Parliament," and between flattery and faithful service, the concepts by which to convey his basic meaning—that the responsibilities of representatives extend beyond the boundaries of the constituents' district. For addressing other representatives, however, Burke found he needed a very different set of contrasts: duty vs. subservience, higher vs. lower political capacities, what the constituent can accurately judge vs. what he cannot, feelings of personal integrity vs. feelings of deceit. What we see is that Burke located a dozen or more *similarities* and *dissimilarities*, all of which could be used to make somebody understand this one idea.[8] Knowledge of one's subject, persistence in preparation and composition, and a bit of ingenuity can overcome very many of the restrictions imposed upon speakers by subject matter, audiences, and occasions.

There is another circumstance in which speakers too easily adopt defeatist attitudes. It develops when the speaker realizes his audience has no strong, initial interest in his subject. One had probably better remain silent than try to discuss the romantic movement in English literature with members of a primitive New Guinea tribe; but there are fewer such im-

[7] "Speech on a Bill for Shortening the Duration of Parliaments," May 8, 1780. *Works* (Boston: Little, Brown, 1869), VII, pp. 71–87.

[8] See Chap. 6, pp. 150–161 for discussion of the speaker's options when his need is for means of amplification as distinguished from proof.

penetrable situations than inexperienced speakers realize. The little narrative that follows is true, and it illustrates how fully respectful, sympathetic adaptations to an audience can overcome ignorance and initial indifference.

Bob Barth was one of a class of fifteen students, all but four of whom were college freshmen. Nine were women and six were men. In conference with his instructor Barth revealed that he would like to explain the operation of jet aircraft engines in his next speech to the class but, he said, this probably would not be wise since it was already clear that only two of the fourteen students who would be his audience had even an elementary knowledge of mechanical and physical principles. Barth's judgment on his audience was exactly right; most knew nothing and seemed to care nothing for the world of physics and mechanics. Nonetheless, Barth's instructor contended that this was a golden opportunity for an experiment with what careful selection of ideas and methods could accomplish with a difficult audience. Barth reluctantly agreed to do what he could and set doggedly to work designing a speech that assumed little interest and no mechanical knowledge on the part of his hearers.

On the day of his speech Barth began by saying:

I'm going to talk to you today about jet engines. I suspect you think you aren't interested. Probably what's in your minds now is something like this.

Here Barth uncovered a rough but clear drawing of a jet engine "pod" covered with such words as "dangerous machine," "complicated," "for mechanics only," "expensive," etc. Barth continued:

The fact is that in principle at least jets aren't complicated. They're rather simple. If you've ever blown up a toy balloon and then let it out of your hands to watch it shoot through the air as the wind escaped, you not only know something about jet propulsion, you've used it. Let's begin right there—with the air escaping out of the balloon.

Barth's speech went on in this vein, covering simply but accurately the elemental facts about the construction and operation of ram-jet and turbo-jet engines. There was nothing unusual about his delivery, except that it was not as direct and forceful as it ought to have been. The language of the speech was simple and the examples were always from everyday life, but there were no other marks of artistry. Even the charts and sketches that communicated things hard to put into words were free-hand crayon drawings on cardboard sheets of different sizes. Yet when Bob Barth ended his talk there was a ripple of applause—the first applause heard in that public speaking classroom. At the end of the hour two young women who had been in the audience exchanged these observations as they walked from the room. "I learned more today than I do in most class periods," said one. Her companion replied, "Yes. And imagine! I even thought I understood that engine."

What happened? A simple but rare thing. A speaker accepted his audience as he found it, adjusted to its limitations and its needs, and gave it as much information as its little knowledge, his inventiveness and art, and the time would allow. Without fanfare Barth offered his listeners two always alluring reasons for attending: I can help you understand a thing that's been a trifle mysterious to you, and you'll find the whole experience much easier than you expect. Scarcely any subject is unusable in speaking if speaker and audience approach it in this spirit. Aristotle said it well:

. . . for style and reasoning alike, . . . in order to be lively they must give us rapid information. . . . What we like are those [arguments and expressions] that convey information as fast as they are stated—so long as we did not have the knowledge in advance—or that our minds lag only a little behind.[9]

To gain attention and interest, no matter how forbiddingly indifferent an audience seems, one must give information the listeners can rapidly comprehend. Adapting to the interests of audiences does not mean we are to tell them what they already know. This is a splendid way to bore them. The single most important task in speaking is to bring "news" at just the rate at which the hearers can absorb it. If one can achieve that, there are few occasions on which a speaker need feel that what he wants to say will be rejected.

Thoughtfulness of others, a willingness to hunt for and experiment with alternative ways of handling ideas, and a reasonable amount of patience and persistence are attributes the composer of speeches needs in large portions. But there are two things for the absence of which no amount of rhetorical skill and ingenuity can ever compensate: a thorough knowledge of one's speech subject and a clear-headed vision of what one wishes to

9 From *The Rhetoric of Aristotle* trans. and ed. by Lane Cooper. Copyright, 1932, Lane Cooper, p. 207, Bk III, Ch. 10. Reprinted by permission of the publisher Appleton-Century-Crofts.

accomplish by speaking. We have explored the avenues along which your mind may travel in search of useful ideas, some considerations relevant to your research, and the problems and opportunities you will encounter in shaping ideas. We shall therefore turn next, in Chapter 6, to the problem of coordinating one's information to form a speech that is both manageable for you and clear to your audience.

Exercises

Written

1. Assume you are to speak to your classmates in favor of majoring in the academic field that interests you most. Identify three lines of thought (topics) that it would be useful to discuss with this audience. Identify three other lines of thought that are relevant to your assumed speech subject but which you would not choose to discuss in a speech to your classmates. Explain the grounds on which you include or exclude each of these lines of thought.

2. Assume you are to give a classroom speech on "Censorship of Motion Pictures Should (or Should Not) Be Discontinued." Which of the sixteen lines of thought listed in this chapter suggest the most promising lines of research for this speech? Explain why the remaining lines of thought are not potentially useful as guides to promising information for this speech.

3. Identify the lines of thought (topics) used in some brief, familiar speech such as Lincoln's "Gettysburg Address," St. Paul's "Sermon on Mars Hill," Shakespeare's version of Mark Antony's speech over the body of Caesar in *Julius Caesar*. Defend or criticize the speaker's choice of these lines of thought. Were there other lines of thought he might as wisely have chosen? If so, illustrate how one of them might have been incorporated into the speech.

Oral

1. Give a short speech in which you explain two different ways in which a specific proverb may be interpreted or a process explained.

2. Give a brief report on a speech or editorial you have heard or read in which you believe the speaker either made exceptionally inventive use of the lines of thought available to him or failed to take advantage of promising lines of thought open to him.

6   *Invention:*

General Tactics

In Chapter 5 we examined the intellectual discipline and outlook public speakers need if they are to be alert to what is sayable about subjects and if they are to maintain the adaptive posture public speaking demands. We saw that a speaker's view of himself and his available materials differs from the view taken by many other creative artists. The speaking-listening relationship is always a highly intimate social relationship, existing in a moment of time which may or may not be ideal from the viewpoint of speaker and listener. As we have noted repeatedly, listeners—those for whom speaking occurs—function under psychological conditions markedly different from those that prevail when the same people become readers, admirers of painting or sculpture, or contemplators of the beauties of nature. Very often listeners to speeches have not even sought out the speaker and his subject as, on other occasions, they seek out the musician when they want music or the actor when they want drama. Much of the time the speaker-listener relationship is an inevitable part of some larger bargain, or even an accident, from the viewpoint of the listener. It is therefore a necessary part of the speaker's art that he transform himself and his subject matter into stimuli capable of inducing predetermined changes in a *particular* group of listeners. This necessity of adapting to the particular, this adaptive posture, differentiates the speaker-as-artist from most other artists. His respondents are special: though they have the traits of all mankind, they possess unique and, for the speaker, crucial attributes induced by the setting and the time in which they enter into relationship with him.

Though a first step in composing a speech must be to adopt an audience-centered attitude toward one's self and one's ideas, the speaker's engagement with other minds is not won by attitude alone. His listeners cannot observe his attitudes toward subject, self, occasion, and audience except through the tactics they see him using as he speaks. Speakers are known by their works; their ideas are known only by the ways in which they handle knowledge. It therefore becomes important to explore those tactics in the management of thought that enable a speaker to establish strong rather than weak intellectual and psychological relationships with particular audiences.

Speeches are always about something. What, then, constitutes a suitable subject for a public speech and how are such subjects found? Speeches are intended to modify the perceptions of those who hear them. What features of a speech effect these changes in auditors? Speeches are messages that are chiefly oral. How does one enhance the likelihood that auditor-viewers will grasp spoken messages as they were intended to be grasped? In this chapter we shall treat the general answers to these three questions; in Chapter 7 we shall examine the special tactics of choosing and using ideas which are peculiarly relevant to the five purposes of speaking: informing, inquiring, reinforcing beliefs and feelings, persuading with a view to altering behavior, and entertaining.

Choosing Subjects

What constitutes a suitable subject for a public speech and how are such subjects found? When you cease to be a student, most occasions on which you make public speeches will probably suggest appropriate subject matter. Your professional and avocational competencies, the setting in which the speech is to be given, or the terms of the invitation you receive will sharply narrow the range of subjects open to you. But as a student of public speaking you will be free to choose your speech subjects more often than not. This means you will have both opportunities and difficulties which may not be available to you outside the classroom.

The specifications of a good speech subject are easy to lay down in general terms: any subject on which you talk ought to be timely, significant for you and your audience, appropriate for you as the speaker and for the audience and occasion, capable of being presented effectively through oral discourse, and manageable in the time available to you. In other words, a good subject for a speech is one that meets the demands imposed by your own capacities, the capacities and readiness of the audience, and the conventions of the situation in which you will appear.

All this is quickly said, but standards give us no procedures by which to locate discussable subjects. And for some students of public speaking finding subjects seems to present more problems than testing their suitability. So, we shall need to see how subjects of any sort can be discovered in the hope that students' perplexity may be assuaged.

To find subjects about which you might sensibly communicate with other people, let your mind run freely over all kinds of subject matters. Suspend your doubts and critical inclinations temporarily. Just try to see what is interesting in the world about you and within you. Use the procedure sometimes called "brainstorming." The next paragraph illustrates how the process can work. The subjects and subject areas discovered are printed in brackets following the stimulus that brought them to mind.

This paragraph is being written in a motel apartment. That fact will affect the thoughts that spring to mind [the power of suggestion; hotel-motel-hostelry operations]. The highway is visible from the window [mass transportation problems, highway construction, auto and truck licensing, highway safety, scenic routes]. A row of shrubs can be seen across the highway [horticulture, landscaping, plant breeding, land use, plant pathologies]. The storm windows are still on the motel [insulating materials and properties, maintenance industries, glass making, fabricating for the construction industries, custom building vs. prefabrication]. A school bus passes [the topic of education calls up too many possibilities to enumerate]. The typewriter is before me [mechanisms of communication, the publishing industry, business machines, automation]. A bookshelf is at my side. On it stands *The Ugly American* [foreign policy, diplomacy, the responsibility of the press], a murder mystery [escapist reading, paperbacks, censorship], Charles Perelman's *Traité de L'Argumentation* [foreign language study, foreign travel, methods of persuasion, the study of philosophy, the relative merits of different academic subjects].

Twelve minutes passed while this little "brainstorming" experiment took place and the results were typed out. By the most conservative count thirty-two different, discussable subjects and subject areas emerged. It is difficult to imagine an educated man or woman who could not, by further narrowing one of these thirty-two topics, find a timely, significant, manageable subject on which to give a worthwhile, ten-minute speech.

"I have nothing to talk about" or "I cannot find an interesting subject" is almost never a statement of fact. Either assertion really means "I have not truly opened my mind to the possibilities." Discussable subjects are everywhere about you. Look at the newspaper headlines. Walk along library shelves noting book titles. Look closely at any group of people, animals, machines, plants, or anything else. Or take any class of things as your starting point and begin enumerating members of that class. Try *vehicles, buildings, clothing, inventions,* or *authors* as a start. The fund of possibly interesting subjects for speeches is virtually inexhaustible if you let your mind run freely in one direction after another. But keep some record of the often strange, often familiar things free-wheeling thought grinds out.

Once you have noted down a considerable list of *available* subjects and subject areas, it is time to reactivate your critical powers and judge the results. Cull the list for timely, significant themes *you* are interested in. Do not ask, yet, whether a subject is manageable, and don't worry about whether your audience will be interested. If a subject is timely and interests *you*, there may be a way to trim or expand it to meet the manageability test. If you are as careful a workman as Bob Barth, whom we described in Chapter 5, you can probably find ways of making it interesting to your hearers. It is also possible that there is a special approach to the subject that will fit the occasion on which you will speak. Your immediate problem is to draw from a random list of ideas those that are potentially timely and potentially significant for *you*.

To be a live option a subject need not be patently within your present knowledge and preparation. It need only be one you can and are willing to learn more about than your audience already knows. Given this much, it is probably within your power to command some phase of the subject and to make it vital for your audience.

Building Proof

What features of a speech effect changes in the viewpoints of auditors? They are several.

PURPOSIVENESS

As we said in Chapter 3, purposiveness in a speech is important both to you and to the listeners whose viewpoints you hope to change. It is therefore imperative that you formulate a clear purpose statement for every speech you plan to make. To be an efficient guide for you and your listeners, your central idea—or specific purpose, as we shall sometimes call it—must be expressed in a concise sentence that specifies two things: (1) the kind of experience you intend your listeners to have, and (2) the essential content you will put into the speech. Some standards for evaluating your phrasing of a central idea have already been discussed in Chapter 3 (see pp. 48–49). Others will be discussed in Chapter 7 (see pp. 166–167; 170–173; 176; 179).

Consider first your own need of a purpose statement. You need such a statement because, as we saw in Chapter 5, any subject can be treated in a number of different ways. One dares not be vague about his purpose. "I want to tell you about psychology" does not declare which of the hundreds of speeches that could be made about psychology is to be prepared *now*. "I want to help you to understand what requirements a psychology major must meet" does identify one particular speech "about psychology." "I shall explain three milestones in the development of psychology as a science" identifies another, different speech "about psychology." "I shall show that important psychological research is lagging for want of public support" identifies still another speech, and so on. In short, you need a precise statement of (1) your aim and (2) the range of subject matter you intend to cover in order to know *what* speech to prepare.

You need a statement of your specific purpose before you from the very beginning of your preparatory work. It will keep your attention focused on your real business throughout the stages of preparation. However, you should always feel free to revise your purpose statement. As you learn more about your subject and think more about your audience and occasion your vision of what you can achieve through a speech will, naturally, change. Be ready, then, to modify your aim and your coverage of subject matter as you need to—but the most recent version of your specific purpose must be in your mind at all times.

It is also important to your listeners that your speech exhibit the unified thrust a precise statement of purpose can give it. Listening is not an especially efficient way of acquiring ideas, and listeners need all the help they can get if they are to extract the right ideas from public speeches. If they know what your specific purpose is, that knowledge will help them to see how the details of your speech relate to one another and to what you are asking of your audience. Hence, telling your audience your purpose often gives you advantages you can ill afford to lose.

There are times, however, when more will be lost than gained if you tell your hearers exactly what you are trying to do and how. This is almost always the case with a doubtful or hostile audience. To tell an audience of scientists, "I want to show you how science is undermining morals," may arouse so much defensiveness in the scientists that they will close their minds to what you have to say. In circumstances like this, experienced speakers usually adopt the tactic of withholding their specific purposes from the audience in order to be sure the listeners give the fullest possible attention to the "proofs" of the speech and are not prematurely disturbed by the conclusions to which these proofs lead.

As in most matters relating to public speaking, the expectations of the audience and the demands of the occasion and the subject must govern whether you reveal your purpose early, late, or not at all. But whether you do or do not reveal your speech purpose remains a matter of tactics only. Whether he knows your purpose or not, your listener will invariably understand a unified message better than a disorganized one, and it is the statement of intent that lies within *your* mind that will give your speech its unity.

Do not mistake the central idea of what has just been said: careful attention to formulating purpose statements for speeches is important, not because a textbook says so, but because speakers and listeners are human beings having the fault that they expend energies inefficiently if they lack the kind of guidance a clear sense of purpose can give. How the forms for expressing purpose statements may vary depending on the response expected from listeners has been touched on in Chapter 3 and will be further explained in Chapter 7. Here, we wish to establish the broader proposition that the demands of subject matter, speakers' capacities, and listeners' capacities all conspire to make formulation of clear and settled speech purposes essential if the viewpoints of listeners are to be effectively changed.

KINDS OF PROOF

However expertly a speech purpose is phrased, it does not, itself, accomplish the work it forecasts. Proofs and amplification—including all the behavior a listener perceives or thinks he perceives in the speaker—do this work. There is no completely reliable way of determining in advance exactly what an idea or way of speaking will accomplish with an audience, but there are fairly dependable ways of making sure that any part of a speech, or the whole speech, has those features of proof that usually make communication acceptable and influential for listeners.

Any well-stated purpose reveals that the speaker is chiefly interested in securing one of five responses. The purpose statement may indicate that the speaker wishes, in the main, to *inform* listeners. A specific purpose may show the speaker aims at leading his listeners into an *inquiring* exploration of a subject. It may reveal that he wants to *reinforce* ideas and attitudes that his listeners already possess in some form and degree. Again, the purpose statement may show the speaker hopes to *persuade* listeners to adopt some view or take some action to which they were not already committed. Finally, the purpose statement may indicate the speaker aims at *entertaining* his listeners. Whatever aim the speaker adopts, he is always seeking to induce some kind of change in his listeners' experience. He must get them to accept information and use it in special ways, if he is to inform; they must experience heightened desire to investigate, if he is to provoke inquiry; they must revalue their prior knowledge, if he is to reinforce their beliefs and attitudes; they must accede to his interpretations of things and of their own interests, if he is to persuade them; they must suspend some practical and serious concerns, if the speaker is to entertain them. Whatever he attempts, the speaker's success depends on his ability to cause some shift in the listeners' outlook. So, to ask what makes people change viewpoints is to ask what people accept as proofs.

One may express in these ways what listeners demand of a communication before accepting the outlook it urges:

1. They demand that either the communication or their own experience reveal a connection between what the communication asks of them and their own personal interest. (See Chapter 4, pp. 72–89.)

2. They demand that either the communication or their own experience provide rational justifications for believing what is said to them.
3. They demand that the source of the communication (the speaker and his sources) seem worthy of confidence—at least on the subject of the communication.

These are general demands a speech, or any part of it, must in some way satisfy, if there is to be change in the attitudes and beliefs of those who listen. You have often made these same demands on speakers, though you expressed them within your mind in question form.

Suppose someone is talking to you about an engineering curriculum. Natural, legitimate questions constantly pop into your mind as the talker moves through his remarks: Why should *I* care about the engineering curriculum? Why bring this up *now?* Why should I believe the curriculum *is as you say it is?* Why is what you urge on me *better* or *truer* than an alternative? Why should I listen to *you* on this matter?

Anyone talking about engineering curricula can expect these questions to arise again and again in any listener's mind. And if we substitute another subject for engineering curriculum, we shall find that listeners hearing a speech on that subject are bound to raise precisely the same set of questions.

Notice that some of these questions ask whether the listener's personal interests are going to be satisfied (Why should *I* care? Why bring this up *now?*); some ask for rational justifications (Why should I believe things *are as you say they are?* Why is what you urge on me *better* or *truer* than an alternative?); and another asks about the speaker's qualifications (Why should I listen to *you* on this matter?). The implications are plain enough: if, as a speaker, you see to it that these five questions are satisfactorily answered either by what you say and do or by something your listeners are already aware of, your speech will have the personal-interest, rational, and source justifications audiences demand as the price of shifting attitudes and beliefs even slightly.

To deal with how one builds up personal-interest, rational, and source justifications, we shall have to talk about these kinds of justification separately, but as you read the discussion that follows you should bear in mind that these sources of influence never *actually* operate separately from one another. For example, if you show a listener it is in his interests to change viewpoints, this will probably make him think better of you as a source, and it may also cause him to ask for far less rational justification than he otherwise would. Likewise, to build good reasons into a speech will make you seem a more reliable and believable person. These forces are always working for and against one another simultaneously, even though we cannot write about them except as individual forces.

Developing Personal-Interest Justifications. "Why should *I* care?" and "Why bring this up *now?*" are primitive questions. They spring from man's basic attributes. We saw in Chapter 4 that listeners are anxious about things that seem likely to affect their private purposes and interests, that people tend to shut out things having no apparent bearing on their immediate affairs as they understand them at the moment, and that all of us behave this way just by virtue of being human. For these reasons it is of the highest importance that each listener whose reactions are important to you shall find satisfying answers to why *he* should care *now.*

To see how listeners may be shown that their own interests justify what you say, we must begin by reviewing some elemental psychological concepts. Many modern psychologists posit that we behave as we do in consequence of internal forces commonly called *needs* and *drives. Drives* are usually thought of as stimuli within us that tend to induce us to act in some way or other. *Needs* give rise to these *drives* and direct them toward simple or complex *goals.* These *goals* are conditions likely to satisfy our *needs* and hence cause our *drives* to cease.[1] Some of our *needs,* and therefore our *drives,* are physiological (e.g., the need for food and drink evokes hunger-thirst drives); some are social as well as physiological (e.g., the basic need for physical safety and the learned need for social approval may evoke a wide variety of drives toward the goal of gregarious experience). Experience teaches us that certain behaviors satisfy specific needs, thus relieving us of the tensions we experience when drives associated with these needs are stimulating us. Thus, we soon acquire many predictable patterns of activity to which we regularly resort when we experience the tensions of specific drives. For example, we learn that to drink a cup of coffee at mid-afternoon "picks us up." So, under tension of drives toward relaxation, we go through what is essentially a thirst-satisfying activity. We do not feel any the less gratified because the drives that induced us to act in this way

[1] This and the immediately following statements are simplifications of highly complex concepts widely and often somewhat differently used in psychological explanations of behavior. They should not be taken as definitive or universally agreed-upon descriptions of reality. We offer them only to furnish a tolerably acceptable framework within which to examine the options a speaker has in trying to reach the interests of those who hear him.

had less relation to bodily need for fluids than to a need for rest or, perhaps, some need for companionship. In similar ways we develop predispositions toward specific, predictable intellectual activities. These, of course, are the behaviors of special importance to speakers. We learn that experienced people are often better advisers than the inexperienced; so, we become predisposed to listen to and accept what, say, a world traveller tells us. Or we learn that Midwesterners are more friendly than New Englanders. We are thereby predisposed to react approvingly to a statement that says we will find it more pleasant to live in Winona, Minnesota than in Pittsfield, Massachusetts. We may know nothing of either place, but our predisposition to respond favorably toward Winona, Minnesota is nonetheless real. In such manner everyone has acquired hundreds of ready propositions—infrequently verbalized, often contradictory to one another—that constitute his fund of *attitudes*.[2] These predispositions to respond favorably or unfavorably become our guidelines in judging what does or does not conform to our own needs or interests. And what is especially important to speakers is that *these attitudes, though infrequently verbalized, are nonetheless expressible in words, as needs and drives are not. Listeners' attitudes, therefore, can be thought of as yes-no propositions capable of taking their places amidst the propositions the speaker, himself, offers.*

Make no mistake, the paragraph above presents a vastly oversimplified view of human behavior. It does, however, present concepts with which we can think meaningfully about the tactics of building personal-interest justifications into speeches. The crucial thing to understand from what has been said is this: we do not, with words, reach human needs *directly;* we can, however, rather directly awaken need-produced attitudes which, being susceptible to verbalization, can in effect become an integral part of language-bound experience within a listener. A speaker can weave a tapestry of need-justified experience within listeners if he sets off attitudes that coherently intermingle with the information his language supplies.

See how a masterful political speaker did this for a Detroit audience during the economic depression of the 1930's. The speaker was Franklin D. Roosevelt. In order that you may see what he accomplished, we have broken a quotation into separate thought units and have suggested, opposite each unit, the kind of favorable or unfavorable predisposition that thought unit probably energized in most listeners.

[2] See Leonard W. Doob, *Public Opinion and Propaganda* (New York: Henry Holt, 1948), pp. 27-30.

Take another form of poverty in the old days.	Unfavorable to "poverty"; perhaps to "old days" also.
Not long ago, you and I know, there were families in attics/—in every part of the Nation—	Unfavorable to attic living and poverty that causes it.
	Increased unfavorableness to *widespread* poverty, etc.
in country districts and in city districts/	Still more unfavorable to *universal* poverty.
—hundreds and thousands of crippled children who could get no adequate care,/	Unfavorable attitudes toward poverty now reinforced by unfavorable attitudes toward neglect of crippled children.
crippled children who were lost to the community and who were a burden on the community.	Earlier attitudes further reinforced by unfavorable attitudes toward *losses* and toward economic and other *burdens*.
And so we have, in these past twenty or thirty years, gradually provided means for restoring crippled children to useful citizenship;/	Now favorable attitudes toward "restoring" actions are evoked. They are the stronger for the "restoring" actions suggest ways of relieving the unpleasant drives caused by contemplating widespread poverty, neglect, losses, and burdens. Moreover, the speaker, FDR, was himself permanently crippled by poliomyelitis.
and it has all been a factor in going after and solving one of the causes of poverty and disease.[3]	Favorable attitudes are now transferred to these ways of acting that promise to eliminate what is unpleasant to contemplate. Some hearers may begin to "learn" a new attitude here —one favorable to governmental action to end poverty and its consequences.

Here, no reasoning is offered nor does Roosevelt make any verbal attempt to justify himself as uniquely qualified to say what he does. The

[3] Franklin D. Roosevelt, "The Philosophy of Social Justice Through Social Action," a campaign address delivered in Detroit, Michigan, October 2, 1932. Text as established by L. LeRoy Cowperthwaite, "A Criticism of the Speaking of Franklin D. Roosevelt in the Presidential Campaign of 1932" (Ph.D. thesis, State University of Iowa, 1950), 2 vols. Used by permission.

thoughts expressed are justified by his own crippled condition and by a series of attitudes that become, in effect, proofs of the goodness or badness of whatever Mr. Roosevelt is mentioning. The speaker evokes these attitudes in series, creating out of them a kind of argument leading to the conclusion: Neglect of the impoverished is thoroughly bad when we know how to get rid of the pitiful and costly effects of poverty from the lesson taught by our good experience with the crippled, including Franklin D. Roosevelt himself. What the speaker did was to set off images, recollections, and ideas in his hearers' minds; associated favorable-unfavorable attitudes did the rest—stamping poverty and neglect as "bad" and "going after and solving . . . the causes of poverty and disease" as "good." By his ideas-borne-on-language and ideas-born-of-his-own-handicap Mr. Roosevelt was regulating the mixture of need-produced attitudes and Roosevelt-supplied perceptions of how things had been and could be.

You, too, will find points in your speeches for which your hearers will have the best proofs already within them. How silly it would be to prove by statistics, quotations, and arguments that skillful teachers are more desirable than unskillful ones if the audience were made up of students! Any student's attitudes will supply proofs far more potent *for him* than any assembled from outside his skin. Every student's needs and experience have taught him such attitudes as: disorganized lectures get in the way of learning; teachers who don't allow discussion are inferior; a showman isn't necessarily a good lecturer; good examinations ought to teach something; good teachers show interest in individual students; and so on. Such attitudinal propositions, whether or not they have ever been voiced as opinions, have only to be triggered by the mention of disorganized lectures, showmen, etc. to become proofs of that which you associate with them.

To identify all the attitudes possessed by even a single audience would require attitude and opinion research by a corps of social scientists. Some political candidates and certain other communicators have the benefit of such research data, but most public speakers must work without these advantages. Most of us must discover the attitudes of our hearers—and thereby the personal-interest justifications open to us—from using less precise generalizations such as those discussed in Chapter 4. We are not wholly disadvantaged.

You will not need Mr. Gallup's polling organization to tell you that the young people in your audience will be more disposed than their parents to endorse idealistic and unqualified propositions. Nor need you be a social scientist to predict that members of a taxpayers' association will be cost conscious and, therefore, favorably predisposed toward ideas that hint at control of public expenditures. What you chiefly need, if you are to compose public speeches effectively, is a readiness to ask yourself what most people of the sort you will address have already learned to identify as "good for me and mine" and "not so good for me and mine." Much of the time, if you will ask yourself this question, common sense will tell you which attitudes can be called up to justify your ideas and which must be carefully skirted lest they leap into your hearer's consciousness as proofs against you.

We began this section by saying that answers to "Why should *I* care?" and "Why bring this up *now?*" must either be obvious to your listeners or supplied in your speech. The rest of what we have been saying can be epitomized in this statement: *one* place where answers for these questions can be found is in the systems of attitudes your listeners bring with them. Your listener may call up an attitude himself, or you may remind him he possesses it. However it arises to his consciousness, the attitude will teach him why *he* should care *now*. It is your task to direct his caring toward the conclusion you have in view, not let it subside or become associated with something other than the viewpoints you are urging. When Franklin Roosevelt juxtaposed the plight of crippled children and poverty, he exercised three such controls at once. He awakened dormant attitudes favorable to the proper care of children, took advantage of strong, depression-bred attitudes unfavorable to poverty in any time or place, and aligned these so they would "prove" that government ought to "go after and solve" other causes and results of poverty. When you wish to use listeners' attitudes to support propositions your hearers have not yet "learned," your method must be essentially the same as Roosevelt's.

Developing Rational Justifications. Sometimes "Why should *I* care?" or "Why bring that up *now?*" cannot be sufficiently answered by triggering attitudes. Then you may need to argue or explain the answers in the same manner you will usually use when answering "Why should I believe things *are as you say they are?*" or "Why is what you offer *better* or *truer* than some alternative?" When this is your tactic, you will not work *pri-*

marily through existing attitudes but, instead, through propositions *you* supply and relate to each other in ways your listener considers rational.

What constitutes a rational justification is a human question, not a scientific one. We can use the example below to illustrate how variable judgments of rationality are, and how rational justifications are created in speeches. The example comes from a speech that was predominantly persuasive, but the lessons that can be learned from it are generalizable to speeches with other aims.

On January 25, 1959, Mr. Oliver W. Hill, then chairman of the Legal Committee of the Virginia State Conference of National Association for the Advancement of Colored People Branches, delivered a radio speech from Richmond, Virginia. His specific purpose was to show that segregation of races in public schools is unconstitutional and unwise. At one point in his speech he argued as follows:

> The segregationists complain that in 1896 the United States Supreme Court decided that racial segregation did not violate the provisions of the 14th Amendment in the case of *Plessy vs. Ferguson*. But for some unexplained reason, they ignore the fact that in the Plessy case—which, incidentally, involved segregation on street cars—the United States Supreme Court arbitrarily determined that racial segregation did not violate the rights of the Negro as guaranteed by the 14th Amendment. No evidence was introduced in the case on this question. In the *Gong Lum* case, in 1928, neither the detrimental effects of segregation nor the right of a state to make racial classifications was an issue, because the little Chinese girl conceded the right of the state to make racial classifications.
>
> But in the School Segregation Cases [1954], for the first time concrete evidence was presented to the Court which overwhelmingly preponderated over any evidence to the contrary that racial segregation was in fact harmful to Negroes.
>
> Faced with this history and these facts, there was no logical or just conclusion that the United States Supreme Court could reach other than to hold racial segregation in public schools unconstitutional.[4]

Here is a relatively uncomplicated unit of speech by means of which the speaker hoped to root out one point of view and replace it with another. It is plain he meant to do this by supplying reasoning and evidence—rational justifications. If we rearrange the leading ideas of the argument we shall

[4] Oliver W. Hill, "Reply to Broadcast Address to the People of the State," *The Crisis,* March 1959, 184–185. By permission of *The Crisis.*

be better able to see what this reasoning and evidence provided to the attentive listener.

The English logician, Stephen Toulmin, has devised a way of "laying out" arguments[5] which, if used here in simplified form, will help us identify the chief constituents of Mr. Hill's rational justifications.[6] Unspoken but implied material is placed on brackets in our layout.

DATA: that from which argument starts

WARRANT: justification for making the CLAIM about the DATA

CLAIM or conclusion concerning DATA

Segregationists [rest their arguments on] the 1896 decision in *Plessy vs. Ferguson*

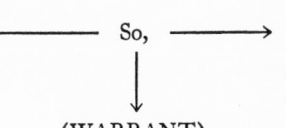 So,

[Segregationists' grounds for believing racial segregation is legal are unacceptable.]

(WARRANT)

Since

[The kind of evidence used in Plessy case was too limited to make it an acceptable precedent for conclusions about the legality of racial segregation in schools.]

(BACKING)

On Account of:

1. Plessy case involved street cars [not schools].

2. The Court was arbitrary [in going beyond its evidence in a case where] no evidence on rights of Negroes under the 14th Amendment was introduced.

[5] Stephen E. Toulmin, *The Uses of Argument* (Cambridge, Eng.: Cambridge University Press, 1958). See especially Chapter 3, "The Layout of Arguments."

[6] Several liberties have been taken with Toulmin's method in the analysis that follows. Toulmin's "layout" scheme permits more detailed and definitive analysis of arguments than the adaptation we use here for expository purposes.

3. In [the related] *Gong Lum* case
neither effects of segregation nor
states' rights to make racial classifications was considered.

4. [When in 1954] the Court did
consider evidence showing the
effects of segregation on Negroes,
it concluded segregation in public
schools was unconstitutional.

We could analyze Mr. Hill's argument by other methods or in more
detail, but this analysis of it will serve our needs. The points to see are
several. First, Hill has (1) drawn his listener's attention to a piece of alleged fact (DATA) and (2) implied a CLAIM or conclusion about it.
Second, he has taken pains to justify his CLAIM by giving reasons why the
Plessy case is a poor precedent (or DATUM) for segregationists to use in
forming their own claims. Third, he has not expressed the WARRANT
for his implied claim. He has left that to be understood by the listener—
presumably to be inferred from the kind of BACKING he gives. Fourth,
his assumption seems to be that if we think his points of BACKING are
convincing, we will then think something like: The kind of evidence used
in the Plessy case was too limited to make it an acceptable precedent for
deciding the present question—thus creating our own WARRANT. It is
clear that if we do this, Mr. Hill's implied CLAIM—which he also leaves
us to discern and formulate for ourselves—will seem justified. Fifth, in
looking at the argument we should notice some options that were open to
Hill but which he did not choose to use. He could have marked out more
explicitly the route his listener was to follow in thinking: by justifying the
truth of his DATA through adding confirming evidence; by expressing
his WARRANT in words so no one could miss it; by providing different
or additional reasoning and evidence as BACKING for the WARRANT;
by expressing his CLAIM in words. He did not do these things; nonetheless, they, plus the things he did do, constitute the options that are open
to a speaker when he undertakes to build rational justifications for any
CLAIM or conclusion.

Now, what if we ask whether Mr. Hill proved his CLAIM about
the segregationists' position? We would certainly get different answers
from different listeners or readers. The answers depend on several things.

The kind of answer we receive will depend on (1) whether the person we consult agrees that the segregationists' position does *in fact* depend on the *Plessy vs. Ferguson* precedent. (2) It will depend on whether the person we consult does supply and accept a WARRANT that would, for him, "register explicitly the legitimacy of the [logical] step involved and refer it back to the larger class of steps [the making of reliable analogies] whose legitimacy is being presupposed."[7] To put the same point another way, anyone who accepts Hill's CLAIM as proved must presuppose that for a legal decision to be a good precedent it must deal directly with the kinds of evidence that are relevant to the situation in which it is being applied. Anyone who does not accept this general rule will see Mr. Hill's CLAIM as unjustified. (3) Whether Mr. Hill proved his point will depend on whether the person we consult agrees that Hill's unspoken WARRANT really applies to the particular DATA about which he is implying a CLAIM. Thus, if we ask whether Mr. Hill proved his CLAIM, we might get responses ranging all the way from "Not at all" to "Absolutely." And every answerer would be able to find some sensible, rational justification for his answer! In such a jungle of differing judgments by listeners, makers of communications must think carefully about their movements before making them.

One would think Mr. Hill must have believed he had few if any listeners who would question his assertion that the segregationists' case did in fact rest on *Plessy vs. Ferguson*. By leaving his DATUM unamplified and undefended, he acted as one ought to act when making a statement certain to be believed by all the listeners he really cares about. It also appears that Hill thought there were listeners, who were important to him, who would have doubts or misunderstandings about his it's-a-poor-analogy WARRANT. At least this would be a sensible reason for offering several pieces of reasoning and evidence as BACKING for the WARRANT. And Mr. Hill apparently felt no one would miss the conclusion he was urging, for he chose not to state it. In general, the only good reasons for not stating one's CLAIM are that it is obvious or that to state it outright might force a listener too fast or too far. In Mr. Hill's case his position in the segregation controversy was well known, so it is unlikely he was trying to be especially gentle with his audience.

Thus the tactics in calculating and building rational justifications be-

[7] Toulmin, *op. cit.*, p. 100.

come clear. Ask yourself what data or datum you are offering a conclusion about. Ask yourself what general idea it is that warrants or justifies or legitimizes making such a claim about these data. And ask what kind of knowledge listeners will need in order to see why the general, warranting idea you ask them to use fairly justifies your particular DATA-SO-CLAIM movement in thought. When you have located these three major points in argument (DATA, WARRANT, CLAIM) ask yourself which of these points are likely to seem troublesome to the listeners whose agreement is important to you. Now, bolster the trouble spots with additional reasoning, evidence, amplification, or all three. Your goal in all of this, as we have said before, is to supply important groups of listeners in your audience with what they will consider sufficient justification for moving confidently with you from one position in thought (DATA) through a suitable bridge-forming idea (WARRANT) to a new position or outlook (CLAIM).

To proceed as we have just outlined and to produce proof that will satisfy those listeners whose agreement is important to you will require some knowledge about people in general. It will also require considerable knowledge about the viewpoints of those who make up your specific audience and some knowledge of what standards of rationality and sufficiency various sections of your audience are likely to apply. In general, when trying to build a piece of argumentation you will be working with several standards of rationality and sufficiency at once—your own, and the different standards of various segments of your audience. A good rule-of-thumb is: (1) *satisfy yourself that you are right*, then (2) build up your argument to the point where you feel it will *satisfy the most skeptical listener whose viewpoint you think you might, possibly, change.*

Any speaker must first be satisfied he is right about the legitimacy of the basic position he takes. Having settled that matter according to his own standards of rationality and ethics, he has to decide what it would take to satisfy those among his auditors whose viewpoints he can, practically, hope to change. For Mr. Hill to try to prove his case to ardent segregationists would have been a waste of time. Consciously or unconsciously, Mr. Hill like any other speaker had to define a certain *part* of his total audience as his *real* audience for this bit of his speech. Every speaker must likewise decide how wide a range of standards it is worthwhile to try to satisfy. In practice this means deciding what are the most demanding standards of rationality and sufficiency your materials and your intentions make it possible and desirable to meet. Ordinarily it is safe to assume that any listeners who neither doubt nor misunderstand your point will be more than satisfied by whatever proof suffices for doubters.

A mistake speakers sometimes make is to give only their own validations of ideas. Those who do this frequently discover their listeners are unimpressed. For listeners who are, or should be, part of the *real* audience may apply more demanding standards of rational justification than does the speaker. Sometimes the speaker bores his hearers by trying to meet higher standards of rational justification than the listeners think necessary.

There is considerable variety in the patterns of our reasoning and in the forms in which evidence occurs. Some of the variations of pattern and form will be examined under the heading *amplification* in a later section of this chapter, others will be treated in Chapters 8 and 9 which deal with organizing speech materials. But for detailed treatments of technical reliability and scientific or statistical validity in reasoning you should consult authoritative works on logic, argument, and statistical and experimental procedures. These matters are not treated here because we believe with the classical—and we think, best—writers on rhetoric and public speaking that the applicable tests of rationality in public speaking are psychological and situational, not philosophical or mathematical. It seems to us that the formal rules of scientific or philosophical reasoning are far too rigid and specialized to be fruitfully applied in speaker-listener relationships where cautiously analytical thought processes are but partially developed at best and where, except when expert addresses expert, private rather than universal standards of validity and adequacy operate. Perhaps it should not be so, but centuries of experience and numerous experimental studies of communicative processes indicate that in the logic of popular communication at least, "One man's meat is another's poison." What constitutes sufficient rational proof of any idea depends on who is the audience. The very degree to which every speaker is, himself, a powerful proof or disproof of his ideas is a further indication that the role of formal logic in popular communication is limited indeed.

The Speaker as a Justification of Ideas. Why should I listen to *you* on this matter? is asked no less often than the related questions we have already discussed. The reasons for the question were pointedly stated by Aristotle:

The character of the speaker is a cause of persuasion when the speech is so uttered as to make him worthy of belief; for as a rule we trust men of probity more, and more quickly, about things in general, while on points outside the realm of exact knowledge, where opinion is divided, we trust them absolutely. This trust, however, should be created by the speech itself, and not left to depend upon an antecedent impression that the speaker is this or that kind of man. It is not true, as some writers on the art maintain, that the probity of the speaker contributes nothing to his persuasiveness; on the contrary, we might almost affirm that his character is the most potent of all the means of persuasion.[8]

At a later point in his great work on the art of speech making Aristotle added:

As for the speakers themselves, the sources of our trust in them are three, for apart from the arguments [in a speech] there are three things that gain our belief, namely, intelligence, character, and good will. Speakers are untrustworthy in what they say or advise from one or more of the following causes. Either through want of intelligence they form the wrong conclusions; or, while they form correct opinions, their rascality leads them to say what they do not think; or, while intelligent and honest enough, they are not well-disposed [to the hearer, audience], and so perchance will fail to advise the best course, though they see it. That is a complete list of the possibilities. It necessarily follows that the speaker who is thought to have all these qualities [intelligence, character, and good will] has the confidence of his hearers.[9]

In the twenty-four centuries since these observations were made neither experience nor research has produced reasons for significantly modifying Aristotle's explanation of how what-the-speaker-seems increases or detracts from his total influence. Some research suggests that perhaps the speaker's "character is the most potent of all the means of persuasion" in the short run only,[10] but no evidence has called into question the general assertion that during and immediately following a speech the listener's confidence or lack of confidence in the speaker is the most potent complex of forces consistently working to justify or undermine the message.

[8] From *The Rhetoric of Aristotle* trans. and ed. by Lane Cooper. Copyright, 1932, Lane Cooper, pp. 8–9, Bk I, Ch. 2. Reprinted by permission of the publisher Appleton-Century-Crofts.

[9] *Ibid.*, pp. 91–92, Bk II, Ch. 1.

[10] C. I. Hovland, I. J. Janis, and H. H. Kelley, *Communication and Persuasion* (New Haven: Yale University Press, 1953), p. 259. "In summary, the available evidence indicates that both positive and negative prestige effects tend to be lost over a period of time."

Two reminders contained in our first quotation from Aristotle deserve special attention. First, the farther removed from "exact knowledge" an idea or contention is, the more heavily listeners depend on their impressions of the *messenger* for indications of how safe it is to accept the message. Herein is an important rule of thumb for the practicing public speaker: *The less his listeners know about his subject matter, the more attention he must give to establishing himself as a messenger worthy of belief.* A second of Aristotle's important observations is: "This trust, however, should be created by the speech itself, and not left to depend upon an antecedent impression that the speaker is this or that kind of man."

It is not just *reputation* that makes or mars a speaker's prestige; everything revealed by the speech—knowledge, analytical power, organizational ability, verbal skill, delivery—plays a part in maintaining, strengthening, or weakening a listener's confidence in what is said. Whether he realizes it or not, each speaker shapes his prestige by every choice he makes or leaves unmade in research, composition, and delivery. This fact is far too often neglected by inexperienced speakers, and it has, until recently, been largely disregarded by social scientists exploring what the ancient Greeks called the *ethos* of speakers. One group of contemporary scholars has had this to say about the complex judgments people make concerning the credibility of those who address them:

In order to understand these various effects and the conditions under which they occur, one is led to a fact which is obvious but has rarely been incorporated into investigations of communicator effects: Attitudes toward the communicator and the cues which elicit them operate in interaction with many other factors of the communication situation. These other factors include such variables as initial attitudes toward the content, cues as to the source's responsibility for the content, the congruence between what is said and prior knowledge about the source's position on the issue, the complexity of the question raised in the communication, the ambiguity of the proposed answer, and the vividness of the source.[11]

And even these authors have only begun to enumerate the variables that may and often do modify our impressions of the worth of a messenger and his message. It is not too much to say that every choice you make or leave unmade in creating and presenting a speech can, potentially, generate proof or disproof of your message for some listener.

[11] *Ibid.*, p. 47.

What you must establish about yourself in order to lend personal justification to what you say is well-enough known. Three things must be shown—or already known—to your listeners. Cooper's translation of Aristotle expresses these as "intelligence, character, and good will." Hovland, Janis and Kelley (who were apparently quite unaware of Aristotle's comments on the subject) inferred from twentieth-century research that "expertness," "trustworthiness," and "intentions" are the qualities that determine how influential the source of a communication can be.[12] In short, if your qualifications are to justify what you say, you must establish in your listeners' minds that (1) you know enough about what you are saying to deserve a hearing (intelligence or expertness); (2) you are dealing with your material and your listeners candidly and honestly (character or trustworthiness); and (3) you have the listeners' interests in mind in all you say and recommend (good will or good intentions).

To see how these impressions are normally established, let us look at some examples illustrating various methods of what we have called "source justification." Consider first two instances in which well-known speakers strengthened their contentions by indicating that they were trying to think broadly and inclusively, not just in the special ways their professional interests might suggest. In each case, too, the speaker draws direct attention to his own fairness in managing ideas and in dealing with his auditors.

Observe the scientist and former President of Harvard University:

> I have purposely placed before you a false dichotomy—the Book of Job taken literally or dialectical materialism. I have already suggested, I hope, my own predilection; I would not repudiate the nineteenth-century optimism about the continued improvement, with the aid of science, of all the practical arts (including the art of human relations). I would not, however, subscribe to any "in principle" argument about what science can accomplish. I would be certain that for the next century, under the best conditions, the areas of uncertainty and empiricism would remain enormous. As to the Book of Job, I would subscribe to the answer that the universe is essentially inexplicable and I would interpret Job's vision symbolically, using this as one entrance to the whole area of inquiry that can be designated as the universe of spiritual values.[13]

---

[12] *Ibid.,* p. 35.

[13] James B. Conant, "Science and Spiritual Values," a lecture delivered at Columbia University in 1952. In his *Modern Science and Modern Man* (New York: Columbia University Press, 1952), p. 92.

By candidly warning his listeners that he has overdrawn, for purposes of emphasis, the conflict between spirituality and the scientific spirit, Dr. Conant encourages a favorable impression of his own integrity and, therefore, his trustworthiness as an interpreter and judge. And does not his caution, his unwillingness to accept any extreme position, also enhance his trustworthiness? That Conant, a scientist, will "subscribe to the answer that the universe is essentially inexplicable" is surprising, perhaps. If so, this may render his viewpoint all the more acceptable because, as a listener might say to himself, "A scientist would hardly say a thing like that unless he had very good reason. If he were just thoughtless, his training would make him give the opposite answer."

On April 5, 1906, President Theodore Roosevelt pled for moderation and due regard for truth in the journalism of the "muckrakers," some of whom had been carried far from fact by their zeal for exposing corruption. At one point in his "The Man with the Muck-Rake" speech Roosevelt said:

> It is because I feel that there should be no rest in the endless war against the forces of evil that I ask that the war be conducted with sanity as well as with resolution.
>
> The men with the muck-rakes are often indispensable to the well-being of society; but only if they know when to stop raking muck, and to look upward to the celestial crown above them, to the crown of worthy endeavor. There are beautiful things above and round about them; and if they gradually grow to feel that the whole world is nothing but muck, their power of usefulness is gone.[14]

Like Dr. Conant, Theodore Roosevelt conveys an impression of trustworthiness through the care he takes in defining his position, between sensationalism and complacency, while keeping himself on the side of reform. He not only implies this is a sane and sensible position, he declares its opposite is not very sane. He further asserts that he has adopted his position just because he is against evil. In these tactics he is more direct and obvious than Conant when claiming credit for intelligence and trustworthiness. He is subtle also. His metaphorical imagery, borrowed from John Bunyan's *The Pilgrim's Progress*, could evoke religious or spiritual attitudes of approval in some listeners—casting an aura of spirituality over Roosevelt's position. Finally, we should note that by casting doubt upon the intelli-

[14] In *American Public Addresses, 1740–1952*, ed. by A Craig Baird (New York: McGraw-Hill, 1956), p. 214.

gence and trustworthiness of those he is criticizing, Roosevelt goes a step beyond Conant. He seeks deliberately to detract from the trustworthiness of his opponents.

These are representative examples of the ways speakers seek to enhance their own images. It is worth recalling that Franklin Roosevelt, in the passage we quoted earlier, worked in like ways. To justify his contention that social action can remove the causes of social evils, it would have been as logical for him to point out that government action had "twenty or thirty years ago" brought sanitation to the slaughter houses of the country. His image as a speaker with warm and sympathetically humane intentions would not have been enhanced by that choice. It was enhanced, however, because he chose to illustrate his point by referring to what governmental action had accomplished for crippled children—and his comments on this topic were doubly strengthened by the fact that he was, himself, a cripple.

There are other more obvious but nonetheless important steps a speaker can take to justify his message through justifying himself as its source. The late Ralph Zimmerman, an undergraduate at Wisconsin State College, Eau Claire, Wisconsin, did this impressively in a speech entitled "Mingled Blood." His opening words were:

> I am a hemophiliac. To many of you, that word signifies little or nothing. A few may pause a moment and then remember that it has something to do with bleeding. Probably none of you can appreciate the gigantic impact of what those words mean to me.

At a later point Zimmerman tellingly used his own disabilities as proofs in his explanation of the disease:

> If internal bleeding into a muscle or joint goes unchecked repeatedly, muscle contraction and bone deformity inevitably result. My crooked left arm, the built-up heel on my right shoe, and the full-length brace on my left leg offer mute but undeniable testimony to that fact. Vocal evidence you hear; weak tongue muscles are likely to produce defective L and R sounds.[15]

Mr. Zimmerman's subject matter is exceptional but his method is not. He is only being more direct than Franklin Roosevelt. He offers the familiar proof: "Believe me because I have experienced it." That every listener could hear his weakly formed "r" and "l" sounds was perhaps more

[15] Copyright by the Interstate Oratorical Association. For a full text of this speech see Carroll C. Arnold, Douglas Ehninger, and John C. Gerber, *The Speaker's Resource Book* (Chicago: Scott, Foresman, 1961), pp. 99–101.

dramatic evidence of "I have been there" than displaying a piece of coal picked up in a mine you visited, but both devices qualify the speaker by displaying concrete evidence of his authority.

Our final example illustrates, among other things, how good intentions toward the audience can be established, even while criticizing:

> I sense this evening that your relationship towards them may be different from mine. Most of you have probably visited skid row areas. Outwardly you express sympathy for these men, but somehow I can't help believing that inwardly you are experiencing a deep sense of satisfaction at being superior to those human derelicts. My relationship was once like yours. Now it's different because as a restaurant owner on skid row I made many acquaintances with these so-called "bums." Although I've now sold the restaurant I still visit them from time to time.[16]

Mr. Karos, an undergraduate at the University of Minnesota when he made this speech, not only establishes his authority on skid-row derelicts, but he offers evidence of friendly yet candid intentions toward his audience. Though he doubts the depth of his listeners' sympathy, he neither blames them nor sets himself morally above them. In effect, he says he is no different from them except for certain special knowledge from which they, too, can learn. Here are signs almost any listener would read as indications of Mr. Karos' expertness, trustworthiness, and good intentions. For as long as the signs indicate Mr. Karos possesses these virtues, his listeners will almost certainly grant him a fair and favorable hearing. Indeed, unless something he says strains their credulity or runs counter to their strongly established attitudes, listeners are likely to accept Mr. Karos' viewpoints simply because they have accepted *him* as worthy of belief on a subject outside the realm of exact knowledge for most listeners.

Other methods of providing source justification can be illustrated briefly. Franklin Roosevelt's famous salutation, "My friends—" or his "you and I know" or any speaker's use of the pronouns "we," "us," "our" instead of "I," "me," "my" exemplify the many small expressions of good will and friendly identification with an audience that are open to anyone's use. Simply to use a cogent argument or to cite the best rather than a second-best authority will hint that you, as speaker, have intelligence and knowledge. A dispassionate recital of arguments for or against the position

[16] Peter A. Karos, "The Haven of the Defeated," in *Winning Orations of the Northern Oratorical League, 1945–1950* (Minneapolis: The Northwestern Press, 1950). Also in Carroll C. Arnold, Douglas Ehninger, and John C. Gerber, *op. cit.*, pp. 160–163.

you are taking can suggest to some hearers: "He knows the facts," or "He's keeping his feelings under control and so is the more to be relied on." Demeanor, too, is an avenue to source justification. Why are conversational directness and unselfconscious action, voice, and diction so much prized by listeners? In large part because these behaviors are interpreted as signs that no ulterior intentions or affectations are influencing the speaker's attention to his business with us, his hearers.

In Aristotle's shrewd observations lies the basic thing every speaker must remember if he is to give his message his own support—as its source: not reputation alone, but everything the speaker does *in his speech* influences the trust his hearers will have in him and in his ideas. Whatever your qualifications to speak, what your *speech* must show is (1) that you know enough to deserve a hearing, (2) that you are dealing honestly with your material and with your listeners, and (3) that you have your listeners' interests at heart.

In this section we have been looking at the kinds of justification listeners demand as the price of acceptance and belief. Although we have discussed personal-interest justifications, rational justifications, and source justifications in separate subsections, these forces cannot be disengaged from one another in reality. To repeat a metaphor we have already used, to compose and deliver an ideal speech for a given occasion is to weave a fabric of thoughts—some having the color of reason, some the color of personal interest, and some the color of *ethos* magnification. The weaver of such a fabric creates the shadings of coloration that will satisfy those who must purchase his cloth—his *real* audience. The metaphor is legitimate at least in the sense that the process of justification in speech making is vastly more comparable to weaving or to painting than to brick laying or assembly-line manufacturing. This is a primary reason this book is entitled *Public Speaking as a Liberal Art* rather than *Public Speaking as an Applied Science*.

Clarifying and Reinforcing Ideas

How does one enhance the likelihood that auditor-viewers will grasp spoken messages as they were intended to be grasped?

In all forms of communication it is essential to take whatever steps are necessary to assure that respondents will accurately perceive the message. When speech is your mode of communication, what you say must be *instantaneously intelligible*, for review and recapitulation are all but impossible unless you provide them. Consequently the methods of clarifying and reinforcing thought are of critical importance to you.

It is customary when writing about public speaking to distinguish "proof" from the clarifying-reinforcing operations called "amplification." Though the distinction has been honored for centuries, the differences between the two kinds of content are inevitably fuzzy. Some of the reasons are these. Most ideas have to be justified in some degree before listeners will accept them. Sometimes this requires that reasons and evidence (BACKING) be furnished, sometimes that need-produced attitudes be awakened as supports, sometimes that the source of the idea be rendered more credible. Of course, any cluster of statements put into a speech for such justifying purposes will furnish some clarifying matter along with justification. But an attitude-awakening statement or a bit of rational justification may not, by itself, convey *enough* knowledge or allow enough time for the listener to apprehend fully what he is supposed to accept as justified. Additional content may be needed to aid his comprehension. It is this additional content, inserted primarily to clarify, to detail or reinforce other ideas, that writers on the art of public speaking have long discussed under the label, *amplification*. To restate (in order to amplify the thought we have just been developing), we have now to consider those materials and tactics speakers use *primarily* to clarify, magnify, or otherwise enhance the likelihood that listeners will understand messages as they were meant to be understood. We shall speak of these as *amplifying* materials and tactics, but you should notice that they often yield justification as well as clarification.

There are at least nine common methods by which speakers clarify or amplify ideas. We shall identify them and briefly discuss their general use in the paragraphs below.

ANECDOTES

An *anecdote* is usually a brief narrative illustrating another idea with which it is connected. For example, to clarify or emphasize the damage a storm can produce, you might tell the story of a family's experience in a tornado. Fables, parables, imagined episodes, or real incidents all provide anecdotal amplification and often, because of their narrative form, dramatization. The chief considerations in using anecdotes are that one needs to keep them short and sharply relevant to the points they are intended to clarify.

An anecdote, like any other form of example, offers some rational justification of what it illustrates and clarifies. But as a narrative, an anecdote can set events before hearers in a dynamic way; this fact makes it easier to enlist listeners' personal interests and attitudes in support of or against the thing being clarified. It is probably fair to say that anecdotes contribute more as proof by eliciting strong attitudes than by furnishing grounds for rational justification.

COMPARISONS AND CONTRASTS

Comparisons and *contrasts* constitute another class of amplifying material. They may be exceedingly concise as in metaphors, similes, or antitheses; or they may be extensive as when anecdotes, examples, or whole arguments and descriptions are compared or contrasted. Since we acquire so many of our new concepts by comparing or contrasting the new with the old, these methods are especially valuable in clarifying because they use learning processes everyone is used to.

The distinction often made between *analogies* used to give rational justification and *comparisons* used to clarify is imprecise at best. Any good comparison yields some rational justification just as any good analogy clarifies. The important thing is that a comparison or contrast, used primarily to prove, needs to be developed with much more attention to literal likenesses and dissimilarities than do comparisons and contrasts used merely to clarify. For example, when Lincoln said, "A house divided against itself cannot stand," he used a metaphor to clarify his view of the divided country's crisis; he was not trying to prove that a nation is so like a family or "house" that precisely the same forces affect both. For his amplifying purpose it was enough to suggest a loose yet clarifying similarity; nonetheless, even this hint at a likeness could function, for some hearers, as reasoned justification for Lincoln's view.

Definitions are of several sorts. Ideas are commonly defined (1) by classifying them; (2) by differentiating them from other things that belong to the same class; (3) by inferring their nature from the contexts in which they normally occur; (4) by referring to the etymological derivations of their names; (5) by explaining what they are *not*; (6) by describing or explaining them from some special vantage point (e.g., specifying what a musical note is if we view it as a complex of sound waves); (7) by specifying how the thing functions, as when a child defines an automobile as a thing to go riding in.

The most formal kinds of definition are too much used in public speaking. Particularly is this true of those "dictionary definitions" that classify terms and define them etymologically. Definitions that compare, contrast, or exemplify are far more interesting and easier to understand. Definitions involving classifications or derivations usually demand that the listener think abstractly. Sometimes he has enough understanding to do this and sometimes he has not. To be safe, it is a good rule to offer classifying definitions only *after* other modes of amplification have been provided. So used, the formal definitions will sum up the other clarifying material as in the first and clearer amplification below.

To understand what a puppet is, think of a ventriloquist's dummy. [Example.] He's a doll of sorts, and a very agile one. [Very broad, hence easy, classification.] If you inspect his limbs you'll find they are specially devised to be moved by hidden hands or wires or strings. [Functional definition.] A puppet, then, is any form of doll with jointed limbs that are controlled by some hidden means. [Classifying definition differentiating "puppet" from all other things in its class.]

The following amplification is less easy to take in at a single hearing and so is less well suited to speech:

A puppet is any form of doll with jointed limbs that are controlled by some hidden means. Its limbs are specially devised to be moved by hidden wires or strings. It is a doll of sorts, and a very agile one, as you can see if you think of a ventriloquist's dummy.

These two explanations are the same in content, but the first proceeds from the specific (example) to the abstract. It carefully prepares the hearer for the final abstraction. The second explanation proceeds in the opposite order, immediately confronting the listener with the most difficult form of amplification and only afterward illustrating what the abstract definition meant.

Etymological definitions are sometimes interesting, sometimes not; sometimes they are genuinely clarifying, sometimes not. It does not help very much to know that the English word *define* comes from the Latin *definire*, meaning "to limit." One could much more easily say simply that *define* means in English to "explain or set forth the limits of something." On the other hand, if you are trying to explain what *habeas corpus* means in law, the shortest, quickest, and most interesting way to do it is probably to tell your listener that the literal Latin meaning of *habeas corpus* is "You may have the body." In short, etymological definitions are always available to you, but they ought to be used or rejected according to the *practical* help they will give your particular audience. That all English words are derived from somewhere does not make discussion of derivations inevitably clarifying.

DESCRIPTION

Description is a process of amplification as the above explanation of puppet illustrates. When Aristotle noted that all men like communications that set pictures before their eyes, he pinpointed the chief standard by which to judge the value of a description used in speaking. The best oral description is one that clarifies by offering word pictures.

Where anecdotes, comparisons and contrasts, definitions, and examples highlight or emphasize *special details* of whatever is being talked about, our descriptions usually aim at setting the *whole* of something before a listener. Generally speaking, a unit of oral description should have these qualities: it should focus attention on significant rather than trivial aspects of what is being described, it should be free from ambiguity, it should make clear the interrelationships or patterns that give the described thing its special nature or character, and it should be as pictorial as the content will allow.

Description can contribute rational justification to communication as well as clarify the communicated concepts. The way we see a thing or process influences our judgment of its plausibility. Since the describer fits together the elements that go into his description, he will always be at least implying that his is the best or true way of understanding what he describes. Observe the dual functions of clarifying and justifying in a bit of description used in a speech by the historian, essayist, statesman, Thomas Babington Macaulay:

> If, Sir, I wished to make such a foreigner clearly understand what I consider as the great defects of our system, I would conduct him through that immense city which lies to the north of Great Russell Street and Oxford Street, a city superior in size and in population to the capitals of many mighty kingdoms; and probably superior in opulence, intelligence, and general respectability to any city in the world. I would conduct him through that interminable succession of streets and squares, all consisting of well-built and well-furnished houses. I would make him observe the brilliancy of the shops, and the crowd of well-appointed equipages. . . . And then I would tell him that this was an unrepresented district.[17]

Obviously Macaulay was clarifying the nature and extent of an unrepresented section of London, but for at least some of his listeners his enumeration of features must have strengthened attitudes favorable to parliamentary representation for the area.

EXAMPLES

Examples are probably the most readily available and most useful of all modes of amplification. Whether factual or hypothetical, examples can focus listeners' attention on just those features of a thing that the speaker most earnestly wants understood. All of us have said in a moment of perplexity, "For instance?" or "Can you give me an example?" We seem to understand specific cases more easily than generalizations, and most of us gain more satisfaction from mentally manipulating specific data than from manipulating abstractions. For such reasons, exemplifying, whether as a part of defining or in the form of anecdotal amplification or as an element in description or in any other connection, is the speaker's ultimate weapon where clarification is his principal concern.

Some writers make a distinction between specific instances cited for clarification and those cited as proofs. The distinction seems to us arbitrary.

[17] "On Parliamentary Reform," an address to the English House of Commons, March 2, 1831. In *Speeches* (New York: Hurst and Co., n.d.), p. 79.

Any example or illustration will, if it is relevant, function as both clarifying and justifying material. Examples, used for the *primary* purpose of justifying, need to be examined carefully to see that they really prove in a rational way what they are intended to prove. But these examples are not fundamentally different from examples used to clarify in less literal ways. Indeed, we are all so used to reasoning from examples to generalizations that we often do it too readily for our own good. Just because this habit of generalizing from specific instances is so well established among listeners you will often need to caution your audiences *not* to reason too far from your clarifying examples. It may clarify the meaning of *tolerance* to cite Prince Hal's amusement at Falstaff's habits, but if you used this clarifying example you would probably be wise to caution your listeners against interpreting your example as meaning that tolerance of wenching and violence is your ideal measure of one man's regard for the rights of others.

QUOTATIONS

Quotations always lend some justification to what is said. If chosen carefully, they can also help to clarify the matters to which they refer. Whenever a speaker shows by quoting that he is not the only person in the world who holds the viewpoint he expresses, he necessarily directs justifying forces toward his listeners. But if quotations are used principally for purposes of amplification, they must do more than lend authority; they must express thought more clearly or more memorably than the speaker can express it. Benjamin Franklin's "A penny saved is a penny earned" may express one of the values of thrift better than you can ever express it. In that case the line is worth quoting as *amplifying* material. But if Franklin's observation had run, "Money not spent becomes as accessible a resource as earnings," you could invent a better way of expressing the same idea, and there would be no point in quoting Franklin unless you needed his reputation as a sage as a further justification for your own position.

REPETITION AND RESTATEMENT

Repetition and *restatement* are amplifying tactics of great importance. As we have said, listening is not a very efficient process for collecting ideas;

that is why speakers have to give their hearers second and third chances to perceive and understand. Research on the usefulness of repetition suggests that with each of your first three repetitions of a given thought you further increase the likelihood that your listeners will actually grasp the idea. It appears that after the third repetition the gains achieved by each succeeding repetition diminish. There is also evidence that repetitions clarify and emphasize more effectively when distributed, when separated from one another. Apparently, however, this is not always true with restatement—phrasing a given idea in several different ways. Note the clarification and the emphatic force Macaulay gave the idea that time might give Parliament no second chance to reform the representative system:

> Now, therefore, while everything at home and abroad forebodes ruin to those who persist in a hopeless struggle against the spirit of the age; now, while the crash of the proudest throne on the Continent is still resounding in our ears; now, while the roof of a British palace affords an ignominious shelter to the exiled heir of forty kings; now, while we see on every side ancient institutions subverted and great societies dissolved; now, while the heart of England is still sound; now, while old feelings and old associations retain a power and a charm which may too soon pass away; now, in this your accepted time; now, in this your day of salvation, take counsel, not of prejudice, not of party spirit, not of the ignominious pride of a fatal consistency, but of history, of reason, of the ages which are past, of the signs of this most portentous time.[18]

Here the tightly packed, paralleled restatements of the time-is-running-out theme make Macaulay's meaning unmistakable and render the idea more impressive as well. A safe general rule for amplifying through repetition and restatement is to *distribute* repetitions of an idea but to use restatements both sequentially and distributively.

Just saying a thing more than once—whether in the same or in different terms—increases the probability that it will be perceived by a listener. There also seem to be ways, which no one fully understands, by which even unvaried repetitions tend to make those who are subjected to the repetitions accept what they hear as true. In both repeating and restating, the method that clarifies tends also to justify. And of course, if one variously rephrases content so as to awaken strong attitudes—as Macaulay did—a great deal of personal-interest justification can be built into speech even though repetition and restatement are essentially amplifying procedures.

[18] *Ibid.*, p. 91.

STATISTICS

Statistics, by which we mean any numerical data, clarify or amplify because they express content in the language of numbers, specifying quantities as other language cannot. Therein lie the strengths and weaknesses of statistics as amplifying materials.

The degree of danger involved in highway travel can be variously expressed. It can be dramatized through anecdote or example; it can be compared to the danger of air travel; congestion and consequent dangers can be described; and so on. Also, this danger can be expressed statistically; but now one shifts from word symbols and real images to numerical symbols that represent quantities of cases and situations. By this shift we gain much in precision of a kind, but we lose much in specificity and imagery. We may say there were 500 traffic fatalities in Powhatan County which has a population of 1,500,000 people. Or we may say there was a fatality for every 3000 people living in the county. Either is a precise expression of traffic dangers in that county. But to get this precision, the conditions under which 500 people died, all the consequences of their deaths, and much other information have to be dropped out of the story. We have chosen to *represent* people and things by numbers. Moreover, the language of numerical expression has specialized rules—a special grammar, so to speak. What is it the numbers represent? Considering what they represent, and how the counting was done, what may or may not be inferred? What kinds of statistical manipulation are allowable, given these numerical representations of reality? Such are the normal questions any use of numbers raises. Unless the speaker tells his listener how his statistics may and may not be interpreted, given the accepted principles of statistical manipulation and expression, his statistical amplifications may confuse or even mislead. This means statistics alone are not very useful to a listener; it is numbers *plus analysis of their meaning* that auditors require.

Even with the limitations we have just outlined, statistics are invaluable amplifying materials wherever quantitative attributes and relationships have to be clarified. Because they are so valuable for these purposes, it is all the more important for you to remember (1) that you must often compensate for the dryness of statistics, and (2) that it is usually not enough merely to *supply* statistics—the interpretations that may and may not be made also need to be explained.

To compensate for the abstractness of statistics and to *focus* attention it is well to round off figures (let 1611 become "slightly over sixteen hundred" etc.). It is also useful to present any series of statistics visually as well as orally if that is possible, for what is both seen and heard is the more likely to be understood. Note, too, that concentrated clusters of statistics become confusing. Distribute them if you would hold attention. Finally, because statistics can only express quantitative attributes and relationships, it is well to amplify them further by using other, more vital and imagistic materials.

Quantitative precision is exceedingly important in clarifying; so is realism. In handling statistics *both* should be thought of in preparation and presentation. It is when realism and vividness are neglected in the presentation of statistics that listeners think, "There are too many dry statistics here."

AUDIO-VISUAL AIDS

Audio-visual aids become valuable amplifying materials when they save or reinforce words, bring ideas closer to reality, or enhance attention through movement or change. Many speakers tend to think only of charts and graphs when they consider whether some external aid might clarify content. This is a mistake. The available resources are much more numerous: photographs, maps, charts or graphs, models, mock-ups, blackboard drawings, assistants who help with demonstrations, sound movies, television kinescopes, musical instruments, disc and tape recordings, and so on. And the most versatile and convenient audio-visual aid any speaker has at his disposal is himself—a fact he should never forget, lest his best resources be neglected out of fascination with gadgets of inferior potential.

One basic principle should be observed in deciding whether to amplify ideas with audio-visual aids: *Unless the aid is less complicated than the idea being clarified it will confuse or distract attention.* Other more specific considerations are important too. Any aid must be relevant and well timed if it is to be genuinely helpful. Your listener demands as the price of his attention that whatever aids you use be: see-able or hearable or both, understandable, and in some degree interesting. The situation under which you speak will determine what is in good taste and otherwise appropriate, and what physical properties the aid must have to be seen, heard, and understood. *You* are also a controlling factor determining the worth of a given audio-visual aid. You (or someone available to help you) must be able to manage and control your aids without disturbing the intimate relationship you need always to maintain with your audience during a public speech. For example, there is nothing intrinsically wrong with an hour-long documentary film or a twenty-minute segment of an opera, but a public speech cannot *contain* either because the speaker cannot maintain a continuing association with his hearers.

There seems almost no end to the ways in which audio-visual aids can be misused in public speaking situations; but almost all misuses grow out of disregard for the fact that audio-visual aids potentially endanger the speaker's own mastery of purpose, audience, and occasion. "Who is in charge?" is always a pertinent question when audio-visual aids are brought in. The following true story presents a set of extreme circumstances, but it tellingly illustrates how and why unsophisticated use of audio-visual amplification can turn what was to have been a public speech into something very different.

The student's chosen subject was "The Treatment of Snake Bites." Having introduced his subject, he startled his audience by releasing a white rat from a cardboard canister. The speaker announced the rat's name was Maudie, and whipped out a hypodermic needle. Plunging the needle into Maudie, he explained that he was giving the animal an injection of snake venom. Maudie would expire within a few seconds, he said. Meanwhile, he would explain what steps a human being should take if bitten by a poisonous snake. To clarify these steps the speaker now drew grease-pencilled lines and circles on his forearm to indicate where incisions should be made in cases of snake bite. But Maudie was dragging herself about, gasping her last in full view of everyone. Naturally, her troubles drew even the speaker's attention away from his explanations. He interrupted himself to comment: "Oh, yes. Bleeding at the mouth—quite natural at this stage." The speech, of course, was a failure, as any thoughtful person could have foretold from the moment this speaker decided to introduce poor Maudie as an "aid."

Quite apart from the charges of cruelty and bad taste with which listener-spectators had every right to counter this speaker's claims to good sense and good character, the poisoning of a rat was foreseeably irrelevant to his purpose. It would set in motion forces he could not control, and it was predestined to direct and hold attention away from his message. Movement, attitudes of revulsion, surprise, the life-death contest, grim realism, suspense, and like forces would be at work to grip audience attention. No comparable forces would be working for the speaker's message—however good his grease-pencil drawings or his exposition of them. To generalize, any speaker who introduces charts that are too detailed or passes items through the audience while he talks or involves himself with overly complicated mechanisms makes the same fundamental mistake as Maudie's executioner: he abdicates his proper position of command.

Audio-visual resources are exceedingly effective means of clarification when judiciously conceived, planned for, and used. Ill-conceived, ill-planned, or ill-used, they supplant rather than supplement the speaker and his speech. Where statistics must be *given* vitality, audio-visual aids have so much potential power over listeners' attention that their influence must be carefully modulated if they are to be constructive, clarifying forces in public speaking.

Just how a public speech is to be composed and of what it shall consist cannot be specified in detail without full knowledge of the special and interrelated demands that will be imposed by speaker, audience, subject, and occasion. We cannot say in a textbook: "Take your pen in hand and compose your speech in precisely the following manner." We can only say: "When you compose any speech, these are the rhetorical resources and tactics available for meeting the demands of your particular subject matter, audience, and occasion." That is the kind of counsel about speech composition we have tried to present in this chapter.

Looking for the resources available to the composer of *any* speech, we have indicated the characteristics a good speech subject must have and how promising subjects of all kinds may be found. In considering what features need to be built into any speech if it is to change the viewpoints of auditors, we found purposiveness, personal-interest justifications, rational justifications, and speaker justifications to be characteristics that any speech needs to possess if it is to be influential. Finally, we observed that at least nine types of material are available for use when one's primary purpose is to clarify, reinforce, or otherwise enhance the likelihood that ideas will be fully and accurately understood by listeners.

These and the products of your preparatory research are the resources open to you as you establish the *content* of any speech you compose. Exactly how you will need to use and blend these resources depends, in part, on the specific purpose you have chosen. In the next chapter we shall deal with special ways of handling these materials and procedures in informing, inquiring, reinforcing, persuading, or entertaining.

Exercises

Written

1. Before beginning other preparation for your next speech write out a "Choice of Subject" paper containing the following information: (a) an exact statement of your proposed speech subject; (b) an exact statement of your specific purpose; (c) a brief essay explaining why your subject and purpose are timely, significant for you and your audience, amenable to oral presentation, and manageable in the time available.

2. Evaluate each of the following statements, indicating how well each meets the criteria for good expression of a specific purpose. Properly rephrase any statement you find unsatisfactory in wording.

   a. Don't adopt the sales tax.
   b. This is a speech to clarify the processes by which committee chairmen are chosen in the United States Senate.
   c. I want to explain that women ought to receive the same pay as men when they perform the same jobs and that in general their equality with men should be universally recognized.
   d. Economic and social effects of the growth in the United States' tourist industries since 1960.
   e. It takes study to appreciate the art of motion pictures.

3. Identify and evaluate (a) the kinds of justification and (b) the forms of amplification used in the following excerpt from Leonard Bernstein's lecture, "The World of Jazz":

   But I find I have to defend jazz to those who say it is low-class. As a matter of fact, all music has low-class origins, since it comes from folk music, which is necessarily earthy. After all, Haydn minuets are only a refinement of simple, rustic German dances, and so are Beethoven scherzos. An aria from a Verdi opera can often be traced back to the simplest Neapolitan fisherman. Besides, there has always been a certain shadow of indignity around music, particularly around the players of music.

I suppose it is due to the fact that historically *players* of music seem to lack the dignity of *composers* of music. But this is especially true of jazz, which is almost completely a player's art, depending as it does on improvisation rather than on composition. But this also means that the player of jazz is himself the real composer, which gives him a creative, and therefore *more* dignified status.[19]

Oral

1. Prepare and deliver a one-point informative speech in which you use at least four different forms of amplification.
2. Prepare and present a short speech on some aspect of a subject you know your classmates disagree about. Try to build enough rational justification into your speech to satisfy a skeptical listener. After the speech, invite a listener who agrees with you and one who still disagrees with you to evaluate how well you proved your point. Conduct a class discussion of their evaluations of your proof.
3. Present an oral report on an advertisement or advertising campaign. Discuss the ways in which personal-interest, rational, and source justifications are used in this advertising.

[19] From Leonard Bernstein's televised lecture "The World of Jazz," in *The Joy of Music* (New York: Simon and Schuster, 1959), p. 97. Used by permission of the author.

Invention in Relation to Purposes

7

This chapter concludes our consideration of the discovery and selection of *what* to say in a public speech. In Chapters 5 and 6 we have sought to generalize about all speeches and all speakers regardless of their specific purposes. But your specific purpose does affect your choice and management of what to say. Here, then, we shall examine how each of the normal objectives in speaking (to inform, to induce inquiry, to reinforce, to persuade, to entertain) influences your choices.

Speaking to Inform

There are times when speakers are fully satisfied if their hearers *understand* what is said. Sometimes such understanding is the sole objective of an entire speech; then we tend to think of the talk as wholly informative. We could as easily call it explanatory or expository. A teacher's lecture or a physician's explanation of how a disease must be treated are examples of this kind of discourse. At other times a speaker may wish, ultimately, to intensify his listeners' beliefs and attitudes or to persuade them to act; yet he encounters moments at which he will still be satisfied merely to attain intelligent understanding. In such moments this speaker, too, takes *informing* as his temporary aim. Whether understanding is a speaker's over-all objective or the objective of only a part of his talk, the aim of informing requires him to find particular kinds of material, use them in certain special ways, and meet the distinctive standards that listeners always impose when they are asked to accept knowledge understandingly.

What kinds of content are appropriate when you set out to *inform* your auditors? We have already said in Chapter 6 that, whatever your purpose in speaking, you always need to discover proofs and materials that clarify and reinforce. What should such materials *do* in order to be especially useful in informing? The closest anyone can come to a general answer for this question is to say any material that clarifies such attributes of a subject as are listed on p. 103, *excepting the attribute of desirability*, will be at least potentially informative. We can also say that whatever clarifies any of the five relationships listed on p. 103 will also be at least potentially informative. But material that concerns the *desirability* of anything is never purely informative. It implicitly or explicitly raises questions about debatable matters: "goods," "bads," "betters," "poorers," etc. In other words, any material that affirms or denies the desirability of something forces speaker and listener into the realm of persuasion. There is nothing wrong with entering this realm. We simply state the fact that, however informative, talk about desirabilities must always be persuasive as well. The result is that the speaker who raises questions of desirability must meet the standards of persuasive speaking as the purely informative speaker need not.

What are the standards peculiar to informative speaking? They could be expressed as (1) *accuracy*, in the sense of being true to fact in both detail and proportion; (2) *completeness*, in the sense of being comprehensive enough to cover the subject promised in the specific purpose of the speech or in any subsection of the speech; and (3) *unity*, in the sense of providing knowledge that will be intelligible as a *whole*, not as a mere miscellany of items. Like many other propositions about oral communication, these standards of good informative speaking grow out of the demands of the audience. When a speaker indicates he wants to make us understand, all of us, as listeners, begin analyzing what he says for its truth; for whether there is enough detail to permit understanding and to justify accepting what is being offered; and for whether what we are told "adds up" to any completed, significant whole.

The speaker who undertakes to explain how a tape recorder works will err seriously if he alleges that all tape recorders use vacuum tubes for sound amplification (many use transistors), he will err in a different way if he neglects to discuss the play-back systems most recorders have, and he will err in another fashion if he does not make it clear that the entire mechanical system exists to preserve sound and re-present it for later examination. If he makes all three errors he will have violated all the basic demands listeners place on those who inform. His listeners may not reject him as a person for his error of fact, his omission, and his disregard for the total meaning of his material; but they will not understand tape recorders unless they understood them before. Why? The speaker did not put into his discourse those things that must be there if talk is to inform or teach: accuracy, completeness, unity.

What we have just considered can be summed up by saying that when you set yourself the task of informing you take on an assignment in *clarifying* and *amplifying*. In informing, proving by direct argument is not your primary business.

It is easy to become imprecise about *what* one is clarifying and amplifying. To become so will surely confuse a listener. In previous chapters we have repeatedly insisted it is never enough to say, "I'll talk to them *about*" this or that. Informative speaking is especially liable to this "about" trouble, but there is a simple preventative. If you will write out your specific purpose, then examine it carefully to see that your statement expresses all, but no more than, you want your listeners to understand, you will seldom confuse yourself or your audience by having an imprecise purpose. A very good practice is the following. Write the words: "When I finish my speech I want my listeners to understand *that*. . . ." Insert after "that," a *single clause* completing the sentence and expressing just what you want to accomplish. "When I finish my speech I want them to understand *that* the Battle of Gettysburg was a battle of maneuver rather than firepower," is a clear and precise subject sentence. "When I finish my speech I want my listeners to understand the Battle of Gettysburg" is virtually useless as a subject sentence because it gives no focus to the speech and promises the listener no clear boundaries for the knowledge you will present.

Even if audiences did not insist that informative speakers be explicit about their purposes, your own needs and convenience would justify taking great care in phrasing subject sentences. Without an exact expression of specific purpose you are likely to try to cover too many points, you will tend to gather material you cannot use, and you will have frustrating difficulties in organizing your materials once assembled. You need to be precise in formulating your subject sentences in all forms of speaking; but in preparing informative speeches the need is greatest because on the one hand your listeners' expectations will be especially exacting, and on the other hand you, as speaker, will be tempted to speak too inclusively and discursively.

The problem of maintaining interest is often harder to solve in informative speaking than in, say, persuasive speaking. Often one must explain abstractions, static things, technical matters unfamiliar to the audience. Such content lacks inherent power to command attention. The material does not, itself, exhibit animation, conflict, realism, suspense, nearness, recency, or like qualities that naturally arouse the interest of an audience. So, if the material will not arouse interest, *you* must.

When subject matter of the kind we are talking about has to be discussed, you will have to search out justifying and amplifying materials that have the interest-enhancing qualities the topic itself lacks. What kinds of materials are these? Specific examples, comparisons and contrasts, brief narratives, real and figurative analogies are especially useful. So, too, are all facts that are close to the experience of your listeners—even facts that appear threatening.

The anatomy of the common housefly does not seem, at first glance, a subject on which to build a speech of consuming interest, but a student speaker did just that by searching out concrete and threatening amplifying materials. The housefly is a hairy creature. This unexciting fact assumed genuine significance when the speaker amplified it by saying that the fly's body hairs are easily befouled as he moves around filth, and the same hairs as easily pollute human food when the fly later alights on it. The fly's digestive system is not a universally exciting object, but the speaker we are thinking of centered her exposition of this part of the fly's anatomy on the fact that the insect's digestive system is not capable of handling dry matter, thus it is necessary for him to salivate or regurgitate on dry food in order that he may wet it and make it edible. In explaining the mouth, legs, and wings of the fly the speaker used visual aids and other attention-compelling ways of treating dull facts. That exposition of the housefly's anatomy did not lack for attention or understanding. Our discussion of Bob Barth's speech on jet engines (see Chapter 5, pp. 122–123) illustrates comparable care and ingenuity in locating the kinds of pertinent information that compensate for remoteness, technicality, or plain dullness of subject matters which must nonetheless be lucidly explained if the world's work is to be done.

Not all topics for informative speeches are inherently uninteresting, of course. Our point is simply that many subjects of indifferent interest still deserve to be explained. Speakers confronted with this kind of subject matter can remedy the situation if they make special efforts to find amplifying materials with unusual power to arouse interest.

There is another opportunity that speakers often neglect when speaking informatively on difficult subjects. It is the opportunity to treat the subject matter *as if* it were other than it literally is.

No one has ever seen a sound wave. Sound waves do not behave precisely like the water waves we call ripples. Nonetheless, it is customary to explain part of the behavior of sound waves *as if* the waves acted as ripples spreading outward when a stone is dropped into water. There are many aspects of sound that cannot be explained properly by this *as-if* treatment; nevertheless, the treatment will do as long as we confine our attention to certain, specific aspects of how sound waves spread out from their source. The whole point of hunting for *as-if* treatments is that people build new knowledge upon the knowledge they already have. In our example, to get a start toward understanding sound waves the familiar ripple pattern serves interestingly and clearly, even though the analogy ultimately breaks down. In the same way, some aspects of a steel rolling mill can be made both clear and interesting if we think of the steel *as if* it were dough and the mill *as if* it were equipped with kitchen rolling pins. One must be careful, of course, that listeners understand that an as-if treatment is not a discussion of actuality; yet, even though there is some danger here, informative speakers are well advised to search more often than they do for such potentially useful ways of explaining. It is worth remembering that this mode of thinking and explaining has become standard in scientific communication just because many concepts that must be communicated can only be expressed in as-if terms or through mathematical symbols.

We have been discussing informative speaking *as if* information-giving really existed completely apart from inquiry, reinforcement, persuasion, or entertainment. It seldom does; but we can talk clearly of only one thing at a time. The facts are that clear explanations persuade us to believe; they encourage us to seek more knowledge through inquiry; they reinforce our feelings about what we already knew; and they are often entertaining in the sense that all new learning is pleasing. It is especially true that good informative speaking frequently persuades. When Winston Churchill explained the battle-front situation to the British people during World War II, he was at the same time persuading and encouraging them to stand firm against Britain's enemies. President John F. Kennedy's broadcast explaining the steps his government had taken in the Cuban crisis of 1962 both clarified the United States' actions and encouraged support for those actions. Speakers too often forget that the strongest persuasion is often simply a clear exposition of how or why the facts are as the speaker knows them.

To summarize, informing is one of the purposes that may dominate a speaker's effort at communication. When it does, it is particularly important that he carefully specify to himself (perhaps to his auditors also) exactly what he wants understood. Information about any attribute or relationship characteristic of the thing he is explaining is potentially useful, except that propositions about desirability automatically involve him in persuasion as well as information giving. Accuracy, completeness, and unity are the qualities that justify what is said to those who are trying to gather information. Informing is thus an enterprise in clarifying and amplifying rather than proving. For these ends, comparisons, contrasts, reference to the familiar, exemplification, narratives, and analogies are especially valuable kinds of material. When the subject matter to be explained is not inherently interesting, these clarifying materials and the as-if treatment may make it so. And if the right kinds of material are found, are carefully developed in ways we have suggested, and are structured so they convey a complete and unified view of what is being explained, it is quite likely that the speech will induce understanding while at the same time stimulating interest, belief, and a sense of personal satisfaction in those who hear.

Speaking to Induce Inquiry

Do speakers ever address audiences without having "the answers"? Unquestionably, though when this happens the audience is likely to be a select and often rather small one. An executive or a chairman presenting a problem to his staff or committee often finds it necessary to set forth the problem before requesting the discussion through which it will be solved. A more formal example of speaking to induce inquiry might be seen when a city manager or other official outlines to a mass meeting the nature of his city's water-supply crisis and presents the alternatives from which the city must choose its solution. In formal as well as informal settings speakers do address audiences without pretending to have the answers. A fraternity member may observe that the porch of the chapter house is deteriorating. If nothing is done about it he may feel moved to introduce the problem at a business meeting. Not having the answers himself, he may choose to discuss the problem and several possible ways of doing the necessary repair work. Likewise, a speaker might be truly perplexed about "What attitude should we take toward conscientious objectors?" and so, wish to set off discussion of the topic. In such moments these speakers are not informants in the usual sense, nor do they have an answer about which to persuade their hearers. Their objective is to set out the conditions within which a solution must be found and to challenge those who listen to evaluate and select a desirable solution. The challenge may be for private thought or for public discussion in the open forums that often follow such speeches.[1]

The subject sentence of any speaker who undertakes to induce inquiry is stated well when it expresses the precise question he believes his listeners can and will attempt to answer. Such a sentence might be stated, "When I finish my speech I want the audience to be prepared and motivated to answer the question, '..?' " The words, "be prepared and motivated," represent key aspects of the inquiring speaker's assignment. Whether he puts these words in a formal statement of purpose or not, his function is always to *pave the way* for a search for answers. To do this he must explain the problem to be solved and at least suggest directions in which a solution might be looked for—insofar as he can foresee those directions. These parts of his task are primarily informative, but unless he can also answer his hearers' ever-present question, "Why should I care?" little will result from his speech. This is why whoever undertakes to induce inquiry must accept the dual responsi-

[1] The best exposition of this kind of speaking to appear in recent textbooks on public speaking is found in J. H. McBurney and Ernest J. Wrage, *The Art of Good Speech* (New York: Prentice-Hall, 1953), Ch. 13, "The Methods of Inquiry." Recognition that formal speaking of this kind does occur can be found in the writings of Cicero and Quintilian and even in the works of lesser but earlier authors. Our discussion of this topic draws upon many of these sources and, at several points, goes somewhat beyond what has heretofore been said.

bility for preparing and for motivating his audience to do the thing he asks—try to solve a problem.

The fact that men who make speeches to induce inquiry do not "know the answers" too frequently keeps them from even identifying the proper questions! Men often are sensitive to difficulties and have standards or goals by which to measure solutions yet possess no clear idea of just what question needs solving *now.* The agriculturist and writer, Arthur Young, observed this state of mind among the revolutionists in France in 1792:

> I have been in much company all day, and cannot but remark, that there seem to be no settled ideas of the best means of forming a new constitution. . . . In these most interesting discussions, I find a general ignorance of the principles of government; a strange and unaccountable appeal, on one side, to ideal and visionary rights of nature; and, on the other, no settled plan that shall give security to the people for being in future in a much better situation than hitherto; . . .[2]

Mr. Young identified one of the great sources of difficulty in the French Revolution: most of the leaders formulating and debating revolutionary measures simply lacked the political wisdom or experience to formulate *political questions.* They framed, discussed, and debated *philosophical propositions* instead. Some excesses of the period followed from this fault, for philosophical propositions are not best settled by popular discussion and debate.

The campus speaker who sets as his purpose, "To prepare and motivate the student council to answer the question, 'What is Student Government for?'" is in the same difficulty as the French leaders. He is aware of a general problem area, but he has not identified any precise question with which to begin a practical inquiry into the topic. No speaker can, in the time audiences give him, lay out the entire subject of student government as an area for inquiry and at the same time indicate the many directions in which we might look to find fractional answers to why student governments should exist at all. But a practical question for inquiry might be, "What role, if any, should Student Government have in regulating student conduct?" Another inquiry might investigate "What administrative functions within the university can be usefully delegated to Student Government?" These are questions for which we might get answers from an

---

[2] *Travels in France.* Quoted in *The Debate on the French Revolution, 1789–1800,* ed. by Alfred Cobban (London: Nicholas Kaye, 1950), pp. 51–52.

audience; from unduly philosophical queries we can only expect aggravating controversy.

It is essential, then, that the subject sentence for a speech to induce inquiry *stipulate in precise language a question that is at least potentially answerable by those to whom it is addressed*—answerable within the time, knowledge, and occasion open to them. But a qualification should be attached to what we have just said. It is that problems or questions need not be *completely* answerable to be worthy of inquiring consideration. If it seems likely that your listeners *can progress toward an answer*, you are surely justified in asking them to make the attempt.

A speech of inquiry is largely but not wholly informative. With a single exception, preparing to speak for the purpose of inducing inquiry is like preparing to speak to inform. The exception is that where an informant has little use for materials relating to the *desirability* of things (a topic that usually raises controversial issues), *desirability is a topic that must be treated in any inquiry into a question involving policies*. Whether student government should regulate conduct, finally becomes a question of whether such regulation would be desirable. Whether student committees should conduct any of a university's administrative functions, likewise becomes a question of whether it would be desirable to give committees these powers. So it is with virtually all questions about courses of action or human values. The desirability of the action or the thing to be judged is a topic that must be explored in settling it. Where the question for inquiry is one to determine a fact or truth or falsity, desirability is seldom discussed.

The relatively distinctive pattern of organization into which main ideas fall in a speech of inquiry are discussed in Chapter 8 (pp. 216–218). These divisions of an inquiry themselves constitute useful guides to the materials needed in developing speeches of this kind.

One other thing should also be said about the general structure of inquiries. Such speeches normally begin with discussions of a problem and proceed toward solutions deserving consideration by reasonable people. This kind of thought movement is not *inherently* interesting to listeners or even to the speaker himself. As in all inductions the mind moves painstakingly over information without assurance that a rewarding answer will be found. The speaker, and therefore the listener, moves in thought from point to point with judgment suspended. Even at the close of the inquirer's talk he may or may not have revealed a preferred solution. There are, thus, few natural climaxes in the communicative experience; there is no built-in sense of energetic progress toward a satisfying ending with attendant release from the tensions always involved in wrestling with the uncertain. In return for asking his listeners to defer judgment and to sustain the tensions of inquiry, the inquiring speaker ought to repay them by using the most interesting amplifying and clarifying materials available to him. He ought to select those amplifying materials that do most to aid his auditors in grasping his message (see Chapter 6, pp. 150–161).

Finally, it deserves to be pointed out that an inquiring speaker assumes a special leadership role. He presides over a collaborative search for a "best choice"—possibly even for the truth. In this role he must be exceedingly careful to demonstrate his own knowledge of the subject, his impartiality concerning the decisions he is asking his listeners to make, and his candor in dealing with both content and listeners. Few things are more resented than attempts to maneuver audiences toward a preselected conclusion under the pretense of inviting them to inquire freely.

Questions, not propositions, stimulate inquiry; so, the subject sentences of speeches to induce inquiry ought to contain clear expressions of potentially answerable questions. Where the issue for inquiry concerns a matter of policy, *desirability* and all the other attributes and relationships we commonly talk about can suggest aspects of the problem and of solutions that may deserve discussion. Because of their inductive character, speeches of inquiry usually need to be specially enlivened with the most interesting amplifying materials that are available and relevant. Those who give speeches to induce inquiry assume the roles of informant and leader; it is therefore essential that all they do and say give evidence of their personal qualifications for these roles.

Speaking to Reinforce Beliefs and Feelings

From time to time we talk to others without intending to establish new beliefs or reverse the directions in which our listeners' feelings run. We often talk simply to *reinforce* beliefs and feelings that already exist. We speak of the values of education on a commencement day; we assure a friend that he is right in asserting that Joe DiMaggio was a better baseball player than Mickey Mantle; and so on. The aim of such talk is to make the listener believe something *more than ever* or to feel *more strongly than ever* that which he already feels in some degree. We seek to put our hearers more completely under the dominion of their existing beliefs and feelings than they were before we began to talk.

Speeches that reinforce beliefs and feelings are a kind of persuasion. The reasons for considering them apart from what we shall later refer to generally as "persuasion" are: the materials one needs to reinforce beliefs and feelings are somewhat unique; and the modes of development, by which speeches reinforce, are more often those that amplify than those that prove.

Whether his subject be education, the importance of physical fitness, testing nuclear weapons, or some other, the speaker who wishes to reinforce beliefs or feelings limits his search for major ideas to the things his hearers already know; and he commits himself to treating them in ways that are at least akin to those his listeners are used to. When reinforcing beliefs and feelings, speakers locate their themes by studying the knowledge and attitudes their listeners already possess, and they develop those themes according to the value systems their hearers already accept. The fact is that speaking of the sort we are now discussing allows the speaker the least intellectual freedom of any customary mode of speech making. This is precisely why speeches to reinforce beliefs and feelings are to be found in all societies no matter how totalitarian their control over men's minds. Even where freedom to change people's minds and freedom to disseminate information disappear, there are always *some* things that are universally held in high esteem and about which beliefs and feelings may still be reinforced even if no other kind of influence through speaking is allowed.

Although the speaker who seeks to reinforce beliefs and feelings is severely limited in what he may use as basic content for his speech, this kind of reinforcement has important social functions in any society. Through such speaking, organizations are unified and kept faithful to their goals, religious congregations are sustained in their faiths, and social and political virtues such as civic pride and mutual respect are maintained as active forces. Indeed, the bonds that give cohesion to all our social groupings are the chief subject matters of society's most important reinforcing communication. And it could be added that without reinforcement through public speeches and other media of communication, social bonds would begin to atrophy and any society would begin a drift toward anarchism.

The audience, then, determines on what subjects speeches of reinforcement may be made. Whatever a given audience already believes or disbelieves and whatever values they hold in high esteem or plainly reject can become the subject matters for speeches of reinforcement. Little else can. (One can reinforce disbelief or rejection as readily as belief or acceptance.) But not every existing belief or disbelief is appropriate for discussion at *any* time. Those who attend graduation exercises indicate by that act that their beliefs about education are just then of high importance; hence, the commencement occasion determines that beliefs about education are to be reinforced rather than, say, beliefs concerning what splendid communities the listeners live in. Carry the example further. Many women attending commencement exercises in a community will also be members of the local chapter of the League of Women Voters. While attending graduation ceremonies these women will not be strongly conscious of their beliefs concerning political action and they will not wish to hear the merits of political action extolled. But the next meeting of their League chapter is likely to be an occasion for a speech of reinforcement on just that theme. Thus, audiences' beliefs and values define the subject matters available to those who speak to reinforce, but the range of these subjects is always further narrowed by the special expectations listeners adopt on specific occasions for speech making.

Generally speaking, the occasions that call for speeches of reinforcement are those of a ceremonial sort (anniversaries, religious or other observances, ritualistic meetings, etc.) and those dedicated to arousing and enspiriting (rallies, pep meetings of every kind, "kick off" meetings of all sorts, etc.).

When you have identified what topics are allowed you by the demands of your audience and occasion and when you have selected a speech subject from among these options, your next problem is to state your subject sentence in a manner that can guide you in research and composition. We have discussed this matter generally in Chapter 6. Here, we need only add that in framing a subject sentence for a speech to reinforce belief or feeling you can help yourself and your listeners a great deal if you adopt the following formula for writing it. Write the words, "When I complete my speech I want the audience to (believe, feel) (more, less) strongly that ...." Strike out either "believe" or "feel," leaving the word that best conveys the response you hope for; and strike out either "more" or "less," leaving the term that expresses the direction in which your reinforcement will tend—toward increasing what is already present or toward further diminishing what is already weak. Now, compose a clause to follow the word, "that." Make it express the *single* proposition you expect to reinforce. Your finished subject sentence might read: "When I complete my speech I want the audience to believe more strongly that Centerville can be made a popular tourist center," or "When I complete my speech I want the audience to feel less strongly that Centerville is an ordinary city."

There are no fundamental differences between these subject sentences for speeches of reinforcement and comparable statements for other persuasive speeches, except that the purpose of a speech to reinforce always indicates that a *degree* of existing belief or feeling is to be changed. If the citizens of Centerville had no previous idea their city might be made a tourist center or if they initially felt theirs was not an ordinary city, the two subject sentences we have just used for illustration could not sensibly include the terms "more strongly" and "less strongly." Without these expressions of *degree,* the sentences would become statements that defined creation or reversal of opinion as the objective in speaking.

Except that it is limited in ways we have discussed, the reinforcing speaker's search for ideas differs little from the kind of searching we have discussed in Chapter 5. Any of the attributes we commonly assign to things and people and any of the relationships we commonly assert or argue (see p. 103) can suggest potentially discussable themes for justifying greater or less belief or feeling. There are, however, two special bits of advice that can help speakers who aim at reinforcement.

The first comes from Aristotle's *Rhetoric* and concerns *how ideas are made impressive.* Aristotle's advice was that a belief or feeling can be made impressive by connecting it with some familiar "good" such as justice, courage, temperance, grandeur, magnanimity, liberality, gentleness, prudence, wisdom, or the like. His reasoning was that ideas are more or less impressive depending on how much they contribute to or are consistent with these qualities which we all admire. The other item of special advice is: it is better to keep the train of thought simple and uncomplicated than to try to render a central idea impressive in too many different ways. Enlargement of the idea to be reinforced is preferable to multiplying its features. In his famous funeral oration commemorating the bravery of Athenians who had died in the first year of the Peloponnesian Wars, Pericles expressed the pith of his whole discourse in this central argument:

> Taking everything together then, I declare that our city is an education to Greece, and I declare that in my opinion each single one of our citizens, in all the manifold aspects of life, is able to show himself the rightful lord and owner of his own person, and do this, moreover, with exceptional grace and exceptional versatility.[3]

The address, as Thucydides preserved it, is but an amplification of these tightly related thoughts concerning the city for which the dead had fought. A lesser speaker might have insisted on discussing the way the heroes died, the justice of the war, the qualities of victories and defeats, and the gratitude of living Athenians—all in a misguided effort to enlarge his listeners' feelings of gratitude to those who had given up their lives. Pericles chose the wiser way. He chose a single theme and amplified it: Athens' worth ennobles them.

If we ask what distinguishes an effective speech to reinforce, one answer must be that it exhibits freshness and originality in amplification of familiar ideas. To achieve more than ordinary success in this kind of speaking, the speaker must offer hitherto unthought-of connections between the familiar belief and such "goods" as Aristotle suggested he use. Or, the speaker must point out hitherto unthought-of attributes belonging to propositions his listeners already believe in. Lincoln did this at Gettysburg when he contended that the *substance* of the dedication ceremony was not really to dedicate a burial ground but to "dedicate ourselves." He thus reinforced existing feeling that the cemetery was a meaningful national monument by adding a new attribute to the dedication process. Winston Churchill, in a moment of reinforcement during a World War II address, similarly enhanced the admittedly impressive achievement of British aviators in the Battle for Britain. He linked the airmen's small number (*degree*) to the large number (*degree*) of those indebted to them: "Never in the field of

---

[3] Thucydides, *The Peloponnesian War*, trans. by Rex Warner (Baltimore: Penguin Books, 1954), p. 119.

human conflict was so much owed by so many to so few."[4] A speaker less adept at reinforcing feelings might have been content to speak in a more usual vein of the airmen's courage. Mr. Churchill did that, but he found another, less familiar attribute of their achievement and thus produced a fresh thought we still quote a quarter-century later.

In summary, speaking to reinforce beliefs and feelings is in some ways a confined and confining enterprise. The commitment to reinforce is a commitment to work with subjects already known to both speaker and listener. Though not always ceremonial, this kind of persuasion is the sort most ceremonies call for. Purposiveness and clarity are no less important when reinforcing belief or feeling than in other kinds of speaking; yet, perhaps because they work so much with familiar ideas, speakers aiming at reinforcement are often less precise than they should be in framing their purposes. The search for materials with which to develop whatever propositions are to be reinforced is like the search for other kinds of speech materials with two related exceptions: (1) reinforcement requires that subject matter be rendered impressive, hence amplifying material rather than material yielding new rational justifications is chiefly needed; and (2) hitherto unthought-of attributes and relationships are the chief sources of that originality which alone can give vigor to the speech of reinforcement and authority to the speaker.

Speaking to Persuade

We have just dealt with a special form of persuasion. Now we turn to the problems of those kinds of speaking more commonly thought of when the term, *persuasive*, is used. These are the speeches in which the speaker aims at *altering* beliefs, attitudes, feelings, or behavior.

Because people associate altered views with persuasion, they sometimes judge persuasion and persuasive speakers unrealistically. The authors of this book contend that the only realistic standard of excellence in persuasive speaking is: Did the speaker engender as much change as the circumstances, including his own sense of responsibility, permitted?

[4] Speech in the House of Commons, August 20, 1940, quoted in *Voices from Britain,* ed. by Henning Krabbe (London: George Allen & Unwin, 1947), p. 59.

Speakers often wish for changes they cannot possibly bring about in everyone. They must then settle for less than their desires. As an example, think of the career of Norman Thomas. Mr. Thomas was a constant spokesman and political candidate for the Socialist Party in America for nearly three decades. Though he was never elected to office and won but a tiny proportion of his hearers to his party, he has been repeatedly credited with popularizing political and social reforms later adopted as their own by Democrats and Republicans. It would be absurd to say that such a persuader's achievements were negligible or that his public persuasion must be called unsuccessful simply because he won no office and no multitude of adherents. The only fair question to ask about Mr. Thomas' powers as a persuader is: Did he engender as much change as the unfavorable views of his audiences and his own sense of responsibility permitted? That question cannot be answered precisely without extensive rhetorical and sociological research, but the general answer must be that Norman Thomas' persuasion was at least creditable, despite his failures at the polls. This, we contend, must be the way of judging all persuasion. It is not the *absolute effect* of a persuasive speech that testifies to its excellence, but *the comparison between the actual effect and what was reasonably possible considering all the circumstances.*

What special demands does persuasion place upon the speaker if we apply the standard of excellence asserted above? The demands characteristic of all public speaking certainly fall upon him. He must be purposive. His subject sentence must be chosen and framed with care, as we have shown in Chapter 3 (see pp. 47–49). But once his subject sentence is clearly formulated there are also necessities that he, more than other speakers, must contend with.

Justifying, as well as amplifying materials, are essential in any attempt at altering beliefs and feelings. Moreover, both must have *motivational* importance for the audience. Ideally, this ought to be true of all content in all speeches; but it is crucial in persuasion. We have repeatedly indicated in Chapters 4, 5, and 6 that listeners have to be motivated to pay attention to what is said; but if hearers are to alter their viewpoints or feelings, their personal interests must supply especially strong justifications for change. This point was forcefully expressed by the Scottish rhetorician, George Campbell. His language and psychological theory now seem somewhat quaint, but his general point concerning persuasion is unmistakably sound:

> . . . when persuasion is the end, passion also must be engaged. If it is fancy which bestows brilliancy on our ideas, if it is memory which gives them stability, passion doth more, it animates them. Hence they derive spirit and energy. To say that it is possible to persuade without speaking to the passions is but at best a kind of specious nonsense. The coolest reasoner always in persuading, addresseth himself to the passions some way or other. This he cannot avoid doing, if he speak to the purpose. To make me believe, it is enough to show me that things are so; to make me act, it is necessary to show me that the action will answer some end. That can never be an end to me which gratifies no passion or affection in my nature. You assure me, "It is for my honour." Now you solicit my pride, without which I had never been able to understand the world. You say, "It is for my interest." Now you bespeak my self-love. "It is for the public good." Now you rouse my patriotism. "It will relieve the miserable." Now you touch my pity. So far . . . [is it] from being an unfair method of persuasion to move the passions, that there is no persuasion without moving them.[5]

A twentieth-century psychologist might reject Campbell's technical distinctions among fancy, memory, and "passion," but he would agree that there is no changing the attitudes or feelings of mankind without engaging the drives or desires that Campbell called "passions." The modern psychologist would agree with Campbell that "the coolest reasoner" must certainly fail to change men's views unless aided by their feelings. This necessity of enlisting active drives and desires in behalf of one's position is one of the special demands the persuader's aim imposes on him.

In order that active drives toward belief and action may operate within hearers, it is sometimes necessary for a persuasive speaker to refrain from expressing all that he himself believes. He may even avoid asking for all the opinion change he would really like to attain. The reason is that what men cannot yet understand, what they are not intellectually or emotionally ready to look upon with receptive minds, is more likely to trouble them than persuade them. St. Paul's sermon on Mars Hill, which we quoted and discussed on pages 115–116, illustrates how such audience-centered restraints affect what persuasive speakers dare say. Paul deliberately claimed less for his religious doctrines than he might have had his

---

[5] *Philosophy of Rhetoric* (New York: Harper & Brothers, 1841), Bk I, Ch. 7, pp. 82–83. Originally published in 1776.

audience of Athenian philosophers been intellectually and emotionally ready to examine his teachings without any sense of bewilderment or unease. Most persuaders find themselves in comparable situations from time to time—situations in which they dare not claim all they would like to claim for fear of losing their chance to change *some* beliefs through asking for too much change too swiftly. Indeed, it might well be argued that St. Paul, himself, pressed a mite too far for his hearers when he introduced the doctrine of resurrection of the dead at the close of his sermon. We are told, "Now when they heard of the resurrection of the dead, some mocked; but others said, 'We will hear you again about this.' "

When he prepares for persuasive speaking, any speaker must also be cautious against being misled by biased sources. All subjects about which we seek to persuade one another are in some degree controversial, else there would be no reason for persuasion. But this means there are probably many sources of information that are so strongly committed to one side of the controversy they cannot give us a *whole* view of the issues and evidence. One does not expect to receive the whole story about a labor dispute at either the labor union headquarters or from the officials of the disputing corporation. Nor is one likely to get all the facts from hearing the witnesses for only one side in a court case. There are other less obvious but equally biased sources of information on almost all controversial issues.

What shall the intending persuader do when researching his case under these circumstances? First, he needs to consult *both* sides: read both *The Nation* and *The National Review*, if his subject involves liberal-conservative controversy in politics; see that he gets the positions of both union and management, if his subject concerns a labor dispute. Getting both sides will not necessarily give him the whole story. He is likely to come away from this kind of investigation with a good deal of information that is not properly part of the story at all. But what he will know is where opponents on the question differ and where they agree. Where they agree, he may probably believe; where they disagree, he must search for more facts by firsthand investigation and by consulting the most impartial sources available. Using both modes of research he will ultimately acquire a reliable body of material for the construction of arguments.

What we have just said may sound idealistic, but it is practical too. Of all speakers, the inquirer and the persuader must be most jealous of their reputations for integrity. Persuaders, like inquirers, presume to lead and advise. Thereby they place their own reliability at issue whenever they speak. You do not readily accept the advice of people who know less about the matter than you do. So it is with all persuadees. What they want from their advisers are two things especially: consistent evidence that the adviser fully understands and reasons well on the matter at issue, and counsel that is in their own best interests. The persuader must meet both demands. The salesman who shows he knows his own product but no other becomes a "salesman" only; the salesman who shows he knows his competitors' products well enough to tell you *why* his is better becomes a persuader in the full sense—a trusted counsellor. One practical reason persuaders must be on guard against becoming victims of one-sided information is simply that if they are so victimized, their limited knowledge may make them stumble in the eyes of their hearers.

There is another equally practical reason. Persuasion that recognizes and successfully refutes opposing positions tends to have more durable influence on audiences than purely one-sided presentations. Experimental evidence seems to indicate that the only circumstances in which one-sided persuasion is more effective than multisided persuasion are where the audience already agrees with the persuader and where the audience never becomes exposed to the other sides of the question at any subsequent time.[6] These are hardly the typical circumstances of important persuasion. This evidence alone should be sufficient motivation for every persuader to prepare himself carefully on the *whole* of every question he discusses.

What we have just said about the importance of recognizing opposing views in persuasive speeches implies that effective persuasion normally involves both constructive and refutational discourse. Constructive argument is that which builds up the persuader's side of his subject, and refutational argument is that which challenges or otherwise exposes weaknesses in contrary views. The technicalities of developing these two sorts of arguments are matters better studied in courses devoted specifically to persuasion and argumentation. As a beginning student of public speaking, you can carry out your work fairly well if you follow these guidelines in developing constructive and refutational arguments:

1. No matter what motivational justifications you offer for your position in persuasion, you must satisfy your listeners that you have not taken up

---

[6] See, for example, C. I. Hovland, I. L. Janis, and H. H. Kelley, *Communication and Persuasion* (New Haven: Yale University Press, 1953), pp. 105–111.

your position irresponsibly. You must give some kind of evidence that you have taken it for sensible and essentially rational reasons. (Concerning the development of rational supports see Chapter 6, pp. 137–143.)

2. Your listeners will expect you to show them why the position you have adopted is *more* sensible and responsible than other positions they may have heard of (or may hear of in the future). This usually means you must give your audience both rational and self-interest justifications for rejecting alternatives to the position you endorse.

3. The ultimate justification for any position you endorse will be, for your audience at least, your constructive proof that your position is *better for them*. Hence, the bulk of persuasion is *constructive*.[7]

One final matter deserves comment in these observations on the special problems of assembling materials for persuasive speeches. It concerns the nature of persuasion itself. What chiefly distinguishes the persuasive speaker from the informant, inquirer, or entertainer is that his *primary* test in choosing among available materials for proof or amplification is always, "Has this piece of potential speech material enough promise or threat for my listeners so I may expect their outlooks to shift a bit because I have used it?" To put the point another way, the persuasive speaker is unusually sensitive to George Campbell's previously quoted reminder: "That can never be an end for me which gratifies no passion or affection in my nature." The informant, the inquirer, or the entertainer may select and use speech material just because the material is a logical part of what he is talking about; the persuader, however, dares not stop his search until he finds materials that will make a *psychological* contribution toward altering human experience.

Speaking to Entertain

The editors of *The American College Dictionary* offer as their first definition of the verb, *entertain:* "to hold the attention of [someone] agreeably; divert; amuse." This definition admirably expresses what a public speaker undertakes when he makes it his purpose to entertain. He commits himself to a speech that will hold attention agreeably by diverting

---

[7] For an excellent, detailed treatment of these responsibilities in argumentation see Douglas Ehninger and Wayne Brockriede, *Decision by Debate* (New York: Dodd, Mead, 1963), especially pp. 81–95 and 252–266.

listeners' thoughts from matters of high seriousness to less demanding things. Often, though not invariably, he adopts the task of holding attention and diverting by providing amusement. Another way of defining an entertaining speech is to say it is a speech that so completely interests the audience they have almost no sense of working to acquire its full significance.

It is exceedingly important to notice that both definitions of *entertain* imply that entertainment *may* be amusing but is not invariably so. We all recognize that a first-rate travelogue can be entertaining and that although some first-rate travelogues are humorous or have amusing undertones, others do not. Likewise, many narratives and many descriptions entertain us; some do so because they are amusing while others accomplish a like effect with very little use of humor. The public speaker who is asked to give "an entertaining speech" should recognize that in choosing his subject and central theme he may elect either a humorous or a nonhumorous subject and still hope to entertain.

Any subject—any theme—that will hold attention agreeably and in a diverting rather than highly serious way is a potential subject for an entertaining public speech. It is not, then, the subject itself that distinguishes the entertaining speech from others we have discussed in this chapter. The *treatment* of the subject matter is the distinguishing mark—it must hold attention with exceptional agreeableness.

Typical occasions for speeches of entertainment allow extraordinary latitude in choosing speech subjects. These occasions are usually either convivial gatherings or those where no stronger motivation than casual curiosity has brought the audience together. Among the convivial gatherings, we all know of the many luncheons, dinners, banquets, fellowship meetings, and periodic "fun nights" arranged by organizations and groups of all sorts. The audiences which congregate at these gatherings chiefly wish their speakers to reinforce the convivial spirit by providing all who have come together a shared, diverting kind of listening experience. Almost any subject in suitable taste, that can by any stretch of reason be connected with the common bonds joining the auditors, will meet their demands.

The occasions where casual curiosity is the chief reason for the listeners' presence are also many. Unless the speaker is known as a humorist, such occasions usually call for light, but essentially straightforward, treatment of whatever subject the speaker is qualified to discuss. To see the difference between the demands of these occasions and audiences and those that confront informative speakers, consider two familiar situations. It is announced by the Rotary Club that the public is invited to an evening meeting at which Mr. So-and-So will talk about his recent visit to India; or, a sorority announces that Miss Blank who won a gold medal in Olympic competition will speak at a public meeting. Plainly Mr. So-and-So's trip and Miss Blank's Olympic achievement prescribe each speaker's general subject, but how will this subject matter be treated? The expectations of the audiences that will attend the meetings will usually dictate that the speakers prepare divertingly informative talks. Few listeners will be deeply informed or consumingly interested in either India or Olympic competition. Many will come to the talks just to *see* the traveler or the champion. In short, casual curiosity and vague interests in the subject will account for the presence of most listeners. The tasks of the speakers, then, will be to present what special information they have in the most popular terms possible. This usually means giving special place to whatever is most colorful, most human, most tantalizing about the subject. Whatever discourse has these characteristics is almost certain to be entertaining. It may not be as impartially objective or as comprehensively informative as a less entertaining speech on India or Olympic competition prepared with a view of giving listeners a *full* understanding of the subject.

From what we have said about the subject matter, occasions, and audiences for entertaining speeches it is possible to draw several important inferences. The first and most important is that *speeches that entertain are not substantially different from other speeches except in the way subject matter is treated.* The more agreeable, the more diverting, the amplification and expression of ideas the more entertaining a speech will be. The difference between informing, inquiring, and persuading on the one hand and entertaining on the other is chiefly a difference of *manner*, not of matter. A second inference to be drawn from what we have said is that *to be entertaining a speaker must regard the pleasure of his audience more highly than the logic of his subject.* This does not mean that to be entertaining one must be inaccurate; on the contrary, accuracy at least in *some* details is essential to entertainment. What arrests us is usually some disproportion of attention to specific details: detailed attention to the colorful garb of Indian women (without much attention to, say, the social significance of their dress) or ludicrously detailed attention to the rigors of training for Olympic competition (without much attention to the reason or results of it). The point the entertaining speaker must keep in mind is that the interesting *parts* of his subject are often more important than the *whole* subject. It is in this sense that he sacrifices the logic of his subject to the pleasure, the agreeable diversion, of his audience. A third inference to be drawn about speaking to entertain is that *while good humor is always entertaining, entertainment does not necessarily hinge upon the presence of humor.* This inference has been amplified by our earlier examples and needs no further discussion.

Since it is the *treatment* of material rather than the subject matter that renders a speech entertaining, you will want to give special attention to stylistic resources in developing any speech to entertain. (See Chapter 10, pp. 265–281.) However, to create entertaining language, it is necessary first to find ideas and aspects of ideas that lend themselves to entertaining treatment. Once again, a review of the attributes things and people may possess and the relationships that may exist among these attributes (p. 103) can suggest potentially entertaining thoughts. Any attribute of anything has potentially humorous possibilities if examined in enough detail or distorted in some fashion. The cartoonist, Rube Goldberg, spent a career reducing the attributes of *possibility* and *feasibility* to absurdity. He depicted fantastically complicated and transparently unreliable machinery for waking people in the morning or closing windows against rain. George Bernard Shaw played trenchantly but amusingly with the attribute of *degree* and with causal relationship when addressing students at the University of Hong Kong:

> That war [World War I] was made by people with university education. There are really two dangerous classes in the world. There are the half-educated, who have destroyed one-half of civilization, and there are the wholly educated, who have nearly completely destroyed the world.[8]

The Reverend Richard Whately, Anglican Bishop of Dublin and also an able rhetorician, developed an entertaining refutation to arguments denying that Jesus lived by applying the tests of *possibility, causality,* and *existence* too strictly to the life of Napoleon. He thereby "proved" that Napoleon could not have lived.[9] Mark Twain once addressed the Lotos Club in New

---

[8] "Universities and Education," delivered February 12, 1933. Reported in *The New York Times,* March 26, 1933. Note Shaw's exaggeration—one of the most common techniques for creating humor.

[9] *Historic Doubts Relative to Napoleon Bonaparte* (1819).

York City soon after returning from England where he had been awarded an honorary doctorate by Oxford University. Members of the Lotos Club insisted Mark Twain put on and display the red-grey academic gown worn by Oxford doctors, which he did. Then, in impromptu remarks, he toyed with the gown's attributes of being red and being a "gown":

> I like that gown. I always did like red. The redder it is the better I like it. I was born for a savage. Now, whoever saw any red like this? There is no red outside the arteries of an archangel that could compare with this. I know you all envy me. I am going to have luncheon shortly with ladies—just ladies. I will be the only lady of my sex present, and I shall put on this gown and make those ladies look dim.[10]

Any subject—idea, thing, or person—possesses diverting attributes and diverting relationships to other ideas, things, or persons. These are what the entertaining speaker looks for in his preparation. Locating them is the first step toward treating the subject in an entertaining manner.

Three lesser and interrelated points must also be made concerning the content of speeches that entertain. They can be stated briefly, but their importance is considerable.

1. *Only in entertainment is it sometimes advantageous to make no sense.* Sometimes what is nonsensical bears just enough similarity to the sensible to amuse us. Here lies much of the fun of Lewis Carroll's *Alice in Wonderland* and comedian Danny Kaye's outrageous double talk. Cautiously and discriminatingly used, nonsense can be entertaining.

2. *What entertains in speaking is that which is quickly and easily understood.* Private jokes or asides and private experience are not entertaining. In entertaining speech all meaning is public—familiar and easily grasped. This must be true even of nonsense for, there, the semblance to sense must be evident or there is no amusement, only bafflement. It is true that working puzzles can be entertaining, but puzzling speech is not. The reason is that speech moves swiftly through time leaving listeners no opportunity to work the puzzles as they appear, one following the other.

3. *An entertaining speaker may properly disregard or even do violence to the natural logic of his subject, but he will please his hearers best if his speech has some kind of thematic logic.* This will give the audience the satisfaction of having been pleased by *something*, not just some *things*. Even the night club gag

---

[10] Last "Lotos Club Speech," January 11, 1908. From the text and incidental remarks as published in *The Family Mark Twain* (New York: Harper and Brothers, 1935), pp. 1175–1178.

man recognizes this audience demand for structure in entertainment. If artful, he will separate his mother-in-law jokes from his insurance-company jokes, giving each group the status of a thought unit within his patter. As though further adapting to the preferences of modern audiences, more and more comedians now develop entire monologues around single themes treated humorously. In so doing, they emulate the practice of the best among entertaining speech makers.

The basic test of a speech to entertain is easy to state: Did it divertingly please the audience? Achieving this goal does not depend upon what subject the speaker chose or on whether he was funny or serious. It depends upon whether he plied his listeners with colorful, humanly interesting, tantalizing ideas about some subject concerning which they already knew something or were at least mildly curious. To judge the speech to entertain by the comprehensiveness of its coverage, the presence or absence of humor, or its conformity to any objective understanding of the facts is to apply standards of judgment which entertainment—in and of itself—cannot accommodate.

But entertainment can be used without being the dominant objective of a speech. There is no reason that comprehensive speeches of serious intent should not contain well-subordinated units of entertainment, provided these entertaining distortions of reality do not becloud the central content of otherwise serious speech.

In closing our three-chapter survey of how content for speeches is discovered and selected we have examined the special opportunities and difficulties that arise when speakers set out to inform, induce inquiry, reinforce beliefs or feelings, persuade with a view to altering belief and behavior, or entertain. We have seen that some of these special purposes limit the range of ideas from which the speaker may draw content, and that each kind of purpose imposes its special manner of treating ideas after they are found. If any generalization is to be drawn from our survey in this chapter, it must be that no speaker can be wholly successful until he has determined exactly what his specific purpose in speaking is to be. Without understanding his task in communication, he cannot know what materials are useful to him nor can he know precisely how to treat them.

It would be an error to infer from what we have said here that mixed purposes never occur in good speeches. Informing, persuading, and entertaining, for example, can all be found in almost any first-rate speech. But if the speech is first rate, *one purpose will dominate the whole composition,* nor will there be any confusion about which purpose dominates any *part* of the speech. If the over-all intention is to persuade, the informing sections will have the features of informative speaking but will plainly subserve the dominant persuasive intention by providing a base for it. Entertaining sub-sections will have the features of speaking to entertain, but the entertainment will provide momentary diversion without distorting the information-giving processes or demeaning the importance of persuasive content.

Exercises

Written

1. Write a brief essay on differences between speech materials that "prove" propositions and those that "amplify" ideas.

2. Choose a general topic such as "The Cost of Living" or "Clothing" and outline three different kinds of speeches that could be given on some aspect of the topic. For example, outline a persuasive, an informative, and an entertaining speech on "The Cost of Food Is Rising."

3. Read a speech of your own choosing and write a critique in which you:
   a. Identify what seems to have been the speaker's dominant purpose in speaking.
   b. Identify any subsections of the speech in which the purpose of communication seems to have shifted temporarily (e.g., from a dominant purpose of informing to a subordinate purpose of entertaining or persuading).
   c. Evaluate the speaker's success in making shifts from primary to secondary aims and back to his primary aim. (Did he indicate to his listeners that he was shifting purpose? Did he indicate why he was doing this? How successful was he in keeping his dominant purpose clear despite temporary shifts? Was the total impact of his speech strengthened or weakened by temporary changes in purpose? If weakened, how might this effect have been avoided?)

Oral

1. Prepare and present an oral report on the kinds of content used in some speech of entertainment you have read or heard. Indicate also what special treatment was given to this content. (Speeches by Mark Twain,

Will Rogers, or speakers of their kind might be chosen for study in connection with this exercise.)

2. Prepare and present a brief talk on why it is unwise for those who speak to inform or to induce inquiry to color their speech content with personal opinions or value judgments.

3. Prepare and present an informative talk in which you assess why some allegedly good speaker failed in a major attempt at persuasion. (William Jennings Bryan, Norman Thomas, Adlai Stevenson, or Richard Nixon might be examined as presidential campaign speakers; or Winston Churchill's "Sinews of Peace," delivered at Fulton, Missouri, March 5, 1946, might furnish a case study for use in this exercise.)

8   *Disposition:*

Organizing

Materials

Therefore when the point for decision and the arguments which must be devised for the purpose of reaching a decision have been diligently discovered by the rules of art, and studied with careful thought, then, and not until then, the other parts of the oration are to be arranged in proper order.

Cicero, *De Inventione*[1]

In a book entitled The Image *Kenneth E. Boulding* points out that the dominant view of physical processes, as they are now understood, postulates that there is an omnipresent tendency "for things to run down." "The end of the universe, according to this picture," he continues, "will be a thin uniform soup without form. It is toward this comfortless end that all physical processes are moving." By contrast, Boulding insists, the record of history exhibits another tendency, "the tendency for the rise of organization." In support of this view he points out:

It is the capacity for organizing information into large and complex images which is the chief glory of our species. . . . Our image of time . . . goes far beyond that of the most intelligent of lower animals, mainly because of our capacity for language and for record. . . . Closely associated with the time structure of his [man's] image is the image of the structure of relationships. Be-

<hr />

[1] Cicero, *De Inventione*, trans. by H. M. Hubbell (Cambridge, Mass.: Harvard University Press, 1960), p. 39, Bk I, Ch. 14.

cause we are aware of time, we are also aware of cause and effect, of contiguity and succession of cycles and repetition.[2]

The organization of a message to be communicated orally is the application of this distinctive human capacity for structuring things, brought to bear upon ideas in such a way as to accommodate the forms and relationships that occur in what *we* think to *other people's* capacities to see forms and relationships. The difficulties of doing this are often severe.

The thought of a swimming pool, in your mind, may be veritably encrusted with what are *for you* related memories of friendships made while relaxing beside the pool; pleasing sensations experienced in cool water on hot days; and, perhaps, of cook-outs and song after sunset. But this cluster of remembered, related meanings can never be verbally implanted instantaneously and whole in anyone else's mind. The elements of the cluster must be detached from one another. They must be verbalized and expressed in some sequence that will enable someone else to create out of his own experiences a cluster of images and sensations comparable to your own. You must verbalize so that connections in the cluster are revealed and so that the sequence emphasizes these connections. Certainly, the more special or private the relationships *you* perceive among the things you think about, the more difficult it will be for you to convey those relationships in familiar, *public* terms. There are, in short, some thoughts and sensations whose significance and interconnections are so highly personal that we almost never succeed in communicating them. One reason is that we cannot, through language at least, line up the aspects of these sensations in any way that exhibits all of them in precisely the interrelationships that make them distinct as experience. Try, for example, to express in words what it feels like to swallow a mouthful of ice-cold water on a day when it is 100° in the shade and you haven't had a drink for three hours. This is a problem for poets, not artisans in public speaking.

Demands for Organization

Happily, most matters about which we normally make public speeches can be verbalized in structured forms that meaningfully convey their in-

[2] (Ann Arbor: University of Michigan Press, 1956), p. 25. See Chapter 2, "The Image in the Theory of Organization." Used by permission.

ternal nature and significance. As Boulding says, the fact that man has a conception of the relationships we call time, cause, effect, contiguity, cyclical succession, repetition, and the like makes it possible to communicate at least the basic natures of the thoughts we acquire. Even listeners, whose perceptions are often not efficient, can see connections and relationships presented by speakers who organize their thoughts with careful regard for the patterns all men are accustomed to perceiving. Three things a speaker must invariably remember, however, are: (1) listeners do not take in as much detail as readers, so he must show relationships among ideas plainly— sometimes obviously; (2) the object of all effort to organize ideas for public speech is to transform the shape of what the speaker thinks into shapes that his particular audience will be able to recognize; (3) as Cicero indicates in the quotation at the head of this chapter, it is foolish to try to organize the ideas of a speech before most of those ideas have been located and the specific purpose of the speech has been identified.

Audiences are insistent that they be able to understand what a speaker says. Much of their insistence is simply an expression of man's unique capacity and wish to reduce chaos through organization. These capacities and needs are satisfied by such perceptions as seeing the interrelationships among ideas; seeing which ideas are primary and which are subsidiary; detecting the rationale behind the over-all pattern of a speech or the chains of reasoning within it. Whoever departs from the order of thought anticipated by his audience, or from an apparently logical order of thoughts, had better explain why he does so, otherwise his hearers will find the flow of thought chaotic and, possibly, suspect the speaker of deliberately trying to mislead them. The gist of the matter is that when listeners cannot make what *they* call "sense" of what they hear the chances are that the speaker is losing his way and is in danger of losing his audience.

Listeners also lose interest in what is said to them when the discourse does not seem *to them* to be advancing toward a psychologically meaningful goal. Just because they are human beings with a capacity and need to organize, listeners demand progression and a sense of constructive variety which produce cumulative, psychologically satisfying effects. A speech, then, must build, point by point. Somewhere a climax must be reached. This high point is usually near the end of the discourse, but it may and sometimes does occur earlier. In either case, it is psychologically satisfying if points along the way are given time, detailed development, and intensity which indicate their relative weights within the total structure. The basic point to be remembered is that listeners anticipate that somewhere a juncture will be reached in your speech when all the facts and opinions necessary are in, or when all arguments have been developed to the point of acceptability. They expect, in short, that all roads will lead to Rome. In this they are simply displaying the chief glory of their species.

Not every decision respecting the organization of oral communication derives from the nature of audiences, though most do. A speaker does well to evaluate his own response to the structure of his ideas. If his proposed pattern for organizing his discourse is so complicated he cannot maintain his grasp of it, he probably has made a poor choice of organizational procedures for his purpose. Weak organization is often a main cause for a speaker's lack of confidence in himself and his materials. Patterns of thought which seem natural and right are those most easily remembered. Only when the speaker is satisfied that he has each piece of supporting material in its proper place is he able to proceed with assurance.

Speech materials often impose specific patterns of organization upon both the audience and the speaker. Once material is discovered and gathered, it requires sorting. Such sorting may mean that anecdotes, questions, examples, and statistics need to be grouped by topic or argument, spatially or chronologically.

As he moves through the period of invention which we have discussed in Chapters 5, 6, and 7, the speaker may envision the proportionate weight in time he would like to give to a particular point, yet when he assembles his data with a view to giving them place and relationship, he may find no support for his pet hypothesis. He may be startled to find that he still has little to say of this matter by way of amplification or support. Then he has the choice of discarding the seemingly weak contention or of backtracking to search out further support. This second procedure will, of course, prove of no avail if he has thoroughly researched his subject in the first place. This is one way material influences structure, but there is another.

It is perhaps more often the case that a speaker finds he has too much material for the available speaking time. Upon sifting and sorting his data he may discover that he has support for twelve or thirteen main ideas. Again, he must choose. He may discard those ideas which are least fruitful, those least likely to gain audience acceptance, or those least necessary or relevant to his purpose. On the other hand, he may decide to regroup and reorganize his material. Very often when material seems to yield too many main points the problem is that lesser ideas are being mistaken for broader ones to which they actually relate as support or amplification.

The processes of elimination or reorganization may seem painful ones. In practice you may find you have to cut your speech almost until the very moment of delivery. Should you discover that your speaking time has been encroached upon by unforeseeable circumstances, still more material must be sacrificed without destroying form. Such was the case when Franklin Roosevelt found it necessary to cut his 1932 speech accepting the presidential nomination. The plane in which he flew from Albany to Chicago was hours late, which meant that he would appear before an audience wearied by waiting to hear him. He wisely decided that the speech would have to be shorter than he had planned. Samuel Rosenman, who assisted him with the speech, writes:

> With each radio report, we were falling further and further behind schedule; and more and more paragraphs came out of the acceptance speech. This lopping off of material on which we had worked so long and so hopefully was a painful process. I know that there were some jewels dropped on the airplane floor that day. It is likely, though, that the cutting process hurt us more than it did the speech.[3]

Such may be your feeling as you discard materials. Yet, rejection and red-pencilling will often result in strengths of conciseness and sharper focus. To drop a jewel-like quotation or fact does not always mar the message as a whole. Often we use too many words or amplify too much. The tightening that comes from excision will very often enhance the speech structure and add to its organic unity.

Should you choose to regroup your materials, you will find you are faced with discovering a new rationale, a new set of topics. Often this regrouping is less difficult than it at first seems. Many good speakers insist the fewer the points in a speech, the better. If you are giving a short speech, under most circumstances you ought to assume that you have time to develop three or four main points at most. Upon close scrutiny and careful weighing you may find that by slicing your material another way those twelve or thirteen points will fit under three or four main heads. What

[3] Samuel I. Rosenman, *Working with Roosevelt* (New York: Harper & Brothers, 1952), p. 75.

seemed main points may in reality be only subpoints or may be made to operate as subpoints with good effect. Again you will keep the audience in mind if you proceed wisely, for you will realize that two or three points acceptably substantiated are more valuable in achieving your purpose than ten or twelve points lightly touched upon and dropped.

The materials of a speech may, upon occasion, make such strong demands that a particular structural pattern is literally dictated to you. Speeches explaining procedures are outstanding examples of such dictation. A demonstrator can hardly demonstrate at whim. A vacuum cleaner cannot pick up lint before it is turned on, and a picture cannot be painted before the colors are mixed. A chemistry professor performing an experiment before a class must follow the order the experiment dictates. He cannot depart far from this pattern without being off on a tangent. In all these cases the path of development is determined in the main by the material.

While we usually think of organization or disposition with respect to the over-all pattern of a speech, the principles of clear organization also operate within the various points of a discourse. If a story is used, chronological or time order is almost inescapable. Only under rare circumstances should you depart from the actual course of events in narration. Interruptions of narrative for the expression of personal opinion are almost always out of place for they divert attention from the main movement of thought. Yet, there may be circumstances where spontaneous insertion of definitions or other clarifying detail is necessary if you are to adapt to the audience at the moment. The questions to be asked about any break in an established or natural order of ideas are: "Is this departure relevant? Will this deviation from the thought pattern aid in the achievement of my purpose?"

Occasions and settings for speaking influence organization of ideas less often than do audience, speaker, and material. The occasion may make acknowledgements or personal greetings necessary at the beginning of a speech, but these are really audience adaptations, for they acknowledge the audience's relationship to the occasion. The setting may also seem to narrow your choice among over-all patterns under certain circumstances. For example, a Washington's birthday celebration may call for a eulogy of George Washington. From experience, speakers have found that eulogies are successful when the praise of the man is set forth by recounting incidents in his life or when the speech is organized around his traits of character.

More obvious structural adjustments made for the sake of the occasion can be seen when speakers depart from the pattern of discourse being pursued because the occasion itself is unexpectedly changed by some distracting occurrence such as the rattle of jack hammers outside the window, a sudden failure in the lighting system, or the unexpected appearance of an important personage. But even here, the modification of organizational pattern is as much a matter of audience adaptation as of adaptation to the occasion.

So we can see that the disposition of ideas, their orderly arrangement, is not happenstantial. Choices regarding organization are wisely made only after careful consideration of the audience's expectations; the speaker's capabilities; the nature of the data used to achieve the speaker's purpose; and, incidentally, the circumstances prevailing at the time of delivery.

Main Components of a Speech

As Plato noted in the *Phaedrus,* a speech is like the human body in that it has a head, a torso, and feet—meaning an introduction, a body, and a conclusion. In most cases the body, often called the "development" or "discussion," is proportionately the largest of the three parts. The conclusion is normally the smallest. Introductions may vary in length or may, upon occasion, be omitted altogether. The proportions of these parts depend upon the subject matter, the occasion, and the speaker himself to some extent, but most often they depend upon the audience's expectations and motivations. If we were to carry Plato's analogy farther, we might say that a speech also contains the equivalents of unifying bodily elements, neck and ankles, which connect the three main portions. These linking parts are major transitions. *Normally,* then, as in other works of art such as plays, poems, musical compositions, a speech has a beginning, a middle, an end, and transitional elements. We shall now consider these separately.

INTRODUCTIONS

The introduction to your speech should fulfill demands made by all of the elements in public speaking. Since it is a beginning, it must (1) attract the initial, favorable attention of the audience; (2) provide necessary background for the audience so they may comprehend the remainder of the speech; (3) be suitable to the occasion; and (4) contribute to your ease during a crucial period of adjustment. In addition, the introduction ought to be coordinated with the body of the speech and be relevant to what follows. It is not a preamble or prelude without relation to the rest of the speech.

At the outset of your speech, attention must be gained in such a way that your listeners will want to go on listening. Any of the methods for achieving attention may, of course, be employed, but the most frequently useful ways of developing introductions are to draw attention by referring to something familiar or something novel. You may start with a reference to the occasion, to its purpose, or to other features which the audience already knows about. You may begin with greetings, a familiar quotation, an anecdote, or analogy. In some cases tradition may dictate what you will say at the very beginning. In others you may need to awaken the audience by sharpening the focus of their attention. Where this is so, unusual facts, strange stories, shocking or startling assertions, unfamiliar statistics, telegraphic headline fragments, or kaleidoscopic elements of a situation may enable you to create curiosity or suspense. Reference to your own interests and needs, especially if they are similar to those of your audience, may create common ground and cause your audience to want to listen. A modest statement of your qualifications for speaking on the subject you have chosen may also make your listeners want to hear more.

Most audiences want to be given reasons for listening. They are always ready to ask, "Why should *I* listen? What's in this for *me?*" They want to be given reasons for listening and, often, they want directions about what to listen for. They want to be invited to pay attention. The ways in which you may touch off an audience's powers of concentration are limitless, yet none is truly useful unless it will at once seize attention and favorably dispose your audience to what follows.

It is often essential for you to include introductory material that provides background knowledge your hearers must have from the outset. It may be necessary for you to provide preliminary information about new materials, details you will use in amplification, or the relationships between main points and your central proposition. Such basic information may be new or it may be old. It may be provided by way of review. Its function will be to provide a context for what you are going to say.

You may find it necessary to define unfamiliar terms to be used later in your discussion or to define familiar terms to insure that the audience understands the meanings you assign to them. A short, historical review of the facts of the case under consideration may prove helpful. In persuasive speeches where argument from precedent is not a main contention or where your subject is one that listeners have not thought a great deal about it is especially useful to employ such a history of the question.

Definitions and histories are sometimes supplemented or replaced by a statement of those aspects of the subject which you will or will not deal with in the body of your speech. Items so singled out because you intend to pass them over or because they seem to be irrelevant are often called "waived materials." You simply state that you will not consider them and give your listeners your reasons. Iteration of main points to be developed later by amplification or support is sometimes called "initial partition." This kind of preview statement acquaints the audience with the structure of the body of your speech. "Initial partitions" are especially useful when your audience needs to know in advance the path you intend to take. Of course, you would not offer such statements if you wished to preserve suspense or feared that revealing your entire plan so early might make some listeners defensive. Initial partitioning is not a useful introductory tactic in speeches developed inductively or in those designed for unfriendly audiences. In such speeches even the subject sentence is often withheld until the end.

In speeches constructed on a deductive pattern you ought to include the subject sentence of your speech as a final item of the introduction, or as an initial item in the body of the speech. As we have already said, the subject sentence is delayed in most inductive sequences. Wherever it appears, it ought to be carefully expressed in a single, economical, unambiguous sentence as was pointed out in Chapters 3 and 6.

Not all the items we have mentioned will be included in any one speech introduction. The amount of time at your disposal and what it is necessary for your listeners to know before you proceed with detailed elucidation or argument will dictate how much and what kinds of orientation materials you will offer.

The introduction is the one part of the speech which, given the right circumstances, may be omitted altogether. It is not necessary if an audience is already attentive and interested in your subject, if they expect you to speak, if they already possess the background information or fully understand your message, if they are highly motivated, or if the occasion exerts no special pressures. College professors often dispense with introductions after the first few lectures. They judge their audiences to be oriented and motivated and so introductory remarks become superfluous. You, however, should use caution in deciding to omit an introduction. Rarely can an introduction be dispensed with when speaking to an audience for the first time; never, when you are aware that your audience is not entirely ready to pay attention to you and your subject from the very outset.

THE BODY OF THE SPEECH

The body of a speech consists of (1) the main points, (2) the material which supports or amplifies these points, and (3) the phrases or sentences which serve as transitions between main points or between supporting items.

Earlier we discussed the sorting and sifting of materials by which you arrive at main points and determine their psychological weighting and placement for the purpose of achieving climax. Once these stages of preliminary analysis have been completed and you know what your main points will be, you are faced with the task of wording the main ideas.

Where possible, main points ought to be worded in parallel phrasings to provide balance in structure. They should also be worded to elicit the responses the speaker seeks from his audience. Main points for speeches purporting to relate, relay, or review information should be simple, clear assertions. In speeches of inquiry the main points are often worded as questions which are then supported with information which provides possible answers or which explores the questions in all their ramifications. Main points for speeches aiming to persuade should be assertions slanted in wording to express the speaker's point of view and to support the main proposition embodied in the subject sentence. They should be "contentions" or "reasons" closely linked to the subject sentence so that they become the foundation stones upon which the core idea rests. Main points for speeches of reinforcement are framed in essentially the same way as those for speeches of persuasion. For speeches designed to entertain, main points again take the form of assertions.

In all cases the determination of the final form which your main points will take rests upon the interrelated demands of the material, the audience, your habitual mode of expression. The ways in which these main points are arranged into patterns will be discussed in the next chapter.

TRANSITIONS[4]

Since your listeners cannot easily review what you have said once it has been spoken, as they might turn back and reread the pages in a book, it will be necessary for you to provide careful transitions if your speech is to be clear at all points. Transitions may be defined as words, phrases, sentences, or groups of sentences which join ideas together. If clear and smoothly worded, they contribute to the organic unity of your speech.

Transitions may be likened to signposts which tell your audience where you have been, where you are, and where you intend to go. They will most frequently occur upon the completion of the consideration of a main idea and before you move on to the next one, but they may also be needed as connections between less important points or as lead-in phrases to the ideas in single sentences.

Transitions are called "internal summaries" when they not only link ideas but, in addition, review key thoughts already covered. Good internal summaries also point ahead to the next idea to be handled. Internal summaries commonly use such wordings as:

> Since we have already considered that . . . , we should adopt. . . .
> In addition to . . . there is another outstanding reason (element, factor, consideration, fact). . . .
> We have seen . . . , yet it remains for us to observe. . . .
> But . . . is only one important viewpoint. Equally as important is. . . .
> Since . . . is so, what can be said of . . . ? (Questions, it may be noted, can often be useful as transitions.)

Where the thought connection to be highlighted is between subpoints, or where the thought relationships are easy to comprehend, a phrase or even a single word such as "so" or "yet" may be adequate to tie ideas together. Some examples of such phrasings are:

[4] This section is based in part upon an explanation of transitions written for the Assignments and Materials Booklet at Cornell University by Harry P. Kerr. Used by permission.

More important than all this is the fact that. . . .
In contrast to. . . .
Looked at from a different angle the problem seems to be. . . .
This last point raises a question: . . .?
What was the result? Just this. . . .
On the other hand. . . .
When this has been done. . . .
And so you can see that. . . .

There is nothing wrong with the following transition: "So much for transitions. Let us now turn to their use."

Variety is to be sought in transitions as in other aspects of speech making. Avoid using only stock phrases or falling into the habit of repeating the same few phrases over and over. While you should not be afraid to be obvious in your transitions, you should avoid being too brief. A mark of the unpolished speaker is his tendency to use only "and" or "also" as transitions. He gives the impression of having tacked his ideas together, of having joined them to one another crudely. Yet he is in a slightly better position than the speaker who melts from point to point or vaguely gropes his way from topic to topic. Good transitions (1) show that the speaker is moving from one idea to another, (2) clearly tie off the ideas just completed, (3) indicate the relationships between the ideas involved, and (4) remind the speaker of his sequence of thought.

CONCLUSIONS

The final segment of your speech, its conclusion, also performs functions demanded by the audience, the material, the occasion, and yourself. In this segment the audience normally expects (1) a restatement of your core idea or (2) a summing up of main points which clarify or prove your thesis. In some instances both restatement and summary may be needed. Almost any body of material needs a final rounding out that sharply focuses on the coupling of subject matter with the speaker's intent. To emphasize a detail or simply to fade into silence obscures meaning. Neither audience nor speakers should feel at the end of a speech that they have been left hanging, that the speech ended too abruptly, or that the subject is still up in the air. The audience should know that the speech is finished, and the speaker should feel satisfied that he has accomplished his purpose and produced an intended final impact. All of this does not mean that the final sentence of a speech ought always to be a restatement or summary sentence. True, recapitulation is the main function of most conclusions, but the last sentences of a speech are often strongest if devised to challenge the audience to further thought or action, or if the closing words operate as a coda to the central theme. At times, the final sentences may echo the beginning sentences or constitute a return to a text or refrain, thus providing a frame for the entire composition. A "thank you" at the very end of a speech may detract from the central idea and an otherwise strong final impression. Indeed, any remarks of appreciation used as last sentences ought to be carefully considered before inclusion since they may destroy the focus of an otherwise effective conclusion.

Introduction, subject sentence, body, transitions, and conclusion will, with rare exceptions, be parts of every speech you will deliver. They may be cast in different designs from speech to speech, but their functions will normally be as we have described them in every speech you construct. It remains for us to consider the most common of these structures or designs, as speakers actually employ them in arranging materials for the purpose of achieving particular audience responses.

Usable Patterns of Organization[5]

The standard patterns commonly used in structuring ideas in speeches include: (1) chronological, (2) spatial, (3) topical, (4) ascending and descending orders, (5) causal, (6) problem-solution or disease-remedy, (7) withheld proposal or indirect sequence, (8) open proposal or direct sequence, (9) reflective sequence or pattern of inquiry, (10) Monroe's motivated sequence, and (11) elimination order.

Four conditions will determine to a marked degree the most appropriate pattern for a given public speaking situation. As a speaker you ought

[5] The descriptions of the cause-effect, problem-solution, withheld proposal, and open proposal patterns in this section are based upon explanations written for the Assignments and Materials Booklet at Cornell University by James A. Wood. Donald E. Williams of the University of Florida prepared the original explanation of the reflective sequence. Used by permission.

to consider (1) the particular type and degree of response you seek to elicit from the audience; (2) whether the audience is favorably, unfavorably, or apathetically disposed toward your subject, your central idea, and you as a speaker; (3) how much knowledge your listeners possess about your subject; (4) how you can best relate your specific purpose to the pertinent interests and desires of your audience.

In using the patterns explained below you should bear in mind that a pattern need not be followed rigidly or in its entirety to be useful as a general scheme for organizing the materials of your speech. These patterns may be used for the organization of the speech as a whole or for only a particular segment of it. In other words, patterns may be combined within a speech. For example, you might have a chronologically arranged section within the introduction to a speech with an over-all problem-solution arrangement; or, you might have a cause-effect pattern for the problem section of a problem-solution speech. Generally speaking, an introduction will need to be organized independently of the body of the speech and the conclusion is likely to be arranged to reflect the pattern of organization adopted in the body.

CHRONOLOGICAL PATTERN

The chronological pattern is a time order, relating occurrences in the sequence in which they happened or giving directions which are to be followed in a prescribed order. The material of a speech will often dictate this kind of ordering. Chronology is an order most useful in recounting events and one that is almost mandatory in narration. Chronological patterns may be used in all kinds of speeches. They are most often used in connection with informative purposes whether to inform be the dominant purpose of a whole speech or of only a segment of it. Aside from the demands of the content, this pattern often meets audience demands for comprehensible order and interestingness. A time sequence usually admits of climactic development, of arousing curiosity and creating suspense. Segments of speeches chronologically developed can be found in the narrations of circumstances leading to crime in Clarence Darrow's famous summation at the trial of Loeb and Leopold, or in Daniel Webster's classic speech for the prosecution in the Knapp-White murder case. Examples of entire speeches developed chronologically would include many eulogies, speeches of nomination, historical lectures, demonstrations, and instructional discourses.

It is a weakness of chronological patterning that such important considerations as cause, effect, desirability, form, etc. cannot easily be emphasized without interrupting the movement-in-time that gives chronology its chief interest value.

SPATIAL PATTERN

The spatial pattern is, as the name implies, a structure which is based on the relationships of the parts of a whole as they exist in space. In using such a pattern, you proceed systematically in your description of how something looks or functions. Normally you will describe from left to right, top to bottom, bottom to top, or front to back. Sometimes you will describe by moving from that portion at the center to those on the periphery. For instance, you might describe the control panel in an airplane by pointing first to those centered instruments most often used, then move out toward the surrounding instruments which are less frequently used. You would then be using a pattern of descending importance which happens here to become identical with the pattern of spatial description. In all uses of spatial arrangement you will need to mention each part or aspect to which you call the audience's attention in the order you have decided upon during your period of preparation.

This sort of structure is especially useful in speeches of information and in those parts of any speech where it is essential to provide information. A fire extinguisher might be described from top to bottom, a painting from right to left, the floor plan of a house from front to back or story to story. The order in which to proceed when describing spatially will ordinarily be up to you. Your decision on which space portion to take up first ought to hinge on your estimation of how you can provide the greatest clarity for your audience while highlighting the *important* relationships among parts. If these standards leave you more than one good way of describing spatially, choose the alternative that is easier for you to present.

TOPICAL PATTERN

The often-mentioned topical pattern is really one in which there is an absence of any easily identifiable speech structure. The label "topical" is affixed to those organizational schemes which we cannot otherwise account for. Some textbooks use the label "classification order" to denote that some kind of orderly categorization accounts for the patterning. Some would say that topical patterns are those which naturally arise from the subject matter. Others, among them Walter and Scott, explain this pattern by saying that it is a pattern evolving out of the natural parts of the subject, its aspects, types, or qualities.[6] The word "topical" gives us a clue. *If there is pattern* in the instances we are considering here, it is one arrived at by finding that no standard pattern suitably orders the data, so we turn to invention. We invent for ourselves a pattern suitable to unique and striking effects. We ask ourselves *where* the places are to which we go for argument or clarification and we come up with such an answer as: "We often look at social, political, or economic aspects of arguments." Thus we arrive at a *special* classification of materials. It is only one of many such schemes of organizing data. Another might have been: public interests vs. private interests. Thus, we think of the topics we might use, select from them; and they, as we choose to arrange them, become the bases for organization of ideas in a speech. We are strongly inclined to think that the topical pattern, as an organizational system, is an arbitrary and artificial one, a catchall category to describe what we really cannot account for in any other way. The only demand made upon such a pattern is that the audience accept as reasonable and suitably comprehensive the speech structure which the speaker has devised.

The so-called topical pattern is adaptable to any purpose but inquiry. In an impromptu speech in Philadelphia, February 22, 1861, Abraham Lincoln adopted a simple but easily understandable topical arrangement treating (1) the principle of unity reflected in the Declaration of Independence and (2) Lincoln's determination to sustain the Union at all costs. He might as easily have chosen to discuss the (1) economic, (2) social,

[6] See Otis M. Walter and Robert L. Scott, *Thinking and Speaking* (New York: Macmillan, 1962), p. 61.

and (3) political benefits of maintaining the Union. Or he might have discussed the (1) legal and (2) historical justifications for the Union. All these arrangements might be identified as topical.

ASCENDING AND DESCENDING ORDERS

Ascending and descending orders resemble topical orders in that, at first glance they seem to be arbitrarily arranged. But in the use of these patterns, aspects, types, or qualities are placed in sequence according to a perceivable rationale that applies to a vast number of subject matters. The speaker, here, proceeds to arrange his points according to their increasing or decreasing importance or familiarity. That is to say, he moves from the most to the least important or from the most to the least familiar points or vice versa. He starts with the strongest argument and moves to the weakest or starts with the weakest and moves to the strongest. He may start on common ground and move into unfamiliar territory, or he may begin with an unusual or rarely thought-of aspect or argument and lead the audience to what they already know or to what is already uppermost in their minds. In the case of descending order, for example, a speaker explaining how pulp is processed for the manufacture of paper would take up the most commonly used process, the ground-wood process, and move through his speech to the soda, sulfite, and alkaline processes, which are used less frequently and are less familiar to most people. Similarly, in a speech on recognition of the Communist government of China, the frequently heard, strong argument that the Chinese government does in fact exist would precede less familiar and weaker arguments concerning the economic or political benefits of recognition. If you simply reverse the sequence so lesser known methods or less strong ideas come first, you achieve ascending order.

As our examples suggest, ascending-descending orders are suitable for use in speeches to inform, to persuade, or to reinforce. The pattern might also be adapted for use in a speech to entertain. In any case, the choice and construction of ascending and descending orders hinge on your judgments of the relative importance of your materials; on your estimate of what will help your listeners to remember and give them a sense of climax; and, sometimes, on whether you have time to develop enough points to make ascent or descent a meaningful pattern.

CAUSAL SEQUENCES

The causal patterns are used in situations where one set of conditions is given as the cause for another set. The speaker may begin with *a given set of conditions as the cause* and allege that these will produce certain results or *effects;* or he may take *a given set of conditions as the effect* and allege that these resulted from certain *causes.*

In most uses of this pattern the speaker's specific purpose is to urge the elimination of those conditions which function as causes. To achieve this specific purpose, however, he may need to persuade his audience of one or more of these three things: (1) that the effects are really undesirable to them; (2) that the alleged causes are truly responsible for these effects; and (3) that elimination of these causes will not result in other, undesirable consequences. Both (1) and (2) must either be self-evident to the audience or the speaker must prove them. The third of these concerns may sometimes be disregarded.

The most common use of this pattern is one in which a speaker points out that certain undesirable conditions (*effects*) now exist and then explains that these are caused by certain other conditions (*causes*). The speaker *may* carry his reasoning through a chain of two or more effect-cause relationships in order to get from the present undesirable effects to the cause which he asks his audience to eliminate. This kind of development might run thus:

I. The nations of the world now spend billions of dollars on armaments. (Present undesirable effect.)
II. This money is spent because the peoples of the world live in perpetual fear of war and aggression. (Establishing first effect-to-cause relationship.)
III. People must live in such fear because there is no international authority strong enough to prevent war. (Second effect-to-cause relationship establishes the *real* cause of the present undesirable conditions.)
IV. Billions of dollars will be saved by the establishment of a federal world government. (Audience urged to adopt proposal eliminating prime cause and thereby eliminating effect.)

Frequently, the speaker will point out that certain existing conditions will cause undesirable effects in the future, and so should be eliminated. The normal sequence in this pattern is to begin with the present causes and then describe the anticipated future effects. Sometimes a more artistic sequence is to visualize the future effects for the audience first, then link these effects to the present undesirable causes. One might structure his speech thus:

I. The free nations of the world are now drifting toward a third world war which will destroy civilization. (Future, undesirable effects.)

II. This drift is being caused by the free nations' present lax attitude toward Communists' piecemeal aggression and flaunting of international authority. (Present conditions cause future effect.)

III. Therefore, the free nations should force Communist nations to recognize international authority. (Appeal to audience to eliminate present causes in order to avoid future effect.)

Sometimes a speaker draws an analogy between a cause-effect relationship and another similar cause-effect relationship which is already accepted by his audience:

I. At the present time, the free nations of the world are permitting the Soviet Union to ignore international authority. (Establishing present conditions as cause.)

II. Because the free nations of the world, acting as the League of Nations, did not force Hitler and Mussolini to keep international peace, a world war was necessary to stop fascist aggression. (Referring to past and accepted cause-effect relationship.)

III. Our present lax policy will eventuate in a world war to stop Soviet aggression. (Drawing parallel undesirable effects from parallel causes.)

IV. Therefore, the free nations should act now to force Soviet obedience of international authority. (Appeal to audience to eliminate present causes in order to avoid future effects.)

Although causal patterns are generally used to advocate the removal of some condition, they can be used to advocate that certain conditions be encouraged. In this usage the speaker will show how something desirable to his audience (*effect*) results from other things (*causes*); therefore, they should set these causes in operation in order to secure the effect. Such a pattern might run:

I. We want permanent peace in the world. (Establishing condition, effect, as desirable to audience.)

II. Permanent peace results from the peace-loving, democratic nations' armed superiority over potential aggressor nations. (Establishing cause for the desirable effect.)

III. Therefore, let us build bigger and better hydrogen bombs and guided missiles. (Appeal for audience to favor conditions designed to cause desirable effects.)

The causal patterns are also often used in speeches to inform to describe the relationships of various factors in the thing being explained, e.g., the causes of inflation during war time or the effects of X rays on human tissue. On occasion, speeches to reinforce and entertain are cast in this pattern.

Often the biggest difficulty in using causal patterns for either persuasive or informational speeches is to make clear that a valid cause-effect relationship actually exists between the two sets of conditions. The demands to be met when these patterns are used are primarily those of the audience for a clear and logical demonstration that genuine and significant (for them) causal relationships do exist. In turn, to use causal patterns requires that the speaker be capable of cogent logical thinking and that the materials used in the speech lend themselves to causal development.

PROBLEM-SOLUTION SEQUENCE

The problem-solution pattern is used in situations where the audience faces a problem which you propose to solve. This pattern is also called the "disease-remedy" or the "need-remedy" pattern. Here, the speaker points first to the existence of a problem or evil and then offers a corrective program which must meet two main criteria: (1) the solution must be *practicable* and (2) it must be *desirable*. The corrective program must be capable of being put into effect, and it must be capable of eliminating the problem or the evil in question. It must also be one which will not introduce new and worse evils of its own. This is the issue long debated regarding the testing of nuclear weapons. Do the defense benefits obtained outweigh the undesirable effects on human beings?

The specific purpose of a speech in which the problem-solution pattern is used urges the audience to adopt the conditions embodied in the solution portion of the address. This type of organization usually serves best in the following situations.

1. Where the audience is aware that a problem exists and is interested in finding a solution to it, e.g., the problem of preventing inflation, you may advocate one solution as the best of several possible answers. Although you will generally describe the problem briefly, you will be primarily concerned with showing how your particular solution will solve the problem in the best possible way and how any alleged disadvantages of your solution may be avoided. This latter concern, avoiding new difficulties, will frequently involve you in anticipatory refutation, which means that you will have to dispel arguments against your proposal even though they have not been verbally advanced by anyone at the time you speak.

2. Where the audience is only dimly aware of a problem or need, the problem-solution pattern still serves well. Listeners can be made specifically aware of the problem's exact nature; then, perhaps, the solution will become evident. Here you are primarily concerned with focusing your hearers' vague *felt* needs upon the specific problem you have isolated. You want the audience to see how their interests are vitally affected by the problem once it has been identified. Although you should at least indicate briefly what the evident solution is, your chief concern is to show that a specific serious problem does exist. Where your audience is not initially aware of their difficulty, it is unlikely that in a single speech you can do more than establish that precise sense of need; but not even in these circumstances can you disregard the solution section of your sequence altogether. If you do, you will leave the hearers up in the air. You must at least indicate that there *are* ways of solving the problem of which you have now made them conscious.

3. There are situations where the major concerns of both the preceding settings are combined. Sometimes you *can* carry your audience from awareness of a problem through to a readiness to act on a particular solution.

Now your task is (1) to sharpen awareness of the problem and (2) to show why your solution is the most suitable. Such a speech might be structured thus:

I. A serious problem of juvenile delinquency now exists in the United States. (Referring to felt need.)
   A. This problem not only poses a threat to our personal welfare and property, but costs us millions of dollars in taxes for police protection. (Establishing importance of problem to audience.)

B. Youths seem to have no sense of responsibility for their actions. (Focusing felt need on specific problem.)

II. This problem can be solved by imposing stiffer fines and jail sentences on juvenile criminals. (Statement of solution to specific problem.)

A. By making youths responsible for the consequences of their actions we will deter them from criminal activities. (Showing *how* proposal will solve the problem.)

B. The use of special jails will keep juveniles apart from older, hardened criminals. (Meeting objections to proposal.)

Variations on the problem-solution pattern are sometimes used in speeches of information, as when you show how people were faced with a problem and how they solved it. One might in this way report how an early-warning radar system was established to protect the United States. The pattern may be used for informational purposes even if the solution is not yet in effect, provided the answer has been decided on and is no longer a question for debate. Problem-solution arrangements may also be adapted for use in speeches to reinforce belief and feeling or, more rarely, in speeches to entertain.

From what we have said it can easily be seen that problem-solution patterns are directly tied to audience demands. The audience must feel or be made to feel that a problem exists or that an evil is present. Often the felt need will originate in the speaker himself so that it is his state of mind that makes the initial demand for this pattern. Where this is true, he must make the audience feel that the need for something to be done is justified— in terms of *their* interests. Speech materials also exert influence affecting one's choice of this organizational pattern. They must be capable of being divided into clear-cut problems and solutions. The occasion will determine to some extent those items which the speaker selects to depict the problem and to explain the solution. Thus, all forces in the communicative setting are at work in the final determination of how and whether a problem-solution pattern can be evolved.

WITHHELD-PROPOSAL OR INDIRECT SEQUENCE

The withheld proposal or indirect sequence is a pattern of organization using inductive development of materials. In this pattern individual cases or instances are used as the basis for a generalization about additional members of the same class.

The most important characteristic of the indirect sequence is that when using this pattern you give your audience examples, or some basic assumptions and facts, *before* you present any generalized inferences or conclusions of your own.

This pattern is especially useful when speaking to a hostile audience. Sometimes it is the only pattern that will enable you to persuade, because it permits you to begin an argument with material your audience knows to be true or with assumptions they accept. A common ground of agreement is established with the audience; when inferences are logically drawn from these accepted materials, the audience must either attack the logic involved or admit that you may be right. This pattern is also effective because it reflects man's normal thinking processes of generalizing from examples and assumptions in order to reach decisions.

Indirectly structured speeches operate generally in one of two basic patterns. In the first a number of examples is given, and a generalization is inferred. The plan might be:

I. As most of you know, Senator Bergen has accused 77 men of being Communists; he has failed to prove these charges.

II. According to the Senate record Senator Bergen has used Congressional immunity to avoid answering questions about his recent income-tax returns.

III. Unquestionable evidence has proved that Senator Bergen has used doctored photographs in slandering his opponents.

IV. Therefore, we must assume that Senator Bergen is dishonest. (Point of speech given as generalization from preceding examples.)

In using this pattern it is essential that your induction meet the logical tests for validity in generalizations.

In a second type of indirect pattern you first give basic assumptions or premises which are acceptable to your audience; then you give the facts of the specific case about which you are speaking; finally, you apply your basic premises to the specific case.

I. A government that is established in a country by popular revolution should be recognized by democratic nations as the legal government of that country. (Statement of basic premise which is acceptable to audience.)

II. The Communist government of China was established by popular revolution against Chiang Kai-shek. (Giving the facts of the specific case.)

III. Therefore, the United States should recognize the Communist government as the legal government of China. (Specific purpose of speech.)

There are several specialized patterns which use an indirect approach in supporting central ideas. One of these is the applied-criteria pattern in which fact and value propositions are argued by first setting up criteria or standards and then showing that the alleged fact or value matches them. Another specialized use of an indirect presentation develops when what at first appears to be a pattern of inquiry (described below) concludes by showing or strongly implying that only one particular solution solves the problem. The so-called implicative pattern resembles an incomplete indirect pattern in that description, narration, and exposition are used for persuasive purposes. Word pictures, stories, and explanations hint at conclusions. The arguments presented may or may not be stated in formal fashion during the course of the speech. In any case, the audience is left to draw its own final conclusion or application.

As we have noted, the indirect sequence meets demands of hostile audiences and of materials which can be divided into acceptable and known, unacceptable and unknown. To these conditions of audience and material which invite use of this pattern, we may add conditions emanating from the speaker himself. He may be more adept at presenting materials indirectly, in the soft-sell manner, than he is at approaching his audience frankly and directly. The mood of the occasion may also prompt the use of this pattern. So, once again all elements of the public speaking situation may exert pressure favorable to adoption of a withheld-proposal sequence. Furthermore, indirect presentation is feasible regardless of the speaker's purpose.

OPEN-PROPOSAL OR DIRECT SEQUENCE

The open-proposal or direct sequence pattern of organization is one based upon deductive order and stands in contrast to the indirect sequence.

The speaker in using this pattern urges the audience to accept a proposition on the grounds that its validity, morality, or practicality necessarily follows from accepted axioms or principles.

The direct sequence is simple to use. Essentially, it consists of telling your audience what you intend to prove or explain and then giving the arguments or clarifications that support your thesis. In many such speeches you will use several different arguments or divisions of clarification supporting your subject sentence, and these can be grouped into categories. A person advocating certain national legislation might develop arguments showing that it was morally right, legal under the constitution, of economic benefit, and practicable. A speaker explaining road building might cover route planning, grading, and surfacing. These categories form the main heads of the body of the speech. Frequently they can be arranged in a sequence giving additional climactic or logical force to the development (e.g., the proposal is *desirable;* it is *also practical;* moreover it will have *no significant disadvantages*). The major concern in applying the open-proposal sequence is that the subpropositions be arranged in the clearest, most natural, and most logical order.

The direct or open-proposal sequence includes, among its variations, the topical arrangements we have already described and which are so common in speeches of information. It also includes the list-of-advantages pattern for persuasion in which the case for a proposition of policy is structured around a list of benefits arising out of the proposed policy. This latter variation is closely related to problem-solution organization in that each alleged advantage implies or demonstrates a problem and solution.

In general, this sequence is most suitable where listeners are fairly familiar with the subject under discussion and where they have favorable or open-minded attitudes toward your proposal or subject of information. The significant advantage of this system of organization is that you can give a number of arguments or categories of clarification efficiently while keeping your audience always informed as to what you are trying to prove or clarify and how you are going about it.

As in the case of indirect sequence, whether one adopts or avoids the direct-sequence mode of presentation depends on the outlook of the audience, the way subject matter may be reasonably divided, the speaker's skill with direct vs. indirect presentation, and the tone or spirit of the occasion.

REFLECTIVE SEQUENCE OR PATTERN OF INQUIRY

The reflective sequence or pattern of inquiry is a pattern of organization based upon the five steps in reflective thinking as outlined by the philosopher John Dewey—(1) locating and defining a problem, (2) describing and limiting the problem, (3) suggesting possible solutions, (4) evaluating and testing the solutions, and (5) selecting the preferred solution.

To use this pattern requires willingness on the part of the speaker to suspend judgment about a problem. This willingness comes from experience and reflection; life teaches us that snap judgments are often wrong, and that sound opinions must be based on careful consideration of numerous factors. The speech of inquiry and its reflective pattern of organization are for those—whether speakers or auditors—who are willing to assemble information and ponder various solutions before they decide.

In a state of mind permeated by doubt the inquirer invites an audience to join him in his quest for the best solution or the best answer to a question. He so develops his speech that his listeners feel the problem under consideration is their problem, not his alone. And he does all he can to give the audience and himself *a better basis for coming to a sound decision.* This is the function of a speech of inquiry and it is the need served by the reflective sequence of ideas.

Such a speech obviously is both informative and persuasive. But it is persuasion that asks hearers to ponder, to weigh and consider, to explore; it is not persuasion that asks audiences to adopt the opinion of the speaker.

The inquirer both resembles and differs from the informative speaker. The man who gives us information is thoroughly conversant with his subject; his sole aim is to impart his understanding to others. The inquirer, on the other hand, does not enjoy the same degree of certainty. Instead, he is experiencing a degree of discomfort about his subject, discomfort caused by his inability to settle on a really satisfactory choice among competing solutions or answers. He is certain, however, of some things, for he has studied and thought about the problem that vexes him. (1) He can formulate and clarify the question. (2) He has analyzed the nature of the difficulty and has penetrated beneath its symptoms to its causes, beneath surface phenomena to basic factors. (3) He understands the criteria for a good solution. (4) He knows what solutions are available. His doubt concerns the relative worth of the solutions or the relative validity of the answers. His aim is to impart to the audience the information he possesses and to enlist their help in the final determination.

To orient his listeners to his subject, the speaker who adopts the reflective sequence first provides his audience with an understanding of the problem before him. He informs them of its troublesome symptoms and of its underlying causes, carefully distinguishing between symptom and cause. He may also review the historical development by which the problem arose if this will provide better understanding of what has to be coped with, or he may give the details of a controversy that needs to be settled.

He doesn't stop there, however. He next considers the criteria which an acceptable solution or answer must meet. He must satisfy himself that he has formulated the right criteria, since the acceptability of solutions will depend on what standards are chosen. Though he must consider criteria in every case, the speaker does not always find it necessary to present and justify them in the speech. Some are obvious and readily taken for granted: safety on the highways, democracy, speed in settling legal cases. Such standards hardly need formal presentation in the speech and require no justification. Sometimes the criteria, though they need be presented, are too complex for explanation apart from the discussion of solutions. This might be the case with the aims of a foreign policy, or with the nature of the good life. In such cases criteria will be presented piecemeal as various solutions are discussed. But consideration of criteria is integral to inquiry, and formal presentation of them is frequently advisable.

Having clarified the problem and said what is necessary concerning standards, the speaker using the reflective sequence now turns to the alternative solutions or answers. This is generally the most important and useful element in the speech; hence, he will be well advised to allow sufficient time for it, restricting the preliminary sections to what is absolutely essential. For each solution the speaker does two things: he explains and he assesses. He explains what the solution or answer involves. He assesses or evaluates the solution or answer thoroughly and fairly in terms of the pertinent criteria, keeping in mind the weight or importance of each of these standards.

In concluding his speech, the speaker should do what he can to make inquiry a continuing process on the part of the audience. Their reflection on the subject should not stop when the speech stops. In fact, inquiry on a larger scale—group inquiry—often begins after the speech has been delivered. The speaker, therefore, may well conclude by presenting the salient questions which his listeners should further consider as they continue their search for the best solution. Or he may point out the direction in which he thinks the best answer will be found.

Thus we see that the speaker who would really inquire may suggest but he will not urge acceptance of a preferred solution. He may omit Dewey's fifth step altogether. We further see that all five steps need not be included in every pattern of inquiry. Indeed, some speeches of inquiry go no further than steps 2 or 3. Others omit step 1. The pattern, in short, is subject to considerable variation according to the demands of speaker, audience, and occasion.

The speaker himself makes the first demand justifying this pattern of organization in that his state of mind initially determines its use. The readiness of the audience to accept a pattern which does not provide for conclusive settlement of a problem is also a factor to be considered. Speech materials are of lesser influence on the selection or rejection of this pattern since they at once lend themselves to informing, persuading, or questioning. The occasion is a determinant in that the situation must be one in which men can deliberate. An atmosphere of puzzlement or bewilderment, of careful consideration, will sometimes suggest to you that a pattern of inquiry is your best scheme of organization.

MONROE'S MOTIVATED SEQUENCE

Arnold, Ehninger, and Gerber describe Monroe's Motivated Sequence as follows:

[It is] . . . a comprehensive pattern of organization based upon "the normal process of human thinking," and for this reason assumed to be particularly effective in motivating listeners to respond to the speaker's purpose.

As developed by its principal exponent, Professor Alan H. Monroe . . ., the motivated sequence provides a basic pattern by which all types of speeches may be organized, "needing only to be modified by omitting or lengthening certain parts according to the particular situation." In speeches to actuate, all five steps of the sequence are present. These bear the functional names of Attention,

Need, Satisfaction, Visualization, and Action. The first step catches the "attention" of the listeners; the second points to the existence of a problem or "need"; the third advances a proposal that will "satisfy" this need; the fourth "visualizes" the benefits to be derived from adopting the proposal; and the fifth, drawing upon the groundwork thus laid, makes a direct appeal for "action." In speeches to inform, only three steps—Attention, Need, and Satisfaction—are present. The function of the first is again to catch "attention"; the second shows the listeners why they "need" to know the information that is to be presented; and the third "satisfies" this "need" by presenting the information. Speeches to entertain may be either an extended development of the Attention Step or a mock-serious treatment of the speech to inform, convince, or actuate.[7]

This motivated sequence, more than any other, is psychologically planned to lead your audience's thinking naturally and easily from a vague interest in your subject to a definite acceptance of the attitude or action you are advocating. Each step in the sequence is built on the preceding steps.

The motivated sequence can be used in a broad variety of speeches, but it is chiefly useful when you face an audience that has little interest in your subject or when you want to arouse a strong and specific response in your audience.

Since this sequence is capable of adaptation to a large number of situations, it is enough to say that all of the elements in the speech situation—the audience, the materials, the speaker himself, and the occasion—are to be considered in successfully executing the particular variation of the pattern appropriate to a given speaking assignment.

ELIMINATION ORDER

"Elimination order" is a pattern of organization wherein several or all possible interpretations of a subject or solution to a problem are considered and all but one are pointed out as undesirable, impractical, or incorrect. This strategy is sometimes called the method of residues because the residue or whatever remains is the matter to be accepted by the audience.

---

[7] Reprinted from *The Speaker's Resource Book* by Carroll C. Arnold, Douglas Ehninger and John C. Gerber. Copyright © 1961 by Scott, Foresman and Company, Chicago. See p. 305.

The method of elimination is often used as the fourth step of what is otherwise a reflective sequence. This adaptation is especially advantageous when the speaker's purpose is to present an investigation for the purpose of persuading rather than inquiring. Thus, at the point of considering solutions, the discussion turns to the elimination of all possible solutions except the one the speaker advocates. The same kind of patterning may be applied during the second half of a problem-solution or need-remedy speech where more than one solution or remedy must be considered. Thus, this pattern may be thought of as a variation which can be adopted within either reflective or problem-solution systems or it may be treated as a scheme of organization applicable to a whole speech.

Influences affecting one's choice of this organizational system arise from the audience and the speaker. Both must be willing to investigate more than one possibility in the given situation. The speech materials, too, must offer for discussion more than one course of action or answer. The occasion also presents influencing factors affecting your choice: time must be available for full explanation and testing of several possibilities, and the atmosphere must be conducive to a several-sided consideration of the subject. Thus, once again, all four elements in the speech situation come into play to determine whether elimination order is a wise choice for disposing your speech materials.

We began this chapter by considering man's special need to find relationships and the public speaker's consequent need to clarify and give evidence of thought progression through his disposition of the ideas he seeks to communicate. Disposition of the content of a speech is, essentially, another form of adaptation to the human propensity to search for structure and unity in all things. Our examination of the normal parts of spoken discourse (introduction, body, and conclusion) and of patterns of organization has been in this sense a survey of how other speakers have learned to answer the universal demand for organization in spoken discourse.

Most of the time, as we have seen, a reasonable adaptation to the demands of audience, subject, speaker, and occasion will make it necessary that a speech begin by orienting the listener to speaker and subject (introduction). The properly adapted speech will continue with a systematically presented message that makes listening easier and surer by conforming to a structural pattern familiar to both listener and speaker. It will conclude with some reinforcement of the total experience that was the speech proper.

We have discussed the standard patterns of organization at length for several reasons. First, because speech making is a *public* art in which relationships must be exhibited in familiar, public terms. The standard patterns of organization are simply the most familiar—the most public—relational systems our society uses in verbal communication. Second, while not every speech can be effectively structured according to one of the standard patterns we have discussed, you will never make a speech having no segment that cannot be best conveyed if structured according to some one of the familiar patterns. These patterns, then, are optional systems among which you will constantly choose. We hope that by understanding what they can accomplish and what they cannot, you will be able to choose wisely, not haphazardly; choose, you will and must. Third, most speeches you will give and most of the situations in which you will give them will, in fact, permit you to elect one or another of the standard patterns as a model by which to dispose the material that constitutes the body of your discourse. And one thing is certainly clear: you *can* adapt to man's need to order his perceptions if you develop the body of a speech in accordance with one of these patterns; if you do not do so, you *may* achieve a uniquely brilliant presentation but, lacking experience, you are more likely to achieve obscurity. Fourth and finally, we have discussed patterns of organization in detail because we wished to demonstrate once more that the art of speaking is an art of social adaptation—one in which the demands of content, speaker, audience, and occasion must always be weighed in forming any artistic decision. This is no less true in the disposition of speech materials than in their invention.

E x e r c i s e s

Written

1. a. Choose a subject area, such as socialized medicine, current methods in secondary education, or the Democratic party in America today.
   b. Carefully write out three subject sentences for the subject area chosen. One sentence should be devised for a speech of *information*, another for a speech of *persuasion*, and the third for a speech of *inquiry*.

    c. Write out the main heads for each of the three subject sentences you
have composed.

2. Write an essay in which you evaluate the following introduction according to the requirements for a good introduction found on pp. 197–200.

The Annual February Phenomenon

    Three months from today, on another Wednesday evening, the
Cornell scene will be a lot different from what it is now. The tem-
perature will be 20 degrees colder; Goldwin Smith Hall will be dark as
final exams will have ended; the Library will be closed; and down beneath the Library, past the Baker Towers, the freshman dorm area will
be empty. The dorms themselves will not be empty, for every window
in the cinder-block cubicles will be brightly lit. We step inside a room
to find its pair of freshmen occupants sitting quietly; their cords are
shined, button-down collars buttoned down, hi-fi's spinning Shearing.
They seem to be waiting for something.

    There's a noise from outside the window. We walk over, look out,
and see the empty quadrangle of a moment before covered with a
writhing sea of tweed and occasional flashes of recognition pins. The
February phenomenon known as rushing has once more begun at Cornell University.

    We can briefly define rushing as the acquisition of new members
by fraternities and the affiliation with fraternities by freshmen. We
know that rushing is a lot more than this, for we have all seen it and
many of us have been through it from both sides.

    Let us consider rushing from the fraternity viewpoint. It often
degenerates into a cut-throat, name-calling conversation with the freshman during contact periods. Here the fraternity lacking positive things
to say about itself employs such vivid descriptions of other fraternities
as: "They're on social pro," or "They're split into cliques." We encounter rushing violations, breaches of the rules written to civilize the
Greek jungle. Two of the fraternity men in this audience are members
of a house that encountered flagrant rule violations by another house
last year. Things such as pickups being made ten minutes before proper
time by a house whose date had been broken are common. In this instance the freshman finds himself at Kappa Kappa Do instead of Delta
Delta Kappa.

    Hash sessions are another part of this February phenomenon.
These selection meetings are reminiscent of a cattle sale, and the inaccurate job of selection they do is apparent from the following anec-

dote, which occurred at one of our more prominent fraternities two years ago. Two members and the rushing chairman created a non-existent freshman named Fred Wendel. Fred was "contacted," brought over for dinner, and discussed that same evening in hash session. One of the men involved in the ruse spoke for Fred and said what a top man the rushee was. His sentiments were echoed by his partner, and a chorus of "Oh yeah, hot man, bring him back" mysteriously arose. Fred was "brought back," the same hash policy was repeated, but a few more men spoke up for Fred. This nonexistent freshman was unanimously voted a bid to the fraternity the following week. How good are the hash sessions?

The freshman, on the other hand, is a great variable. He may be a bubbling, extroverted individual, or he may be shy and withdrawn. Most freshmen are scared and ignorant when rushing begins; many are more ignorant when it ends. The intensive eight-day period puts them under great pressure, for the quick decision they are forced to make is probably the most important of their college careers. It decides where they are going to live and whom they are going to live with for three and a half years.

The manner in which rushing occurs, the attitudes displayed by the fraternities, and the tremendous pressures exerted so intensely on the freshmen indicate that a re-evaluation with regulation and modification of this February phenomenon is needed at Cornell.[8]

3. Assume that the following sets of main heads have been taken from the "bodies" of outlines for *informative* speeches. Evaluate each set in terms of (a) the wording of the main points, and (b) the over-all pattern of organization. Give detailed reasons for your judgments.

    a.   I. Every speech should have an introduction, body, and conclusion.

           II. Should the introduction get attention and make the speaker's purpose clear?

          III. A conclusion should summarize and put the entire speech into focus.

    b.   I. The social, political, and economic instability of underdeveloped countries is a potential breeding ground for Communism.

           II. We must increase our financial aid and technical assistance to these countries to head off the threat.

[8] This introduction was composed by Ronald Demer for an all-male class in persuasive speaking. Used by permission.

c.   I. Cornell University has a long and varied history.

           II. It is often called the "cow college of the Ivy League."

           III. A new library complex provides excellent facilities for research and study.

           IV. There are many fraternities and sororities on campus.

           V. Cornell is truly "an institution where any person can find instruction in any study."

           VI. What about Ithaca weather?

           VII. There is a varied program of extracurricular activities open to the student.

           VIII. Many distinguished professors.

           IX. There are many free lectures and other cultural events, including a fine art museum, concerts, plays, and athletic events.

4. Locate the text of a speech in an anthology of speeches, an issue of *Vital Speeches*, or a volume of the Reference Shelf series (H. W. Wilson Co.) devoted to speeches. Read the speech carefully. Identify the over-all structure of the speech. Support your labeling of the pattern in a paragraph or two in which you cite specific portions of the speech which led you to choose the label you did.

Oral

1. a. In class discussion choose several subject sentences for impromptu speeches. Such sentences as: "The automobile is primarily a vehicle for human transportation"; "Donation of blood to the Red Cross is worthwhile"; "Grades in college should be abolished" will serve well.

    b. Assign each of the subject sentences chosen to three different members of the class, and also assign to each of them *one* of the usable patterns of organization discussed in Chapter 8, e.g., chronological, spatial, problem-solution, causal, etc.

    c. Allow time for each of the three students to prepare a two- to three-minute impromptu speech utilizing the pattern assigned.

    d. After hearing the speeches, discuss orally the suitability of the pattern used in relation to the subject sentence assigned. Also evaluate the speaker's ability to produce a recognizable pattern of organization on short notice.

9   *Disposition:*
Outlining

Outlining the speech on paper is essential for careful disposition (ordering) of materials and adequate preparation for extemporaneous and manuscript speaking. Limited use of outlines is possible in impromptu speaking. Outlines are usually skeletal maps by means of which speakers design and review the structural details of speeches, though sometimes these plans are made so complete they almost become manuscripts.

Functions of Outlines

The speaker must decide in his planning what kind of outline is best for him. He must employ full sentences, phrases, or words to keep thoughts clear and sharp. Beginners find sentence outlines most helpful, since full sentences express the complete thought to be presented at each point in the speech. Use of full sentences insures that the speaker has framed each complete thought and understands its juxtaposition and relationship to other complete thoughts. While a thought may stand in the mind of the speaker and be symbolized on paper by a word, indeed by a symbol even simpler than a word such as a cross or a circle, most beginners find themselves handicapped when using shorthand outlines resembling grocery lists. The more experienced the speaker is, the more likely he is to be successful in using abbreviated methods in outlining. It is well to recall, however, that some of the most famous speakers, Woodrow Wilson and Franklin Roosevelt for example, wrote out every word of their important speeches.

If outlining is to function with maximum effectiveness for the speaker, his method must be suited to his individual needs. Outlining serves the speaker chiefly; the audience seldom sees the outline. Utility and speaker-adaptation are the marks of a good outline; no rigid set of rules for structuring a speech on paper are possible.

Speakers may resort to various devices to jog their memories. One speaker may underline main heads in his outline in red; another may place asterisks at various points. Still another will draw pictures. Yet another will include notations of the kinds of material he is including, e.g., example, story, statistics; he may even mark the vocal variations he wants to produce, e.g., loud, soft. No one can say that any of these practices is wrong; for the outline is an instrument, a tool for the speaker. To this there is but one exception and that occurs in the learning situation.

When you are asked to submit an outline to your teacher, you are asked to do so in order to receive helpful, constructive criticism. Your outline, then, is no longer a private paper. It is, instead, a record of preparation to be shared with another interested person who is to make suggestions. This shared paper must be understood by your teacher as well as by you. Since this is so, you, as the writer, must take special care to make ideas and their relationships clear both visually and verbally. You and your reader must both agree upon a system of outlining. You may be asked to employ full sentences, at least to begin with, for the simple reason that they will promote fuller comprehension than phrases or words. A single word offered in support of another single word may not be comprehensible to your teacher and it will not indicate whether you have thought through your ideas. For instance, you may know what you will say when you have written the word "Economic" and listed "Cost" and "Profit" as supporting ideas, but your teacher, functioning as a critic, may not see clear-cut connections between these sketchy symbols. He may be led to conclude that at this particular stage of speech preparation your ideas have not been fully enough refined, that they are still in vague or fuzzy condition. You must take special care in preparing your papers so that ideas and their relationships are kept clear.

As a teaching device your instructor may prescribe that you not only construct a "content" outline showing the ideas in your speech but that you add technical labels. He may ask you to indicate your kinds of proof and amplification, sources of attention, or the pattern of structure exemplified. When these labels are added to an outline, you have in reality two outlines. One maps the ideas to be uttered; the other maps the strategy and tactics. It is common for the inexperienced to mix these two types of mapping. In making outlines you will not give symbols to Introduction, Body, Conclusion, because these are not part of the idea structure of the speech. It is useless to write simply "story" or "statistics" beside a subpoint number without indicating what you intend to say. To identify your tactics or methods is useful for learning or teaching purposes. It enables you to straighten out in your own mind just what it is you are doing as you order ideas and just what kinds of ideas you are ordering. Sometimes your teacher may ask you to use these technical labels in order to test you. But such labels *alone* are not sufficient for you to tell others what you will say. Alone, they produce an unsatisfactory paper for you to refer to should you decide to deliver a second version of your speech before a second audience. You can readily see that an outline reading as follows would be of little help were you to try to determine what the speaker who made it intends to say or has said.

Introduction

   I. Story.—Using novelty, stereotypes, familiarity. Chronological order.
  II. Subject sentence.
 III. Definitions.
     a. By function.
     b. By classification.

Body

 IV. Argument.—Open proposal pattern.
     a. Quotation—familiar.
     b. Statistics—visual aids.
  V. Argument.—Developed inductively.
     a. Report of Experiment.
     b. Report of Second Experiment.

Conclusion

VI. A Summary.

This record of a speech would be of little value to either a critical teacher aiming to evaluate supports or proofs, subject sentences, or attention values, or to a speaker trying to recapture from his personal preparation files what he said six months ago.

Common Practices

There are no hard and fast rules for making outlines for speeches, but there are universal practices which have been found trustworthy. These practices in speech composition satisfy the requirements of the speaker, the material, the audience, and the occasion. They promote the clarity, the organic unity, and the adaptation so necessary for successful speaking. Recording your plan in systematic fashion results in a visual image of the speech which is helpful to you and indirectly to your audience. Exact and methodical planning insures audience understanding and your own control over your material.

What, then, should you do in constructing an outline which will assist you in remembering what to say when? What should you look for as you check over your outline? Provided you are following commonly accepted practices, you should look for:

A clear indication of the basic divisions of the speech: Introduction, Body (sometimes labelled Discussion or Proof), *and Conclusion.* Since these labels are not parts of the idea structure of the speech but are technical notations, they will not normally be given symbols. Symbols such as *I, A,* 1, *a,* etc. ought to be reserved as indicators of relationships. Usually the names of the basic divisions of your speech are centered on the page and go unsymbolized. To place them so insures that you have an introduction and a conclusion and that you are aware of what constitutes these portions of your speech. In those infrequent instances when no introduction is used, its absence is readily apparent if one forms the practice of formally identifying each division actually to be included.

A consistent system of (a) symbolization and (b) indentation. The designation and physical arrangement of ideas are distinct aids in clarifying relationships within the speech and in helping you to remember those relationships. The system of symbols you use is of little consequence, but consistency in their use is essential. It matters little whether Roman numerals, capital letters, or Arabic numerals are used to indicate main heads and subheads. What matters is that each time a type of symbol occurs it signifies that the ideas thus identified are of approximately the same importance or weight. Uniformity in symbolization will clearly indicate the value you assign to your material and the different symbols assigned will show which ideas are subsidiary to which. Since you will be working out a structure idea by idea, you should place only one symbol before any one idea. This serves as a caution against composing compound sentences containing more than one thought. If you follow the rule: one symbol for *each* idea, you will be reminded to break compound statements in two, giving each of the ideas a separate symbol. You will need to check very carefully in making a phrase outline to see that each symbol does stand beside an idea rather than beside a fragment of one or a phrase that represents—for you—several ideas.

Indentation, the physical arrangement of ideas, is a further aid in revealing values assigned and in stirring the memory. If each major and minor new idea is indicated by a particular indentation, that fact announces to the speaker that it is time to embark on a new phase of his thought structure. Ideas subsidiary to other ideas should be indented under the subsuming thought. In this way it will be easy to *see* that support and amplification are subordinate points. Your visual image of your speech will then be a network of ideas with the least important ones indented farthest from the left-hand margin of the page. Though it may be that none of the ideas you set down on the page is, ideally, expendable, it will in all probability be less of a calamity should an idea given minor weight (one farthest indented) be forgotten.

Absence of single subpoints. Wherever one idea is subordinated to another, it indicates a splitting of the subsuming idea for purposes of amplification or support. Usually more than one idea, that is to say more than one piece of information, is needed for adequate development of a point. Yet, there are instances where one definition, one example, or one opinion may suffice to clarify or prove to an acceptable degree. The audience needs may on some occasions be met with one and only one item of amplification. More often it will happen that a single subordinate item would be better reinforced if there were other, parallel items. If not, it may very well be combined with the idea which envelopes or stands above it. An outline containing a multitude of single subpoints should be viewed with suspicion. It is likely that the ideas contained in it have not been developed to the point of audience acceptance and that necessary information and proof have been overlooked. Only when you are absolutely sure that one and only one piece of proof is necessary and desirable should a subpoint be allowed to stand alone.

Discreteness of ideas. In outlines, ideas should not be lumped together nor should they overlap. An outline is a structure intended to insure clarity of relationships, which dictates that each idea stand separately within the structure. The need to reveal clearly the relationship of each idea to other ideas is an additional argument for full-sentence outlining. Sentences, if correctly constructed, are expressions of complete thoughts the precise nature of which cannot be easily missed. You must be wary of the compound sentence in outlining since it contains more than one idea, making it impossible to follow the principle of one symbol, one idea. "Ands" and "ors" should rarely appear in the sentences of an outline; they bear special checking when they do appear. Only so can you be sure that relationships are clear.

Appropriate symbolization and placement of subject sentences. Since the core idea (subject sentence, main proposition, central idea, or specific purpose) is the most important idea in the speech and is the focal point about which all other development revolves and from which all details fan out, it deserves the highest rank in symbolization. This main proposition or assertion should be unmistakable in your outline. It should never appear as a subpoint nor should it be indented beneath any other point. In deductive speech patterns this sentence will usually appear near the end of the Introduction or near the beginning of the Body of the speech. No matter where it appears, the central idea should be designated by the symbol indicating the most weight or value. Graphically, it should at least have the same rank by indentation as the other most important items in the section. The same is true in symbolizing and in indenting the central idea when outlining inductive patterns, such as the withheld-proposal sequence. The main idea should be given the symbol and indentation that will reveal at a glance that it is a statement not outranked in importance by any other ideas in the section of the speech in which it appears. Whether the central idea appears in the Introduction, Body, or Conclusion, it is *the* important idea in that division of your outline.

Clear transitions. Transitions should be uniformly indicated and set off from the rest of the structure. Points of linkage and internal summaries, parts of the over-all speech structure, should be clearly indicated. If they are symbolized and indented in the same manner as other parts of the outline, they should be given technical labels such as "Transition" or "Internal Summary." A common practice is to treat these portions of the speech differently from main points or subpoints, omitting symbols, but marking them off by enclosing them in brackets or parentheses. This practice shows that the speaker gave careful attention to how he would move from one point or subpoint to another and to the necessity for repetition and review.

If the above practices are observed, a diagram of an outline may well look like this:

Title
Introduction

I. ....
   A. ....
   B. ....
II. ....
      (Transition: ....)

Body

I. ....
   A. ....
   B. ....
      1. ....
         a. ....
         b. ....
      2. ....
         a. ....
         b. ....
   C. ....
      1. ....
      2. ....
         a. ....
         b. ....
            (1) ....
            (2) ....
      (Transition: ....)
II. ....
   A. ....
      1. ....
         a. ....

b. ....

c. ....

2. ....

(Transition: ....)

B. ....

1. ....

a. ....

b. ....

(1) ....

(2) ....

(3) ....

(a) ....

(b) ....

c. ....

d. ....

(1) ....

(2) ....

2. ....

a. ....

b. ....

(Internal Summary: ....

....)

III. ....

A. ....

1. ....

a. ....

b. ....

2. ....

B. ....

(Transition and/or Internal Summary ....

....)

Conclusion

I. ....

A. ....

B. ....

C. ....

II. ....

Bibliography
(or Statement of Sources)

....
....
....
....
....
....

Two items appearing in this diagram remain to be considered, title and bibliography or statement of sources.

Titles

The final act in the composition of your speech is ordinarily the selection of a title. Informal situations make titles less necessary than those in which you will be introduced, but formulating a title is an excellent practice, giving the discourse a finished quality. A title provides a short label for use by those reporting your speech or recording the event of which your speech was a part. Titles are normally composed last since that is when you can best cast your eye back over the total composition and decide upon a phrase characterizing it. There are times, however, when a title will evolve from the very first pieces of data you encounter in the process of invention.

Good titles meet demands made in the main by the audience and the subject matter of the speech. Good titles (1) attract attention by their brevity and provocativeness, and (2) reveal to some degree what the speech is about by emphasizing its theme.

A title must be brief for practical reasons. Sentences rarely serve, and even phrases can be too long. An audience stops listening before the end of a title such as: "The History and Significance of the Indian Tribes in the Western New York Area from the Years 1770 to 1790 with Special Emphasis upon the Youth Between the Ages of 12–18 and Their Role in War Making." A better title would be "The Warring Indian Braves of Western New York During the Late Eighteenth Century." A long title is usually impractical for publicity purposes. A well-designed title should be short enough to fit on a poster or into a one- or two-column newspaper

233

head. When a speech has no title or a long and unarresting one, the news-papermen or poster makers often invent one. Reporters did just that when they retitled Franklin D. Roosevelt's "Speech to the Teamsters' Union, September 23, 1944," the "Fala Speech." They also shortened the title of his "Speech at the Dedication of the Outerlink Bridge, Chicago, Illinois, October 5, 1937," to "The Quarantine Speech." The second of these "tag titles" does identify the essential theme of the speech but the first does not.

Your titles must arouse the curiosity of audiences if they are to hold interest. Images can help since they serve as shorthand symbols which stir up mental pictures. William Jennings Bryan's "Cross of Gold" is a classic example, yet we can think of other lesser-known titles such as "Skeletons All" or "Little Fences and Barriers." Such images in titles not only arouse initial attention but they are remembered long after the speech has been delivered.

But the three titles given as examples in the preceding paragraph do not fulfill all of the functions of a good title, because they do not tell us with much clarity what the speech is about. They are riddle metaphors but not good ones, for they do not meet the requirement Aristotle wisely noted when he said, ". . . the metaphors by which we give names to nameless things must not be farfetched; rather we must draw them from kindred and similar things; the kinship must be seen the moment the words are uttered. . . ."[1] The three titles under consideration are not as poor as other titles chosen by undiscerning students: "A Hope for the Future," "You Ought to Try," "A Happy Solution." These are not only vague and uninteresting but could fit any number of speeches. These are "waste-basket" or "umbrella" titles. They contain or cover everything and noth-ing. A good title at least hints at the core idea of the speech. F. Paul McConkey's title, "Roses in the Snow," for a sermon on the beauties of old age is a good one in that it is not only brief and provocative but relevant. "Idle Worship" as a title for an attack on Madison-Avenue religion, and the title of a eulogy of Henry Ford, "The Man with the Model-T Dream," are titles that fulfill their functions better than others considered here. Lest these seem too cute, which becomes the danger when we strain

[1] From *The Rhetoric of Aristotle* trans. and ed. by Lane Cooper. Copyright, 1932, Lane Cooper, p. 188, Bk III, Ch. 2. Reprinted by permission of the publisher Appleton-Century-Crofts.

too hard for good titles, consider Andrew Dickson White's title, "The Battlefields of Science" or Nancy Myers' indictment of television entitled "Moppet Manipulation."

Bibliographies

It may be said that the educated man is one who knows the sources of his knowledge and his opinions. He is able to acknowledge how and where he acquired his ideas and facts, and he often does so voluntarily. In preparing outlines and manuscripts he annotates ideas and quotations not his own as a natural recognition of other people's contributions.

You may be asked to include a bibliography or "Statement of Sources" with your outline. Occasionally acknowledgements of sources may appear in the outline proper, especially where these sources are to be mentioned in the speech itself. More often such acknowledgements will be appended at the end of the outline as a communication to the instructor or other reader. Your teacher, as a critic, wants to know *what you actually found useful.* There are many forms for bibliographical entries. The important things are to be complete and consistent. The following forms may be used when you are asked to cite your sources. Note that comment on the scope and value of printed sources is enclosed in square brackets. The notes on other materials are given in informal description.

Observation:
During the week of August 11–17, 1963, I took part in ROTC naval maneuvers and saw the things I describe under Point I of the Introduction.

Interview:
On May 12, 1963, I talked with President J. B. Smith of X Company for about an hour and got the ideas on management's problems which appear in Section III of this outline.

I have drawn at many points on the courses I have taken in business, economics and oral and written communication.

Articles:
    A. From Periodicals:
        Faulkner, William, "On Fear: The South in Labor," *Harper's Magazine,* CCXII (June, 1956), 29–34.

[Emphasizes the place economic and social fears have in Southern resistance to racial integration in schools. Ideas from this source are incorporated in supporting material for the second main division of my argument.]

    B. From Books:

        Spencer, Herbert, "The Philosophy of Style," in W. T. Brewster, ed., *Representative Essays on the Theory of Style* (New York: Macmillan, 1921), pp. 167–208.

[Ideas on the principles of economy in style which I explain under Point II are taken from this essay.]

    C. From General Reference Books:

        "John Donne," *Encyclopaedia Brittanica*, 9th ed. (New York, 1878).[2]

[This account provided me with most of the biographical facts used in my speech.]

Newspapers:

    A. From signed articles, editorials, and news accounts:

        Folliard, Edward T., "As a Thousand Cheer," *The Washington Post* (September 24, 1944), p. 1.[3]

[Information on audience reaction to Franklin Roosevelt's "Teamsters' Union Speech," September 23, 1944, and some of the details of the speaking occasion were drawn from this article.]

    B. From unsigned articles, editorials, and news accounts:

        "Bushwhacking," *The Washington Post* (September 25, 1944), p. 10.

[This single, critical reaction to Franklin Roosevelt's "Teamsters' Union Speech," September 23, 1944, furnished amplification for Point III, b.]

Pamphlets (where the author or editor is not credited):

    The High School in a Changing World, The American Association of School Administrators (Washington, D.C., 1958).

[This pamphlet provided me with the classification of current trends in high school curricula.]

Sample Outlines

The two outlines which follow are the work of students and will serve to illustrate good outlining procedures. The first is an outline for a

---

[2] In citing any *Brittanica* since 1932 it is advisable to use the date of printing: "John Donne," *Encyclopaedia Brittanica* (1952).

[3] If the article appears in a numbered section of the newspaper, the citation would then read: ". . . (September 24, 1944), sec. 5, p. 1.

speech of information twelve minutes in length. It contains good examples of structure and of outlining mechanics.

Tornado[4]

Introduction

I. It is obvious that most of us here are not particularly worried about the possibility of a tornado in Ithaca.

    A. But, did you know that a tornado can hit any part of the United States during any season?

        1. (Visual Aid Number I—A Chart showing tornado incidence.)

        2. In 1958, there were 19 tornadoes spotted in the middle of the winter over Lake Champlain.

        3. Some of you may remember the tornado which hit Worcester, Massachusetts in 1953.

    B. Since 1953, many large cities have been hit by these violent storms.

        1. In the latest issue of the *Saturday Evening Post*, Mr. E. D. Fales, Jr. states in his article, "The Tornado Hunters," that "twisters in recent years have smashed into Flint; Waco; Cleveland; Chicago; St. Louis; Miami; Vicksburg; Dallas; Fargo; Worcester, Massachusetts; and Columbus, Georgia."

        2. A tornado warning radar has been set up on top of the RCA Building in New York City.

        3. During 1960, 1,200 tornadoes were spotted, of which 600 touched the ground.

            a. Again, in the latest *Post*, Mr. Fales states that since 1953, 1,200 people have been killed and 13,000 injured by tornadoes during a period when there were 5,000 confirmed storms.

            b. Over $200,000,000 damage has occurred during the past year.

    C. It is estimated that more damage and loss of life could occur in Central New York State than in any other part of the country.

        1. It is the only part of the whole nation that has *no* tornado warning system.

        2. Even if there were a warning, most of the residents wouldn't pay attention to it.

II. In all of nature there is no storm which concentrates as much fury in a single area as the tornado.

III. Let us investigate some of the theories as to how tornadoes are formed, what their characteristics are, and how they are detected and predicted.

[4] By Jonathan E. Emerson. Used by permission.

Body

I. There are several theories about how a tornado originates.

   A. First, there is the lightning theory of Dr. Bernard Vonnegut of Arthur D. Little, Inc., a research firm in Cambridge, Massachusetts: "When lightning occurs it may flash so often in one path that it heats up a 'chimney' in the atmosphere; this 'chimney' sucks up air in a great swirl, the tornado is started, and opposing electrical charges in the clouds help keep it going."

   B. Second, there is the warm air—cool air theory.

      1. A layer of cool air forms above a layer of warm air.

         a. A hole develops in the cool air.

         b. The warm air rushes through the hole, like water going down a drain.

         c. The resulting swirling funnel contains 600 mph winds.

   C. Finally, there is the Venturi Theory that a tornado is caused by the prevailing westerlies.

      1. They blow across a hole in the clouds creating suction which starts the tornado.

      2. Electrical charges which are a cause of the whirling motion serve to concentrate the tail after the start.

(These three theories as to how tornadoes originate lead us to speculate on just what it is that happens when a tornado is experienced.)

II. Eyewitnesses of these fierce storms have noted some of the characteristics of a tornado.

   A. Tornadoes sound like:

      1. A humming or buzzing of a million bees;

      2. The sound of a thousand locomotives.

   B. The storm's tail is usually black and vicious.

      1. This tail is from 10 to 400 feet in diameter.

      2. Its color is due to dirt and debris that have been sucked up.

      3. There is often a strange blue glow over 100 feet thick at the top.

      4. There is also a strange blue fire around the base which is accompanied by the smell of sulphur.

   C. In an interview after a tornado near Hickman Hills, Missouri, Robert Jackson of that city said: "I noticed the house next door just kind of raise up on its foundation as if you put a bomb in it. The whole thing just seemed to lift up off the foundation—kinda sideways—kinda raised up and veered off a bit. Then it exploded. It caved in in every direction and the wood went everywhere." Mr. Jackson continues: "I saw several cars go off the lot across the highway. The wind is getting rough when it can throw these cars up. I remember seeing one car sailing right along the outside of the funnel—the black, dirty, filthy part of it. There it was, just one car sailing through the air 30 to 40 feet high."

(Such descriptions as Mr. Jackson's prompt us to inquire into just what efforts are being made to detect the onslaught of such mass destruction.)

III. The effort to predict tornadoes has yielded several important discoveries about these cyclones.

   A. There are several things which must occur before a tornado can develop.

      1. There must be two large air masses.

         a. One must be of rich, warm moisture (90 degrees F.).

         b. The other must be dry and cooler (60 degrees F.).

      2. There must be a disturbance in the area such as a front of giant electrical storms.

         a. Huge thunder clouds are necessary.

            (1) Some are 12 miles in height.

            (2) They can't be any lower than 10,000 ft.

         b. There must be high lightning frequency of at least 20 bolts per second.

      3. Low- and high-pressure centers must run together.

         a. (Visual Aid Number 2—A chart showing juxtaposition of low- and high-pressure centers.)

         b. A large pressure drop must precede the tornado.

   B. Once the storm is formed it is almost impossible to tell how powerful it will be or where it will go, for it is as the author of an article in the *Senior Scholastic* has said: "Tornadoes are fickle. Most travel at a speed of 25 to 40 miles per hour. Still others vary. Some 'live' just a few minutes. But one lasted five hours. It visited destruction on town after town for more than 220 miles. On some terror-filled days, as many as 28 twisters hammer the nation."

   C. The Severe Local Storm Warning Center (better known as SELS) was formed in 1958 to warn people of possible tornadoes.

      1. It is described in the latest issue of the *Saturday Evening Post*.

      2. This system has saved thousands of lives.

(And so we have seen how tornadoes originate, their characteristics, and several important discoveries concerning them. What can we conclude, generally?)

Conclusion

I. There is no justification for the local complacency with regard to tornadoes.

II. More and more is being uncovered about this kind of storm.

III. The information presented here is helping the U.S. Weather Bureau, through the Severe Local Storm Warning Center, to predict where and when these storms will occur, thus enabling it to warn citizens in these areas.

IV. Clayton F. Van Thullenar, research chief and top administrator of the Severe Local Storm Warning Center, has declared: "We go from mystery to mystery. The more we learn, the more impossible it seems that tornadoes can really exist. By all the rules, Nature can't possibly put so much violence in a dot. And yet, there you are."

Bibliography

1. Anonymous, "Best Pictured Tornado; Dallas," *Life*, XLII (April 15, 1957), 48–49.
[Material here, including pictures, enabled me to describe vividly tornadoes under Point II of the body.]

2. Anonymous, "Definite Weather Pattern Needed for Tornadoes," *Science News Letter*, LXXIII (June 21, 1958), 392.
[Subpoint A under Point III of the body was derived largely from this helpful account.]

3. Anonymous, "Hope for Tornado Control," *Science News Letter*, LXXI, (April 20, 1957), 246.
[Supplementary material, in the end not very valuable, on Point III, C of the body was found here.]

4. Anonymous, "New Warning System for Tornadoes," *Look*, XXIII (October 13, 1959), 60 ff.
[Information on the Severe Local Storm Warning Center was supplemented by material found in this article.]

5. Anonymous, "Scientist Has Method for Detecting Tornadoes," *Science News Letter*, LXXI (June 8, 1957), 360.
[This was an extremely interesting article on a particular person's idea as to how tornadoes might be predicted. It would have been included under Point III, C of the body but my time limit prohibited me from including it.]

6. Anonymous, "Seeing Them Coming: Doppler Radar," *Newsweek*, LI (May 5, 1958), 79.

[This article provided information on the radar system mentioned in my introduction.]

7. Anonymous, "Tiros I Photographs Tornado-Producing Cloud," *Science News Letter*, LXXVIII (August 6, 1960), 88.
   [Interesting and clarifying photographs but not really very helpful in the construction of my speech.]

8. Anonymous, "Tornadoes: How, Why, When, and Where," *Senior Scholastic*, LXXIV (February 27, 1959), 35.
   [This article was helpful in the development of Point II of the body of my speech.]

9. Armagnac, A. P., "Tornadoes: Giant Electrical Machines," *Popular Science*, CLXXVI (April, 1960), 100–102 ff.
   [Armagnac aided me in the construction of the explanation under sub-point A of Point III of the body.]

10. Fales, E. D., Jr., "The Tornado Hunters," *Saturday Evening Post*, CCXXIV (May 20, 1961), 24–25.
    [Fales was most helpful to me in providing the figures on incidence and life damage of tornadoes used in my introduction.]

11. Lear, J., "How Stormy Weather is Born," *Saturday Review*, XXXXII (July 4, 1959), 31–36.
    [This account contained particularly good material on how a tornado originates.]

The second outline presented as an example of proper procedures is for a persuasive speech. This outline is reprinted here just as it was submitted by the student. It is for a speech six minutes in length.

Vacation Time[5]

Introduction

I. When we go home this Thanksgiving many of us will again be confronted by our parents or by our former high school teachers with many questions.

   A. "Now that you've been away to school," they will say, "what do you think of the education you received in high school? What suggestions can you give us to help our students?"

   B. This morning I would like to suggest the answer that you should give to these questions this Thanksgiving.

II. I'm pretty sure that many of you here, especially those who are engi-

[5] By William Aylesworth. Used by permission.

neers now, were in some type of accelerated or experimental science course in high school.

A. In fact, ever since Sputnik I in 1957 our nation's high schools have greatly accelerated their science programs.

B. However, during this same period, and with the possible exception of foreign languages, there has been little or no change in the liberal studies given in high school.

C. By liberal studies I, as an engineer, mean everything except science and mathematics.

III. Therefore we should answer our former teachers' questions by saying that we must improve the liberal studies given in our high schools.

A. Our teachers and you might now ask, "Why should we change?"

B. Here are three reasons.

Discussion

I. First of all, the liberal courses now being taught in high school do not fit today's students and today's problems.

A. Let's look at two lists—the first a part of a list of the major problems of teen-agers as reported by 6,000 representative American teen-agers to the Mid-Century Committee for Children and Youth in 1959.

1. War

2. Sex

3. Racial and Religious Discrimination

B. The other list is a list of the major social issues most frequently *banned* as taboo for discussion in high schools according to over 500 school superintendents who reported to the National Education Association Committee on Tenure and Academic Freedom.

1. Communism, Socialism, and National Politics

2. Sex

3. Race Relations

C. It seems obvious that the very issues which should be most discussed in a high school liberal studies program—the teen-agers' problems —are in fact the things that are often left out of the curriculum altogether.

II. Secondly, among those courses that are included in liberal studies, there are very few that are accelerated or taught with the gifted student in mind.

A. When all the tenth and eleventh graders of a large suburban California high school were asked to name the elective courses they would like to take, they named the following: Russian, psychology, sociology, modern philosophy, and anthropology.

  B. Yet William Brickman, the editor of *School and Society* magazine, gives this remarkably similar list of areas of liberal study that would enrich the high school education of the academically endowed but are *not* commonly taught in U.S. high schools: comparative literature, psychology, philosophy, sociology, and history of science.

  C. And what about the subjects that are available in high school?

    1. Many of the courses sound like these examples given by John F. Gunmere of the Wm. Penn Charter School in Philadelphia— "Clicking with the Crowd," "My Duties as a Baby Sitter," or "Developing School Spirit."

    2. How do these subjects compare with literature or sociology— not too accelerated, are they?

(We have seen that high schools may steer clear of many liberal subjects altogether, and offer only limited material in others. Now let's look at the actual methods of teaching these subjects.)

III. These methods constitute my third reason why we must improve our high school liberal studies program.

  A. As many of us who did not exactly "bomb" English I and II know, liberal studies must teach us to think, not simply memorize.

  B. Our high school courses must be more than just guessing games.

    1. What is more valuable in an English course, memorizing the names of the characters of a novel, or comparing and contrasting selections as to mood, author's intent, or use of literary devices?

    2. And what is the use of a U.S. history course like the one I had in high school in which every test was either true-false or multiple choice?

  C. Julian C. Stanley of the University of Wisconsin sums this point up by saying that getting true enrichment from liberal studies takes more finesse than finance, and that we need as much of this finesse as can be developed through the ingenuity, resourcefulness, and energy of our high school teachers.

Conclusion

I. So if you stop in at your old high school this Thanksgiving, tell your former teachers why the liberal studies they teach need improvement.

  A. Too many subjects are taboo—the curriculum should be more inclusive.

B. The courses available are not a challenge—they should have accelerated or advanced sections.

C. Too many of the courses are taught for memory—they should be taught for enrichment.

II. The advice you give this Thanksgiving may have an important effect on the class of 1970.

Statement of Sources

1. Anonymous, "The Inspector General," *Time* (Sept. 14, 1959), 70–72.
2. Anonymous, "How Good Is Your High School?" *U.S. News and World Report* (January 9, 1959), 51–53.
3. Anonymous, "Conant on High Schools," *America* (February 21, 1959), 590.
   [These three sources provided general information on American education.]
4. Brickman, William, "A Secondary Curriculum for the Academically Minded," *School and Society* (April 11, 1959), 177.
   [Brickman gave information useful for topic II in the discussion.]
5. Gross, Richard, "Education's Central Dilemma—What Knowledge Is of Most Worth?" *School and Society* (February 13, 1960), 66–69.
   [This source formed the basis of my discussion of topic I.]
6. Stanley, J. C., "Enriching High School Subjects for Intellectually Gifted Students," *School and Society* (April 11, 1959), 170–171.
   [Useful statistics and information for topic III.]

An outline is the basic tool by which extemporaneous speakers fix the design of their speeches as compositions, test the reasonableness of that design, represent to themselves and others the relationships among their thoughts, and fix their speech plans in their own minds. A completed outline is a visual representation of how speech materials are going to be disposed or handled in the speech to come. Both the making of an outline and review of it are invaluable aids to what ancient writers on rhetoric had in mind when they used the Latin term, *memoria*—the speaker's ultimate command of his material, his plan, and his own thinking processes in the moments of delivery. These things being the justifications for making outlines, the only legitimate justifications for any formal procedures in outlining must be that they are practically helpful. It is on just such a practical basis that we have tried to weigh the merits of outlining procedures in Chapter 9.

The mechanics of outlining are good or bad in proportion to how well they serve your needs and the needs of any constructive critic. Six common practices in outlining are invariably helpful:

1. Clear identification of the basic divisions of the speech: Introduction, Body, and Conclusion.
2. Use of consistent systems of symbolization and indentation to signal the relative importance of the relationships among ideas.
3. Recognition that the appearance of single subpoints in an outline is likely to indicate that a relationship has not been clearly thought out.
4. Firm adherence to the rule of discreteness in outlining: one thought per symbol; one symbol per thought.
5. Clear and unmistakable identification of the central idea or subject sentence.
6. Clear and unmistakable identification, in uniform fashion, of important transitions and internal summaries.

The sample outlines we have provided for your study and analysis conform to these practices in most details. They illustrate the general principles of disposition we have discussed in Chapter 8.

Exercises

Written

1. Arrange the ten statements below as an outline for the body of a speech. There is no title, introduction, or conclusion. Select the subject sentence and give it proper place and status in your outline.

   In Mississippi there is one doctor for every 1500 inhabitants.
   One and a half million man-years of work are lost annually in the U.S. because of illness.
   There is an uneven distribution of doctors in the country.
   Thirteen hundred counties have no hospital facilities.
   There is need for a change in the present system of medical service.
   In New York State there is one doctor for every 487 inhabitants.
   The nation sustains large losses from preventable illness.
   Medical services are not available to all parts of our population.
   Thirty thousand cancer victims could be saved each year through more surgery and radium treatment.
   Hospital services are unevenly distributed in the country.

2. Make a list of suggestions for improvement of the outline by William Aylesworth entitled "Vacation Time." (See pp. 241–244.)
3. In a sentence or two evaluate each of the following speech titles:
   a. "What You Must Do"
   b. "Acres of Diamonds"
   c. "Billy the Kid—Juvenile Delinquent?"
   d. "A Case for Socialized Medicine in the United States Today with Special Emphasis upon the Role of the General Practitioner in the Rural Areas"
   e. "Goya"
   f. "From Trees to Paper"
   g. "Suburbia: A New Way of Life"
   h. "Some Evidences of the Pedagogical Philosophy and Techniques of Quintilian as They Are Found in Modern Speech Education"
   i. "The Sleeping Dragon"
   j. "The Eternal Verities"

Oral

1. Outline a speech by one of your classmates as you listen to him deliver it. Arrange for a conference with him during which you compare the outline you composed with the outline he used in preparing the speech. In your conference look for similarities and differences between the outlines and discuss why these occurred as they did.
2. Compose an outline for a six-minute speech of information or persuasion. Observe the suggestions made in this chapter and in Chapter 8.

10   *Style*

Among all other lessons this should first be learned, that wee never affect any straunge inkehorne termes, but to speake as is commonly received: neither seeking to be over fine, nor yet living over-carelesse using our speeche as most men doe, and ordering our wittes as the fewest have done.

THOMAS WILSON, *Arte of Rhetorique*[1]

Man's true expression of inner self probably emerges more clearly in style than in any other aspect of his speech making. The study of the ways in which a speaker symbolizes his thoughts reveals his capacities to discriminate among meanings, to conceive his ideas clearly, and to represent them to others precisely. The study of men choosing and refining their ideas leads us to generalizations concerning human behavior. Styles reflect men's adjustments to their times. The relatively unguarded expression found in speaking of all kinds mirrors habits of thinking with special sharpness. Thus it is that examination of style provides information for conclusions about men's accommodations to society and in turn about society itself. Words, figures of speech, and images alone and in combination reflect the minds of men so well that the study of spoken style is humane in the truest sense.

Speeches consist of ideas converted into words. *Acoustic* words are essential for all *oral* communication and expression. Whenever we say anything *orally* acoustic symbols stimulate the audience. These sounds are the symbols that stand for our ideas. We encode our thoughts and express our emotions. We depend upon the listener to decode the message and to arrive at the intended meanings and feelings. Ideas may be located and organized with skill and great care, as we have shown in the preceding chapters; but the work of speaking is not finished until the ideas are couched in the

---

[1] Thomas Wilson, *Arte of Rhetorique* (London, 1585), p. 162.

language of speech, voiced, and given further meaning through bodily action.

It is readily apparent that the words we choose as symbols of our ideas, their capacity to stir up meanings in our listeners' minds, and the influence of their combination and structuring are inseparable from the ideas themselves. For instance, one may say, "I think I'll go to bed and go to sleep." Or, "Methinks I will betake me to my nocturnal couch and lie in the arms of Morpheus." Or, "I guess I'll hit the sack and konk out." Even though basically similar in idea, none of these three sentences expresses exactly the same meaning. Since the primary concern in public speaking is to arouse exact meaning, success in speaking depends very much upon the speaker's ability to choose and combine language symbols for aural reception. To put it another way, if we are to be practical we must be concerned with the creation of "style" in public speaking.

Style in speaking is that part of the art which emerges from choices and combinations in language, their grammatical construction, and their psychological impact. Style, this third canon of rhetoric, stands for some of the most complex and personal of all the processes involved in speech making. These are the processes that become our concern once we have selected ideas and arranged them in the logical and psychological sequences we deem most effective. Inevitably some language decisions are made during stages of invention and disposition; but *whole* speeches almost never exist, even in the mind, until after the problems of language have been faced *directly*. Our purpose in this chapter is to discuss the nature of style and the role it plays in oral composition.

At the outset we must make it clear that we shall be using the term "style" in a limited sense. It is true that style may be thought of as pervading all of the finished speech including the way it is uttered. Gestures and facial expression may operate as symbols to stir up thought so that style in delivery is a topic worthy of consideration. Here, however, we shall consider style only as it relates to the process of speech composition, the conversion of ideas into words. We shall explore the role language plays as the vehicle of thought. The selection of words, their combination and structuring into thought units, and all that these entail are our special topics for reflection in this chapter.

Misconceptions About Style

A prevalent misconception about style is that it is decoration. This attitude stems from such dicta as Lord Chesterfield's: "Style is the dress of thoughts." From this viewpoint style is thought of as clothing or covering, as something you *put on* ideas or *do to* ideas. Ideas are looked upon as windows to be trimmed; composition becomes something from which you occasionally step back to see if the baubles and tinsel applied give a beauteous effect.

This concept of style as exornation, as superimposed beautification, is often associated with an equally erroneous conception that style is something to be exhibited, to be manufactured for the perceiver's delight. Speakers who try to dazzle their audiences with clever wordings or impress them with long or archaic words or quaint expressions misconceive the function of style and its relationship to idea, audience, and occasion.

We cannot accept these two conceptions of style. We believe that wordings are part of the meaning, that if truly effective they are inherent in or *at one with* the thought. Rather than worry about what to do with the idea or how to exhibit it once it is conceived, we believe that one should think clearly in the first place so that the chosen words say accurately and clearly what one is thinking. We would say with George Henry Lewes:

> We see at once the mistake directly we understand that a genuine style is the living body of thought, not a costume that can be put on and off; it is the expression of the writer's mind; it is not less the incarnation of his thoughts in verbal symbols than a picture is the painter's incarnation of his thoughts in symbols of form and colour. A man may, if it please him, dress his thoughts in the tawdry splendour of a masquerade. But this is no more Literature than the masquerade is Life.[2]

What Lewes says of writing and literature applies as well to public address.

[2] George Henry Lewes, "The Principle of Beauty," in *Representative Essays on the Theory of Style*, ed. by William T. Brewster (New York: Macmillan, 1921), p. 217.

What Is Style?

In the field of rhetoric, including composition and grammar, the English word "style" has referred historically and etymologically to manner of writing. The word was taken from the old French "style" which was derived from the Latin *stilus*. The spelling with the "y" is due partly to the French influence and partly to confusion of *stilus* with a Greek word *stylos* meaning "pillar." In classical Latin the term *stilus* came to have a meaning similar to the later English word. *Stilus* was a term applied by early Romans to a number of different writing instruments. These instruments, usually of metal or bone, had a sharp point on one end for writing on wax tablets and a blunted surface on the other for erasing. *Stilus*, later applied metaphorically, came to mean the distinctive characteristics of a man's handwriting. It was then extended to mean composition and subsequently to connote good expression in speech and writing.[3]

Between 1650 and 1750, this word "style" displaced the Latin word *elocutio* as the name of the third canon of rhetoric. *Elocutio*, as the term had been used, embraced the proper choice of words and their collocation. As *elocutio* ceased to mean style it displaced another Latin term, *pronuntiatio*. Thus, *elocutio* came to mean the study of delivery. Completing the changes in the language of rhetorical theory, *pronuntiatio* ceased to mean the study of voice and bodily action in delivery, and by 1850, *pronuntiatio* or "pronunciation" meant simply the study of the correct phonation of English words.[4]

As a consequence of these shifts in meaning, the history of the word "style," in its modern sense, begins in English rhetorical textbooks in mid-fifteenth century. By 1720, Jonathan Swift was declaring, "Proper words in proper places make the true definition of a style."[5]

Subsequent definitions give us insight into the nature of style in rhetorical composition as we conceive it today. Before we devise a defini-

---

[3] This discussion is based upon the *Oxford English Dictionary*, Smith's *English-Latin Dictionary*, and Liddell and Scott, *A Greek-English Lexicon*.

[4] These shifts in meaning are discussed in detail in Frederick W. Haberman, "The Elocutionary Movement in England 1750–1850" (unpublished Ph.D. thesis, Cornell University, 1947).

[5] Jonathan Swift, "A Letter to a Young Clergyman," 1719/20, in *The Works of Jonathan Swift*, ed. by Walter Scott (Edinburgh, 1814), VII, 337.

tion of our own it will be well to look at some of the definitions arrived at by those who have given the matter serious thought.

Perhaps one of the most famous definitions of style is that of Comte de Buffon, who in his speech to the French Academy in 1753 said, *"le style est de l'homme même"* or "style is the man himself" and: "Style is simply the order and movement one gives to one's thoughts. If these are connected closely, and rigorously compressed the style will be firm, nervous and concise. If they are allowed to follow one another loosely and merely at the lead of diction, however choice this be, the style will be diffuse, nerveless and languid."[6] These definitions, we see, introduce the ideas that style is individualistic, depending to a great extent on the total personality, and that it is in essence "movement" of idea.

Fifty years after Buffon, Hugh Blair in his book *Lectures on Rhetoric and Belles Lettres* emphasized ideas and thinking in a definition of style, saying that style ". . . is the peculiar manner in which a man expresses his conceptions by means of language. . . . Style has always some reference to an author's manner of thinking. It is a picture of ideas which arise in his mind, and of the manner in which they rise there."[7]

Coleridge, in 1818, contended that style is not translatable, saying that words cannot be changed without changing meaning. He insisted, "Style is, of course, nothing else but the art of conveying the meaning appropriately and with perspicuity, whatever that meaning may be, and one criterion of style is that it shall not be translatable without injury to the meaning."[8]

In 1886, John F. Genung highlighted dignity and distinction as ends of style when he said: "By style is meant, in general, manner of expressing thought in language; and more particularly, of giving such skillful expression as invests the idea with fitting dignity and distinction."[9]

The attempts to define this most complicated and elusive part of rhetoric do not stop with the nineteenth century. Thonssen and Baird, in 1948, broadened the scope of style in public speaking when they declared, "The expression which he [the speaker] then gives to his ideas, together with

[6] Buffon, "Discours sur le Style," in *The Art of the Writer: Essays, Excerpts, and Translations*, ed. by Lane Cooper (Ithaca: Cornell University Press, 1952), pp. 153–154, 148. Copyright, 1952, Cornell University. Used by permission of Cornell University Press.
[7] Hugh Blair, *Lectures on Rhetoric and Belles Lettres* (London, 1783), pp. 101–102.
[8] Samuel Taylor Coleridge, "On Style (1818)," in *The Art of the Writer*, p. 180.
[9] John F. Genung, *Practical Elements of Rhetoric* (Boston: Ginn, 1892), p. 13.

whatever rhetorical devices he uses to enhance effectiveness, may be called his style."[10] The "rhetorical devices," of course, might range from word choice to intonation and gesture.

Finally, Porter G. Perrin defines style by distinguishing it from grammar:

> But whatever *style* may mean to critics and philosophers, for a student or writer, it is most helpfully taken in a more concrete sense, to mean a speaker's or writer's use of language, the sources of the reader's or listener's impressions of his manner of thought and expression. The connotation of *style* is of the effectiveness of the expression (rather than of description of usage or questions of correctness). In contrast to grammar, the typical structure of the language, style refers especially to the words and expressions in which the speaker or writer has a choice among the resources his language offers. An analysis of a writer's style takes into account the qualities of words, phrases, idioms, sentences, and arrangement of material.[11]

Keeping in mind these definitions and what we have already said about style and its inseparable linkage to ideas, we would assert that style, as applied to the rhetoric of oral discourse, may be defined as *the personal manner of utterance or expression giving ideas impact and movement.*

Descriptive Versus Prescriptive Treatments

The study of style has evolved descriptively rather than prescriptively. Writers on style have described and classified styles more often than they have given advice on how to achieve them. This is so because it is relatively easy to label parts and figures of speech, kinds of imagery, and grammatical constructions. These can be identified in a finished speech, viewed as a composition. Over the centuries theorists have found as you may find, that given a knowledge of the terms used in identifying stylistic phenomena, describing a style is not an insurmountable task. Once you know the vocabulary, it is not difficult to identify a simple sentence, a metaphor or simile, an allitera-

---

[10] Lester A. Thonssen and A. Craig Baird, *Speech Criticism* (New York: Ronald, 1948), p. 429. (Italics mine.)

[11] Porter G. Perrin, *Writer's Guide and Index to English,* rev. ed. (Chicago: Scott, Foresman, 1950), pp. 773–774.

tive passage or an image which is chiefly visual or auditory. But it is quite another matter to tell anyone how to achieve style that fits a given speech situation.

Theophrastus, Aristotle's successor as head of the Peripatetic School in Athens, is credited with originating "plain," "middle" and "grand" as epithets describing levels of stylistic elevation. "Plain" style was designated as that nearest to everyday speech; "grand" was the ornamented style of greatest elegance and, presumably, passion. "Middle" style fell somewhere between the two. This classification was preserved in the *Rhetorica ad Herennium,* the oldest extant Latin textbook on public speaking. Cicero also emphasized the same stylistic categories. Some writers of antiquity equated the "plain" style with the ancient Attic orators and called it "Attic," meaning a style characterized by expression which was succinct, energetic, and free from redundancy. They labelled the "grand" style as "Asian" and linked it to the ancient Asian orators whose utterances were thought to be verbose, inflated, lacking in force, judgment, and restraint. The term "Rhodian" was applied to the style midway between these two which was thought best exemplified in the qualities of the orators from Rhodes where the prevalent style was a blend of the plain and the grand. This threefold classification of styles has been preserved down to our day for descriptive purposes. At times even more elaborate systems of dividing style into classes have been adopted. G. F. Quackenbos, as Thonssen and Baird point out, made a most elaborate division of classes of style in his book, *Composition and Rhetoric,* published in the United States in 1862.[12] He affixed descriptive adjectives to ten allegedly distinct qualities of style: dry, plain, neat, elegant, florid, simple, labored, concise, diffuse, and nervous. He illustrated each with the work of great writers or orators.

There have been a few theorists who have attempted to deal with style functionally, assessing what happens to ideas in the speech when they are made acceptable to the particular audience involved. De Quincey, one of those who considered the functions of style, viewed style as having both "organic" and "mechanic" influences. He clarified his position thus:

Now the use of words is an organic thing, in so far as language is connected with thoughts and modified by thoughts. It is a mechanic thing, in so far as words in combination determine or modify each other. . . . It is of great

[12] See Thonssen and Baird, *Speech Criticism,* pp. 407–410.

importance not to confound the functions: that function by which style maintains commerce with thought, and that by which it chiefly communicates with words.[13]

We find, as did De Quincey and others, that it is easier to describe style than it is to determine the functions of language management.

The Development of a Style

Each of you has his own particular manner of utterance or expression, his own speech style—good or bad as that may be. Consider the members of your class in public speaking. You will notice that some of them stand out from the rest insofar as style is concerned. One may have a more poetic style than the others—use more imagery, savour his words more. Another may be somewhat rough-hewn in style—terser, plainer, or more homespun in his wordings. Still another may be abstract, use colloquialisms or slang, or be exceedingly precise in technical explanations. Why these styles impress you as distinctive may be difficult for you to determine, but the probability is that each speaker habitually uses a particular kind of language or a specific set of stylistic devices such as imagery or rhetorical questions. Each may be consciously or unconsciously endowing his speeches with a particular characteristic of style; the style of each has hallmarks, and it is probable that yours does too.

You and your classmates have different styles in part because you work differently. When you revise and reword, you modify and change ideas in order to come to exactly what you intend the meaning to be. Sometimes you back track to a prior wording when you find that it more specifically expressed intended meaning. If you speak impromptu or extemporaneously, however, you will have no opportunity for such polishing. You must say what you mean as accurately as possible the first time. In the extemporaneous mode you may, of course, try out wordings as you work from your outline during oral rehearsal, but you usually do not freeze wording in quite the way you would if you were to memorize or work from a manuscript. At every point in composition you make choices which give your style the qualities that distinguish it as yours. In all cases, you must remember that

[13] Thomas De Quincey, "Philosophy of Style" in *Representative Essays*, ed. by Brewster, p. 64.

while readers may flip back through the pages of a book to reread thoughts, listeners can never turn back to the earlier minutes or seconds of a speech to relisten to that portion which was not clear to them upon first hearing.

In your work in public speaking you will seek to improve your style. You will not fashion a style from nothing. You already have a style of some sort. You have a vocabulary at some stage of development and special habits of expression peculiar to you. Your background, prior education, and methods of writing have exerted influence on your style. Some of your habits of expression are good ones which need highlighting and emphasis. Others are faults to be eradicated insofar as that is possible.

Your task is to improve your style, to use words singly and in combination judiciously so that what you say will be even more correct, more clear, more appropriate, more economical, forceful, striking, and moving for your audience than it is now. You must start by surveying what you have in the way of a speech style and work from there. Always remember that it takes a long time to change the tenor of a style. You cannot expect a new style to emerge overnight, but you will be surprised at the modifications in your style which can take place through conscious attention and experimentation.

Your aim ought to be to nurture variety within your distinctive style. An extremely inflexible style cannot suffice because it will not meet the demands of enough different speech situations. As Herbert Spencer once said, "To have a specific style is to be poor in speech."[14] Distinctive styles in speech are unavoidable but the same style for all occasions would be ineffective. The nature of public speaking with its many, constant, and close adjustments to the particulars in the given instance precludes the use of any one style in all cases. The style of a chemistry or mathematics lecture would hardly be suitable for a popular lecture on the advancement of science. Similarly, a sermon on an inspirational theme would seem ill expressed if couched in the jargon of a salesman. Since adaptation is the key to all good public speaking, since the meeting of constantly shifting demands is of primary concern, variety in style is essential if you are to reach the crest of development in your speech making.

We are of the opinion that there is *no* special style of speaking for each different speech purpose. Aristotle intimates that style varies with different kinds of speeches, that controversial style differs from others, that

14 Herbert Spencer, *The Philosophy of Style* (New York: D. Appleton, 1920), p. 47.

ceremonial speaking is more literary than courtroom address.[15] Blair also matches styles with various speech types and assigns special stylistic characteristics to occasional, legislative, courtroom, and pulpit speaking.[16] He says, for example, that courtroom speaking requires more orderliness, conciseness in narration, purity, and plainness than pulpit speaking. What Blair really does is to assign characteristics in varying degrees, characteristics which we shall subsequently consider in this chapter. Note, however, that the classification of speeches which both Aristotle and Blair employ is based not upon speech purpose but upon situation. These authors do not show that particular styles suit particular responses sought by the speaker; they actually observe that some kinds of speaker-audience-subject-occasion relationships call for this or that manner of address. In fact, then, it is not *purpose* but *situation* that governs the potentialities of stylistic attributes.

There are those who would say that informative speaking is distinguished by language of fact and explanation, the diction of definition, example, comparison and less figurative vocabulary. The same people tend to add that persuasive speaking uses emotional language associated with appeal, exhortation, and power in distinctive ways. We believe that such broad generalizations are less than satisfactory for the reason that situations for informing and persuading rather than the purposes themselves determine what is appropriate in the given case. This is why there is no section in this book in which style is matched to speaking purposes. All the characteristics of style are present in every speech in some degree. No one characteristic is exclusively associated with any one purpose. The demands governing style are more fluid and flexible than those governing invention and organization. What should be sought is a personal, distinctive style within which many variations may be made, arising from adaptations to the requirements of idea, audience, occasion, and the speaker himself.

Language Related to Style

The qualities of language in any speech are in part determined by the speaker's understanding of the resources offered by the meanings of words

---

[15] From *The Rhetoric of Aristotle* trans. and ed. by Lane Cooper. Copyright, 1932, Lane Cooper, p. 219, Bk III, Ch. 12. Reprinted by permission of the publisher Appleton-Century-Crofts.

[16] See Hugh Blair, *Lectures on Rhetoric and Belles Lettres* (Philadelphia: Hayes & Zell, 1860), Lectures XXV, XXVII, XXVIII, XXIX, pp. 261–264, 284b–292, 298b–305, 312b–322.

and the ways in which words may be combined. Words are neither fixed in meaning nor do they combine in only a few ways. Every language is more or less flexible. Spoken language is generally more flexible than written because there are opportunities to add meanings through voice quality, inflection, and action. Thus, if you are to develop variety in your present command of language you must know the wealth of variations available to you in spoken English. Then, learn to use them more extensively.

CONNOTATION AND DENOTATION

As we pointed out at the beginning of this chapter, all *oral* communication involves the use of an oral language. Words are symbols for meanings since they stand for our ideas. No word has exactly the same meaning for any two individuals. Words are black marks on paper or combinations of sounds which travel through air. *We* endow them with meaning. The meaning assigned depends upon the human being who perceives the words, for no meanings exist without the human mind. Our backgrounds make us interpret word symbols in particular and sometimes peculiar ways. Parental authority, environment, and learning experiences all combine to determine just exactly what a word will mean to us. When we are at a loss as to how to interpret a word, we turn to a dictionary or a glossary or some other person for the meaning. Even then we find that the meanings we gather from these sources do not always suffice.

Words always have at least two kinds of meaning: denotative or connotative. Some words denote much and connote relatively little—for most people. Denotative words are thought to be more logical, objective, impersonal, and extensional. They point with explicit reference to objects and actions outside the mind which are verifiable through observation. Purely denotative words require few further words to explain what they mean. A fairly denotative statement would be, "President Jones called the meeting to order. Secretary Smith read the minutes of the last meeting."

Connotative words are those which, for most people, have important emotive, subjective, personal, and intensional meanings. Their meanings are turned toward the self, are private, suggestive, and depend upon the individual's emotions. Such words as "mother," "homecoming," "democracy,"

"Communist," and "lover" are rich in connotation. They arouse emotional responses, create images in the mind, and evoke the established attitudes of the listener. These words can be explained—rendered precise or "public"— only through the use of other words.

Many words, of course, are both connotative and denotative because their objective meanings touch off very personal reactions. The word "house" can in many cases be considered denotative, as in a sentence reading, "There were twenty houses in the three-hundred block of Elm Avenue." This same word in other contexts may call to mind a particular house or a particular experience with a house and thus becomes strongly connotative.

In distinguishing between the two kinds of meaning, Professor S. I. Hayakawa is helpful when he says:

. . . the extensional meaning is something that *cannot be expressed in words*, because it is what the words stand for. An easy way to remember this is to put your hand over your mouth and point when asked to give the extensional meaning.

The *intensional meaning* of a word or expression, on the other hand, is that which is suggested (connoted) inside one's head. Roughly speaking, whenever we express the meaning of words by uttering more words, we are giving intensional meaning, or connotations. To remember this, put your hand over your eyes and let the words spin around in your head.[17]

WORD CHOICE

Our discussion of connotation and denotation has shown that our systems of language are at best imperfect ones. Semantics, the science of word meanings, deals in many ways with some of these imperfections. It is enough to say here that confusion in word meanings poses many a problem for the public speaker. It is almost too much for him to hope that he will stir up the exact meanings he intends, since almost any symbols may mean one thing to him but quite another thing to his listeners. He is constantly making choices and revisions in order to maintain practical control over his intended meanings.

A word choice is a mistake, of course, if it implants a distorted message

[17] S. I. Hayakawa, *Language in Action* (New York: Harcourt, Brace, 1946), p. 47.

in the mind of a listener. As the illustration at the beginning of this chapter suggests, word choices *can* and *do* change meanings. Mental pictures are altered and modified by changes in wording. To say, "I saw a *red* wagon" prompts a different image from "I saw a *pink* wagon" or "I saw a *fuchsia* wagon" or "I saw a *vermilion* wagon" or ". . . a *Chinese red* wagon" or ". . . a *Coca-Cola red* wagon." The manufacturers of nail polish could extend the list of reds *ad infinitum*. Similarly, to say, "The child skipped *gaily* down the street" is different from saying the child skipped "merrily" or "joyously" or "boisterously," or even "happily." But a change of adjective or adverb is secondary to a change of noun or verb. Substitute "lad" or "youth" or "teen-ager" or even "girl" or "boy" for *child,* and the meaning changes instantly. Or substitute "shuffled" or "skated" or "strolled" for *skipped* and the mental picture is again modified drastically. To stir up an intended meaning, just any word will not do even though it conforms to all grammatical conventions.

At times the wrong choice of word, a malapropism, can make meaning ludicrous or spoil the mood created by a speaker, undoing several minutes' work. We think of the student who said that a speaker's body was "stagnant" when he meant "static," and of the student who spoke of "illiciting" rather than "eliciting" audience responses. We also think of the student speaker who, in describing a thief's actions during a robbery, coined a new word when he declared that the thief "slurked" around the corner. Whether the intended meaning was "slunk around" or "lurked at" or "sneaked around" was found out only by questioning the speaker. When he was questioned something fundamental came out: the idea, the image, was not exactly clear in the speaker's own mind. His coined word was in fact a way of evading clear, denotative meaning. From these examples two basic propositions about word choice can be inferred: (1) The first thing to determine is your own *exact* meaning. (2) Once your meaning is clearly known, the next problem is to select the terms whose meanings *as generally understood* conform most closely to the meaning in your own mind.

WORD CHANGES

We must also note that language is in a state of flux, that the meanings of words change with time and locality. The general meanings of a given time or society cannot be relied upon in every circumstance. Wordings are often peculiar to geographical areas. In one region of the United States you may purchase "hot dogs and pop," in another "frankfurts and soda," and in yet another "wienies and tonic." Verbal expressions are also often fads or sayings used by particular in-groups at particular times. "Sharp" and "crummy" have been replaced on college campuses by such words as "smooth" and "grubby." "Big shot" has been replaced by "BMOC," and even "hot" has become "cool." "Straight-arrow" and "turkey" have come to have special meanings as descriptions of college men, but they may soon be replaced by even newer words. The jargon of professional groups also changes with time. Anthropologists, philosophers, semanticists, educationists often use specialized vocabularies which exclude outsiders, and these vocabularies are continually modified. Some words are added, some are replaced, and others are dropped. It appears to be the nature of words and expressions that they become tired and worn out. Certain expressions become clichés: "black as pitch," "blue as the sky," "sore as a boil," "happy as a lark." It is rare for a vocabulary, in any locale or society not to shift. It grows, it shrinks, and the word shadings change.

Shifts in man's way of symbolizing meaning present a major problem to the public speaker. In deference to his audiences he must often speak their particular language at their particular time and according to their judgment of what is appropriate to the occasion. He may, as we have said, place his basic reliance on that language which would convey his meaning clearly throughout *most* of the culture to which his hearers belong. He will err often if he does not also study the particular language usages of the time and place in which he will speak. Let him also remember that here are opportunities as well as cautions.

FIGURES OF SPEECH

Our consideration of the role of language in speech making would be incomplete without a recognition of the place and functions of figures of speech in oral communication.

Figures of speech are forms of expression other than those normally used. They serve to intensify meanings. They make their points indirectly by stating things vividly in terms of something else. They are not literally meant or interpreted. They enhance ideas by making them more graphic and appealing. Like all comparisons, contrasts, and exemplifications, figures of speech are especially useful in translating the unknown into terms of the known.

There are some thirty identifiable figures of speech which are commonly used in written and spoken discourse. It is not as important to know their names as it is to recognize them as resources. Among those most often used in speech making are the following, illustrated with excerpts from speeches.

Simile is a stated comparison between things which are essentially dissimilar except for the particular qualities alluded to in the simile. Such comparisons contain the words "like" or "as." For example, "There are voices hot, like scorching blasts from a furnace . . . and others cold as if they came from frozen hearts" (Peter Marshall, "Letters in the Sand")[18] or "In all things that are purely social we can be as separate as fingers, yet one as the hand in all things essential to mutual progress" (Booker T. Washington, "Atlanta Exposition Address").[19]

Metaphor is an implied comparison between two essentially dissimilar things. Linking words such as "like" or "as" are omitted. For example, "Said the old priest, 'A diamond is a congealed drop of sunlight' " (Russell Conwell, "Acres of Diamonds").[20]

Antithesis is the parallel construction of words, phrases, or sentences which contain opposed or sharply contrasting ideas. The fact that the antithetical ideas are expressed in similar language gives the hearer a sense of balance. For example: "Let us never negotiate out of fear. But let us never fear to negotiate" (John F. Kennedy, "Inaugural Address").[21] When no opposition of ideas is involved in parallel language structures the terms "balanced construction" or "parallel construction" are usually used to identify the figure.

Onomatopoeia is word choice in which sound suggests the meaning of the word. For example, "The wind whispers them, the birds whistle them,

[18] In Catherine Marshall, *A Man Called Peter* (New York: McGraw-Hill, 1951), p. 322.

[19] In W. M. Parrish and Marie Hochmuth, eds., *American Speeches* (New York: Longmans, Green, 1954), p. 464.

[20] In Ashley H. Thorndike, ed., *Modern Eloquence* (New York: Modern Eloquence Corp., 1923), VIII, p. 139.

[21] In Carroll C. Arnold, Douglas Ehninger, and John C. Gerber, eds., *The Speaker's Resource Book* (Chicago: Scott, Foresman, 1961), p. 257.

the corn, barley and bulrushes hoarsely rustle them . . ." (Ralph Waldo Emerson, "The Memory of Burns").[22]

Alliteration is repetition of the initial sounds in words or in stressed syllables within words. For example, "The first duty of law is to keep *s*ound the *s*ociety it *s*erves" (Woodrow Wilson, "First Inaugural Address").[23]

Personification is endowment of objects, animals, or ideas with human attributes. For example: "To-day learning no longer hides in the convent or slumbers in the palace. No! she comes out into every-day life, joins hands with the multitude and cushions the peasant" (Wendell Phillips, "The Lost Arts").[24]

Synecdoche is the substitution of parts for wholes or of wholes for parts of things. For example, "We tie all countries close together, put each doorstep on a universal ocean, but how are we to direct these accomplishments to improve the basic qualities of life?" (Charles A. Lindbergh, "The Future Character of Man").[25]

Hyperbole is exaggeration or overstatement for the purpose of emphasizing without deceiving. For example, "He whispers in a shout, and converses, in ordinary, confidential moments in a shriek" (Robert Burdette, "The Rise and Fall of the Mustache").[26]

Irony implies something different from, usually the opposite of, what is stated. Sarcasm is a form of irony. For example, ". . . as I have spent several months in the [Sandwich] Islands, several years ago, I feel competent to shed any amount of light on the matter" (Mark Twain, "On the Sandwich Islands").[27]

Metonymy is substituting the name of some closely associated thing for the real name of what is referred to. For example, "Then Texas responded to the bugle calls of liberty, and the march of the flag went on!" (Albert J. Beveridge, "The March of the Flag").[28]

Climax is the arrangement of words, phrases, or sentences in series

---

[22] In Lewis Copeland and Lawrence Lamm, eds., *The World's Great Speeches*, 2nd rev. ed. (New York: Dover Publications, 1958), p. 654.

[23] In Parrish and Hochmuth, *American Speeches*, p. 470.

[24] In Thomas B. Reed, ed., *Modern Eloquence* (New York: The University Society, 1900), VI, p. 845.

[25] In *Vital Speeches*, XX (March 1, 1954), 294.

[26] In Ashley H. Thorndike, ed., *Modern Eloquence*, VIII, p. 108.

[27] *Ibid.*, p. 131.

[28] In F. C. Hicks, ed., *Famous Speeches by Eminent American Statesmen* (St. Paul, Minn.: West Publishing, 1929), p. 197.

according to increasing value or strength of impact. For example: "Therefore, in this campaign, the question is larger than a party question. It is an American question. It is a world question" (Albert J. Beveridge, "The March of the Flag").[29]

Repetition is the reiteration of the same words or phrases or sentences in order to reinforce ideas. For example, "We must imagine greatly, dare greatly and act greatly" (Adlai E. Stevenson, "The People's Natural Resources").[30]

A *pun* is substitution of one word for another having different meaning but similar sound. For example: "And so I say it is not capital you want. It is not copper cents, but common sense" (Russell Conwell, "Acres of Diamonds").[31]

There also are several lesser known figures of speech which deserve attention here because they are used by speakers more often than by writers.

Aposiopesis is the practice of breaking off utterance of one thought without finishing it, in order to express another, due presumably to the emotional state of the speaker. The cause of self-interruption might be anger, sorrow, fear, or some other strong feeling. Many sentence fragments, though not all, will fall in this category. For example: "Only yesterday, it seems to him, the little baby girl, bringing the first music of baby prattle into his home; then a little girl in short dresses, with school-girl troubles and school-girl pleasures; then an older little girl, out of school and into society, but a little girl to pa still. And then—. But somehow, this is as far as pa can get; for he sees, in the flight of this, the first, the following flight of other fledglings; and he thinks how silent and desolate the old nest will be when they have all mated and flown away." (Robert Burdette, "The Rise and Fall of the Mustache.")[32]

Apophasis is the ostensible omission or concealment, through denial, of what the speaker has really in fact declared. For example: "I am not pleading so much for these boys as I am for the infinite number of others to follow, those who perhaps cannot be as well defended as these have been, those who may be down in the storm, and the tempest, without aid. It is

---

29 *Ibid.*, p. 189.

30 In Adlai E. Stevenson, *Major Campaign Speeches of Adlai E. Stevenson*, 1952 (New York: Random House, 1953), p. 90.

31 In Ashley Thorndike, ed., *Modern Eloquence*, VIII, p. 151.

32 *Ibid.*, p. 128.

of them I am thinking, and for them I am begging of this court not to turn backward toward the barbarous and cruel past." (Clarence Darrow, "The Plea of Clarence Darrow.")[33]

Epanorthosis is the retraction or cancelling of what the speaker has already stated. For example:

In olden times it used to be popular to call the Sandwich Islanders cannibals. But they were never cannibals. That is amply proven. There was one there once, but he was a foreign savage, who stopped there a while and did quite a business while he stayed. He was a useful citizen, but had strong political prejudices, and used to save up a good appetite for just before election, so that he could thin out the Democratic vote. (Laughter.) But he got tired of that, and undertook to eat an old whaling captain for a change. That was too much for him. He had the crime on his conscience, and the whaler on his stomach, and the two things killed him. (Laughter.) He died. I don't tell this on account of its value as an historical fact (laughter), but only on account of the moral it conveys. I don't know that I know what moral it conveys, still I know there must be a moral in it somewhere. I have told it forty or fifty times and never got a moral out of it yet. (Laughter.) But all things come to those who wait. (Mark Twain, "On the Sandwich Islands.")[34]

The catalogue of figures of speech could be continued, for there are many other standard ways of bending language to the service of special or emphatic meanings. Those we have identified are those you are most likely to find use for—those you have probably been using in conversation and formal speaking simply because you have heard others use them. There is not a great deal to be gained from learning exotic names merely because they are given in a textbook. The practical worth of knowing one figure of speech from another comes from the fact that only in this way can you realize the special resources language management offers. Only so can you discover the out-of-the-ordinary way to symbolize a thought.

Each of the figures we have identified above is common in English usage. If your thought is well adapted to your speech situation, you need not fear that the language device itself will seem so strange as to draw attention away from your idea. These figures of speech are relatively famil-

---

[33] In Maureen McKernan, *The Amazing Crime and Trial of Leopold and Loeb* (New York: The New American Library, 1957), p. 192.

[34] In Ashley H. Thorndike, ed., *Modern Eloquence*, VIII, p. 135–136.

iar to most competent users of English, but they are still not standard or everyday usages. Each startles the listener mildly when it occurs in speech and so momentarily rivets attention on what is being said in that instant. Each is, therefore, a means of emphasis. It is as instruments for emphasizing or intensifying meaning that you should use figures. As we have already said, adornment or embellishment of language is destructive of clarity and directness, hence inappropriate in most public speaking.

A competent public speaker needs to know there are special ways in which he can give exceptional emphasis to his thoughts. The speaker who does not know and understand at least the sixteen usages we have discussed as figures of speech simply does not know his art or its possibilities. He is somewhat like a landscape contractor who knows everything about his business except the conditions under which plants thrive or die. It is as inept for a speaker to disregard how climax, antithesis, metaphor, or repetition could aid him in driving home the problem section of a problem-solution speech as it would be for an alleged expert in landscaping to plan and establish a golf course without inquiring into the nitrogen and water supplies so essential to proper turf. Our advice is, then, that you study carefully the figures of speech we have identified. Look for them in speeches you hear and read. Learn to distinguish between functionally useful and ostentatiously distracting usages of these kinds. In composing your own speeches, review the services figures might render at points where special touches of emphasis or vividness are needed if your listeners are to grasp your full meaning.

Now let us turn from considering word meanings, word choices, and the figures of speech created by words to the general characteristics or traits of style which result from over-all management of words in combination.

Characteristics of Style

We shall consider the characteristics or traits of style in traditional fashion, by looking at the virtues of *good* style. In various proportions these stylistic qualities combine to create the speaker's personal, distinctive style and the variations within it.

ACCURACY

All style has a degree of accuracy; the thought is expressed with either precision or fuzziness. As a speaker your accuracy depends upon your ability to choose the words which best express your thoughts to your listening audience. Your store of word symbols will determine your degree of precision as well as your audience's understanding of that store of symbols.

In addition to bearing in mind the accuracy or precision of your terms you should attend to grammatical accuracy in fashioning your symbols into meaningful clusters. Slips in grammar affect the audience's image of you as a person and of your ability to express yourself. Good grammar is assumed by the audience. As Cicero said:

. . . nobody ever admired an orator for correct grammar, they only laugh at him if his grammar is bad, and not only think him no orator but not even a human being; no one ever sang the praises of a speaker whose style succeeded in making his meaning intelligible to his audience, but only despised one deficient in capacity to do so.[35]

So a second attention to accuracy should be to the accuracy of grammar.

A third concern in investing style with accuracy calls for a consideration of what is correct on the specific occasion. Here, correctness and accuracy blend with propriety, a virtue of good style which we will consider later in this chapter. Yet, the style producing correct tone or feeling for the particular occasion will only result from judicious selection of words with due attention to level of difficulty and kind. Formal, stately occasions call for more formal language than informal classroom situations. The level of abstraction and the technicality of wordings can be accurate or correct only if the audience understands what is said and the occasion justifies the way it is said. The most convivial gathering of astronauts would allow levels of technicality and precision that would prove bafflingly imprecise and incorrect to a high school class in general science.

Accuracy, determined by speaker, audience, the idea to be expressed, and the occasion is the first concern of any speaker.

[35] *De Oratore,* trans. by H. A. Rackham (Cambridge, Mass.: Harvard University Press, 1948), pp. 41–42, Bk III, Ch. 14.

CLARITY

Once you are sure that you are accurate or correct in symbolizing and blending your idea, your next concern becomes clarity. Aristotle, at the beginning of his discussion of style in *The Rhetoric*, said: "We may therefore . . . regard it as settled that a good style is, first of all, clear. The proof is that language which does not convey a clear meaning fails to perform the very function of language."[36] So you must ask yourself, "How clearly have I expressed the idea? How *completely* does the audience understand me?"

Aristotle went on to say, "Clearness is secured through the use of name-words [nouns and adjectives] and, verbs, that are current terms. . . ."[37] We would add that concrete rather than abstract words will help; so will good transitions and simple, familiar sentence structures. The more directly you say what you have to say and the less strange your wordings are the more likely you are to be clear.

Once again, clarity is a matter of degree. The more obscure the expression of idea, the more inefficient the communication. How far you go in amplification, in detailing your explanations and arguments according to what you know about your audience's requirements, will determine how clear you will be. Your care in choosing words will also determine your degree of clarity.

As a speaker you must remember that unless you are clear you will be misunderstood, and that if you are misunderstood you cannot hope to achieve the purpose of your speech. It is easy to confuse clearness and accuracy. An accurate and grammatically correct symbolization of idea may still prove unclear to an audience. An audience may simply not understand symbolization that is accurate on a level of comprehension too high for them. On the other hand, clarity of expression does not necessarily guarantee accurate symbolization of ideas. Misinformation may be transmitted clearly. Ideally, a speaker is both clear and accurate in expression, but it does not always follow that accurate or correct ideas are clearly worded or that clear wording and clear structuring of symbols guarantee accurate transmission.

[36] From *The Rhetoric of Aristotle*, trans. and ed. by Lane Cooper, p. 185, Bk III, Ch. 2. Reprinted by permission of the publisher Appleton-Century-Crofts.
[37] *Ibid.*

The primary demanding element for clarity is, as we have already indicated, the audience. The idea itself is next in the hierarchy. Ideas cry out for clear treatment. The occasion may exert some pressure for clarity if it is of a special nature. The speaker demands least, since his ideas are clear to him even though they may not be clear to anyone else. There, is the rub! Your clarity, for yourself, will tempt you to disregard your listeners' clarity, the opportunities your subject offers you, and special aspects of your occasion.

PROPRIETY

Propriety, or appropriateness, is also characteristic of a good speech style. Style for good public speaking, unlike that for an essay or a novel, is meant for a particular audience in a particular place at a particular time. Particularity and close adjustment are the goals of oral style, not universality or adaptation to respondents in all places at all times.

The style adopted in speaking must, of course, be appropriate to the subject matter treated. "The style again," as Aristotle declared, "should not be mean nor above the dignity of the subject, but appropriate. . . ."[38] To describe a plain, simple, commonplace operation, such as changing a tire, in flowery, poetic language would be ridiculous. Such low subjects are not good ones for stylistic experimentation. To depict a sunset in plain vernacular is to rob the subject of meaning and inherent emotional quality. To say "the sky was kind of red, sort of like a tomato or a radish," would be just as inappropriate as to say of a tire, "the shiny black vulcanized rubber besmirched by dust and grime, ought to be carefully loosened from the band which girdles the wheel."

Style must also be suited to the particular audience if it is to be appropriate. You would hardly use the same vocabulary level or informality in phrasing for speeches before a group of college alumni and before a group of boy scouts or persons lacking in formal education. The word symbols used for these groups would vary as would the amount of elaboration necessary for clarity and interestingness. Yet, in adapting to the particular audience, you must be careful to be always yourself. You must not sell yourself or your listeners short. A college graduate who tries to sound like a farmer at a grange meeting, a juvenile delinquent at a boys' reformatory,

[38] *Ibid.*

and a college professor in the classroom is play-acting. He becomes ridiculous. So in tailoring your style to the audience, do not forget that it must also be tailored to yourself. Your style, as Buffon noted, is you, yourself. It is a very personal thing—your manner of expression. Consciously straining too hard or trying too strenuously for adaptation to the particular audience or striving for a special kind of speaking style, as some beginning students do, usually results in a style which smells of the lamp or sounds like a caricature of someone else.

If style must be appropriate to the subject matter, the audience, and the speaker himself, it must still be appropriate to the particular occasion. To use the same style in a corporate business meeting as you would use for informal remarks at a fraternity meeting would be to court disaster. On certain occasions it would be traditional to be dignified and formal and to strive for niceties of expression. On other occasions it would be more appropriate to be relaxed, informal, and to indulge, with taste, in slang and colloquialisms. In composing your speech the setting, its physical aspects and emotional tone, must be taken into account if your style is to be appropriate to the occasion as well as to subject, audience, and self.

ECONOMY

A glaring fault in most speech making is the use of too many words. We spend words unwisely, using several where one would do. We clutter thoughts so that even when we do not obscure, we irritate with unnecessary circumlocution. For this reason if for no other economy is an attribute of desirable style.

By economy in language we mean the right choice of words, in right amount and best order for instantaneous intelligibility. We mean economy of the listener's attention.

Herbert Spencer in his essay, "The Philosophy of Style," emphasized the importance of economizing the "mental energies" and "mental sensibilities" of auditors or readers. "To so present ideas that they may be apprehended with the least possible mental effort, is the desideratum towards which most of the rules . . . point," he said.[39] Spencer claimed language is a hindrance to thought even though a necessary instrument of

[39] *The Philosophy of Style*, p. 11.

it. He held that economy of the respondent's attention is the secret of effect and depends upon the right choice and collocation of words, the best arrangement of clauses to clarify the ranks of principal and subordinate propositions, the judicious use of figures of speech, and the rhythmic sequence of syllables. Spencer summarized his "principle of economy" thus:

A reader or listener has at each moment but a limited amount of mental power available. To recognize and interpret the symbols presented to him, requires a part of this power; to arrange and combine the images suggested requires a further part; and only that part which remains can be used for realizing the thought conveyed. Hence, the more time and attention it takes to receive and understand each sentence, the less time and attention can be given to the contained idea; and the less vividly will that idea be conceived.[40]

We would agree with Spencer that we ought to use the fewest words possible for proper expression and that extreme brevity is characteristic of passionate language, but we would caution that the fewest number of words for *proper* expression is not always the smallest number possible. Economy of attention is economy only if the idea is fully clear and understandable. At times, economy in style means not brevity or frugality in wording but the necessary amplification. The proper amount of wordage needed in developing an idea, either in clarifying or in proving, will produce the most concise statement possible given the circumstances and the subject matter. And speakers must remember that one of the circumstances governing their art is that listeners cannot review or reexamine unless speakers provide the necessary words.

Saying things the easiest, simplest way without downgrading your vocabulary to an inappropriate level is a very good way to be economical. If you see to it that you have excised superfluous introductory lead-ins to sentences or that you have avoided unnecessary adjectives and adverbs and unnecessarily inverted word orders, you will contribute significantly to your conciseness and you will promote clarity.

FORCE

A good speaking style has drive, urgency, and excitement. It compels the listener to pay attention through its strength as it propels ideas forward. We often equate force with intensity, but we must remember that force or

[40] *Ibid.*

intensity in style is often greatest when language is of a quiet rather than a blatant sort.

Economy and preciseness produce force. Spencer supplies the link when he says, ". . . other things equal, the force of all verbal forms and arrangements is great in proportion as the time and mental effort they demand from the recipient is small."[41] Shortness, terseness, and the resulting abruptness all produce force in style. Even short words help, for as Spencer elaborates:

> . . . the shortness of Saxon words becomes a reason for their greater force. One qualification, however, must not be overlooked. A word which itself embodies the most important part of the idea to be conveyed, especially when the idea is an emotional one, may often with advantage be a polysyllabic word. Thus it seems more forcible to say, "It is *magnificent*," than "It is *grand*." The word *vast* is not so powerful a one as *stupendous*. Calling a thing *nasty* is not so effective as calling it *disgusting*.[42]

Spencer was probably wrong in thinking Saxon words have special forcefulness, but he was right in believing that, in general, the quick blows of short words yield force in style.

We can see the connection between force and preciseness if we note the greater strength of images and shapes which are definite in outline over those which are ragged or vague. Solidly massed units are stronger than scattered ones. An argument has more force when it has perceivable form. Conversely, a point is weakened by asides, irrelevant excursions, or supporting material which so separate and prolong that we stand too far from the centrality of the idea. The single well-defined bullet hits home harder than a scattering of buckshot. So it is with spoken statements.

Force is required in the service of all elements in a speech situation. Sometimes the best adaptation to the audience requires that they be told things strongly. Sometimes the ideas demand forcefulness if they are to be given proper significance. Sometimes the speaker's physical mien dictates that he speak strongly, with real verve and vigor. Finally, some occasions demand a powerful, direct approach in contrast to what has been called "lemonadey utterance."

[41] *Ibid.*, p. 33.
[42] *Ibid.*, pp. 13–14.

STRIKING QUALITY

The characteristic of good style which we choose to call "striking quality" has as its constituents heightened effect and sublimity. In some instances writers have called this characteristic "interestingness," "impressiveness," "ornateness," "vividness," or "beauty."

We reject the term "beauty" with reference to rhetorical composition, because speech making is a utilitarian art. Its primary function is never to be beautiful. While we may admire the imagery and the grace of utterance, it is difficult to conceive of any speech as good simply because it gave aesthetic pleasure. A speech admired for the sole reason that it aroused the imagination as a poem might would be suspect as rhetoric. Similarly suspect would be one whose main virtue was that it was euphonious. Some words are beautiful, others are ugly in sound. Some mental images produced by words are lovely, others are repulsive. The revolting as well as the attractive can draw our attention and subsequently have an effect. Beauty has place as a constituent of striking quality, but it is not the only element in the quality. The unknown writer called "Longinus" said in *On the Sublime:*

. . . the choice of proper and striking words wonderfully attracts and enthralls the hearer, and that such a choice is the leading ambition of all orators and writers, since it is the direct agency which ensures the presence in writings, as upon the fairest statues, of the perfection of grandeur, beauty, mellowness, dignity, force, power, and any other high qualities there may be, and breathes into dead things a kind of living voice. All this it is, I say, needless to mention, for beautiful words are in very truth the peculiar light of thought.[43]

Ruskin, in discussing beauty of style in fine art, enumerated as its qualities: infinity, unity (with variety), repose (even in motion), symmetry, purity, and moderation. He added that the last quality girdles and safeguards all the rest, and "in this respect is the most essential of all."[44] In a chapter on the "Greatness of Style" Ruskin named as the requisites of style: love of beauty, wise choice of noble subject, sincerity, and invention produced by imagination.[45]

[43] Longinus, "On the Sublime," trans. by W. Rhys Roberts, in J. H. Smith and E. W. Parks, *The Great Critics,* 3rd ed. (New York: W. W. Norton, 1951), pp. 95–96.

[44] John Ruskin, *The True and the Beautiful* (New York: Wiley and Halsted, 1859), p. 4.

[45] See John Ruskin, *Ruskin's Works* (Boston: Estes and Lauriat, 1897), XXII, p. 46–70.

Ruskin's emphasis on moderation in the use of the striking is in key with the theories of both "Longinus" and Buffon. "Longinus" points out, ". . . stately language is not to be used everywhere, since to invest petty affairs with great and high-sounding names would seem just like putting a full-sized tragic mask upon an infant boy."[46] Buffon echoed him: "Nothing is more inimical to this warmth [the luminosity of style] than the desire to be everywhere striking."[47]

While good style, it is true, will have a distinctiveness that is striking, beauty alone, even in moderation, will not prove to be the only attribute of language that achieves grandeur in the illumination of ideas. Beauty is relative and dependent on individual tastes. Striking quality is something easier to measure and detect. It too is subjective, but its effects are more readily perceived.

Striking quality in speeches comes from the ability of the speaker to combine words in euphonious combinations, his ability to give poetic turns to wordings yet keep them prose, and his ability to paint word pictures which stir the listener's emotions. The farther the speaker moves in the direction of poetry and uniqueness of expression, the more striking we are apt to think his speaking is. "Hence," as Aristotle advises, "it is well to give the ordinary idiom an air of remoteness; the hearers are struck by what is out of the way, and like what strikes them."[48]

Perhaps this liking for the remote and striking is the explanation of why striking quality in style attracts and holds attention and creates pleasant or disturbing reactions within the individual listeners. If so, we are led back to the speech material and the audience as the primary constituents of speaking situations that demand something striking in acceptable style. The speaker's individual desire to be aesthetically pleasing is another force demanding that utterance be striking. He may be fond of imagery, pleasing sound combinations, and attractive rhetorical figures. As long as his fondness does not produce exhibitionism as a goal, it is all to the good.

The occasion may require style of striking quality. For example, there are occasions where it is difficult to find new ideas in key with the circum-

[46] Smith and Parks, *The Great Critics*, p. 96.
[47] Cooper, *The Art of the Writer*, p. 151.
[48] From *The Rhetoric of Aristotle*, trans. and ed. by Lane Cooper, p. 185, Bk III, Ch. 2. Reprinted by permission of the publisher Appleton-Century-Crofts.

stances. The presentation or acceptance of an award or situations calling for welcomes or farewells may pose such problems to a speaker. He must say something, but it has all been said many times. So he must find a unique or striking way to word his familiar message. By his listeners' standards, originality may in such cases consist chiefly in producing striking variations on familiar themes.

LIVELINESS

Force, economy, and striking quality contribute to *liveliness* in oral communication. If the mission of rhetoric is to endow ideas with movement and its goal is, as C. S. Baldwin said, "the energizing of knowledge and the humanizing of truth," then there is no more important stylistic quality in oral discourse than liveliness. But "propulsion" or movement must be accepted as aspects of this *liveliness*. If speeches are to reach climaxes of reason and emotion, there must be both energy and the kind of movement that carries the idea forward and propels it toward its ultimate, most influential form. For this effect there must be not only energy and movement but some degree of suspense.

Aristotle hints at the importance of keeping auditors in some degree of suspense when he says that listeners ". . . like words that set an event before their eyes; for they must see the thing occurring now, not hear of it in the future, the speaker must aim at these three points: Metaphor, Antithesis, Actuality."[49] He thereafter advises that we make our verbal pictures move—that we make them motion pictures rather than still photographs. Not still-life images but "objects invested with life, and thereby an effect of activity" is the goal.[50] The successful stylist to Aristotle is one who ". . . makes everything live and move; and movement is activity."[51]

In discussing "actuality" Aristotle says,

We have said that liveliness is secured by the use of the proportional metaphor, and by putting things directly before the eyes of the audience. But we still have to explain what is meant by setting things "before the eyes," and how this

[49] *Ibid.*, p. 207, Bk III, Ch. 10.
[50] *Ibid.*, p. 211, Bk III, Ch. 11.
[51] *Ibid.*, p. 212, Bk III, Ch. 11.

is to be effected. What I mean is, using expressions that show things in a state of activity.[52]

Liveliness, then, comes from animation, conflict, actuality (or realism), suspense, and proximity. It comes from the use of present tense and active voice. It comes from economy in wording, from simple rather than complex structuring, from vividness in imagery, and from any other resource of language that sets moving images before the minds of listeners.

How much more effective it is to relate events in a *"you are there"* rather than an *"I was there"* fashion. How much better to take your audience with you as you relive the suspenseful moment when your boat capsized or your car crashed. Let the audience feel the tape breaking across your chest at the finish line of a race, the touch of your friend's hand at the moment of good-bye, the pull of your muscles as they lift a rock or kick a football. We are merely saying *use lively imagery*. Let your audience *feel* with you. Make your images cumulate and build. Let your appeals to sight, touch, taste, hearing, and smell, to thermal and kinesthetic sensitivity, so combine that the images rising in the mind *are experienced*. Consider a sentence like: "I smell the pines in the crisp morning air and hear the crunch of snow beneath me as I plod up the path with weary muscles crying out at every step." In this single sentence four kinds of sensory appeal combine to bring the experience to reality. Experiment with animation, actuality, and imagery and you will find that your speeches have movement. They will run to their goals rather than limp to their conclusions.

The demands for liveliness in speaking come above all from the audience. Hearers want to be moved, to respond empathically, to be excited by ideas. Then, at times, they want to be lulled. Bouncing, vigorous, hard-muscled style must be used in moderation as must striking qualities. A racing style may be out of place at eight o'clock in the morning, for occasions also determine the appropriate degree of liveliness. The solemnity of a commencement or a worship service may call for subdued and gentle pace rather than for vigorous movement. But for speaker and listener alike, whatever the occasion, appeals to experience, to active exercise of mind and body carry with them influences toward strength in all aspects of communication. Speakers do well to remember that liveliness through metaphor, antithesis, realism, and progressive movement of ideas is possible

[52] *Ibid.*, p. 211, Bk III, Ch. 11.

with or without high excitement. They do well to remember also that some speech materials lend themselves better to lively discourse than others. Narratives are especially susceptible to animated treatments while inquiries often demand that the means to liveliness be diligently searched for and found.

To say that liveliness is the most important of all qualities of good oral style is no exaggeration; it is a forthright summary of all we have just said. Accuracy, clarity, propriety, economy, force, and striking quality are virtues of good oral style but they are, as it were, preliminaries to the ultimate virtue of discourse that influences—liveliness. The time-bound, audience-bound, occasion-bound speaker cannot safely disregard this hierarchy of stylistic values peculiar to his art. It is fitting then that we turn next to the peculiarities of oral discourse as contrasted with written composition.

Oral and Written Style

At first glance it may seem fairly obvious that there must be some differences between oral and written style. Both deal with words, sentences, and language in general. Yet, written style often has oral elements, and many fine writers tell us to give our writing the quality of conversation. If we do so, of course, our writing enhances our speaking and vice versa.

James A. Winans once said, "A speech is not an essay on its hind legs." What he meant was that the essay is not oral even though it may be rhetorical. And the chances are that your essays, themes, and term papers, if read aloud would lack some of the traits your writing for speaking ought to have.

Little research and scholarly experimentation have been done to investigate the differences between oral and written style. Much credit must be given to Gladys Borchers for her work in this area, to Gordon Thomas, and the few others who have written on this problem.[53] But their conclusions are based, we think, upon such limited samples that they provide us

---

[53] See Gladys L. Borchers, "An Approach to the Problem of Oral Style," *The Quarterly Journal of Speech*, XXII (1936), 114–117; Gordon Thomas, "Effect of Oral Style on Intelligibility of Speech," *Speech Monographs*, XXIII (1956), 46–54.

with points of departure rather than decisive pronouncements. These studies do provide us, however, with generalizations worthy of testing by experience. These general conclusions on differences in the two kinds of style, we are quick to add, are differences not of kind but of degree.

Drawing upon the research just mentioned and upon our personal observations, we arrive at the following hypotheses which we invite you to test in your speech making. In contrast to written prose style, oral style uses:

1. More personal pronouns.
2. More variety in kinds of sentences.
3. More variety in sentence lengths.
4. More simple sentences.
5. More sentence fragments.
6. Many more rhetorical questions.
7. More repetition of words, phrases, and sentences.
8. More monosyllabic than polysyllabic words.
9. More contractions.
10. More interjections.
11. More indigenous language.
12. More connotative than denotative words.
13. More euphony.
14. More figurative language.
15. More direct quotation.

Aristotle recognized these differences when he said:

> . . . each kind of rhetoric has its own appropriate style. The style of written prose is not that of controversial speaking. . . . A knowledge of both the written and spoken style is required. . . . The written . . . style is more finished; the controversial is far better adapted to dramatic delivery. . . . On comparison, speeches of the literary men sound thin in the actual contests; while those of the orators sound well but look crude when you hold them in your hands—and the reason is that their place is in a contest.[54]

We urge students, when working with them on speech manuscripts, not to worry whether the speech looks well on paper. Any manuscript ought to be neat and readable in the mechanical sense; the important point is that if one brings only the standards of writing for the eye to bear upon

---

[54] From *The Rhetoric of Aristotle,* trans. and ed. by Lane Cooper, p. 217, Bk III, Ch. 12. Reprinted by permission of the publisher Appleton-Century-Crofts.

writing intended for the ear, he will end by applying some criteria of excellence that have no relevance. He will fail to apply criteria that are exceedingly important. For example, the principles of paragraphing have limited relevance to the composition that will be heard. Reading copies of manuscript speeches by outstanding speakers exhibit widely varying practices for marking off major and minor ideas on the manuscript page. Some such manuscripts show very little paragraphing while others show every two or three sentences indented as though they constituted a formal paragraph. Whatever is done, it is the convenience of the speaker, not of the general reader, that must be served.

The same is true of sentences. Speaking appropriately uses many more sentence fragments than formal writing. Every novelist who is expert in writing dialogue and every playwright of worth knows this well. So, to apply formal standards of sentence construction and sentence completeness in evaluating the manuscript for a speech would be to force the communication into forms it need not and does not normally fit. Consider the fragment we quoted from Franklin D. Roosevelt's address, "The Philosophy of Social Justice Through Social Action" (pp. 135–136). The text as printed here is based on an official stenographic report, President Roosevelt's own manuscript, and a recording that seems to have been made either before or after the address to the actual audience. Using all these resources L. LeRoy Cowperthwaite's best judgment of what Mr. Roosevelt actually said in Detroit yields the passage quoted again below. Notice how little the language resembles what we ordinarily call polished writing *for the eye*. Notice the broken sentence structures. Doubtless they were rendered smoothly meaningful by pause and vocal inflection. Notice the reinforcement gained by repetition of the words "crippled children"—reinforcement that writing for the eye would surely achieve in less obvious ways. Plainly, this is not the style of excellent essay writing; it is a very carefully established sample of the *oral* style of one of the most polished and successful political speakers in the history of the United States. This is the way he *talked:*

Take another form of poverty in the old days. Not so long ago, you and I know, there were families in attics—in every part of the Nation—in country districts and in city districts—hundreds and thousands of crippled children who could get no adequate care, crippled children who were lost to the community and who were a burden on the community. And so we have, in these past twenty or thirty years, gradually provided means for restoring crippled children to useful citizenship; and it has all been a factor in going after and solving one of the causes of poverty and disease.

Our point is not that good communication composed for the ear must look exactly like this on the page. The page of a speech manuscript should, however, display the variety of language forms and the plethora of reinforcing and emphasizing devices that listeners require in order to keep control over thoughts that are being developed *acoustically*.

Impaled on paper, some sentences of a speech will look strange, and many constructions will depart from the standard patterns of good communication for the eye. There will be other differences, reflecting the fifteen qualities we have listed above. Usually, the page ought to exhibit fewer words like "however," "thus," "therefore" than an essay might; it ought to reveal in their places such words and phrases as "but," "and so," or "the result of high cost is." These last are simply the connectives of normal conversation.

Speeches ought to contain few indefinite pronouns. "This" and "that" are exceedingly ambiguous words for a listener. They always require him to locate *in his memory* some noun used earlier. If the referent occurred in the preceding sentence it is often just too hard to recall that the "this" now heard actually means the "cathedral" heard five or ten seconds before.

Whether one is writing or speaking, he will convey his meaning more forcefully and usually more clearly if he uses verbs in the active voice. There is more efficient meaning and more action in "The dog bit the man" than in "The man was bitten by the dog." "It is believed by most observers that a decision will be made by the President on Thursday" is just bad writing. But it is stupid speaking. Listening is neither easy nor a highly efficient way of absorbing information. Good oral style should compensate for these limitations by its directness, and one of the easiest, most obvious compensations is to keep verbs in the active voice as much as possible and in the present tense where that is appropriate.

There is not enough scientific evidence to justify an unqualified declaration that if you incorporate in your speaking such qualities as the fifteen we have enumerated and if you keep your talk in the active voice as much as possible, you will achieve a successful oral style. There can be no question but that the basis of good style in speaking is largely the same as the basis for good style in writing, but oral style needs to be adapted to the special circumstances under which speaking takes place. A crucially important fact is that speaking is heard, not read. This is why oral style must be conversational, personal, and responsive to the thought processes of listeners. We believe that if you try to inject such qualities as we have been discussing into your spoken language, you will at least begin to increase your conversational quality and rid your speaking of the written or essay-like sound that disturbs and hampers efficient listening.

Improving Your Style

In looking back on what we have said concerning the nature and characteristics of style, you may be moved to say, "That's all very well, but what can I do to meet the demands for sound management of language in speaking? What sort of program for long-range improvement should I follow?" We advise you to:

1. *Become language conscious.* Sensitize yourself to good and bad uses of words. Discover your faults in grammar and those points of style where you seem to be most limited. Ferret out such weaknesses as want of vividness, poor syntax, malapropism, use of clichés. Listen carefully. Read widely. At times read aloud to test the "orality" of your prose.

2. *Increase your speaking vocabulary.* Make conscious efforts to extend the number of words and phrasings at your command. Reading will help. So will writing. Do not go out of your way to master unusual words and unique phrases; learn the meanings of language you encounter but do not understand. You are after the most accurate and most appropriate words. Keep a dictionary handy and refer to it. *Roget's Thesaurus* will also prove helpful. *Use* these references when words you do not know fall under your eye or upon your ear.

3. *Write.* By expressing yourself on paper you will learn to make conscious word choices. Writing will improve your vocabulary and the accuracy with which you use words. Aim for the best written expression when writing for the eye and the best oral expression when writing for the ear.

4. *Rewrite.* Once you've written it, put your speech aside; but come back to it, and rewrite it. The best speech makers who work from manuscript often put their speeches through several drafts. Franklin Roosevelt, master of the craft as he was, put some of his speeches through as many as twelve drafts before he was satisfied that he was saying things the right way. Benjamin Disraeli wrote, rehearsed alone and before friendly critics, and rewrote again—in order to speak extemporaneously! In rewriting, smooth out wordings, correct unclear constructions, tinker with phrasings, rearrange language and ideas. By polishing your utterance on paper you will make it more precise and vivid whether you are to speak from manuscript or extemporaneously.

5. *Study published and live speeches.* Note what makes for success and failure in style. Take cues from the good models. Avoid the faults of bad ones. Go so far at times as to imitate the style of others, but for practice and exercise only. Do not study the style of great speakers to copy them in your own original efforts but study them with an eye to incorporating their best attributes in a distinctive style suited particularly to you.

6. *Speak in public.* Take advantage of opportunities to refine your expression of ideas in both conversation and public address. Speak as often as possible. The more you speak, especially in the extemporaneous and impromptu modes, the better you will become at finding ways to finish phrases and statements effectively no matter how you started them. The more experience you have with thinking on your feet and symbolizing your ideas as they develop in your mind, the more fluent and attractive your style will become.

Style is that part of the art of public speaking which emerges from our choices and combinations of language. Its grammatical aspects and its psychological impact have been the subjects of investigation in the preceding pages. "The personal manner of utterance which gives movement and impact to ideas" is not decoration to be exhibited but that facet of speech making derived from reasonable and imaginative management of words.

Wording and thinking are inseparable processes wherever communication deserves its name; hence, style in speaking must always be viewed as one more means to winning a particular response under particular circumstances. The origins of the word, *style,* and the meanings assigned to it through history remind us that what we call oral style cannot be separated from the whole act of speaking, except for purposes of discussion. Style, good or indifferent or bad, is present in all speaking; and it colors listeners' perceptions of other qualities the speaking exhibits. But there seem no grounds for supposing that *a* universally suitable style can be described either for the individual speaker or for any of his customary purposes: informing, inquiring, reinforcing, persuading, and entertaining. We have therefore contended that it must be the business of each speaker to understand the resources of language for effective expression of ideas and to develop through practice and experience that style best suited to his needs and talents.

As we have seen, it is easier to describe style than to determine exactly how language usage affects those who listen or to prescribe the processes by which stylistic excellence is to be acquired. What speakers must come to appreciate is that the evocative power of language may range from "plain" to "grand," that words have multiple meanings—denotative and connotative, and that the many minor devices of language manipulation called figures of speech offer resources for achieving special degrees of clarity and force. Given these understandings of the resources of language, sensitive judgments concerning the demands of subject, audience, occasion, and self must guide the speaker toward those choices that yield the stylistic virtues of accuracy, clarity, propriety, economy, force, striking quality, and—above all—liveliness.

The resources of language are so diverse and the powers of language so subtle no one has ever yet understood either fully. But college students, statesmen, ministers, lawyers, teachers, and hundreds of others have consistently demonstrated that, given *some* understanding of language, thoughtfulness, readiness to adapt, and intelligently planned and evaluated practice can yield what we have defined as style: *The personal manner of utterance which gives movement and impact to ideas.*

E x e r c i s e s

W r i t t e n

1. Select the definition of style which you consider to be best from the standpoint of public speaking. Write an essay in which you defend your choice.

2. Choose a speech from *Vital Speeches* or from an anthology of public addresses. Study it carefully. Write an essay in which you (a) identify the stylistic devices the speaker has employed in his use of language as support for his ideas; and (b) point out particular word choices marked by clarity, propriety, and economy.

3. Rewrite the following sentences for oral delivery:

   a. Therefore, it is evident that before you can provide an elucidation of the operational functions of the system for the propagation and dissemination of information you would be required to make a thorough investigation of the public relations branch of the corporation.

   b. If one had one's preference, one would be likely to hold a preference for one's own photographic equipment with which to photograph one's own favorite subjects.

   c. Easily seen is the fact that the playing field is surrounded by a large metal fence over which the ball often passes when a home run is made.

   d. Even although I had been selected to represent my college, had planned my itinerary to the meeting, which incidentally was held sixty miles from the college itself, had packed my clothing for the journey, which I did the night before, had reserved my seat in the airplane, which was a jet and was flight 107, and had persuaded my close friend, whose name was Mark Smith, to convey me to the airport, I was still in fear that the weather would prevent my going to the convention at all.

   e. "Like I said," she said, "Jane's cheeks looked as red as roses, however, I discovered that the effect was all due to the application by her of cosmetic in large quantity."

4. Rewrite the following paragraph in such a way as to give it the motion-picture quality discussed in the section of this chapter devoted to Liveliness.

   My most embarrassing experience was when I was a boy. It was the result of my getting into a place I had no business being. I had crawled under our old back porch and had found some paint cans. I had pried off the tops with a stick. Then I had put my hands into one can after another. First I put them into a can of green paint. Then I put them into a can of red paint, and then into a can of yellow. The color which resulted was an ugly brown. When I finally finished, my clean clothes had paint dribbled all over them. I was a mess. What was embarrassing though was that I couldn't get the paint off. After a licking by my mother, a bottle of turpentine was given to me, and I tried to get the paint off with that. I rubbed and rubbed with a cloth, but there was so much paint it just wouldn't come off. I was embarrassed for a whole week because it was summertime, and I looked as if I were wearing a pair of brown gloves. I guess I felt most foolish when my piano teacher came to give me my lesson, and I had to explain why my hands were as they were. I also felt very foolish on Sunday. I was sure that everybody was looking at my hands when I was up there singing in the choir.

5. a. Identify the kinds of imagery used in the following passage taken from a speech by a college student.

> The quiet rural atmosphere had been effectively shattered. Chickens and feathers flew fast and furiously from both sides of the road. Cattle, only a moment before peacefully pastured, ran in aimless directions. Farmers' horses became frightened and reared into the air. A low-slung sports car, flashing and brilliant yellow in the afternoon sunlight, thundered through the rural village, a beautiful blonde movie queen at the wheel. An aroused policeman hauled the straw-haired beauty over to the side of the road, arrested her, and brought her before a justice of the peace who fined her five dollars. The indignant beauty thrust a 10 dollar bill into his hand and stalked out of the courtroom. "Just a minute," shouted the judge, "your change." "Keep it," she hurled back as she hopped into the auto, "I'm going out of here a hell of a lot faster than I came in."[55]

b. Identify the figures of speech used in the above passage.

c. List the kinds of imagery *not* used.

d. Write a paragraph commenting upon the strengths and weaknesses in the rhetorical style of the passage.

Oral

1. Compose and deliver a two-minute narrative in which you use (a) at least three different figures of speech and (b) at least three different kinds of imagery.

[55] From the manuscript of a speech entitled 'Seven Years of Silent Excitement," by Nelson T. Joyner, Jr. Used by permission.

2. Take a speech you delivered during a prior session of your class. Drawing upon what you now know about style, redo the speech or a portion of it and deliver it again. Discuss the effects of the deliberate stylistic changes with your listeners.

11   *Delivery*

The utterance of a message in the presence of other people is an intimately revealing act, probably the most intimately revealing public behavior in which we engage. We know that when we speak to others we lay open for inspection our minds, knowledge, integrity, social grace, and even our muscular coordination. For most people this is, at least at first, a worrisome business. As a consequence, many cast about for *rules* of physical action. Presumably they hope to discover in prescriptions the means of seeming knowledgeable, poised, and self-controlled. This is one reason no facet of public speech has been more discussed than delivery.

Theorists have explored the mechanics, the patterns, and the potentialties of vocal and gestural expression with astonishing patience and detail. Natural gestural communication has been charted and reduced to rule. Natural vocal patterns have been analyzed and recorded in complicated notational systems so that what is natural might be imitated precisely. This and more has been done in the interests of enabling men and women to speak their meanings clearly and conventionally in public. The assurance with which such efforts have been carried out is suggested by the following statement written less than a hundred years ago:

By the study and work of Delsarte a science has been created, every fleeting sign of emotion has been fixed, and may be reproduced at will; and this for the instruction of the artist who may never have observed them in another, nor himself felt the impressions that give rise to them.[1]

The explanations for such avid interest in the physical aspects of public speaking are doubtless many and subtle. Some of this interest, it appears, developed from the ancient tendency to treat the five canons of rhetoric

[1] Angelique Arnaud, "Arnaud on Delsarte," in *Delsarte System of Oratory* (New York: Edward S. Werner, 1887), p. 246.

as individual arts of speech. Unquestionably, much interest in studying delivery for its own sake also grew out of a feeling that if we could learn enough about bodily action, we would find that all men have an elemental gestural language in common. And, of course, much attention to voice and action stemmed from the belief that related principles must govern the artistic use of the human body in dance, music, speech, and acting. We think, however, that the most common reasons for the consuming interest laymen and students of public speaking always have in delivery are traceable to feelings we all share about ourselves and our relationships with others.

To try to communicate with another—to seek to influence his experience by speaking to him—is to take risks. There is the possibility of succeeding in the influence we attempt, but there is also the risk of failing to influence. There is the possibility of achieving a strong and favorable personal relationship—of being well thought of, but there is the peril of revealing some incapacity or unconventionality that will cause one to lose face. There is the possibility of so coordinating thought, language, and action in speech that the communication represents one's inner experience precisely as intended; but there is the hazard that something will go wrong with this attempt at coordination and the resulting behavior will convey what was not intended.

It is normal that we should be anxious to insure ourselves against the uncertainties of speech, and it is certainly not abnormal that we should in consequence seek precise, sure ways of regulating external actions. Thus, as men have asked for centuries, we too ask, "How *should* body and voice, the physical instruments of speech, be managed?" It is, after all, the body our listeners see and the voice they hear.

Speech *is* intimately revealing. Speaking *does* involve us in risk taking. Physical and vocal activity *do* furnish cues by which other people form judgments of our worth and self-control. The crucial question for those who practice the art of public speaking is: Can the risks of speaking be minimized by adopting *rules* of delivery? This is the question men and women of Western culture have been disputing since the days of Gorgias and probably before, yet every speaker must settle it for himself—by choice or by default. Before trying to establish your own answer, you ought to know something about answers others have made to the question.

Schools of Delivery

THE IMITATIVE SCHOOL

In his book, *The Province of Expression,* S. S. Curry says that what is probably the oldest method for developing delivery can be labelled the "imitative." He adds: "Many in every age have practiced this method; but the teachers who have practically followed it while not theoretically believing in it are numerous. . . . Those who believe in this method quote from Aristotle and contend that art is founded upon imitation, or at least must begin in imitation."[2]

Those committed to imitative action argue that the only way to get at a subjective art like delivery is by imitation. They contend that all art requires example. For them, the teacher serves as a model whom his students ought to imitate. The "touchstone technique" is the key to learning. The art of delivery is supposedly so subtle that analysis of it is impossible; therefore, the best method of improving delivery becomes direct or indirect copying. Little attention is paid to action of the mind during speaking or to the adaptation of the speaker's delivery to a particular audience. Direct study of the elements of delivery, movement, and voice are often bypassed. Such a method, as Curry insists, appears to violate the laws of nature which remind us that all expression comes from within, that everything in nature is original. Imitative delivery takes no account of the fact that individual temperaments differ, audiences differ, occasions differ.

THE MECHANICAL SCHOOL

The general characteristic of the mechanical or elocutionary view of delivery is that it begins with analysis of the vocal and visual elements of presentation. It is rooted in careful study of vocal modulation, inflection and stress, posture, facial expression, and gesture. From such empirical study, rules for the correct or natural expression of thought and emotion are then derived.

[2] S. S. Curry, *The Province of Expression* (Boston: Expression Co., 1927), p. 301. Professor Curry discusses "imitative," "mechanical," and "impulsive" schools of delivery.

One of the founders of this approach to delivery was Thomas Sheridan, dramatic coach, father of Richard Brinsley Sheridan, the British dramatist. He wrote several works on elocution, the most important of which was his *Lectures on Elocution,* published first in London in 1762. Sheridan's attempt to discover a mechanical method of explaining delivery was followed by the attempts of many others. Joshua Steele's *Prosodia Rationalis,*[3] with its system of musical notation for the speaking voice, and Gilbert Austin's *Chironomia,*[4] with its painstaking descriptions and prescriptions for achieving correct posture, gesture, and movement, are books which illustrate ways of pursuing the method. One of the books to carry the mechanical method of studying delivery nearest to perfection was Dr. James Rush's *Philosophy of the Human Voice,* published in 1828. Every passion, Rush thought, had a particular stress. He divided stress into categories with such labels as "radical," "medium," "intermittent," and "compound." He further held that such qualities of voice as stress and inflection could be regulated by rule. Like Steele, he believed that the proper natural passions could be represented by printed notations such as those found in musical scores. Though books such as those just mentioned are rare today, there are still some contemporary works which recommend careful annotation of scripts to remind the reader of intended vocal and bodily manipulations.

Those who have approached the study of delivery through mechanical methods have sought to improve upon nature by providing rules whereby ideal delivery may be attained. Nothing is left to chance or inspiration. All elements of the performance are prescribed; how a thing is to be said must be decided before any utterance takes place. Impromptu and extemporaneous modes of delivery are poor vehicles for achieving perfection under such a system. The mind of the speaker using the mechanical method usually dwells upon the manner of speaking more than upon what is being said. Correctives based upon rules are prescribed for particular imperfections, and the danger is that picayune details receive a disproportionate amount of attention. Even though the mechanical approach to delivery emphasizes the importance of thorough, scientific knowledge about the behaviors of the voice and body during speaking, it makes no allowance for adaptation at

---

[3] *Prosodia Rationalis: or An Essay Towards Establishing the Melody and Measure of Speech, to Be Expressed and Perpetuated by Peculiar Symbols* (London, 1779).

[4] Gilbert Austin, *Chironomia or a Treatise on Rhetorical Delivery* (London, 1806).

the moment of utterance and produces inflexibility if adhered to completely. It is a method alien to audience-centered performance.

Curry attributed the popularity of mechanical delivery to human nature.[5] Men like to think all that is needed to produce good speech are a few rules for vocal and visual action. They want to ignore the action of mind, for criticisms of one's ideas are taken far more personally than criticisms of one's techniques in transmitting them. The mechanical or elocutionary system appeals particularly to those who are certain that the substance of what they say is above reproach. It also appeals to those who search for a scientific base, rooted in fact, for their conduct during delivery. Its difficulty is that it emphasizes the external aspects of speaking above the creative processes that are the justifications for speaking at all.

THE IMPULSIVE SCHOOL

At the opposite pole from the speaker who follows a mechanical method is the speaker who allows impulse to govern his communication. The impulsive school of delivery is founded erroneously upon the writings of Richard Whately.[6] From Whately's criticisms of mechanical delivery and from other sources, certain teachers derived an anti-elocutionist viewpoint which has persisted in some quarters to the present day. Those who hold this extension of Whately's position contend that it is best to leave delivery to impulse. They advocate no system at all. Total naturalness is their goal. They overlook the fact that art demands skill and control as well as spontaneous inspiration. They also overlook the unconventional habits and abnormal conditions which ought to be corrected by training. They advocate allowing the feelings one has at the moment, whether relevant or not, to hold sway. They would say that when the feeling predominates, delivery becomes what it was meant to be—natural.

THE THINK-THE-THOUGHT SCHOOL

As we have indicated, the impulsive approach to delivery was not a true interpretation of Whately. Whately insisted that a speaker ought to

[5] S. S. Curry, *The Province of Expression*, pp. 324–325.
[6] See his *Elements of Rhetoric*, of which there are a number of printings published in England and the United States.

concentrate upon what he is saying. It is evident from his writings that he did not advocate impulsive delivery. He did say:

The practical rule then to be adopted, in conformity with the principles here maintained, is, not only to pay no studied attention to the voice, but studiously to *withdraw* the thoughts from it, and to dwell as intently as possible on the Sense; trusting to nature to suggest spontaneously the proper emphases and tones.

* * * * *

He who not only understands fully what he is reading [aloud], but is earnestly occupying his mind with the matter of it, will be likely to read as if he understood it, and thus to make others understand it; and in like manner, with a view to the impressiveness of the delivery, he who not only feels it, but is exclusively absorbed with that feeling, will be likely to read as if he felt it, and to communicate the impression to his hearers. But this cannot be the case if he is occupied with the thought of what their opinion will be of his reading, and, how his voice ought to be regulated;—if, in short, he is thinking of himself, and, of course, in the same degree, abstracting his attention from that which ought to occupy it exclusively.[7]

At another point Whately said,

When however I protest against all artificial systems of Elocution, and all *direct* attention to Delivery, *at the time*, it must not be supposed that a *general* inattention to that point is recommended; or that the most perfect Elocution is to be attained by never thinking at all on the subject; though it may safely be affirmed that even this negative plan would succeed far better than a studied modulation.[8]

It is apparent that Whately really recommended thinking the thought, occupying the mind with ideas, rather than with worry about prescribed behaviors in delivery.

We see, then, that Whately put ideas at the center of his theory of delivery but that he did not recommend that *no* attention be paid to the use of body and voice. There are some extremists who would go farther. They would say that all you need to do is to think the thought; delivery will then take care of itself. They are a bit like the followers of the impulsive school who admonish, "Feel the feeling." We would say neither thinking

[7] Richard Whately, *Elements of Rhetoric*, 6th rev. ed. (London: B. Fellowes, 1841), pp. 401–403.
[8] *Ibid.*, pp. 392–393.

the thought or feeling and reacting will alone generate good delivery. One may do either with his back to the audience, while mumbling into his beard, or while focusing his gaze on the rafters.

Delivery as Adaptation

The approach to delivery which we advocate is a modification of Whately's theory reinforced by the teachings of James A. Winans. We hold that to think the thought is not enough, though it is primary. We propose that one ought to achieve both a keen sense of communication and a vivid realization of one's idea at the moment of utterance, and, moreover, be able to *control* all the channels of action—mental, physical, and vocal—to support and reinforce ideas. We say there are no hard and fast rules for delivery. Delivery must be adapted to all the demanding elements in the speech situation: the material, the audience, the occasion, and the speaker himself. None of these aspects of the situation is ever frozen or absolutely set; they make fluctuating demands. Even so, there are principles which may be followed to achieve effective, adaptive delivery, and these are in accord with the point of view we have just expressed.

GENERAL PRINCIPLES

We hold that in all delivery there is a fundamental axiom which all public speakers ought to bear in mind. *Good delivery helps the listener to concentrate upon what is being said; it does not attract attention to itself.* If this is adopted as a governing premise, we can further say that in reaching this objective:

1. *You should remember that you are not speaking to perform or to exhibit yourself.* Delivery should be viewed as a means to an end, not as an end in itself. During public speaking the message is the most important thing to be exhibited. It is more important than you are. Your mission should never be to show off your body, your grace, or your clothing. It must be to communicate ideas.

2. *You should realize fully the content of your words as you utter*

them. Following this precept, originally formulated by Professor Winans, means that you must concern yourself with the full process of communication during the moments of delivery. To create or re-create ideas vividly at the moment they are being uttered means that you reactivate a subject and ideas to support it, that you regenerate the enthusiasm that led you to speak in the first place. This enthusiasm must last from the first moments of preparation through the last syllable of your speech. You must be in control of assimilated ideas so that they are at your bidding. You must have become so intimately acquainted with them as you structured, worded, and orally rehearsed them that no matter what happens during the actual presentation of your speech, you will be master of your speech, your feelings toward its substance, and your audience's response to it. Professor Winans put your needs well when he said:

. . . there should be full and sharp realization of content. And this includes more than bare meaning; the implications and emotional content must also be realized. The reference here is not merely to those striking emotions commonly recognized as such, but also to those attitudes and significances constantly present in lively discourse: the greater or less importance of this or that statement, the fact that this is an assertion and this a concession (with an implied "granted" or "to be sure"), this is a matter of course while this has an element of surprise, and so on through all possible changes.[9]

The ideas you work with must be in your grasp so that you can support them through your own behavior, vigorously and forcefully. The ideas you have painstakingly worked over must come alive. They must flow. You must be running over with them, yet in control of them and your thoughts about them. You must be able to lose yourself in your speech and still maintain control of your experience.

No matter how well you know your materials, the impression you ought to give during extemporaneous delivery should be of meeting the ideas for the first time. You ought not be serving up limp remnants from creative experience. What was alive as you prepared and as you rehearsed orally must come to life again in the actual speech situation. Overrehearsal, loss of enthusiasm, repetition to the point of being "sick of the whole

[9] From *Speechmaking* by James A. Winans. Copyright, 1938, D. Appleton-Century Company, Inc., p. 25. Reprinted by permission of Appleton-Century-Crofts.

thing" will promote mechanical, boring, dull delivery. The process of speaking, you must remember, is one of creation and re-creation.

3. *You should cultivate a keen sense of communication.* This second step which we borrow also from Professor Winans is closely allied to the first. Enthusiastic response to ideas and supporting materials is again a necessity. A keen sense of communication is more easily felt than described. Thinking of public speaking as dialogue rather than as soliloquy will help. Talk *with* the audience not *at* them. Dwell on ideas until you are sure of the response for which you work. Try to feel on the platform what you experience during verbal exchanges with your friends over the dinner table, on the athletic field, or in bull sessions. We experience this keen sense of sharing minds daily; trying to recapture the same sense in public speaking makes for lively delivery. By assuming a false, tense, artificial mood we rob public speaking of the urgency and eagerness it ought to have. As Professor Winans said:

> We should make sure in our efforts to bring this communicative tone into our delivery that it springs from mental attitudes; for it, no more than other tones, should be assumed as a trick of delivery. The attempt to assume it is likely to result in an over familiar confidential or wheedling tone which is most objectionable.[10]

4. *You should be direct.* People are seldom evasive when they are in earnest. Look the audience in the eye. If you look elsewhere, so will your audience. If you look at your audience, they will look back at you. Looking at a spot on the back wall will not produce directness. You will give the impression that you are in a trance. A dead-fish stare while you call up ideas and wordings will not do. Neither will darting your eyes from person to person in the audience or addressing one side of the audience to the exclusion of the other. In the first instance eye contact will be so fleeting that it will be no contact at all. In the second, a whole segment of the audience will think that you have ignored them.

Your eyes are the most expressive parts of your face. Haven't they been called "the windows of the soul"? More than any other part of your body they reveal your emotions. And it is your feeling for content that that delivery must convey. So you should face front and direct your eyes to

[10] *Ibid.*, p. 28.

your listeners. Try looking at a segment of the audience or at one or two people in a particular area of the room as you develop an idea. When you have finished with that idea, and as you start the next one, direct your gaze to another part of the audience. As you move to subsequent ideas, refocus each time. Then you will talk *with* your audience, not *at* them or *past* them.

Directness is fundamentally a matter of direct eye contact. Attain this much and the probabilities are that you will also be tolerably direct vocally and in movement.

5. *You should punctuate and support your ideas with your body and your voice.* Channel your physical resources to the reinforcement of your message. Let your bodily actions and your vocal intonations operate as means to the end of warm, emphatic communication. In speech making, gestures, pitch changes, variations in vocal rate and volume, pauses, shifts in posture, and walking take the place of the commas, italics, exclamation points, and question marks in written communication. Intelligibility and clarification often depend greatly upon support and emphasis from your physique. Learn to use *yourself* often and with control. Some special considerations in this connection are discussed below under the heading "Bodily Action" (pp. 297–300).

6. *You should remember that emotional and physical responses are generated by your delivery.* What you do with your body and your voice will stimulate your audience to respond in like manner. In a later section of this chapter we shall discuss the nature of these empathic responses more fully. As a guiding principle, however, we observe here that you ought to be aware that what your listeners see and hear will cause them to have physical and emotional reactions. If you are nervous and fidgety, your audience will become so. If you sound as if your throat hurts, theirs will hurt. If the audience detects that you are tense and rigid, they will experience the same physical states. If you are confident or indecisive, smiling or depressed, tough or soft in manner, the listeners will feel so too. Your auditors will respond to what they perceive; therefore, it is up to you to control what they take in. Your manner will determine the experiences they will have. These experiences may be pleasant or unpleasant, relaxed or tense, casual or formal according to your behavior. Once you have made your decisions in invention, disposition, and language choice, you are

responsible for making the audience aware of them by the visual and vocal cues you provide for them.

7. *You should focus the attention of the audience.* Realize that your task is to control your audience and that in doing so you must direct their attention to whatever heightens your meaning, be it an image created with words or a visual aid. It is not enough merely to gain attention at the outset of a speech; you must maintain it by constantly directing attention to the stimuli playing the most important roles in stirring up meanings in each moment of discourse. You are remiss if you allow audience attention to wander. You are also remiss if you do not replace an irrelevant stimulus with a relevant one. Displace distracting stimuli—a flapping window shade, a smell from the laboratory down the hall, your listener's fatigue—with strong stimuli bearing upon your message. Bodily movement and vocal variation are resources always available to you for this purpose. Control of attention through these means is normally as necessary as control achieved by selection of material, structure, and style.

8. *All aspects of your delivery should promote conversational quality.* We noted differences between conversation and public speaking in Chapter I (pp. 10–12). We observed there that public speaking contrasts with conversation in that we speak more loudly, are relatively uninterrupted, focus attention more sharply, are more systematically prepared, and have less opportunity to perceive the responses of our auditors. But effective public speaking has important characteristics of good conversation: directness, spontaneity, animation, and emphasis. It is therefore conversational *quality*, not conversational *style*, that ought to be sought for the most effective delivery. Reproduced conversation will not satisfy. While speeches ought to be so delivered that they sound like conversation, they must still be more dignified, more eloquent, and more forceful than conversation itself. Alertness, the working of mind and body in lively response to the meanings of ideas and audience reactions, is the goal in speech making. Even the strong emphasis and sudden outbursts that characterize good conversation ought to be characteristic of your public speaking.

Public speaking is not exhibitionism; it is sensitive re-creation of ideas by a speaker whose *whole being* directs, punctuates, stimulates, and focuses meaning—after the manner of a conversationalist now aware of his enlarged responsibilities.

BODILY ACTION

We have several times implied in the earlier pages of this chapter that the chief instrumentalities of delivery are physical actions involving the face, limbs, and torso and expressive use of the voice. The broad principles we have just outlined apply to any aspect of delivery, but there are some special considerations having to do with bodily communication that deserve discussion.

To begin with, any speaker must understand that his actions are of two kinds: overt and covert. Overt action is open to inspection and is easily perceived by the audience. Covert action is covered or concealed. An audience may sense concealed action in the organism of a speaker even though the action cannot be seen. For example, the contractions of hidden muscles of the throat or leg are actions audiences may sense through perceiving the speaker's tension but without being able to locate the on-going activity itself. Both overt and covert action take place during speaking and the speaker is aware of both.

Strong feeling often turns covert action into overt action. A spectator at a football game may so strongly wish his team to score that he actually crouches, reproducing the thrust he wants a ball carrier to prepare for. On the other hand, the spectator may not go all the way in his response and may perform the action only partially. For fear of audience censure, he may inhibit his actions allowing only muscular contractions well hidden beneath his skin or clothing. Less dramatic but similar behaviors occur constantly on the public speaking platform. It is not unusual to see speakers sufficiently moved by indignation or determination to bring a clenched fist into sight from behind the lectern or to hear the rap of hidden knuckles as he utters his strongest words.

All action, then, is covert or overt. And whether evident or concealed, actions associated with speaking express *something*. The practical questions about these actions concern whether they express relevant meaning and whether they do it conventionally. In order to talk clearly about whether given actions serve their practial ends, however, it is useful to have a few agreed-upon terms by which to refer to specific kinds of bodily action.

Descriptions of action. It is common practice to refer to categories of action when describing or evaluating movement. "Eye contact" is the phrase used to denote the focusing of the eyes upon the audience. "Posture" or "stance" usually refers to the position of the whole body. "Movement" is the label ordinarily used to indicate walking or movement of the entire body. "Gesture" is the word used to indicate movement of the hands and arms. "Facial expression" is self-explanatory, as are "head action" and "shoulder action."

Adjective labels are also applied to aspects of the broad categories of these actions. Postures are often characterized as "parade rest," "limp rag," "skating," "whipped dog," "the Colossus of Rhodes." "On the balls of the feet" is a phrase used to describe good posture.

Gestures are labelled in three ways. One set of terms indicates their functions: emphatic, descriptive, and suggestive. Other terms indicate the position of the hand at the time of gesture: palm up, palm down, clenched fist, and index finger. Still another set is based upon inherent qualities of gesture: habitualized, natural, nervous.

Good gestures we are told, and we agree, are gestures characterized by vitality, proper coordination, good timing, integration with other bodily movements, habitualization, appropriateness, and the ability to hold some energy in reserve. We would add that good gestures employ broad strokes in large situations and subtle movements in small ones, and usually just precede the idea they reinforce. It is useful to have names for familiar patterns of behavior. It is more useful to have principles by which to govern behavior.

Principles of Good Bodily Action. The questions students ask are: "How shall I walk?" "How shall I stand?" "How shall I move?" "What shall I do with my hands?" "How can I register feeling in my face?" There are, of course, no prescriptions. Action suitable to an instant of speaking on a particular subject in a particular place at a particular time cannot be rigidly prescribed if the circumstances are to be taken into consideration. Mechanical planning and execution, which prescription implies, do violence to the individualized nature of the public speech. There are, however, generalized hypotheses that can be made about the successful use of action. Exceptions to these are effective only under unusual circumstances. We may say:

1. Action should be in key with audience temperament and should prompt the sought reactions.

2. Action should be appropriate to the occasion.
3. Action should reinforce, enhance, emphasize, and convey meanings.
4. Action should never detract from what the speaker is saying.
5. Action should refine the focus of attention.
6. Action should provide for the speaker's comfort by being easy and un-labored.
7. Action should reveal total concentration of the organism upon the expression and communication of the message during presentation.

The Demands for Action. Demands of the audience with respect to action are demands for stimuli to hold its attention and add to its understanding. They are demands for animation. The interest and understanding of the audience are sustained by moving, vital, graphic, and realistic meaning if the speaker uses action well. The audience nods if the speaker's body is asleep, if movement and gesture are vague, unchanging, or monotonous. A speaker who is eager to express himself will reveal his attitudes by bodily tonus and expression and his listener-viewers will respond in kind.

Further audience requirements for action derive from the ages of listeners. A group of kindergarten children listening to a talk on Africa may wish the speaker to be the elephant he describes. The five-year-old demands much action, for his attention span is short and his comprehension level, comparatively speaking, is low. His imaginative level is high so he responds with great delight when the speaker is literal and offers representational action in amplification of ideas. On the other hand, if the speaker were to address a gathering at the home for the aged, he would disturb his audience if he were to use a great deal of action or action that was especially fast. Unless his aim were humorous effect, this speaker dare not assume his hearers have never seen an elephant. The postures and gestures that gave joy to the child by seeming to represent the trunk of the animal are absurd in the sight of the mature. The younger the audience, the more plentiful and suggestive action may be. The older the audience, the more likely it will be that reserved and subtle action is meaningful and fitting.

The message, too, exerts pressure for bodily action. Since the listener's eye reads only the speaker's body and its surroundings during a speech, it receives whatever signals the speaker chooses to make in order to clarify his message. As we have noted, action is part of the punctuation of a speech. It is evident to the sensitive listener that an index finger shaken in the right way or brought down forcibly upon a table is in reality an exclamation point, just as a spread palm in horizontal motion may serve the same function as underlining. So it is that material often requires bodily action for proper emphasis. Often, too, action serves to clarify. A step or two in a new direction during a transition breaks and refocuses audience attention as a speaker moves from point to point in his speech. Other action is directly suggested by material, especially material involving literal description. For example, the easiest way to suggest spherical or square shapes is by gestures. During demonstrations of techniques necessary in military, gymnastic, or dance instruction, action is not just inherent in the material, action *is* the material, a part of the message to be conveyed.

The occasion may also govern action by requiring traditional action as in church ritual, or by requiring action suitable to the mood of the occasion. Quick, jerky movement in a softly lit, sedate ceremonial setting would normally be as inappropriate as would lazy, languid movement at a political rally. Even the time of day also exerts influence upon action. When it is late and the audience is tired, speakers do well to increase the flow and variety of their movement. Action must suit the setting and the time of day.

The action of the mind and the action of the body seek coordination. Action aids the speaker as a tension reducer even as it conveys his attitudes and feelings to listener-viewers. The speaker who is afraid, who lacks confidence, will feel better when he moves. Unhappily, such movement can take the form of fidgeting. Excess energy engendered by defense mechanisms when the speaker feels danger needs to be controlled. But if the speaker will direct his action toward reinforcing his message, it will be appropriate to his speech, to his audience, to the occasion and he will gain relief from it.

VOICE

Those who define speech broadly argue that a shrug of the shoulders or a crook of the finger is "speech," but it is impossible to conceive of public speech consisting of gestures alone. All public speaking requires at least tolerable vocal ability.

Management of the voice, then, ought to be a serious concern of every public speaker. He must be able to control his voice and use it flexibly. Yet, a sound course in public speaking cannot be a course in voice training.

To take time for vocal exercise in a public speaking class is usually inadvisable unless all members of the class possess identical weaknesses in vocal habits. Voice improvement is most wisely achieved, we think, by individual work on poor habits or by a separate course of study. Poor vocal habits ought to be remedied by private exercise and practice. Public, group exercises consume valuable time which ought to be devoted to speech making.

Minimum skill in vocal performance for public speaking meets the demands of the audience, the speech content, the occasion, and the speaker. You, as a speaker, must at least (1) be heard, (2) be understood clearly, and (3) be free from annoying vocal habits and distortions. Most of us can fulfill these minimal requirements. But there are some who do not meet the requirements simply because they have acquired poor habits in the formation of particular sounds—a "p" sounds like a "b" or an "l" like a "w." There are also those whose voices sound so unpleasant that the quality distracts from what is being said. It is obvious that any public speaker who forms sounds that are mistaken for other sounds, who cannot be heard, or who produces sounds so unpleasant to the ear that listening is made difficult is not going to achieve maximum effectiveness on the platform.

There is no one who cannot improve the vocal aspects of his performance. The great majority of us are endowed with adequate physical equipment for acceptable voice production. We do make sounds which are *usually* heard and understood, sounds which are adequate for communication. We may be sloppy and inaccurate or lack distinctness, but every day we convert ideas into sounds which convey meaning. But it is still universally true that anyone, no matter how pleasant his voice and clear his diction, can make it pleasanter. Witness those who have the most musical and flexible voices, the Laurence Oliviers and Maurice Evanses, who after years of experience continue to exercise their vocal mechanisms to improve intelligibility and quality.

It is not our purpose to provide a manual for those with defective voices or for those who wish to improve voice and diction through drill and exercise. Therapy to remove defects or to improve manipulative skill is a highly individual matter to be undertaken in addition to, and many times before, work in speech composition. Here, we intend to explain some of the aspects of normal vocal behavior as they relate to public speaking.

As we have already indicated, we believe that voice, like action, must be under the speaker's control, if a speech is to be effectively delivered. We agree that you must think what you are saying and that you ought not to be affected or "speak with your mind on your larynx," but to say you ought to pay no attention to understandability or to vocal flexibility could very well lead to failure. As we see it, for a good public speaker to attain clearness and variety, he needs to be generally acquainted with the process of producing meaningful sounds and with the variables of vocal expression: articulation, volume, rate, pitch, and quality.

Voice production. Speech is an "overlaid function" of the speech organs because each of them has some other primary purpose such as breathing or swallowing. Inspiration takes place as air is taken into the lungs through the nose and/or mouth, passed through the pharynx (throat), the larynx (voice box, vocal folds, or Adam's apple), the trachea (windpipe), the bronchi, and bronchial tubes. As air fills the lungs, they expand; the chest walls within which they are contained move outward and upward to create the partial vacuum that causes this lung expansion. The scaleni, intercostal, and elevator muscles which control the actions of the ribs come into play in this raising of the ribs and consequent expansion of the rib cage. During this action, the front wall of the abdomen also expands as the diaphragm—the muscular floor of the chest and the roof of the abdomen—moves downward compressing the visceral organs. When the rib muscles and the diaphragm relax, the latter moving upward in a recoiling action, the size of the chest cavity is again reduced and the air forced out of the lungs and through the trachea. As this exhalation takes place, the air passes through the larynx and between the vocal folds which vibrate to produce sound as the air passes through the glottis (the opening between the vocal folds). The length and thickness of the vocal folds and their state of tension are responsible for the pitch of the voice produced.

The sounds produced by the vibrating vocal folds are given character and quality as they are resonated from the surfaces of the pharynx, mouth, and nasal cavities. They are reflected from these surfaces and reinforced by them. Finally, certain sounds some of which are thus modified are turned into consonants by the articulators: the tongue, the teeth, the lips, and the soft palate which controls the passage of air between the mouth and nose. These sounds combine to form words, and the cycle is complete.

From this simplified description we see that the production of voice is a motor process involving breathing; a phonation process involving the vibration of the vocal folds; a resonation process involving the reinforcing surfaces of the mouth, throat, and nose; and an articulation process involving the formation and codification of specific sound symbols.

The cycle we have described repeats itself over and over again as we speak, and what happens at the various stages in the cycle is responsible for the distinctive attributes of the voice. The physical adjustments and modifications which take place during voice production and the general physical condition of the speaker are responsible for the individuality of each human voice. It has often been said that our voices are as distinctive as our fingerprints. Certainly we know we can readily identify one another by voice alone, that by the sound of the voice we know who is at the bottom of the stairs or around the corner.

Articulation. The most effective public speakers attain a high degree of clear, distinct sound formation. They articulate sounds well. They are not content to slur over words, to drop off word endings, to run together sounds which ought to be kept separate even though such slovenly practices do not always lead to misunderstanding. They aim for distinctness. Where the elision of sounds is called for, they naturally blend the sounds skillfully. They carefully guard against mistakes in articulation which result from addition, omission, or substitution of sounds. That is to say, they do not add sounds as in "athalete" for "athlete," "exscaped" for "escaped," "acrost" for "across." Nor do they omit sounds by saying "reglar" for "regular," or " 'nuff" for "enough." Nor do they substitute one sound for another by saying "hypmotism" for "hypnotism," "cartoon" for "carton," "ya" for "you," or "fella" for "fellow." They pronounce words in accordance with the conventions acceptable to their particular audiences. Generally speaking their authorities are dictionaries, community leaders, or experts in the field in which a given word is commonly used. They attack words with definiteness and end words crisply unless the word is supposed to die away gradually. They are attentive to "-ing," "-tion," and "-nd" word endings. They aspire to neat, businesslike utterance that is relaxed and unlabored. Through such considerations as we have enumerated here, they aspire to meet the demands of their audiences and their content for clear, controlled, understandable utterance. Meanwhile, they seek to create a personality image which pleases their audiences and themselves. And lest all this seem idealistic, let it be said that no speaker loses influence by conforming to the *best* standards of content, audience, and occasion. He does lose standing if he falls short of these demands.

Volume. The effective public speaker keeps himself in good physical condition and sees to it that he is sufficiently rested to produce appropriate volume or force. When we say *appropriate* volume, we mean that degree of loudness which meets the needs of the audience and the physical setting for the speech. Without straining, an audience ought to hear every word a speaker says, no matter what the size of the place in which he speaks. To be effective, speech must be easily heard. Where loud, strong utterance is required, the speaker ought to be able to produce it, but where the situation calls for soft or soothing utterance the speaker must be equal to that necessity.

Force is described in some textbooks as explosive, effusive, and expulsive. Explosive force is loudness characterized by violent changes in volume. Effusive force is gentle, sustained, and flowing. Expulsive force is somewhere in between and is marked by abruptness of initiation of the sounds.

Beginning speakers are often unskilled in assessing the audience and occasion demands for force due to a lack of speaking experience. Some speak in tiny, whispery, subdued voices which cannot be heard beyond the first row, because they are unable to judge how forcefully sounds must be produced in order to reach the rear of the room. Just as often, the beginning speaker speaks with too much volume. He unnerves his audience with too much force because he erroneously thinks that all speeches ought to be delivered loudly. He is like those people who think they must shout into the telephone in order to be heard at the other end of the wire. Too often a speaker mistakes force or loudness for intensity. He thinks that to be intense he must increase volume. Much intensity is, of course, of a very quiet sort which achieves its influence by its very want of force.

To make proper adjustments to situational demands for volume requires experience and practice. Where a student speaker repeatedly misjudges, a hearing test is in order. It may be that he does not hear himself accurately and as a result is using more or less force than needed.

Rate. Optimum effectiveness in public speaking requires a rate of speaking suited to the abilities of the audience to comprehend and to the emotional coloring or mood to be conveyed. Beginners tend to race through their speeches, stumbling over words, slurring them and blurring articulation. The audience cannot then keep up with the speaker. He passes from one symbol to another so rapidly that his listeners grasp them erratically. Ultimately, listeners may come to feel they are running a losing race and so give up, exclaiming to themselves, "What's the use?" The remedy is disciplined self-control on the speaker's part. If he thinks the thought, means the thought, and *paces utterance to meaning*, his listeners will have no cause to complain.

Where ideas are not under control, are not at the speaker's beck and call, rate may become inappropriately slow, lagging behind the audience's abilities to comprehend. Again, the result is irritation. The audience wishes the speaker would "get on with it."

Where rate is either too fast or too slow the speaker has disregarded his audience and his own meaning. Usually he is speaking *at* his listeners rather than thinking out his material *with* them. The cause of slowness may be poor preparation. Perhaps he is birthing his ideas, finding them for the first time in slow, disjointed wordings while his audience waits impatiently. The cause of undue rapidity may be want of the keen sense of communication we have already discussed. Meaningfulness, self-discipline and consideration for the audience are the only serviceable roads to improvement.

Ineffectual pausing and phrasing are characteristic of poorly managed rate. The too-rapid speaker does not take time to group words into meaningful thought units; nor does he stop at intervals frequent enough for the audience to catch up with him and absorb his ideas. The too-slow speaker breaks ideas within thought groups so that meaning is distorted or lost; his pauses are simply stops during which he collects his thoughts. He hesitates, often filling the resulting silence with vocalizations—"uhs" and "ers." His disfluency destroys meaning, destroying effectiveness also.

A mark of the skilled speaker is that he controls rate as he observes audience cues which signal that listeners are or are not absorbing his message. He responds to his audience as he observes them. If he sees frowns or puzzled looks, he may slow down, at the same time modifying content by repeating what he has already said or by adding new ideas to make his point clearer and more acceptable. If he sees his listeners staring vacantly or assuming lolling, indifferent bodily postures, he may speed up or slow down in order to produce variety and thus recapture attention. If he sees knowing smiles or heads nodding in agreement and understanding, he may speed up since he has been given a "go" signal which says that what he is saying is readily understood and he need not belabor it. Speed ought to match the rate of comprehension.

The content of the speech often demands variations in rate and certain quantities (meaning elongation of particular sounds, usually vowels). A blow-by-blow description of a boxing match would sound ludicrous if delivered at largo pace and with elongation of vowel sounds within each word. Similarly, to describe a quiet, calm, romantic canoe ride in the still dusk with rapid rate, shortened duration of sounds within words, and abrupt, staccato rhythms would neither reinforce meanings nor create appropriate mood. Just as rate ought to match comprehension, it ought to be suited to the material's meaning and tenor.

If rate is to be correlated with reception, meaning, and mood, it will, of necessity, be varied. To speak at the same rate throughout a public speech produces monotony and invites the audience to turn its attention elsewhere if, indeed, it does not lull them to sleep.

Pitch.   Flexibility in pitch is a further indication of the skilled speaker, for it shows that he knows a lack of variety in pitch is just as hampering as a lack of variety in volume or rate. A lack of variety in all three, as most of us are aware from listening to lecturers who have droned their ways through an hour without any vocal adjustments, can destroy the meaning of even the best ideas and the attentiveness of even the most willing listeners.

Each of us has a pitch level which is natural and normal. Hanley and Thurman say, "Research findings for superior young adult male and female speakers are that their average (habitual) pitch levels are C_3 and $G\#_3$ respectively . . . or one octave and two musical notes, respectively below middle C."[11] They, as others who have made a special study of voice, recommend that no one institute a program for the relocation of pitch without medical consultation. They further add:

> Pitch (frequency) is a function of balances among length, tension and mass in the vibration of a taut string, which your vocal cords resemble to a considerable degree. In your vocal mechanism these balances or this adjustment has been arrived at over a span of years. Your average level changed from infancy to childhood to young adulthood, where you now stand. In the absence of better information, we believe, it should be assumed that your physiological maturation has been as normal in the larynx as it has been in your upper arm, or ankle, or any other anatomical locus. If this is true, if you have normal cords which vibrate under normal tension, then the frequency at which they vibrate most often is

[11] Theodore D. Hanley and Wayne L. Thurman, *Developing Vocal Skills* (New York: Holt, Rinehart and Winston, 1962), p. 144. By permission of Holt, Rinehart and Winston, Inc.

the best, the one at which you can produce sounds longest, with least effort. Temporary movements away from that frequency are good, for obvious reasons. But an ill-considered shift of any magnitude away from that habitual level can result in vocal strain and other more serious effects. . . .[12]

We may note, however, that a number of people unintentionally key their speech too high or too low. This is true in general and it is especially true at the outset of a speech or at points where tenseness and nervousness impair ability to vary pitch levels. If a speaker selects an artificial basic pitch to begin with, it will be difficult for him to inflect upward or downward for emphasis or meaning. If he does not take such steps to reduce tension as discussed in Chapter 3, he will also find himself adopting pitch levels that do not allow reasonable expression of meaning.

Changes in pitch are effected by raising or lowering the key of the voice either gradually or abruptly between or within words. Gradual changes in pitch are referred to as "slides," since we actually slide from one key to another. Abrupt changes are called "steps." The way in which we modify pitch oftentimes determines what we mean and the degree of emphasis we place upon the idea. In fact, through inflection, it is possible to convey a meaning opposite to that inherent in the words used. "Oh no" can convey a variety of meanings depending upon the way it is inflected. "Oh, no" inflected upward by means of a step may convey disbelief. "Oh, no" inflected downward by means of a slide may indicate indecision. "Oh no" inflected downward by means of a slide may indicate dismay or may mean "yes." When pitch varies within words or individual sounds we call the inflection "circumflex."

The demands for appropriate pitch most often come from the material in the speech. To give the material meaning it must be inflected. In daily conversation we do not think much about the matter of inflection or changes in key, for we automatically make changes consonant with meanings. We inflect upward at the ends of questions which are to be answered "yes" or "no" without thinking and downward on questions to be answered with other than "yes." At the same time we stress words to produce shades of meaning. "*Did* he go?" is different in meaning from "Did *he* go?" or "Did he *go?*" because the word stressed varies even though in each case we have inflected upward. By changing the pitch through steps or slides upward and

[12] *Ibid.*, p. 145.

downward and by stressing or giving force to a different word each time, we can see that it is possible to effect a variety of meanings though we have not in any way changed the word symbols conveying our message.

The demands of the audience for variety in pitch are demands for interestingness and for comprehension of meaning. A further demand is for comfortable empathic responses which result from the appropriateness of the speaker's basic pitch. If an audience perceives from inflections that you are not thinking what you are saying or that you lack enthusiasm for your ideas or are falsely enthusiastic, if they see that you are uncomfortable and unable to move freely within a pitch range, you cannot expect them to respond appreciatively to your message.

The speaker's need for flexibility of pitch arises from his need to avoid feelings of strain. Also, he listens to his own voice as he speaks and is in some degree stimulated or bored by what he hears.

The occasion or setting must be considered in establishing pitch controls. Pitch helps to establish mood. High pitch can create impressions of tension and excitement while low tones can help to convey solemnity or calmness. Pitch and the power to project adequate sound are related. To fill a large hall or to speak above competing noises one must adopt his most comfortable and efficient pitch range so that all resources of a relatively relaxed vocal mechanism are at his disposal in overcoming the difficulties imposed by unfavorable conditions of the setting.

Quality. Quality is produced by changes in the shapes and sizes of the resonators, e.g., pharynx, mouth, nasal passages. No uniformly accepted set of labels exists for describing vocal qualities, but labels have been attached to various types of voices.

In criticizing the vocal aspects of a speech it is common practice to say that a speaker's voice is breathy, nasal, denasal, pectoral, oral, guttural, metallic, strident, or orotund. These terms are really attempts to explain vocal resonance or placement, to say something about what is happening along the path of the breath stream which produces sound. To say a voice is *nasal* means that an unusual amount of the breath stream emanates from the nose strongly reinforced by resonance in the nasal passages. To speak of a voice as *denasal* means that there is little nasal resonance on the "m," "n," and "ng" sounds due to some closure or obstruction of the nasal passages. What we have called nasal is sometimes spoken of as positive nasality; denasal quality is sometimes called negative nasality.

To say a voice is *pectoral* is to imply that the sound seems to be rein-forced in the chest or pectoral regions. To refer to a voice as *oral* is to indi-cate that vocal placement seems forward in the mouth so that sound seems to be reflected off the teeth and gum ridges. *Guttural* voices are those that seem especially reinforced low in the back of the throat. *Metallic* or *strident* voices are those that sound as though they are heavily supported by strained and tense surfaces, presumably those within the mouth including the hard palate (roof of mouth). *Orotund* voices are those thought pleasant because they seem reinforced by a suitable balance of relaxed surfaces which suggests that the cavities involved must be rounded. The truth is that none of these descriptive terms accurately describes acoustic phenomena in any precise way, but the terms do describe our psychological reactions to what we hear and they enable us to talk meaningfully about these perceptions.

A more precise term is *breathy* or *aspirate* when used to describe voices produced by inadequately controlled use of the breath stream. When more breath is released than is used in vibrating the vocal folds efficiently, the re-sult is a whispery sound, usually of inadequate volume. Often the reason for this phenomenon is that the vocal folds are not firmly approximated; the air passing between them causes *some* vibration but also some sheer escape noise comparable to the sound of whispering.

The ways a speaker tenses his muscles, particularly those involved in voice production and resonation, and his general physical condition deter-mine his vocal quality to a large extent. Tensed muscles are likely to pro-duce *metallic* quality; too much relaxation of muscle is likely to produce un-conventionally *nasal* sounds. A person in excellent physical condition is likely to manipulate his resonators so as to produce rich voice with pleasing overtones. A person in full control of all his muscles is likely to produce full, resonated tones. An invalid or aged person who lacks control over his gen-eral musculature has poor control of his speech.

Good quality, defined by Hanley and Thurman as "absence of certain negative tonal characteristics," is in large part desirable for the speaker's own well being. It is also highly desirable for the empathic effects it has on audiences. Strained voices produce comparable strains within those who hear them. And, of course, "negative tonal characteristics" are incapable of pro-ducing affirmative aesthetic experience in those who listen.

In summary, knowing how voices are produced, how vocal sound is articulated and what effects flow from various qualities of voice and diction is a necessary basis for exercising that self-control all effective public speaking requires. The public platform is no place to perform vocal or articulatory experiments, but it is a place for revealing the precision of muscle and quality control that comes from private experimentation and reflection. You ought to experiment with your vocal resources, as with your bodily resources. Only so will you establish the habits of self-control and versatility essential to strong, favorable, empathic responses on the part of listeners.

EMPATHY

As we have already implied, the bodily action and vocal quality of a public speaker are visual and acoustic stimuli that subtly affect listeners. Since what the listeners see and hear has an effect upon their inner experience, *empathy* needs to be discussed.

Empathy is defined as, "The ascription of our emotional feelings to the external object which serves as their visual and auditory stimulus."[13] The German word for empathy, *einfühlung,* provides a clue to the distinctions which must be made between sympathy and empathy. Sympathy is a feeling the observer experiences *toward* the speaker, a feeling he has *for* him. Empathy is a "feeling in with" the speaker. The psychologist, Woodworth, says, "As sympathy means 'feeling with,' empathy means 'feeling into,' and the idea is that the observer projects himself into the object observed and gets some of the satisfaction from watching an object that he would get from being that object."[14] Shaffer, Gillmer, and Schoen add that, "These empathic actions, postures or expressions are not deliberate mimicry and the persons displaying them are usually unaware of what they are doing. As non-voluntary acts, therefore, they are explained in the same manner as suggestion."[15]

The implications for you as a public speaker are apparent. You must so act and sound that the audience receives the sensations (or suggestions) you wish them to have. They must perceive you in such ways that they wish

---

[13] *Funk & Wagnalls New Standard Dictionary of the American Language* (New York: Funk & Wagnalls, 1960), p. 813.

[14] Robert S. Woodworth, *Psychology, A Study of Mental Life* (New York: Holt, 1921), p. 491.

[15] Laurance F. Shaffer, B. Von Haller Gillmer and Max Schoen, *Psychology* (New York: Harper and Brothers, 1940), p. 195.

to take part in what is going on, to participate with you in your speech, and find doing so an experience appropriate to your meaning.

Most of us have had the experience of watching a speaker teeter on the edge of the platform so that his balance seemed precarious. We have heard speakers whose rates and bodily actions were so slow that we wanted to push them along. We have listened to speakers so gravel-voiced that we came away with a sore throat. As we literally "take in" speakers, we sometimes do so so strongly that we ourselves make movements in imitation of them. In all such cases we manifest empathy. Some other examples of empathy at work can be seen in persons at the theatre who cry with the tragic hero, persons at a track meet who lift their bodies as the high jumper clears the bar, or persons at a circus who shift their bodies as they watch a tightrope walker balancing and shifting in a dangerous position above the crowd.

There are more subtle empathic reactions than these. They include our responses to an architecturally unbalanced building, our muscular tonicity in reaction to chamber music, our empathic reactions to sculpture or to paintings. It is not necessary to go deeply into the theories of empathy advanced by Theodor Lipps, Vernon Lee (Violet Paget), or Karl Groos. The theories of empathy as a largely mental-psychological activity, a kinesthetic motor response, or awareness and inner-mimicry are interesting and bear inspection. But no matter what theory one accepts, the fact remains that empathy is inevitable during normal perception and therefore is a significant factor in response to public speeches.

Since the public speaking situation is one in which normal perception is continually taking place, we must control the visual and auditory cues we provide audiences. Undesirable empathic responses are taking place when the members of an audience squirm, close their eyes, look out the window, or yawn. When a listener nods his head in agreement with you, smiles when you smile, laughs with you, leans forward in his seat when you lean forward, you may be sure that he is "feeling in" with you. To be a truly able speaker you must become sensitive to audience reactions and learn to elicit, identify, and react to audience responses which indicate that the listener is not only listening but is participating in your speech and reacting with you. Finally, the primary reason for developing conventional expressive vocal and bodily action is to assure that relevant rather than irrelevant empathic responses will be generated by your delivery.

All aspects of bodily and vocal expression in public speaking must help the listener to concentrate upon what is meant by the speaker. Empathy, "feeling into" ideas and behaviors the speaker presents, is the mark of listeners' deep and full concentration upon the event that is the speech. If the thought and behavior on which they so concentrate reinforce the speaker's purpose, the impact of content and delivery nears the ideal. But this coordination of matter, manner, and listeners' perceptions is less often the product of the inspired moment than of moments carefully prepared for by planning and rehearsal. We have discussed the various aspects of planning speeches and rehearsal for extemporaneous speaking in earlier chapters,[16] but effective delivery and compelling empathy are hardest to achieve when speeches are delivered from manuscript or when portions of material within extemporaneous speeches must be read. We turn next, therefore, to the topic of reading for public speaking.

Reading for Public Speaking

THE SPEAKER BECOMES READER

Public speakers become public readers in one of three ways. They may read an entire speech from manuscript. They may memorize a speech and read it from memory. They may find it necessary or desirable to read quotations, prose or poetry, as parts of a speech. In each of these circumstances the method of delivery changes the role of the speaker. We pointed out in Chapter 1 (pp. 12–14) that the person who reads aloud becomes an interpreter—one who stands between the author of the material and the audience. When he presents his work from memory, a speaker stands between the author he was and the speaker he is. Since the position of the reader is in all events an intermediate one, it is easy to see that the primary demands upon him come from the material. Elements in the particular occasion and the conventions of the audience may make for minor modifications in a reader's behavior. His personal skill may affect his communication, but the

---

[16] For extended discussion of extemporaneous speaking and rehearsal for this mode of delivery see Chapter 3, pp.54–56; 60–61.

material to be read stands as the central determinant of what ought to be done in the speech situation.

In reading any piece of material aloud, whether it be a whole speech or an excerpt from someone's writing, we must remember that there are two reasons for reading: (1) to bring something new and unusual to the fore or (2) to give listeners meanings which they would not get from reading the material by themselves either silently or orally.

Reading a speech or some portion of it involves stirring up meanings in those who listen. By uttering the sounds signified by black marks on a white page, the reader seeks objectively or subjectively to translate the marks into meaning. He seeks to endow the printed words with the meanings their composer, or he, if he happens to be the actual author, intended them to have. Where he has done the composing, the reader, of course, knows clearly what the words mean; the problem becomes one of revitalizing his own ideas. Where he has not done the composing, he must assure himself that he understands what the author meant before he can give the meaning to others. Whether he undertakes to revitalize his own ideas now consigned to cold, frozen symbols on the page or to bring to life what another author meant, a reader has analytical work to do before he reads.

Most students read badly because they are not aware of what work is involved in getting and giving meaning. This is a sufficient reason for discouraging beginners from reading their speeches. At the beginning of their study most students read even short quotations so poorly they distort meaning and rob the material of its sense. We cannot attempt in this book to present a full treatment of oral interpretation, but we can offer basic suggestions to the public speaker who must sometimes read and ought to do so better than his unstudied practice allows. Since the public speaker's reading is primarily for utilitarian rather than aesthetic purposes, the observations that follow focus on reading to convey practical meaning, leaving out of consideration the equally legitimate object of reading to create aesthetic pleasure.

GENERAL PRINCIPLES

The stages of preparing one's self to read meaningfully are not always exactly the same nor do they follow in prescribable sequence, but the following suggestions are arranged in the approximate order in which you are likely to confront the problems discussed.

Discover author's purpose and method. To determine the author's purpose and method, sift the material for clues. Try to perceive the purpose. Is the communication essentially utilitarian? Aesthetic? Or does the author's intent fall somewhere between these extremes? At the utilitarian end of this imaginary continuum might stand a technical report or the minutes of a business meeting. At the aesthetic end you would expect to find emotional love lyrics. Any author's purpose in composing will lie somewhere along the line between these types. Consider the differences in communicative purpose that distinguish a news report, an editorial, a personal essay, a fictional narrative, a scene from a play, a ballad, a sonnet.

When an author's purpose is practical, as the news reporter's and editorialist's purposes usually are, he will be concerned with explaining how a thing can be done, why it should be done, or how to get people to do it. He may simply describe. Or he will undertake to explain the nature of things through abstract proof. But some editorialists, many essayists, and most narrators try to bring meaning to readers by giving significant form to selected portions of human experience. Most authors from whom you will have occasion to read have the same purposes you have as public speaker: to inform, persuade, reinforce, inquire, or entertain. You must discover *which* purpose dominates in each passage. You must ascertain the writer's central idea, the theme of his work. This tells you what tone or mood to adopt in your general delivery of the material. It also gives you a framework for further analysis of the material.

Discover the complete meaning. One of the chief causes of poor reading is failure to obtain *complete* meaning from the material. To discover the over-all purpose is not enough. You should learn what the material says and what the author's philosophy or attitude is. In so doing, you may have to turn to other materials and read about the author or read critical essays written about the material.

Getting the full meaning entails knowing the meaning of all the words you read. You must ascertain not only their dictionary meanings but their denotative and connotative meanings as well. You will also have to view words in their contexts before you can interpret them precisely as *this* author meant them; you may even have to analyze syntactical structure to know what the passage means. You should realize that words mean little in and of themselves. It is the associations and the responses they touch off that are important. Make sure, then, that you are aware of the referents intended by your author. Examining language carefully, a task which you may tend to find laborious, will be essential to your intellectual grasp of the material, your capacity for reconstructing suggested meanings, and your ability to respond emotionally to the ideas before you.

To achieve complete meaning you will sometimes have to study the setting for the material. The historical period depicted or to which the piece belongs will be as much a matter for concern as its objective meaning. You may have to answer for yourself such questions as: "Who is saying this?" "Why is he saying it?" "Who is the intended listener?" Whether the words to be read were spoken at Gettysburg National Cemetery or in the give-and-take of a Lincoln-Douglas debate will affect the manner in which you read them.

Knowing the author's mood is a related requirement for attaining complete meaning. Mood is the author's inner expression of attitude. It will color your selection. If you express a wrong mood, the result can be shocking. You, as the middleman, must reflect feelings in harmony with the author's temper and for that reason, sight reading, unless you are an experienced and accomplished reader, can be dangerous. The establishment of mood is especially important to effective presentation of materials with aesthetic purposes. You cannot read poems and stories effectively unless you understand and are able to transmit mood. Even your reading of utilitarian material is enhanced if you can adopt the manner that reflects your author's attitude toward the subject about which he wrote.

Sometimes paraphrasing a passage or writing a précis will aid you in assimilating its full meaning. You must undertake whatever research, peripheral reading, or repetition is needed to discover complete meaning. Only if you understand the *whole* can you understand how to read a work or any of its parts.

Discover the structure and unity of the selection. Every well-written composition has perceivable structure and unity. Some planned development of ideas dominates the work. If you know what lines of thought or feeling are those that contribute most to the structural pattern and the unity of the material, you have important leads toward what to emphasize in reading. You have need, then, to examine the form the author has chosen as his medium of expression. News story, prose narrative, ballad, sonnet, and dramatic scene all have their distinctive structural patterns. For example, the most important facts or meanings are not usually found at the *end* of a news story, but they *are* likely to be found near the end of a dramatic scene. What is worth quoting, what is representative of the author's meaning, and what must be high-lighted if an entire selection is read are all revealed by attention to the structure and unity of the work.

Discovering structure means examining grammatical constructions so you can clearly see minor relationships. It means paying close attention to transitional portions of the work. Whether they are minor or major structural features that you explore, your purpose is basically to discover what relational patterns *you* must express by manner of utterance.

Cultivate a sensitivity to rhythm. Some of the subtlest shadings of meaning achieved through language are conveyed by changes in rhythm, changes in the beat or measure of sounds. This is especially true of poetry, but it is also important in some prose. If you choose to quote Daniel Webster, Winston Churchill, Adlai Stevenson, or John F. Kennedy, you will seldom convey the full meaning of the passage if you do not give some expression to the rhythmic patterns so characteristic of these speakers' oral expression. Only by preserving rhythm, or by breaking it, can the meanings of some authors be realized. It is seldom necessary to break prose rhythms but it is frequently necessary to do so with poetry. You should be careful not to let meter dominate your utterance to such a degree that you destroy meaning. The extreme example of this fault is the small child's sing-song recitation of poetry. In all written and spoken forms, rhythm is an important element of meaning; therefore, your control of it will be a great aid in conveying that meaning.

Cultivate imaginative capacities. A further requisite for good reading is imagination, the power to see what others cannot in a particular circumstance or combination of words or emotional undertone. Develop your ability to perceive the author's uniqueness and his abilities to create new patterns of expression, new relationships between ideas, and new word pictures. The more aesthetic the author's purpose the more valuable imagination is in interpreting his material.

Imagination comes from experience and from the ability to divorce yourself from reality. It comes, in part, from a capacity to dream. We do not advise that you take yourself out of this world. We do advise that you let your mind range as you work over material to be read. Visualize the possibilities. Create several versions of possible meaning in your mind, then choose the one most true-to-purpose for your final interpretation.

Bringing the imagination to bear is especially important in the preparation of fictional and poetic materials. Without the imaginative component, the reading of make-believe writing is lackluster, pedestrian. The interpretation of fantasy requires imaginative abilities of the highest degree.

The development of imaginative capacity will stand you in good stead generally. Imagination is often necessary if you are to find and present complete meaning, and imagination adds vividness and dramatic quality to your reading.

Cultivate ability to group and pause.   Grouping or phrasing is the art of breaking a text up into ideas or speech units. A word is a grammatical unit; the idea is the speech unit. According to W. M. Parrish:

> When we are creating thought as we go along, as in conversation, we generally make the grouping clear to our hearers, that is, make our ideas distinct. In reading from the printed page, our eyes must be trained to run quickly along the succession of words and organize them into proper groups before the voice attempts to utter them. If the voice fails to communicate this grouping to one's hearers, it fails to communicate meaning, for meaning lies in the grouping. Just as in written language we group letters into words, and separate these words from one another, so in spoken language we should group words together and separate the groups from each other. If we fail to do so, we throw upon our hearers the burden of sorting our words apart, a task as difficult as sorting out the words from an unspaced sentence in print.[17]

In reading poetry the inexperienced tend to group mechanically at the end of each line. Such practice is to be avoided. You must learn to group by thought, and the more determined you are to give the meaning, the more groups you will make.

You should be aware that there are two types of punctuation, oral and written. Oral punctuation makes meaning clear to the auditor by some noticeable change in voice or action, as written punctuation makes similar meanings clear to the reader. The two kinds of punctuation do not always coincide. There are many times when you will want to ignore the written punctuation altogether. Pausing at every comma, semicolon, or period does

[17] Wayland Maxfield Parrish, *Reading Aloud,* 3rd ed. (New York: The Ronald Press Co., 1953), pp. 24–25. Copyright 1953 The Ronald Press Company. Used by permission of the publisher.

not always enhance the meaning. It may confuse. One who reads aloud must determine which written punctuation assists him in grouping audible thought and which does not. Punctuation in oral reading and in public speaking, as we have already noted, is achieved by oral inflection; change in volume, rate, or pitch; and by gestures and other bodily movements which make groups of words clearly convey ideas.

A pause is a psycho-physiological event. Proper pausing does more than any other one thing to make reading natural and realistic. "There is never any need to pause for breath alone, as the pauses for thought are so many that the lungs may always be full, a necessary condition for good voice support. . . . We must learn to fill the think tank and the lung tank, automatically and simultaneously."[18] A pause is not *mere* silence. It is not a dead stop. To be a true pause, the silence must be pregnant with meaning. When the voice stops for a true pause, the thought continues to manifest itself. The reader sees ahead and gains command of the next idea; the listener digests what has been said and becomes curious about what is to come. Pausing helps both the oral reader and the listener to apprehend clearly the relationships between the words and phrases.

Professor Parrish gives two very good reasons why young readers do not pause. He says:

First, they lack confidence. The excitement of reading before others causes a nervous acceleration of what is normally too rapid a rate of utterance. Under such circumstances the cessation of vocal activity for a fraction of a second seems an ominous silence full of dreadful possibilities. The reader begins to wonder whether he has not broken down. . . .

A second reason why young readers seldom pause is just that they do not deliberate. They skim. Their minds do not dwell upon the ideas to be communicated. So surely as the mind begins to dwell upon the words being expressed there will be a focusing on separate word-groups (how else can one think?), and these word-groups will generally be separated from each other by pauses.[19]

Cultivate ability to subordinate ideas. You must realize that in oral reading and in speaking, ideas are not all of the same value. Some ideas are

[18] S. H. Clark and M. M. Babcock, *Interpretation of the Printed Page* (Englewood Cliffs, N.J.: Prentice-Hall, 1940), p. 5.

[19] Parrish, *Reading Aloud*, p. 41. Copyright 1953 The Ronald Press Company. Used by permission of the publisher.

less important, are subordinate, to others. They support and amplify. In your analysis of material to be read you must, of course, discover these idea relationships. We have discussed the relations of structural analysis to this discovery. You must learn to *convey* relationships by voice, gesture, and movement, to emphasize the most important ideas and deemphasize the less important ones. Some readers read every word in the same way, with the same rate, pitch, and volume, even the same gesture. Their reading is boring and monotonous. It lacks variety, and what is more important it is valueless for the clarification of the meaning inherent in the material. Thinking the thought, feeling the meaning, and releasing voice and body to reinforce these experiences offer the best means of expressing discovered relationships.

Cultivate ability to maintain visual directness. The ability to preserve visual directness is an even greater problem when reading to an audience than when speaking to them. Readers who bury their noses in books or who direct their gazes to papers on the lectern break the flow of communication and destroy the sense of liveliness which ought to prevail during public speaking. As Henneke says,

> The reader has a special eye problem. He must look at his manuscript and still maintain eye contact with his audience. His best answer is a compromise. His eyes should follow the manuscript until he is certain of what he is going to say. Then he may look at his audience until he has completed saying that phrase or group of phrases.[20]

In this way readers may read without wholly destroying the intimate speaker-audience relationship that gives speech its special social meaning.

We would add that the preservation of visual contact with an audience during reading is a skill attained only through much practice. To take in a group of words, then to lift the eyes and focus upon the audience as these words are uttered requires that you remember what the eye first took in long enough to deliver it meaningfully and without interruption. The process demands a high degree of physical coordination plus memory and self-control. Some beginning students who find it difficult to achieve all this resort to memorizing quotations. Others who do not memorize choose a better way, they make themselves thoroughly familiar with all quotations or excerpts before speaking. If they proceed wisely in this task they find they

[20] Ben Graf Henneke, *Reading Aloud Effectively* (New York: Rinehart, 1954), p. 143.

are following precisely the steps of analysis and practice we are recommending on this and the immediately preceding pages.

In short, visual directness—or its absence—usually reveals whether the reader has thoroughly or haphazardly prepared to read.

Cultivate the "illusion of the first time." Flexibility and variety are essential for all good speaking or reading. Where in extemporaneous speaking one thinks anew and responds afresh to ideas sifted and structured but never unalterably fixed by preparation, in reading from memory or the printed page it is fixed content and form that must be recaptured. The speaker's stimulus in the moment of speaking is never quite static, unless he overprepared; the reader's stimulus is inevitably static. It is precisely that thing to which he responded again and again during hours of preparation. Only *response* to content and form is variable for the reader. Thus, the illusion of fresh experience with content is much harder to convey when reading than when speaking.

For most people operating under the circumstances that control oral reading, it is not limitations of vocal and bodily equipment that constrain; it is inability to recapture whole meanings and to respond with full powers of intellect and imagination while under the stresses of public communication. There is no easy remedy. As is true with other arts, so it is here: given understanding of how to study material and of the resources of delivery, only practice, evaluation, and more practice can produce the controlled but lively responses to static stimuli that superior reading requires. The "illusion of the first time," to which audiences so enthusiastically respond, is largely the result of experience and painstaking practice. But for the speaker who reads only brief passages in the midst of extemporaneous speaking there is this encouraging fact: careful analysis, modest experiments with the resources of delivery, plus less than formidable amounts of practice can produce meaningful readings of utilitarian prose and uncomplicated kinds of poetry.

In this chapter we have examined delivery as a means to an end rather than as an end in itself. The schools of delivery that have held influence in modern times are, if nothing else, reminders of the fascination men have always had for the part of speech making that is most personal and most intimately revealing. For our day, and on the basis of man's experience with the various schools of delivery, it seems sensible to approach personal presentation of speeches by first recognizing that constructively communicative physical behavior arises as controlled but free response to thought and feeling fully experienced. If physical and vocal behaviors are means rather than ends in speaking, a general standard for good delivery is easily found: *Good delivery helps the listener to concentrate upon what is said; it does not attract attention to itself.*

There are, as we have tried to show, general principles of bodily and vocal action which encourage free and full use of the human body in reinforcing thought and feeling. We have noted, too, that empathic reactions to delivery deeply influence audience response to the speaker's message. In essence, however, it is the speaker's attitudes toward the ideas he communicates, himself, and his audience that govern the functional value of his delivery. We have offered suggestions concerning constructive use of the body and voice, and on reading for public speaking. But our belief is that it is through knowing and reflecting upon the possibilities of communicative action and by private drill to achieve conventional and variable habits that effective delivery ultimately emerges on the platform.

Exercises

Written

1. Write a description of the bodily action used by one of the following:
   a. A professor during the course of a lecture.
   b. A classmate delivering a speech.
   c. Your roommate as he goes about his daily activities.
2. Write an analysis of your voice after listening to a recording of it. Comment specifically upon volume, rate, pitch, and quality.
3. Listen to a live speech delivered in person or over television. Write a description of the speaker's delivery with these questions in mind: What did the speaker do to support his ideas visually and vocally? What did he do with his body and voice which detracted from what he was saying?
4. Observe one of your classmates as he delivers a speech and during an informal conversation. Write a comparative account of his use of body and voice in these two situations. Note the similarities and differences in vocal and visual elements.

Oral

1. Deliver a short speech during which you read aloud from at least three different literary forms, e.g., news account, scientific report, fictional prose, sonnet, ballad, essay, or dramatic scene.

2. Prepare and deliver a speech three to six minutes long in which you explain some procedure requiring much action of the body, e.g., how to do a dance, how to perform artificial respiration, how to handle a fencing foil, how to execute wrestling holds, how to gesture on stage, how to direct calisthenics.

3. Prepare a two-minute speech requiring gesture for description, explanation, and emphasis. Practice the speech aloud outside of class, deciding upon which bodily actions to employ. Deliver the speech in class *without words*. Use only eye contact, movement, posture, and gesture to convey your ideas. Discuss what you have done with members of your class in order to determine how much of your intended meaning was conveyed.

4. Assign each of the following sentences to three or four members of your class. Ask each person to say or read his sentence with a different emphasis from the person preceding him, changing the meaning of the sentence each time it is read. Following the readings, discuss the differences in volume, pitch, and rate employed to achieve the differences in meaning.

    a. Who do you suppose I saw in class today?
    b. Oh yes, I'd love to go.
    c. You aren't really sure of that are you?
    d. I've never seen such food.
    e. There are always a lot of men at the movies on Saturday night.
    f. It was the most spectacular yet peculiar race you ever saw.
    g. There was the book just where I'd left it rain-soaked and falling apart.
    h. No I simply can't believe that that is so.
    i. Whoever heard of a person doing such a thing.
    j. Oh my dear what have you done?

12   *Judging the Speech*

A liberally educated citizen ought to be able to explain what happens when he is addressed by a public speaker. He ought to be able to describe the speech he hears and to explain why and how it contributed to the results that followed. If people could do these things expertly in all cases, judging speeches would be a science, and public speaking would be human engineering. But none of us has achieved precision in observing and analyzing public speech, nor are we likely to achieve it soon.

Even the highly educated find it difficult to perceive the components of speeches as they listen. They find it even more difficult to judge what effects speeches have on people other than themselves. Those who have carefully studied the theory and practice of speech making judge qualities and effects somewhat more reliably than those who have not, though they are by no means infallible. Like reliable criticisms of fiction, poetry, or painting, reliable evaluation of speeches depends greatly on practical and theoretical knowledge about what is possible and impossible given the resources of the art.

The basic justification for criticism of speaking is that here, as in other arts, criticism is both the way we tell ourselves what is going on and the way we learn how to practice the art with greater insight. We are not likely to reduce speaking or any other art to science, but we still have both need and responsibility to bring as much knowledge as possible to bear when we respond to the discourse about us. To equip us for such informed responses is, indeed, a primary object of all liberal education.

At various points in this book we have said that public speaking is a liberal art. The broad aims of a liberal education are to stimulate you to

323

think in a variety of ways, to increase your ability to judge, to enable you to choose among alternatives, and to prepare you to take a responsible place in the world. We have explored theories with you to enlarge your understanding and described procedures and methods to enable you to fill your roles as public speaker and listener to speeches. As a final matter we invite you to consider how to form useful critical judgments.

We know there are those who believe that students are too young and inexperienced to be critics. But we believe criticism of live speeches is an important and necessary aspect of your study of public speaking. You were not prepared to function as a critic during the first rounds of speaking, but with some theories at your command you are ready and able to evaluate speeches with regard to those principles at least. Most important, critical activity will benefit you both as a speaker and as a private person.

The audience reactions revealed to you in early speeches are valuable. By knowing what your audience thought of your first speeches, you can discover ways to improve your adaptation to the group in your later efforts. We are not saying audiences ever stay the same. By living a day longer your classroom audience changes each time you meet. Nonetheless, there are some criteria by which they measure effective speaking which do not change from session to session. Your colleagues' reactions of today never change so much or so fast that they can be totally discounted tomorrow.

Criticism in the classroom is a reciprocal activity. By openly registering your responses to your peers, you will aid immensely in their improvement. Conversely, their frank responses to your speech making will often provide you with directions for improvement and always with insights into how others judge speaking.

To exercise full responsibility as a critic, you need to develop powers of discrimination and to know the methods and standards for criticism. We believe that oral and written criticism of live speeches and written criticism of the texts of outstanding speeches are constructive experiences. We say with Dean Everett L. Hunt that

. . . we might be better satisfied with the returns from the money and energy spent on rhetorical training if we cared more about producing educated and critical audiences. . . . Critical and analytical study of rhetoric and oratory should not be limited to those who expect to become professional speakers or writers, or to those who expect to teach it; it should be offered to all students who desire to understand the significance of rhetoric in modern life.[1]

Whether or not you are invited to criticize spoken or written public speeches at any juncture in your course in public speaking, you owe it to yourself as a part of liberalizing education to develop standards of judgment and critical acuity toward the speeches you will hear, read, or deliver in future days or years.

If you are to make informed judgments of the speaking that goes on about you, you must understand the nature of criticism, the standards and methods commonly employed in evaluating speeches, and the tasks you can effectively undertake as a critic of the speeches you will find in the laboratory atmosphere of the classroom and elsewhere.

The Nature of Speech Criticism

Criticism of any kind is judgment and/or appreciation. To evaluate or criticize implies analysis and comparison, approval or disapproval, commendation or censure. All reactions to objects, ideas, actions, and persons are critical or noncritical. Assessments or evaluations are criticism. Descriptions, reviews, commentaries, and surveys, unless interpretative, are not.

Criticism is essentially a comparative activity involving discrimination. Whenever we make a judgment or register appreciation, we do so with some standards of perfection in mind. Where we are subjective in our judgments, our standards are likely to be very personal. We may not even be conscious of them. Where we become objective, we tend to become consciously aware of our norms and to identify them in our minds or on paper. Whichever cast of mind characterizes our criticism, we have some standards and our judgments place what we judge somewhere along a continuum of excellence. The object of our appraisal is contrasted to norms, or measured by them, and found to correspond in some degree. Either the item being criticized corresponds closely to the standards or it does not.

---

[1] "Editorial: 'From Rhetoric Deliver Us,'" *The Quarterly Journal of Speech*, XIV (April 1928), 266–267.

The Critical Object

A focus upon some object to be scrutinized and judged is essential in any type of criticism. The object may be tangible or intangible. It may be a material or combination of materials, an action or an idea. In aesthetic criticism this object may be a specific painting, such as Picasso's "The Lovers"; a pattern of sounds such as Beethoven's Fifth Symphony interpreted by a great orchestra; or physical action performed by dancers, such as the *pas de deux* from *The Firebird*. Objects for literary criticism are novels, short stories, poems, or essays, usually in the tangible form of printed words on a page. Whatever the kind of criticism, some object exists to be appreciated and/or evaluated and perhaps to be praised or condemned.

The critic who assesses a live speech, the speech as it is delivered, deals with a distinctive *critical object* which has its own distinctive features. The object he examines, appreciates, and judges consists of a combination of sounds and actions, symbolizing ideas, existing in time, and cutting through air. This object is in constant flight, not static, not arrested. It is unlike some other critical objects. It is not a statue which can be placed on a pedestal and viewed from all sides. It is not a musical score nor a play script which can be consulted. It is not a painting which can be gazed at for hours on end. It is not print which can be pored over. The critical object in speech making cannot be taken in with the eye or ear *alone*. It must be seen and heard, perceived by eye and ear, all in the moments of its creation. Like the dance, it does not stand still for examination, yet its verbal nature makes it seem analogous to objects of literary criticism. And while it is true that a critic viewing a painting takes in first one part then another, and the critic of music hears sounds in sequence in time, the critic of a speech faces a more exacting assignment, he must see *and* hear in sequence. Often he will not even have the drama critic's advantage of being able to consult a script before or after seeing and hearing the object he is to criticize.

The speech critic deals with a critical object which usually exists once and only once. There may be no public prevision of the object and there may be no subsequent record. Speeches may be delivered on identical subjects and in identical words, but the very nature of public speaking prevents exact duplication of a speech. The components in the speech situation are constantly shifting; the critic perceives a *whole* speech only once. He must scrutinize a speech on the wing. He may record judgments and reactions after the event, but he cannot depend upon repeated exposures to the critical object.

To complicate matters further, the speech critic cannot always be present when the speech he wishes to criticize takes place. For example, he may choose to criticize a speech delivered in the past. Or he may decide to criticize a piece of oral utterance only after finding that it was of some importance to society or exerted some particular influence. Or, even if present at the moment of utterance, he may not have intended to appraise the speech and so may have failed to take full advantage of his attendance. In any of these situations he is unable to experience the *real* speech. Nonetheless, several alternative critical objects are available to him.

The most advantageous of these alternatives rarely exists. It is conceivable, though not very likely, that our would-be critic could obtain a sound motion picture of the speech that made all necessary observations of visual and audible elements possible. A film of this sort would come closest to reproducing the real speech, but it cannot reproduce the speech situation because it will lack three-dimensional factors. The film of the event is obviously not as reliable as on-the-spot observation for assessing such factors as actual environment and audience reaction. But seldom will this alternative be open to the critic, for even where films are available they usually contain only portions of major speeches.

A second alternative critical object for the speech critic is some form of electrical transcription of the sounds of the speech. This form of the speech eliminates all possibilities for considering its visual aspects, but it does allow some evaluation of vocal performance. The current practice of many on-the-spot speech critics is to tape the speech at the time of observation and then to use the tape as a check on the accuracy of their impressions. If the critic cannot make his own electrical recording, he may try to obtain one through a radio or television station or buy one which has been commercially marketed. The availability of such recordings is limited, and, of course, obtaining a recording of an orator who spoke in the early days of sound recording provides a critical object of dubious quality.

More often, the critic who was not present when the speech was delivered, or who made inadequate observations while in attendance, will have to content himself with some written record: a handwritten manuscript, a typed or mimeographed script, or a printed page. Fortunately, he may pore over, analyze, outline, and study this kind of record. He may be able to supplement the script with other written accounts that help him reconstruct the milieu, the occasion, and audience reaction. He may be able to read the criticism others wrote subsequent to the delivery of the speech. In his over-all appraisal he may, and often does, use any of the various methods for historical, literary, and experimental studies. But even with all these aids his critical object remains the least satisfactory of those we have discussed.

The critical objects for critics of speeches, then, are of four types. The object may be the live, pulsating, reacted-to utterance of the moment; a film; an electrical transcription; or a manuscript or printed text. It is the unique nature of these critical objects that chiefly distinguishes rhetorical criticism from other kinds of criticism.

The purpose of public speaking also influences the character of speech criticism. Public speaking is a utilitarian rather than an aesthetic art. It seeks to gain immediate or long-range response or both, and it must be judged in the light of its purpose. It is possible to judge the literary value, the historical significance, and the moral qualities of speeches, but these judgments alone cannot yield full appreciation or analysis of a speech. They do not produce evaluations recognizing that the primary purpose of speech making is a practical one.

Wichelns, in his now famous essay entitled "The Literary Criticism of Oratory," says of rhetorical criticism,

. . . we find that its point of view is patently single. It is not concerned with permanence, nor yet with beauty [as may be the case in the judgment of literature]. It is concerned with effect. It regards a speech as a communication to a specific audience and holds its business to be the analysis and appreciation of the orator's method of imparting his ideas to his hearers.[2]

Wichelns was thinking mainly of criticism as a scholarly activity involving the analysis of speech texts, but what he says applies to critics who hear and see speeches as well as to those who read them. His elaboration upon what rhetorical criticism is bears quotation.

[2] Herbert A. Wichelns, "The Literary Criticism of Oratory," in *Studies in Rhetoric and Public Speaking in Honor of James Albert Winans* (New York: Century, 1925), p. 209. Reprinted in Donald C. Bryant, ed., *The Rhetorical Idiom* (Ithaca: Cornell University Press, 1958), pp. 1–42.

Rhetorical criticism is necessarily analytical. The scheme of a rhetorical study includes the elements of the speaker's personality as a conditioning factor; it includes also the public character of the man—not what he was, but what he was thought to be. It requires a description of the speaker's audience, and of the leading ideas with which he plied his hearers—his topics, the motives to which he appealed, the nature of the proofs he offered. These will reveal his own judgment of human nature in his audiences, and also his judgment on the questions which he discussed. Attention must be paid, too, to the relation of the surviving texts to what was actually uttered: in case the nature of the changes is known, there may be occasion to consider adaptation to two audiences—that which heard and that which read. Nor can rhetorical criticism omit the speaker's mode of arrangement and his mode of expression, nor his habit of preparation and his manner of delivery from the platform; though the last two are perhaps less significant. "Style"—in the sense which corresponds to diction and sentence movement—must receive attention, but only as one among various means that secure for the speaker ready access to the minds of his auditors. Finally, the effect of the discourse on its immediate hearers is not to be ignored, either in the testimony of witnesses, nor in the record of events. And throughout such a study one must conceive of the public man as influencing the men of his own times by the power of his discourse.[3]

Another way of putting it, in line with the demands we have discussed in this book, is to say that as the critic analyzes and evaluates he ought to keep the demands of the audience, the material, the occasion, and the speaker uppermost in his mind. The assignment that faced the speaker should be a primary consideration as the critic assesses and imaginatively sets forth what ought to have been said and how it ought to have been said under the peculiar circumstances which constituted the demands of the speaker's situation.

It is also of value to turn to what rhetorical criticism is not. Loren D. Reid, in reflecting upon the myopia of young critics, warns:

Rhetorical criticism is not simply a discussion of the speaker's ideas, . . . not simply a narrative of the circumstances under which a speech is delivered, . . . not simply a classification or tabulation of rhetorical devices, . . . [and] not primarily an excursion into other fields of learning.[4]

[3] *Ibid.*, pp. 212–213.
[4] "The Perils of Rhetorical Criticism," *The Quarterly Journal of Speech*, XXX (December 1944), 416–422.

The perils Reid enumerates all lead to mere description or too-simple comment on a speech. A preoccupation with any of them will produce something less than significant critical judgments.

Critical Points of View

THE PRAGMATIC VIEWPOINT

Value systems underlie all our judgments of speech making. Whether we wish to call them critical standards or philosophies, we all hold basic tenets which determine qualities we emphasize in our assessments. Perhaps the most important of these viewpoints is the pragmatic, that which in speech criticism stresses the *effects* of the speech. As we have seen, this emphasis underlies Wichelns' distinction between rhetorical criticism and other kinds of comment about speeches. Weaver, Borchers, and Smith call it the "empirical standard."[5] McBurney and Wrage label it "the results theory" of criticism.[6]

Under this philosophy, the consideration of the speech becomes an especially practical matter. We ask, "Was the speech effective? Did it elicit the response sought? Did it achieve the intended result? Did it fulfill its purpose?" In the classroom we are also likely to ask, "Did the speech fulfill the assignment for which it was designed?"

We tend to measure the success of a speech on the basis of *immediate* rather than *long range* effectiveness, forgetting that failure to attain an immediate, visible response may not mean the speech was a failure. A speech may not elicit on the spot the response the speaker hoped for, but it may have effects that operate over a period of time. Who can declare that the speeches proposing the St. Lawrence seaway in the 1920's had absolutely no favorable effect? Eventually the seaway came into being. Some of the persuasive speeches given a generation ago may have contributed toward producing the final decision. So many outside factors impinge upon the

[5] See Andrew T. Weaver, Gladys L. Borchers and Donald K. Smith, *The Teaching of Speech* (Englewood Cliffs, N.J.: Prentice-Hall, 1952), pp. 497–498.

[6] See James H. McBurney and Ernest J. Wrage, *The Art of Good Speech* (New York: Prentice-Hall, 1953), pp. 22–24.

speech situation that to base our judgment of over-all quality on immediate response alone is not entirely fair. The speeches of a political campaigner may be excellent in many respects, but due to extrinsic forces it may be impossible for *any* speaking to win an electoral victory.

Of course, we cannot dismiss *effect* completely. Practically, the speech must get an effect to do its work. Yet, we should remember that although effect is a decisive consideration in passing judgment on a speech, to consider *only* immediate or even long-range effects will produce but a partial evaluation.

THE ETHICAL VIEWPOINT[7]

A second value system underlying speech judgments arises from a special interest in judging intention. If the motives of a speaker are in line with ours and if his intentions are admirable, we may praise him for taking or upholding what we think is the right position. In viewing a speech from such a vantage point we ask, "Is the speaker honest, sincere, courageous in the beliefs he enunciates? Is he truthful? Is he consistent? Is he on the side of good?"

These are all good questions which should not be overlooked by any thoughtful critic. Certainly, as critics, we would not wish to hold up as exemplary that which is untrue, biased, or designed to hurt the audience. We cannot underscore strongly enough that lying, cheating, plagiarizing, and speaking with bad intent are reprehensible. We must pause, however, to consider that an oral discourse may be filled with truths and be based on the soundest motives and still not represent an intelligent or artistic use of the resources of human speech. Who would deny that many clergymen and professors honorably present what they believe to be truth and still prove poor preachers and lecturers?

So, we say first, that ethical merit, even though highly prized, cannot guarantee quality or even competence in speech making. Secondly, we would remind you that it is very hard in some instances to discover a speaker's motives. It is not always possible to declare he is sincere, honest, acting

[7] This viewpoint, as we discuss it, involves both ethical and truth considerations. McBurney and Wrage see these as separate theories. See *ibid.*, pp. 24–28.

with goodwill, or appealing ethically to the feelings of his auditors. Lastly, we would say that it is well to bear in mind that ethical standards vary from society to society, group to group, era to era, and age level to age level. Ethical standards are relative. And the question, "How can we know truth?" is still in dispute among philosophers. What is thought valuable or true by an Eskimo may not be thought so by a Samoan. What may be ethically necessary to a Mennonite may not seem so to a Mohammedan. What was moral and commendable to the ancient Greeks may not seem so to us today, and what is "right" for teen-agers is not always "right" for thirty-year-olds. Judging ethical worth is no easy matter. This is not to say that we, as critics, can dodge responsibility for making those ethical judgments that are plainly and defensibly open to us. A function of humane education is to aid discovery of truth and formulation of a system of values. Still, even where we *can* make fair and supportable judgments on the ethical merits of a speech these cannot be made the sole standards of judgment applied to rhetorical efforts.

THE ARTISTIC VIEWPOINT

A third value system holds artistic excellence in high esteem. It calls upon the critic to judge on the basis of the skill with which the theories and principles of an art have been applied. It

. . . holds that speech is an art reducible to principles. Good speech is constructed on these principles, exhibits these principles to the discerning critic, and may be judged by these principles. Any speech in any situation for any purpose is good in the degree to which it measures up to or incorporates these principles, and is poor speech in the degree to which it does not.[8]

An artistic value system sometimes places great weight upon the skill with which the resources of an act have been used. It is really eclectic in nature, for it formulates criteria to be applied with an eye to both effectiveness and ethical worth. It calls upon the critic (1) to know the particular methods and norms to be applied to speeches, (2) to perceive whether or not these standards have been applied skillfully and unobtrusively, and

[8] *Ibid.*, pp. 28–29.

(3) to offer what judgments he can fairly defend concerning the public worth of the speech as a whole. To the authors of this book the artistic viewpoint seems most likely to produce comprehensive and practically useful speech criticism.

Critical Criteria

It is not enough to base criticism of speeches upon a value system. You must also be specific in passing judgment on the choices a speaker makes. When you have made general judgments of effectiveness, of ethical worth, and of artistry, the next decision you make must concern the speaker's purpose. His purpose will determine which aspects of his speaking are crucial to success and which are not. You must move from reactions to the total speech to specific judgments on how well principles and techniques were applied in the particular situation.

CRITICAL HIERARCHIES

The aspects of speaking which you choose to evaluate will vary in relative importance as you move from speech to speech. They will form a hierarchy in your mind as you approach the task of judging. On one occasion, the organization of the speech may be the item at the top of your hierarchy, the most important aspect of the speech to be judged. On another, structure will not stand at the top but near the top. On still other occasions, structure will be far down the list. This is particularly true when you are judging classroom speeches. When you have been concentrating on organization and outlining in class, structure may loom as the most important thing to be considered in oral criticism or in the notes you provide for the speaker. Because organization is what you are studying, it becomes the primary feature of rhetorical skill to receive attention. In listening to a lecture by a learned professor or to a court plea, structure may be important but not as important as the speaker's selection of topics or arguments or the evidence he uses as support. Structure then moves down from the head of the list of rhetorical resources under critical consideration to second or third place.

But there are other situations where structure will rank rather low in the hierarchy of achievements to be weighed. In criticizing an occasional speech, for instance, you may find yourself discounting both disposition and invention while weighing the speaker's stylistic achievements much more seriously. You may conclude that the ideas are well worn, that structure was dictated so the speaker had little choice of patterns, given his situation. The topical or chronological patterns may seem to you about the only appropriate ones for this speaker to use. Given such circumstances, you may decide that originality in wordings and the use of images were the chief resources open to the speaker in his effort to produce response through artistic utterance. So you may move style, delivery, invention, and all their attendant aspects ahead of structure in your evaluation of this speaker's accomplishments.

Thus, you can see that the critic's hierarchy of criteria shifts constantly depending upon the aims of the speaker, his subject matter, and the occasion. You must decide what your critical hierarchy will be each time you criticize a speech. As you listen or read to evaluate, you must separate the important from the unimportant qualities of discourse. If you do not, you may end by concentrating on trivial matters to the neglect of crucial items that deserved most attention from the speaker whose work you are judging.

You will need to guard against developing fixations, as some students do. For some, voice or bodily action always occupies first place. They seem easiest to comment on. In your critiques of classmates the danger sign is present if you always say: "Jim doesn't make any gestures," or "John has too many breaks in fluency," or "Sandra mispronounces cement, column, and coupon," or "George rattled the keys and change in his pocket— most distracting!" All you have said may be true, but you are not focusing on the total speech or its most important aspects, unless delivery is your main concern.

DETAILING THE CRITERIA

Once you decide which matters are most important in criticizing a specific speech, your concern will become specificity of judgment. Usually you will start with the broader aspects of the speech and work to the details.

In assessing a speech of information, for example, you will want first to ask yourself questions about the speech as a speech: "Did it have a clear, identifiable central purpose? Did it elicit a favorable response? Did it have a recognizable introduction, body, and conclusion? What was its total impact?"

Next, you will want to ask questions about the speech as a speech of information. You might ask the general question, "Does the audience *understand* the subject better now that they have heard this speech?" Then you may pose questions relating directly to expository techniques: "Was there justification in the subject matter and in the audience's interest for the way this speaker used exposition, description, and narration at various points in the speech? Did this speech meet the special demands for good expository speaking by being accurate, clear, and interesting? Were visual aids used to clarify points or for their own sake?"

From these kinds of questions you may turn to those relating to specific details which may or may not be exclusively applicable to informative speeches. Here you will ask such questions as: "Did the story of the male student who knitted his own socks and ate light bulbs illustrate *originality* or merely *peculiarity?*" "Were the statistics used to show the relation between monetary support and the quality of higher education from a reliable source? Were they truly representative?" "Were the gestures used to support the idea that schools are bursting with students appropriate? Well coordinated? Definite enough?" "Isn't the word pronounced gri-*mace*, not *grim*-ace?" These and like questions complete your movement through the speech, evaluating the speech as a speech, then as a particular kind of speech and finally as a work consisting of detailed strengths and weaknesses.

Criticism sheets used to assess classroom speaking sometimes will assist you in deciding which questions to ask and which questions are most important. The criticism sheet we have designed for classroom use is reproduced below. It provides for both structured and unstructured comment. Aspects of speech making that need to be held in mind when considering any kind of speech are arranged along the left side of the paper with spaces in which quick reactions can be entered while the speech is being delivered. The right half of the sheet provides space for personal notations and revised, final reactions to the speech. The box in the lower righthand corner encourages the user to recommend areas for improvement and so points up the constructive aspect of the critic's task.

NAME: SPEECH NO.:

SUBJECT: DATE:

Symbols:
  X—No
  √—Yes
Grades:
  Papers:
  Speech:
  For the round:
  Consult Instruc-
    tor?_____

SUBJECT AND PURPOSE
  Subject worthwhile?_____
  Purpose delimited?_____

CONTENT AND ORGANIZATION
  Introduction
    Get attention?_____
    Needed information given?_____
    Purpose made clear?_____
  Development
    Organization—soundly planned?_____
      —easily followed?_____
      —transitions effective?_____
      —internal summaries appropriate?_____
    Supporting Material—clear?_____
      —interesting?_____
      —convincing?_____
      —visual aids effective?_____
  Conclusion
    Provide a note of finality?_____
    Whole speech in focus?_____

DELIVERY
  Mental Alertness
    Realize each idea as uttered?_____
    Keen sense of communication?_____
  Body
    Eye contact adequate?_____
    Posture acceptable?_____
    Movement meaningful?_____
    Gestures effective?_____
  Voice
    Distinct?_____
    Vocal variety adequate?_____
      Rate?_____ Pitch?_____ Volume?_____
    Fluency adequate?_____

LANGUAGE
  Have good oral qualities?_____
  Convey ideas clearly?_____
  Grammar correct?_____
  Pronunciation correct?_____
  Increase interest and impact?_____

NEXT TIME work especially for:

OVERALL EVALUATION
  Adapted to situation and audience?_____
  Purpose fulfilled?_____
  Make good personal impression?_____
  Interesting?_____

T he   C r i t i c a l   A c t

A good classroom critic, like a good speaker, considers the import his observations will have for his audience. He aims for and expresses judgments which cast the most light for the largest number. This means that he carefully edits his criticism as he goes. In public evaluations he side-steps purely personal preferences and those problems of concern only to a particular speaker. Instead of commenting orally on one speaker's peculiar vocal habit, he dwells on problems common to all speakers. He does not concentrate on strengths or faults not generally found in the speeches heard in class. All faults treated constructively are fair game for the critic, but in the classroom as elsewhere some matters having general application deserve public comment; others concern basically personal matters and are best criticized in private conferences or in tactfully worded notes.

Your education as a speech critic begins in the classroom. To make the most of it and to give others greatest benefit from it we suggest you approach classroom criticism in the following ways.

1. *Ready yourself for your critical task by preparing to concentrate on what you will see and hear.* Focus, visually and aurally, upon the speech being made. You must listen intently (see Chapter 3, pp. 61–65). Insofar as possible rid yourself of distractions from without and within. Once you have excluded all bids for attention except those emanating from the speaker, you are ready to go to work.

2. *Locate your critical criteria consciously.* Decide what you are listening for, what aspects of the speech deserve your special consideration because of their importance in this speaking situation. In other words, decide which aspects will rank highest in your critical hierarchy. By directing attention to the facets of speech making being studied at this juncture in your course, you will give your criticism purpose and clear direction. The more specific you can be in determining your critical purposes, the more specific will be the criticism you produce.

Do not try to observe every aspect of the speech at once. Try to feel its full impact, of course, but select several *important* items for scrutiny

337

and register your reactions to those. Scattering your attention over too many items will be of little service to the speaker and will impede the development of your own critical faculties. A speaker will not be helped by superficial comments about a dozen things. You will not be helped by trying to judge a host of items in haphazard fashion. Aim to develop and substantiate a few major critical judgments.

3. *Adopt a constructive attitude.* As you listen purposefully to detect the choices the speaker has made, consider the alternatives. As you note merits and flaws, ask: "What *might* have been done in this situation given the speaker's purpose?" "What *constructive* suggestions can I offer for future improvement?" Negative comment registering only personal impressions and without substantiating evidence or affirmative suggestions will be of little help. To say, "Your speech was poorly organized" or even, "Your economic argument was unsound" does not get to the heart of the matter, because it does not get to the "why" of the trouble. It does not offer *full* analysis of the critical object. "You didn't look at your audience," "Your sentences were clumsy," or "You committed several grammatical errors" may be useful lead-off generalizations in evaluating a speech, but unless they are accompanied by suggestions for correction they offer no comparison of the speech as-it-was with the speech as-it-might-have-been. Such comments illustrate criticism but not rhetorical criticism.

Starting speech criticisms with the positive things, the strong points of the speech, and leading to the less praiseworthy works well. The speaker will listen to what you say, will know that you are not picking him apart for selfish reasons, and will be likely to remember both the things he did well and those he did poorly. It is natural to blot out the unpleasant. By starting with what is pleasant to the speaker and working to the unpleasant, you will be on sounder ground if your aim is to be truly helpful, and it is. It has been said, "Only those who have the heart to help have a right to criticize."

4. *Measure the speech against the criteria you are applying.* Set clearly in mind the three basic aspects to be examined in a speech: effectiveness, ethical worth, and artistry. Be prepared to measure what the speaker does against specific criteria relating to ideas, proofs, arrangement, style, and delivery. Keep the situation uppermost in your mind as you make your educated guesses on the effectiveness, truth, and skill of what the speaker is doing.

Jot down reminders of the criteria you are applying as you listen, then of your judgments on them along with some examples and illustrations. A few notes to serve as reminders will do. Do not become a stenographer. You are a member of the audience and so should remember that a speaker cannot be at his best when trying to address a roomful of bowed heads nor can a critic function effectively if he does not take in the visual as well as auditory elements of communication.

Remember that your job is to judge the speech making, not the personality of the speaker per se. Of course, there is never a speech without a speaker, but your business is to assess his platform personality *as a part of the speech*. Consider how his ethos contributes to the speech not what contributes to your like or dislike for him as a person.

5. *Make a judgment.* This admonition may sound superfluous to you, but we make it because we have found it is often needed. In too many cases you will be tempted merely to describe what you see and hear. Description is, to be sure, a first step in fruitful criticism, but not your main business as a critic. Your ultimate function is to deliver a decision—a judgment—based upon the relationship between what you perceive and what you know. Comment alone will not serve nor will wishy-washy observations delivered with an air of doubt. To be an effective critic you must avoid straddling the fence. Make up your mind. Decide whether the aspect of speech which you are considering is effective or ineffective, true or untrue, adequate or inadequate, skillfully or unskillfully handled, successful or unsuccessful in its results.

6. *Be as specific as possible in formulating your judgment.* Document your criticism with concrete evidence. Refer directly to the speech whenever you can, to specific arguments, illustrations, and wordings. Provide examples to back up both favorable and unfavorable evaluations. If, for instance, you are criticizing style, strive to identify portions of the speech where style was effective and portions where it was not. Refer to specific sentence structures, phrasings, and images. This will reveal that you have been both perceptive and thorough in arriving at your judgments. It will also be constructively useful to all who hear your criticism. Find segments of the speech illustrating strengths and weaknesses in clarity, correctness, liveliness, force, and the like. The more precisely you can put your finger upon exactly *what was done* and exactly *why* it was effective or ineffective, the more worthy of attention your observations will be.

7. *Register your judgment.* When you are asked to present your critical assessments orally or in writing, do not sit back apathetically. Articulate your convictions. Silence during the oral criticism period following a speech or submitting doodlings on a scrap of paper will contribute nothing to the speaker or to your own development as an intelligent, informed critic. Do not feel that you must couch your judgments in rhetorical jargon. Do feel that you must be tactful in wording and frank in your remarks. Clear, direct, precise expression of your position and the reasons for it are required.

IN EVALUATING TEXTS OF SPEECHES

Your task as a critic of a tape-recorded, printed, or manuscript speech will be more complicated than your task as critic of the live utterance in the classroom. What appears before you on paper or what you hear over the amplifier is all that remains of a speech. It is as if an archaeologist gave you only some of the pieces of a Greek vase and then asked your opinion of the whole. Some of the things you will have to do in criticizing texts of speeches arise from the fragmentary nature of your critical object.

Most differences in your critical procedure will result from your lack of knowledge about the speaker and about the historical and immediate settings for his speech. This means the steps required to supplement the text will precede those we have suggested for actual criticism of the live speech. You will find it necessary to substitute reading for listening. You will be taking words in with only the eye *or* ear, not seeing and hearing a speaker as he delivers his speech. Delivery cannot be evaluated *in toto*, if at all. Voice may be judged from a recording, but not bodily action, unless you have access to a sound film. Most judgments on delivery will be far from satisfactory since they must usually be made by using accounts written by others who saw and heard the speaker in action.

In all ways your criticism of texts will be post-mortem evaluation. This means that you will substitute "read" for "listen" in the steps of criticism we have already given and your perceptions will be restricted to word symbols since you are denied the stimuli in the real situation.

What, then, are the tasks to be accomplished prior to those necessary for and similar to evaluating classroom speeches?

1. *Determine the authenticity of your speech text.* Determining the genuineness of the text may not be an easy job. Unless you are convinced of the trustworthiness of the editor or of the accuracy of the source, you will have to match the text you use with others in order to produce a reliable one of your own. You will wish to work with the best text available. You must also be as sure as possible that this speech was actually composed and delivered by the orator in question.

2. *Inform yourself of the milieu.* For a full understanding of the speech you must have knowledge of the time in which it was given. You must learn what ideas were in the air, what philosophies prevailed, what historic events occurred, and what were the day-to-day concerns of the people. In other words, you must reconstruct the temper of the times if your educated guesses about the importance of the speech and the possible effects it had are to be of any worth. To accomplish this you will have to read historical and interpretative accounts of the cultural, economic, religious, and moral activities of the particular society in which the speaker moved. You will also have to acquire a sense of the chronology of events. This is a large order, but only by filling it to the best of your ability can you hope to judge fairly a rhetorical effort designed for a particular audience, particular place, and particular time in the past.

3. *Inform yourself of the immediate speech setting.* Once again, to make judgments you must focus on the particularities of the situation. You must know where the speech was delivered, when it was delivered, and to whom it was delivered. To put it another way, you must know the details of the specific occasion. Gaining this knowledge, like gaining knowledge about the milieu, calls for historical research. This research will lead you to sources bearing more directly upon the speech than the research you will do on the temper of the times. In the course of your work you will peruse those writings that specifically concern the subject of the speech, the circumstances determining its composition and delivery, the physical setting for the speech, and the particular audience which assembled to listen to it.

4. *Inform yourself about the speaker.* A study of the speaker will further your understanding of the recorded or printed speech. You will need to acquire information as to his identity, his place in society, his habits

of mind and life, his sense of values, and his impact on other people. To gain insights into the speaker as a person you will need to study autobiographical and biographical materials, diaries, memoirs, photographs, and books of letters. Your task will be to produce a portrait of the speaker *as a speaker*. To do this you will have to sift through your resource materials to find whatever information is available on the orator's speech training, his methods of speech composition, his way of thinking, and what people influenced him in ways that might have affected his speaking. You will also need to look for descriptions and evaluations of his speaking and of his speeches.

5. *Read the criticism written by others.* Turning to see what others have done or how they have treated the speech you are studying will prove rewarding to you. The amount of published speech criticism is not great and you will sometimes find it difficult to locate. But there are essays, head-notes, and journal articles containing critical evaluations of many speeches and speakers of the past and present. Often you have only to turn to the newspapers published the day after the speech to find an appraisal of what was said and of the orator's performance. It must be clear to you, however, that your purpose in all such reading is to form your own point of view about the speech. You are not reading the criticism of others so that you can parrot or imitate. Your purpose is to synthesize what you have read and then to arrive at your own decisions.

You can see that criticizing a speech when only the recorded or written text is available is much more laborious and difficult than criticizing speeches you can personally witness and hear. In the latter case, you hear and see the speaker and are normally acquainted with the historical and immediate settings because you are a part of them. You may even know a good deal about the personality who addresses you. The job of criticizing a speech from a text adds many preliminary tasks to all the things you do to criticize a live speech. The object of most of this research is simply re-creation of the attendant circumstances. These attempts at re-creation will lead you into many fields of knowledge—history, philosophy, literature, sociology, psychology, religion. You can readily see why some teachers insist that no one is ready to criticize speeches until he has passed considerably beyond a beginning public speaking course. Yet, you may be asked to evaluate representative or great speeches as part of your basic study of the art of speaking. We think such research and criticism benefit all who undertake them. This is why we have discussed the kinds of inquiry this mode of criticism demands.

Criticism is judgment and/or appreciation, essentially comparative activity. In every art the critical act calls into play one's full knowledge of the art's resources and potentialities, and one's capacity to take in or understand the critical object to be examined. When this critical object is a speech, whoever would fully appreciate or informedly judge it must understand what is possible in speaking and how to analyze the constituents of a speech.

The form and content of any criticism are largely determined by the creative purposes that brought the object of judgment into being. The purposes dominating the creation of most speeches, as we have seen, are utilitarian. Thus, *effect* is usually placed above such criteria as permanence or beauty in evaluations of speeches. Nonetheless, judgments that evaluate only effects are but partial. Ethical and artistic considerations, too, are relevant. It is the contention of this chapter that criticism which focuses upon the artistic achievements of speakers—the degree to which they fully use the resources of their art in seeking utilitarian and ethical effects—is that which produces the most comprehensive and constructive judgments.

In the classroom or out of it the criticism of speeches requires method and wisdom if it is to be worthy of credit. Criticism, we think, requires (1) concentration on the speech as a critical object, (2) conscious identification of relevant criteria for evaluation, (3) constructive attitudes toward the critical process, (4) comparison of speeches-as-perceived with criteria that define the ideal, (5) formulation of judgments that are specific and cogent, and (6) documented expression of the criticism itself.

Exercises

Written

1. Identify in advance some speech which is going to be delivered on some future date in your community. The speech must be one which you can both see and hear. Prepare to criticize this speech by systematically writing down pertinent information about the speaker and his purpose, the audience, and the occasion. Attend the speech. Make notes during its

343

delivery using a body of criteria which you have decided to make the basis of your criticism in consequence of preliminary analysis of speaker, audience, and occasion. Finally, write a balanced evaluation.

2. Select a famous speech from a past era. Obtain the best text of the speech available to you for analysis and criticism. Read background materials on the period, including writings on the prevalent culture, living habits, and beliefs. Also read autobiographical or biographical materials about the speaker. After achieving an understanding of the total situation and of the total speech, choose one of the following topics for detailed written analysis and criticism:

   a. The speaker's logic.
   b. The speaker's use of supporting and amplifying materials, e.g., example, narration, statistics, definition, etc.
   c. The structure of the speech as it relates to the subject matter, the audience, and the occasion.
   d. The speaker's style.
   e. The authenticity of the text of the speech studied.

Oral

1. Listen intently to a particular classroom speech assigned to you for evaluation. Keep in mind the requirements set forth in the directions for preparation and delivery. Take written notes where appropriate. Structure your judgments on the various aspects of the speech as clearly as possible. During the oral criticism period reserved for the speech assigned, deliver a one- or two-minute extemporaneous speech working from your notes.

2. Prepare and deliver a speech in which you discuss one of the following:

   a. The essential considerations involved in appraising one of the canons of public speaking: invention, disposition, style, delivery, *memoria*.
   b. The differences between the procedures for the criticizing of a live speech and those to be used in criticizing the text of a speech.
   c. The distinctions to be made between the critical object in speech making and in other arts.
   d. The problems involved in arriving at a set of criteria to be applied in judging a particular speech.

Special Index for the
Study of Types of Speeches

This index is designed as an aid to students and teachers who wish to structure the study or preparation of speeches around purposes for which speeches are made. The general section of the index identifies treatments of topics pertinent to all or to several speech purposes. Subsequent sections indicate the portions of this book which relate directly or with special relevance to a specific type of speech.

Index